July 29, 1992

Portland, Or 97236

W9-AJU-462

*M*ARRIAGES
of
*W*ILSON *C*OUNTY, *T*ENNESSEE

1802-1850

MARRIAGES
of
WILSON COUNTY, TENNESSEE

1802–1850

Compiled by
EDYTHE RUCKER WHITLEY

With an Index by Eleanor R. Antoniak

Baltimore
GENEALOGICAL PUBLISHING CO., INC.
1981

Clearfield Co.   200 E. Eager   Baltimore, Md. 21202
410-625-9004

Copyright © 1981
Genealogical Publishing Co., Inc.
Baltimore, Maryland
All Rights Reserved
Library of Congress Catalogue Card Number 80-85115
International Standard Book Number 0-8063-0927-X
Made in the United States of America

Introduction

 ILSON COUNTY was created on October 26, 1799 from a part of Sumner County. It was named in honor of Major David Wilson, a native of Pennsylvania, who came to Sumner County while it was yet part of North Carolina and who was Speaker of the Territorial Assembly before the county was created.

It is not known what became of the county's marriage records for the period 1799-1801. Until January of 1841 the marriages were not recorded in a register, the bonds and licenses merely tied in packages and stored away in the courthouse. It is entirely possible, therefore, that some early marriage records were lost or misplaced.

This present compilation represents all the marriages for the period 1802-1850 that I know anything about. There is a gap of a few months in 1840-41 which I have been unable to fill, either from loose papers or from the register. However, it is possible that marriages during this period were not recorded.

Edythe Rucker Whitley
Nashville, Tennessee
1980

WILSON COUNTY MARRIAGES

Section 1: 1802-1840

John W. Baker & Polley Boleman, Sep. 16, 1802. Benjamin
Baker, BM.

Robert Eason & Lydia Hariss, Sep. 16, 1802.

Lynsey Martin & Nancy Stacy, Nov. 4, 1802. Joseph
Stacy, BM.

John Cothon & Perthana W. Rutland, Nov. 18, 1805.

Samuel Thomas Sr. & Barbary Petner, Dec. 12, 1805.
Samuel Thomas Jr., BM.

John Sinsett & Jenny Jones, Dec. 30, 1805. Levin Wilson,
BM.

Benjamin Alexander & Sarah Cloyd, July 21, 1802. Sam'l
Hogg, BM.

George Allin & Sally Johnson, Aug. 28, 1806. Solomon
Harpole, BM.

John Afflett & Nancy Taylor, Aug. 27, 1806. Dabid
McMurry, BM.

Julus Alford & Ann Hays, Feb. 18, 1806. Harman Hays,
BM.

Philip Anderson & Polly Macnatt, Feb. 24, 1806. Levin
Macnatt, BM.

Kenedy Bass & Fanny Barnett, Oct. 9, 1806. John Gray,
BM.

John B. Belford & Ruth Brown, July 7, 1806. John
Pursley, BM.

Wyett Bettis & Melly Powers, Aug. 7, 1806. John Bettis,
BM.

Robert Boyd & Elizabeth Gardner, Aug. 11, 1806. John
Boyd, BM.

Vachel Blalock & Patsey Chapple, Jan. 19, 1806. Aley
Elkins, BM.

George Allen Brough & Mirah Bone, Nov. 18, 1806. William
Bone, BM.

Elisha Brown & Polly Allen, _____, 1806. Jesse Cage.

Avery Brown & Sarah Marlow, Sep. 22, 1806. Rich Marlow,
BM.

George Brown & Polly Thompson, April 10, 1806. Jony
Williams, BM.

Edward Brown & Sally Bandy, Sep. 12, 1806. Richard
Bandy, BM.

Thomas Clifton & Letty Rogers, Dec. 22, 1806. John
Tucker, BM.

Christopher Coonce & Polly Brinson, Jan 27, 1806.
_____ Amos Small.

Peter Cotton & Levinah Tucker, May 20, 1806?. Jeremiah
Tucker, BM.

Anthony Copland & Nancy Craig, March 24, 1806. David
Craig, BM.

Jesse Cunningham & Rossey Beasley, June 30, 1806. Dillard Beasley, BM.

Thomas Dell & Agness Hopson, July 3, 1806. John Harpole, BM.

Samuel Dickings & Clampet, April 11, 1806. Henry Truet, BM.

Joseph Dixon & Polly Clark, July 23, 1806. Spencer Bevers, BM.

John Schols & Judith Compton, July 3, 1806. William Allin, BM.

Walter Eddey & Elizabeth Grimes, July 12, 1806. Michael Carter, BM.

James Elliott & Polly Carlock, June 16, 1806. John Quesinberry, BM.

John Fergeson & Patsey Harris, Jan. 18, 1806. Eli Harrell, BM.

Sam'l Gibson & Sally Browning, Nov. 3, 1806. Joshua Gibson, BM.

Jno. Givins & Jenny Berry, May 26, 1806. John Bradley, BM.

Elijah Gwyn & Sarah Idlett, Jan. 1, 1806. John Rise, BM.

Andrew Hays & Susanah Enoch, Aug. 4, 1806. Campbell Hays, BM.

Philip Hintson & Elizabeth Tucker, May 28, 1806. John Simpson, BM.

William Holebrook & Sarah Davis, Feb. 9, 1806. Arthur Davis, BM.

William Holland & Fanny Still, Nov. 14, 1806. Richard Holland, BM.

Levi Holland & Nancy Siddle, Aug. 26, 1806. Aaron Anglin, BM.

Stephen Hopkins & Polly Adamson, Oct. 21, 1806. George Peu, BM.

James Johnson & Elizabeth Nixon, Feb. 18, 1806. Samuel Johnson, BM.

Guyn Johnson & Nancy Bamett, Feb. 24, 1806. John Bamett, BM.

Elijah Jones & Patsey Browning, Oct. 15, 1806. David Hooks, BM.

Isaac Johnston & Prissola Arnton, ___ ___ ___ 1806. Charles W. Arnton, BM.

Noah Kelly & Hannah Hicks, July 8, 1806. Richard Hicks, BM.

Joseph Ladwin & Mary Vanhooser, July 26, 1806. Isaac Barlett, BM.

Stephen Lankford & Lear Herrod, July 5, 1806. Samuel Herrod, BM.

Levi Lannon & Rachael Gibson, Aug. 30, 1806. Samuel Gibson, BM.

George Lockmellor & Polly Porter, April 30, 1806. Samuel Caple, BM.

Hugh McCoy & Caty Watson, Aug. 2, 1806. James McCoy, BM.

McElyea & Polly McElyea, Sep. 2, 1806. William
Donnellson, BM.

Leven McNatt & Nancy Smith, Feb. 24, 1806. Phillip
Anderson, BM.

Donald McNickols & Betsey Bradley, Sep. 23, 1806. John
Patton, BM.

Andrew Morrison & Jane Robertson, Sep. 6, 1806. Mosses
M. Robinson, BM.

James Newby & Sally Beetley, Dec. 22, 1806. John Hallum,
BM.

John Pankey & Peggy Smith, June 15, 1806. George Hallum,
BM.

John Phillips & Elizabeth Scott, Jan. 6, 1806. John
Phillips, BM.

Hardy Pemmel & Lucy Patterson, Jan. 1, 1806. John
Fonville, BM.

John Powel & Sally Boothe, June 23, 1806. David Boothe,
BM.

George Ross & Lydia Dockings, Jan. 25, 1806. Allen Ross,
BM.

John Scoby & Ann Speers, Jan. 21, 1806. Thomas Bradley,
BM.

William Sysom & Aldey Munday, Dec. 15, 1806. John
Quick, BM.

James Smith & Christian Donnell, Dec. 4, 1806. Peter
Donnell, BM.

Amos Small & Polly Koonce, Jan. 27, 1806. Christopher
Koonce, BM.

Alexander Steele & Lucy Compton, Aug. 28, 1806. James
Steele, BM.

John Stockard & Polly Thomas Flood, May 2, 1806. Thomas
Flood, BM.

Zachariah (Zachariaiah) Tait & Rebecca Williamson,
Dec. 22, 1806. Nathan Clampet, BM.

Garland Tedwell & Susanah Magness, July 8, 1806. James
Higdon, BM.

Peter Walker & Drucilla Hendrix, Sep. 2, 1806. John
Smith, BM.

David Walls & _____ Bugg, Jan. 11, 1806. David Fields,
BM.

Benjamin Winford & Elizabeth Babb, Nov. 19, 1806.
Thomas Wilson, BM.

Amos Winsett & Polly Phillips, May 3, 1806. John
Winsett, BM.

Anthony Winston & Sally Ann Watson, Aug. 27, 1806. Joel
Jones, BM.

Thomas Woolridge & Jenny Bradley, July 17, 1806. Thomas
Bradley.

Isham Wynne & Sally Schols, April 5, 1806. Jesse Cage
& Benjamin Winford, BM.

Patrick Youree & Rispey Chapman, Aug. 6, 1806. Silas
Chapman, BM.

Burtis Alford & Mary Bryant, Feb. 21, 1807. Achilus
Bryant, BM.

James Anderson & Elizabeth Chapman, Aug. 13, 1807. John Crawford, BM.

Joshua Anderson & Polly Patton, April 4, 1807. Thomas Poteat, BM.

William Anderson & Elizabeth Greenwood, March 4, 1807. Urica Anderson, BM.

John Ashford & Jensey King, Aug. 26, 1807. Alston Elkins, BM.

Joshua Bains & Nancy Ruiff, Jan. 10, 1807. Henry Rieff, BM.

Zebulon Baird & Cloey Hunt, Nov. 14, 1807. John Searcy, BM.

Adams Barus & Polly Leonard, Feb. 1, 1807. Joshua Barus, BM.

Dread Bass & Nancy Brian, Aug. 7, 1807. Jacob McDermet, BM.

John Barnet & Polly McAdow, Sep. 23, 1807. James McAdow, BM.

Stephen Barton & Ellennor Baird, Feb. 14, 1807. Zebulon Baird, BM.

Middleton Bell & Rebecca Gibson, Aug. 11, 1807. William Gibson, BM.

John Bettis (Bettie or Betty?) & Sally Bradley, Jan. 10, 1807. Hugh Bradley, BM.

Jonathan Biles & Polly Barnet, Aug. 6, 1807. John Barnet, BM.

Jacob Boring & Ann Ross, Jan. 4, 1807. Samuel Ross, BM.

Thomas Bowen & Lucy Drew, Jan. 24, 1807. William Drew, BM.

Alexander Boyd & Rosanah Boyd, June 2, 1807. John Boyd, BM.

John Braddock & Nelly Leonard, Feb. 9, 1807. Richardson Bery, BM.

John Brown & _____ Bumpass, April 10, 1807. William McAdow, BM.

James Broadway & Elizabeth Foster, Jan. 14, 1807. Henry Foster, BM.

Edward Bruce & Nelly Burns, March 30, 1807. John Burus, BM.

David Burton & Ann Davis, Oct. 8, 1807. Ebenezer Donelson, BM.

James Byrn & Rebecca Word, March 23, 1807. J. Jetton Thomas, BM.

James Carruth & Sally Williams, March 20, 1807. W. Bradley, BM.

James Carter & Polly Davidson, Jan. 23, 1807. Moses Carter & John Brown, BM.

Samuel Dickings & Nancy Heflin, July 28, 1807. Jacob McDumet, BM.

Larry Epps & Elizabeth Craton, Jan. 26, 1807. John Bradley, BM.

Daniel Forbes & Elizabeth Horn, Oct. 11, 1807. John McDaniel, BM.

James Gray & Patsey Denton, Sep. 13, 1807. Edmund W. Vaughan, BM.

John Gray & Fanny Die, June 22, 1807. John Brady, BM.
John Hallum Jr. & Polly David (or Davis), Aug. 22, 1807.
Authur Davis, BM.
James Hicks & Tabitha Standeford, March 2, 1806. Noah
Kelly, BM.
Henry Howel & Polly Eagon, Aug. 1, 1807. William Eagan,
BM.
John Jennings & Fanny Word, March 24, 1807. James Cross,
BM.
Joseph Johnson & Nancy Brown, Dec. 17, 1807. Jesse
Cage, BM.
Hartwell Keeling & Nancy Grimes, Aug. 26, 1807. John
Wilkinson, BM.
John Keeling & Polly Manning, July 13, 1807. Thomas
Bradley, BM.
Ezekiel Lindsey & Elizabeth McNeeley, July 22, 1807.
William McNeeley, BM.
David London & Polly Partin, April 16, 1807. John B.
Walker, BM.
William Milligan & Nelly Meehee, Oct. 8, 1807. Samuel
Elliott, BM.
John Mooney & Lydia Burns, Feb. 25, 1807. Thomas
Patterson, BM.
John Morris & Nancy Walls, June 13, 1807. Ransom Stroud,
BM.
John Nicks & Anna Richard, Dec. 8, 1807. Robert
Alexander, BM.
Richard Ramsey & Patsey Bloodworth, Jan. 6, 1807.
William Bloodworth, BM.
John Rice & Nancy Ramsey, Oct. 8, 1807. Parvan Bandy,
BM.
Reuben Searcy & Hearty Bass, June 8, 1807.
John Smith & Polly Warnick, Jan. 24, 1807. William
Warnick, BM.
Thomas Smith & Sarah Meredith, Dec. 14, 1807. Samuel
Meredith, BM.
William Smith & Suckey Hail, July 15, 1807.
Samuel Smith & Polly Roach, Oct. 10, 1807. William
Smith, BM.
Abner Stewart & Nancy Gray, Oct. 8, 1807. James Gray,
BM.
Samuel Thomas & Ann Eathridge, Aug. 6, 1807. Moses
Odom, BM.
William Thompson & Rebecca Wilson, June 2, 1807. John
Davis, BM.
James D. Walker & Nancy Davis, Jan. 30, 1807. Arthur
Davis, BM.
William Webb & Rachel Godfrey, March 9, 1807. Burtis
Alford, BM.
Simeon Wherry & Ann Sypert, Sep. 4, 1807. Henry Bradley,
BM.
John Whitson & Nancy Keeling, Aug. 27, 1807. John House,
BM.
John Wilkinson & Elizabeth Thomas, Feb. 16, 1807. Rodham
Allin, BM.

William Adamson & Demorris Bledsoe, June 7, 1808.
George Pue, BM.
Willsher Brandy & Nancy Johnson, Jan. 6, 1808. Jesse
Cage, BM.
Robert Bogle & Sally Brison, June 2, 1808. Thomas
Leech, BM.
John Bond & Sarah Cummings, Oct. 5, 1808. James Bond,
BM.
Joshua Brown & Prudence McMin, June 27, 1808. Solomon
George, BM.
Reason Byrn & Francis Craddock, Oct. 13, 1808. James
Byran, BM.
John Campbell & Pheby Casady, Nov. 2, 1808. Samuel
Barton, BM.
Hezekiah Cartwright & Elizabeth Maholland, Sep. 2, 1808.
Matthew Cartwright, BM.
John Clemment & Jane Pullem, Sep. 27, 1808. Samuel
Barton, BM.
Henry Cocke & Elizabeth Tipton, Nov. 21, 1808. Joshua
Tipton, BM.
James Cropper & Peggy Purvine, Aug. 17, 1808. John
Purvine, BM.
James Craton & Jenney Wamack, Dec. 31, 1808. Richard
Diskill, BM.
John Davis & Polly McAlpen, March 14, 1808. Jesse Holt,
BM.
Humphrey Donelson & Sally Kelly, Feb. 17, 1808. Obediah
Woodwine, BM.
John Fakes & Mary Edwards, Nov. 7, 1808. Robert
Edwards, BM.
John Green & Nancy Myrick, April 25, 1808. Walter
Myrick, BM.
Beunajah Gray & Eloner Warnick, March 1, 1808. John
Roach, BM.
Robert Harris & Elizabeth McCown, Nov. 16, 1808. Isham
Webb, BM.
William Hartgrove & Jane Greenwood, April 21, 1808.
Benjamin Williams.
Melby Hearn & Hiskey Muckle, Jan. 18, 1808. Isaac Van-
houser, BM.
Jeremiah Hodges & Peggy Brown, Nov. 5, 1808. Thomas
Leech.
Micajah Hobbs & Fanny Hodges, April 6, 1808. Jeremiah
Hodges, BM.
Jonathan Hunt & Hannah Hendricks, June 21, 1808. William
Pratt, BM.
Graham Jackson & Betsey Smith, Nov. 5, 1808. William
Cople, BM.
Edward Jones & Margaret Thomas, June 5, 1808. John
Winsett, BM.
Grissam Moyers & Sarah Bradberry, Jan. 23, 1808. Jesse
Cage, BM.
William Palmer & Polly Bond, Aug. 19, 1808. John Bond,
BM.

Thmomas (Thomas?) Smith & Sousannah Hill, Aug. 29, 1808.
James Anderson, BM.
Tavner Spradley & Sousan Shours, Feb. 23, 1808. James
Barton, BM.
Joel Swindle & Nancy Hudson, Jan. 20, 1808. Samuel
Harris, BM.
Dabney Paton & Polly Whitson, Jan. 9, 1808. Jackson
Brown, BM.
Thomas Telford & Elizabeth Chowning, Oct. 13, 1808.
Sam'l Tilford, BM.
Luke Tippet & Jenney Cooksey, March 12, 1808. Henry
Carson, BM.
Braswell West & Rebecca Levins, April 1808, Thomas
Drennon, BM.
Jeptha Williams & Cinthy Rogers, Nov. 9, 1808. George
Rogers, BM.
Duke Wortham & Betsey Norton, June 3, 1808. Walter
Clopton, BM.
Simon Adamson & Susanah Hopkins, Feb. 22, 1809. Stephen
Hopkins, BM.
Gabriel Anderson & Polly Truet (?), May 23, 1809.
Joshua Anderson, BM.
Joshua Anderson & Peggy Thomas, Feb. 1, 1809. Henry
Thomas, BM.
John Anglin & Elizabeth Carver, Sep. 1, 1809. Aaron
Anglin, BM.
John Baker & Jenney Bearding, Feb. 13, 1809. John
Powel, BM.
Parran Bandy & Lytia Rice, Dec. 25, 1809. Ransom Gwyn,
BM.
David Barret & Jemima Allin, Nov. 11, 1809. Johnson
Bandy, BM.
Sion Bass & Polly Perry, Feb. 25, 1809. Richardson
Perry, BM.
John Berry & Elizabeth Campbell, Oct. 12, 1809. John
Givins, BM.
Tillman Bettis (Bettie or Betty) & Sally _____,
May 10, 1809. Richard Carr, BM.
Jesse Bloodworth & Narcissa _____, Dec. 11, 1809.
William Bloodworth, BM.
Solomon Brill & Nancy Jacobs, March 25, 1809. Andrew
Baird, BM.
John Brown & Rachel Lomax, Dec. 16, 1809. Jonathan
Picket, BM.
Robert Campbell & Tilley Stewart, Nov. 3, 1809. Joseph
Kirkpatrick, BM.
Samuel Cannon & Polly Alexander, Aug. 21, 1809. Robert
Alexander, BM.
Richardson Carr & Milly Sawyers, Sep. 6, 1809. Thomas
Carr, BM.
Thomas Carver & Margaret Donelson, Dec. 4, 1809. Humphry
Donelson, BM.
William Cartwright & Patsey Fuller, June 3, 1809.
William Draper, BM.

Benjamin Castleman & Polly McFarlin, Sep. 7, 1809.
Samuel Meredith, BM.
Isham F. Davis & Rachel S. Hays, Oct. 10, 1809. Sam'l
Meredith, BM.
James E. Davis & Polly Taylor, April 15, 1809. Jones
Hudson, BM.
Eli Donnell & Peggy Tague, Sep. 30, 1809. Robert
Donnell, BM.
James Drennon & Fanny Devault, June 21, 1809. Mathias
Devault, BM.
Jonathan Eatherly & Jenney Thompson, Sep. 27, 1809.
Warren Eatherly, BM.
Spencer Edward & Sally Wilson, Feb. 21, 1809. Bradford
Howard, BM.
John M. Garrison & Patsey Cannon, 1809. Samuel Cannon,
BM.
Rutland W. Grissam & Betsey Rathers, Dec. 6, 1809.
James Rathers, BM.
James Hall & Prudence Hern (Horn?), Aug. 16, 1809.
Thomas Bradley, BM.
Richard Hancock & Mary Cooper, Nov. 10, 1809. John
Fuston, BM.
Zachariah Hardwidge & Peggy Dodds, Dec. 28, 1809. John
Patterson, BM.
George Harpole & _____, Feb. 4, 1809. Adam
Moser, BM.
Jas. Horton & Rebecca White, Dec. 21, 1809. Robert
Ross, BM.
Joseph Hubbard & Susanah Womack, March 22, 1809. Richard
Womack, BM.
Josiah Impson & Polly Smith, Aug. 26, 1809. Thos.
Bradley, BM.
Isham Johnson & Sally Carroll, June 17, 1809. Jeremiah
Taylor, BM.
John Jones & Frances Knight, Nov. 7, 1809. William
Mount, BM.
Joseph Knox & Jane Crocket, Sep. 13, 1809. Archibald
Crocket, BM.
John Leech & Jensey Stuart, June 20, 1809. James Stuart,
BM.
Alexander Marrs & Marthew Donnell, Sep. 20, 1809.
Robert Donnell, BM.
John Marshall & Ann Donelson, July 6, 1809. William
Marshall, BM.
William Marshall & Milly Hargis, Sep. 25, 1809. Samuel
Moore, BM.
George Martin & Patsey Dillard, March 20, 1809. Sam'l
Hogg, BM.
John Martin & Patsey Lane, Oct. 5, 1809. Auron Lane,
BM.
John McKnight & Margaret Alexander, Oct. 2, 1809.
Andrew M. Alexander.
Lewis McCartney & Polley Anderson, May 8, 1809.
Gabriel Chandler, BM.

Daniel McCoy and Jane _____, April 27, 1809. John
Hamilton, BM.

Robert Morrison & Edy Sharpe, Sep. 2, 1809. William
Campbell, BM.

Andrew Morrison & Lydia Alexander, April 1, 1809.
Ezekiel Alexander, BM.

Richard Mount & Polly Martin, Jan. 16, 1809. John
Pirtle, BM.

William Petty & Elizabeth Johnson, March 1, 1809. Oran
Riddle, BM.

William Porterfield & Myrandy Young, March 29, 1809.
Joseph Young, BM.

John Robertson & Elizabeth Williamson, March 9, 1809.
John Williamson, BM.

John Ruff & Hanah Ross, April 19, 1809. Samuel Bryant,
BM.

Rhoford Rutland & Sally Cawthon, Jan. 20, 1809. John G.
Graves, BM.

Archibald Sherrill & Elizabeth Anderson, Sep. 26, 1809.
Gabriel Chandler, BM.

Philip Smart & Rebecca Gorge, March 6, 1809. Charles
Blalock, BM.

Thomas S. Smith & Margaret Cannon, Jan. 21, 1809.
Samuel Cannon, BM.

Charles B. Smith & Elly Hutson, Dec. 26, 1809. William
Scott, BM.

Richard Tally & Tabby Taylor, July 25, 1809. Martin
Tally, BM.

Jeremiah Taylor & Milly Mitchell, Oct. 3, 1809. Sam'l
Meredith, BM.

George Tedford & Elizabeth Galbreadth, Feb. 3, 1809.
Gilbert Cribbs, BM.

Isaac Thomas & Nancy Jones, Aug. 22, 1809. John Winset,
BM.

William Tolbert & Jane Parks, Oct. 12, 1809. Sam'l
Meredith, BM.

Nathaniel Wade & Polley Melton, March 27, 1809. Aaron
Lambert, BM.

Joseph Walley & Jenney Thaxton, Nov. 20, 1809. Richard
Top, BM.

Bryant Ward & Polley Wynne, Sep. 23, 1809. Hardy
Hunter, BM.

Abraham Whitson & Rutha Brown, Nov. 18, 1809. Dabney
Tatum, BM.

George Whitson & Polly Meredith, Feb. 25, 1809. Thos.
Bradley, BM.

John Wooddall & Polly Collings, June 30, 1809. Thomas
Bradley, BM.

Samuel Vick & Drucilla Neil, March 27, 1809. David
Heflin, BM.

Esekiel Alexander & Polly Cooper, Oct. 8, 1810.
Abraham Cooper, BM.

Samuel Alsup & Elizabeth Jennings, Dec. 26, 1810. Author
Harris, BM.

Robert Anderson & Nancy Sands, Dec. 1, 1810. John
Roberts, BM.
Daniel Baker & Sally Woodward, May 4, 1810. Benja.
Baker, BM.
Thomas Bonner & Polly Granade, Oct. 1, 1810. James L.
Rawlings, BM.
Jesse Bowers & Nancy Mann, Nov. 8, 1810. Thomas
Bradley, BM.
Leeroy Brawley & Sally McSpedden, March 14, 1810. Jno.
McSpedden, BM.
Nathaniel Brown & Sally Scott, Jan. 24, 1810. Thomas
Donnell, BM.
Breedlove & Nancy Breedlove, Feb. 10, 1810. Martin
Breedlove, BM.
Samuel Cartwright & Letty Moore, March 20, 1810. Jno.
Tipet, Sam'l Harris, BM.
Gabriel Chandler & Jenney Thomas, Jan. 30, 1810. Samuel
Sherrill, BM.
Andrew Creswell & Anna Brown, Feb. 6, 1810. Wm. Holbrook,
BM.
Henry Dawson & Sally Wright, Dec. 5, 1810. Ebenezer
Gilbert, BM.
James Dickings & George McWhirter, Feb. 27, 1810.
George McWhirter, BM.
John Donnell & Elizabeth Davidson, Jan. 27, 1810. Jesse
Donnell, BM.
George Donnell & Armelia Shanks, May 14, 1810. Abel
Williams, BM.
William Dunn & Elizabeth Brady, Dec. 11, 1810. John
Dunn, BM.
Isaac B. Eslick & Jenney George, April 30, 1810. Joseph
Sharp, BM.
Merrel Elkins & Thankful Maddox, April 16, 1810. Jacob
Castleman, BM.
Alsey Elkins & _____, April 2, 1810. Mevell Elkins,
BM.
Benjamin Ferrell & Polly M. Davis, Nov. 18, 1810.
Benjamin Hobson, BM.
Miles Gay & Rhoda Harkins, April 17, 1810. Jordan Ross,
BM.
John Galloway & Sally Barret, May 9, 1810. A. Robertson,
BM.
James George & Elizabeth Eslick, March 13, 1810. Isaac
B. Eslick, BM.
David Gibson & Purely Bloodworth, Jan. 13, 1810, by
Ransom Gwyn, J.P., Jan. 18, 1810. John Barber, BM.
John Harris & Sally Cartwright, Feb. 7, 1810. Samuel
Cartwright, BM.
John Harris & Catherine Baker, Nov. 30, 1810. Harris
Smith, BM.
Jeremiah Hendrick & Nancy Farmer, March 17, 1810.
Thomas Wilson, Wm. McClain & James Smith, BMS.
Charles Henry & Nancy Cutrull, Sep. 3, 1810. Aron
Spring, BM.

WILSON COUNTY MARRIAGES

James W. Herron & Mary Godfree, April 4, 1810. James
Godfree, BM.
Gabriel Higdon & Rebecca Davis, April 29, 1810. Alex
Bevely, BM.
William Hollandworth & Jensey Walker, April 7, 1810.
James Hollandworth, BM.
James Holland & Elizabeth Walker, March 4, 1810. George
Michie, BM.
John Hubbard & Elizabeth Jennings, June 11, 1810.
Presley Lester, BM.
Josiah Jackson & Nancy Clampet, March 17, 1810. James
Clampet, BM.
David Johnson & Elizabeth Walker, Jan. 8, 1810. James
Higdon, BM.
Cornelius Joiner & Sucky Carey, July 21, 1810. Moses
Odom, BM.
Tyry Laine & Nancy Ligon, July 17, 1810. John Martin,
BM.
Edward Lawrence & Delilah Woodward, Jan. 29, 1810.
Joshua Harris, BM.
William Mann & Francis Turner, Jan. 4, 1810. Saml.
Meredith, BM.
John Martin & Rebecca David, Sep. 18, 1810. James E.
Davis, BM.
James McCartney & Sarah Lowery, Sep. 4, 1810. Archibald
Davis, BM.
John McNeely & Belinda Carson, March 8, 1810. John
Travillion, BM.
William Nicks & Sally Pugh, Dec. 31, 1810. Thos.
Bradley, BM.
William Overall & Terry Humble, Sep. 29, 1810. Jase
(Jesse ?) Overall, BM.
Richard Perry & Frankey Joiner, July 21, 1810. Moses
Odom, BM.
Justes Ruleman & Ruth Standford, Jan. 25, 1810. Abner
Moran, BM.
Sam'l Scott & Anny Donnell, March 27, 1810. Sam'l
Meredith, Jno. Foster, BMS.
John Seabolt & Mahaley Kelley, Aug. 14, 1810. Abner
Wason, BM.
James Shorter & Margaret Smith, Aug. 18, 1810. Ralph
Smith, BM.
Stpehen Smart & Kindness Shorter, Jan. 24, 1810. Alsey
Elkins, BM.
William Stacy & Polly Sherrell, Dec. 19, 1810. B. Howard,
BM.
Moses Sterritt & Sarah Witherspoom, Aug. 11, 1810.
Galley Swann, BM.
John Thompson & Peggy Wilson, March 27, 1810. Eze_iel
Bloyd, BM.
John Travillion & Mary Carson, March 8, 1810. John
McNelly, BM.
John Walker & Nancy Wilson, Jan. 8, 1810. James Hodges,
BM.

Obadia Woodrum & Dolly Bradberry, Jan. 29, 1810. John
Bradberry, BM.
William Williams & Nancy Brown, Feb. 1, 1810. John
Tuder, BM.
Frances Woodward & Jenney Brannon, Feb. 21, 1810.
Boswell Pearcy, BM.
William Young & Hannah Bridges, June 2, 1810. Beverly
Young, BM.
Abraham Adams & Nancy Adams, Jan. 7, 1811. William
Kennedy, BM.
Reuben Allin & Jemima Lewis, Jan. 21, 1811. William
Lewis, BM.
Sampson Allen & Polly Somers, July 10, 1811. William
Makwell, BM.
Sam'l R. Anderson & Fanny Parish, Feb. 20, 1811. George
Still, BM.
David Barton & Sarah Borum, Oct. 7, 1811. Richard
Borum, BM.
Thomas Barton & Tabitha Hodges, Oct. 6, 1811. Jesse
Hodges, BM.
Jones Bass & Kissiah Rowland, Sep. 10, 1811. Green
Williams, BM.
Beurriah Batman & Sally Magness, June 7, 1810. Drury
Reeves, BM.
Kenneth Bethoon & Delilah Ragsdale, June 4, 1811.
Richard Ragsdale, BM.
Samuel Bettis & Achaza Chapman, Oct. 12, 1811. William
Bettis, BM.
John Jordon Birch & Sally Caldwell, Sep. 13, 1811.
David Caldwell, BM.
John Blurton & Sally McMinnaway, March 29, 1811.
Ebenezer Donelson, BM.
Thomas Bogle & Rachel Brison, Feb. 26, 1811. Joseph
Brison, BM.
Morris G. Burton & Polley Reading, Feb. 13, 1811. Lewis
(Leevis) Reading, BM.
Randal Carter & Polly Johnson, May 11, 1811. Harrison
Akin, BM.
John Cartwright & Polly Dillard, March 16, 1810. W. P.
Pool, BM.
Banard Carter & Rasey Benthal, March 23, 1811. Benthal,
BM.
Jacob Casselman & Anne Moore, Aug. 29, 1811. Benjamin
Casselman, BM.
Eddins Chandler & Huldy Sherrill, Jan. 11, 1811. Sam'l
Meredith, BM.
Pitts Chandler & Permilia Henderson, May 11, 1811.
Wm. Moss, BM.
Levin Clark & Patsey Doak, Dec. 26, 1811. Thos. Bradley,
BM.
Stephen Cloyd & Polly Wilson, June 8, 1811. Edmund
Cruther, BM.
Isaac Coe & Patsey Rather, Aug. 1, 1811. James Rather,
BM.

James Crawford & Anny Thrower, April 20, 1811. William Crawford, BM.

John Davis & Theodelia Marton, April 16, 1810. Nathaniel Davis, BM.

Nathaniel Davis & Elizabeth Mcfarlin, April 16, 1810. John Davis, BM.

Mathew East & Jinsey W. Peak, June 4, 1811. Aaron Sheron, BM.

Robert Irwin & Mary Leech, Feb. 23, 1811. John Leech, BM.

Benjamin Fisher & Peggy Crawford, Nov. 17, 1811. Anderson Fisher, BM.

Samuel Givin & Lucy Howell, Jan. 9, 1811. Henry Howell, BM.

Lewis Hancock & Franky Adams, Jan. 21, 1811. Abraham Adams, BM.

Hugh Henry & Phebe Oneal, July 10, 1811. Charles Henry, BM.

James Lasiter & Susannah Allin Celchem (?), Dec. 11, 1811. Jacob Laciter (Lasiter), BM.

William Lewis & Casady Knight, Dec. 28, 1811. Reubin Allin, BM.

James Mays & Polly Tucker, Jan. 21, 1811. James Munnett (Monnett?), BM.

Stephen Medlock & Sarah Tucker, Jan. 28, 1811. Littleberry Medlock, BM.

Richard B. McCorkle & Ibby Campbell, Jan. 1, 1811. Thomas Hobbs, BM.

John W. McSpaden & Rachel Brady, May 30, 1811. Collin C. Stoneman, BM.

Benjamin Morris & Naomi Flowers, Dec. 23, 1811. Isaac Sanders, BM.

Joseph Oranduff & Lilla Harlow, Feb. 7, 1811. Tom Bradley, BM.

Everd Parker & Nicey Johnson, Oct. 8, 1811. John Bryan, BM.

Robert W. P'Pool & Polly Cartwright, March 16, 1811. John Cartwright, BM.

Thomas W. Porterfield & Cinthea Ireland, Aug. 27, 1811. David Ireland, BM.

James Prim & _____ Eason, Nov. 20, 1811. Benjamin Bowers, BM.

John Quarles & Lockey Quarles, Dec. 17, 1811. Abraham Trigg, BM.

Luke Ray & Elly Daniel, Dec. 25, 1811. John Eagan, BM.

Henry Robertson & Polly Lambert, April 7, 1811. Jeremiah Taylor, BM.

Henry Rogers & Slly Jones, Oct. 20, 1811. John Fergington, BM.

James Scott & Lyssa Bone, Sep. 25, 1811. Wm. Scott. BM.

Robert Shannon & Rachel Osmit (Osment?), Aug. 21, 1811. James Steele, BM.

Robert Smith & Polley Marshall, Oct. 15, 1811. William Marshall, BM.

John Smith & Hannah Cannon, July 19, 1811. Sam'l Cannon, BM.

Aaron Springs & Rachel Oneal, March 6, 1811. Charles Henry, BM.

William Sypert & Patsey Dew, Dec. 17, 1811. Thomas Sypert, BM.

Nathaniel Thomas & Nancy Tally, Oct. 22, 1811. Pleasan-Tally, BM.

James Thomas & Nancy McMinn, Aug. 26, 1811. Jacob Thomas, BM.

Andrew Thompson & Anna Retta Kelly, Oct. 19, 1811. Isaac Williams, BM.

James Tipton & Polly Gray, Feb. 16, 1811. Thomas Ford, BM.

Sam'l Vanhouser & Sally Upchurch, Feb. 5, 1811. Joseph Godwin, BM.

Ross Webb & Elizabeth Moore, Oct. 9, 1811. Thomas Watson, BM.

John Wheeler & Anne Clark, June 8, 1811. A. J. Jennings, BM.

John W. White & Susanah Bradley, Sep. 14, 1811. John Bradley, BM.

Lamark Whitworth & Polly Mitchell, Nov. 29, 1811. Isham Webb, BM.

Green Williams & Sally Reed, Dec. 10, 1811. Henry Rieff, BM.

Patrick Anderson & Fanny Chandler, May 13, 1812. Richard Anderson, BM.

Elijah Armstrong & Peggy Higgins; Jan. 18, 1812. Joel Willard, BM.

Smitile Belote & Nancy Gill, Nov. 2, 1812. William Gill, BM.

William Benson & Fanny Dodd, Feb. 22, 1812. Moses Pruett, BM.

William Bettis & Winney Lambath, March 17, 1812. Samuel Bettis, BM.

John Blackburn & Caty Carver, Feb. 23, 1812. William Blackburn, BM.

Henry Blackwell & Patsy Brown, June 14, 1812. Moses Brown, BM.

Brient Blurton & Nancy Ross, Oct. 31, 1812. Hinton Blurton, BM.

Robert Bonds & Polly Benton, March 31, 1812. Alexander Carter, BM.

Benjamin Bonner & Lucy Look, Aug. 10, 1812. Thomas Locke, BM.

Hugh Bradley & Patsey Hunter, Aug. 10, 1812. James Bradley, BM.

Lemuel Bricham & Polly Logan, Feb. 28, 1812, by Ransom Gwyn, J.P., March 1, 1812. David Logan, BM.

Joseph Bridges & Elizabeth Gill, Aug. 24, 1812. Thos. Bridges, BM.

Jesse Brinson & Susanah Moss, Jan. 29, 1812. Jacob Cook, BM.

Dudley Brown & Edness Henderson, May 30, 1812, by Isaac
Winston, J.P., June 3, 1812. Cornelius Organ, BM.
Thomas Calloway & Celia Griffin, Nov. 25, 1812. James
Coats, BM.
James Calhoon & Winney Woodward, Nov. 7, 1812. Joseph
Barton, BM.
John Caplinger & Catherine Harpole, July 24, 1812. Adam
Harpole, BM.
James Cawthon & Sally Peak, Sep. 29, 1812. John Cawthon,
BM.
John Compton & Lucinda Travilion, June 9, 1812. Wm.
Harris, BM.
William Cooper & Mary Blaylock, Jan. 17, 1812. Eli T.
Hunt, BM.
Jesse Dickins & Polly McDerment, Sep. 10, 1812. Adam
Vinyard, BM.
Lewis Dickings & Hannah Ashford, Aug. 26, 1812. Moses
Ashford, BM.
James Drew & Rebecca Brown, Feb. 22, 1812. Moses Brown,
BM.
John Eagan & Margaret Wray, May 16, 1812. Luke Wray,
BM.
Nicholas Edwards & Milly Powers, Oct. 24, 1812, by
Winston, J.P., October 25, 1812. David Moses, BM.
Martin Franklin & Nelly Watson, March 21, 1812.
Bethleham Estes, BM.
Charles Golston & Elizabeth Neel, Aug. 28, 1812. Robert
Goodman, BM.
Joseph Gray & Agness Gray, Jan. 4, 1812. John Gray, BM.
George Hamilton & Doluthea Hamilton, Feb. 5, 1812. Hugh
Bradley, BM.
William Hancock & Neely West, Aug. 23, 1812. Major
Hancock, BM.
Overton Harlow & Betsey Hunt, Aug. 1, 1812. James
Anderson.
Adam Harpole & Polly Bettis, April 15, 1812. George
Harpole, BM.
John Hays & Betsey Estes, July 26, 1812. Sam'l Hays,
BM.
Joseph Hays & Susanah Adamson, April 25, 1812. John
Hays, BM.
Levis (Lewis) Howel & Polly Jennings, Jan. 7, 1812.
Henry Howel, BM.
Joseph Humphrey & Nancy Brown, Jan. 4, 1812. Edward
Brown, BM.
Eli T. Hunt & Sarah Webb, July 11, 1812. Thomas Bradley,
BM.
Pleasant Irby & Kezia Lambert, Oct. 5, 1812. John
Irby, BM.
William Jennings & Elizabeth Gibson, April 10, 1812.
Jesse Jennings, BM.
William Jewell & Anny Thomas, Oct. 2, 1812. Jacob
Thomas, BM.
Lewis Johnson & Edy Wright, Sep. 10, 1812. John Bryan,
BM.

Robert Johnson & Susan Adams, July 15, 1812. Isaac McKee, BM.

William Kelly & Dellornan Keeton, March 2, 1812. Jas. Hollingsworth, BM.

Luke Kent & Polly Mann, April 2, 1812. Harry Brown, BM.

John Kimbro & Nancy Beardon, March 13, 1812. Jones Mitchell, BM.

Robert King & Lyda Keeton, March 2, 1812. James Hollingsworth, BM.

Thomas Knight & Rebecca Jones, May 20, 1812. Aquilla Knight, BM.

Thomas Knight & Alley Martin, Dec. 24, 1812. Charles Warren, BM.

Dempsey Lambuth & Hicksey Bettis, March 17, 1812. Samuel Bettis, BM.

Carter Marlow & Leslater (Lester?) Bryant, Aug. 1, 1812. Richard Marlow, BM.

McKensey Marlow & Nancy McMillin, Aug. 1, 1812. Richard Marlow, BM.

William Marshall & Catharine Marshall, July 23, 1812. Thomas Bradley, BM.

James McAdow & Judeth Smith, July 4, 1812. Harris Smith, BM.

James McDaniel & Peggy Green, Jan. 31, 1812. Harvey Young, BM.

James McDaniel & Anny B. Vaughn, Feb. 10, 1812. Amy B. Vaughn, BM.

Norman McDaniel & Mildred Perryman, Oct. 21, 1812. Samuel Dodd, BM.

William McHaney & Sally Word, March 23, 1812. John Lester, BM.

Robert Mitchell & Agey Moore, July 28, 1812. Ishmeal Bradshaw, BM.

John Morrow & Sally Hall, Nov. 10, 1812. Charles Fox, BM.

William Mount & Mary Jones, March 25, 1812. Robert Whitton, BM.

John Oneal & Dorcas Midget, Feb. 24, 1812. Joseph Midget, BM.

William Parrish & Martha Davis, Feb. 11, 1812. Benjamin Hobson, BM.

Thomas Patterson & Mary Harpole, Dec. 3, 1812. Wyat Bettis, BM.

Joseph Phillips & Martha Williams, Oct. 14, 1812. Abel Williams, BM.

Isham Quarles & Polly Paschal, July 7, 1812. Elisha Chastain, BM.

John Ragan & Caty Hurmbell (?), June 2, 1812. Wm. Bone, BM.

Aaron Romine & Polly Wells, Jan. 21, 1812. Thos. Conger, BM.

Samuel Reedy & Cinthia Waller, Sep. 28, 1812. Eli Herrel, BM.

16

Lewis Riding & Elizabeth Johnson, Feb. 5, 1812. Isam Johnson, BM.

Michael Johnson & Mary Hank, Jan. 3, 1812. Sam'l McAdams, BM.

Thomas Robertson & Betsey Wooten, Oct. 17, 1812. Thomas McKnight, BM.

Theodore Ross & Peggy Garmany, June 23, 1812. Ephram Farr, BM.

Alexander Rutledge & Nancy Cox, March 30, 1812. Stephen Barton, BM.

Henry Shelby & Hannah (Martha?) Brown, March 10, 1812. Thomas Bradley, BM.

Byrd Smith & Martha McAdow, Dec. 3, 1812. William Brown, BM.

David Smith & Priscilla Bennett, May 4, 1812. Joseph Call, BM.

George Smith & Ally Martin, March 21, 1812. Joseph Stacy, BM.

Harris Smith & Nancy Flood, Nov. 27, 1812. Samuel Kelly, BM.

Sharach (Shadrack?) Smith & Nancy Howard, Oct. 15, 1812. Lewis Patterson, BM.

Arden Somers & Nancy Tucker, Feb. 16, 1812. Cornelius Organ, BM.

Lawrence Sypert & Polly Lambert, March 3, 1812. Thos. Sypert, BM.

John C. Tippet & Caty Hail, March 14, 1812. Stephen Barton, BM.

William Terry & Betsey Marlow, Jan. 29, 1812. B_____ Marlow, BM.

Isiah Tribble & Patience Pemberton, May 23, 1812. William Johnson, BM.

James Wier & Caty Shaw, N.D. (about 1812). William Steele, BM.

Wiley Whitley & Polly Snoody, Dec. 3, 1812. J. Lyvet, BM.

David Williams & Betsey Hoover, June 23, 1812. Geo. Rogers, BM.

Dukeson Williams & Patsey Dickson, April 20, 1812. Valentine Hooser, BM.

Robert Wilson & Jenny Donall, Aug. 29, 1812, by David Foster, V.D.M., Sep. 8, 1812. Alexander McNeely, BM.

Richard Womack & Agey Smith, Sep. 12, 1812. John Smith, BM.

William Woods & Elizabeth Harris, April 29, 1812. John Dew, BM.

William Woodward & Jane Bradley, Dec. 24, 1812, by Thos. Calhoon, V.D.M.

Henry Wright & Sally Ensley, Nov. 17, 1812. Hugh Ensley, BM.

Joseph Young & Peggy Stewart, March 24, 1812. James Stewart, BM.

James Adams & Jenny B. Thomas, Sep. 10, 1813, by David Foster, Sep. 23, 1813. James Thomas, BM.

Abner Armstrong & Sally Young, April 27, 1813, by Thos. Calhoon, V.D.M., April 28, 1813.

Jno. Bachelor & Nancy Clarkston, Nov. 17, 1813. Asa Godd, BM.

Robert Barskin & Rachel Rickett, Nov. 3, 1813. James McKnight, BM.

Dillard Beasley & Sally Harris, Oct. 26, 1813. Thomas Lock, BM.

John Berry & Elvira Harris, Aug. 13, 1813. Sam'l Harris, BM.

Polemy Bledsoe & Margaret Allin, Feb. 4, 1813, by James McAdow, J.P.

Moses Brooks & Nancy Tait, July 14, 1813. David Tate, BM.

Aaron Climer & Rebecca Sullivan, Sep. 20, 1813, by Jacob Sullivan, Sep. 23, 1814. James Ozment BM.

John Cooper & Piney Rogers, Dec. 6, 1813. W. Wooward, BM.

Elijah Cherry & Jenney Chadock, July 31, 1813, by Thos. Calhoon, Aug. 29, 1813.

Elijah Curry & Margaret Law, July 16, 1813, by David Foster, July 20, 1813. Robert Telford, BM.

Joshua Dillard & Catherine Quinn, Oct. 9, 1813. Alexander Chambers, BM.

James Dolley & Nancy Woodward, June 5, 1813, by Thos. Calhoon, V.D.M.

Frederick Foster & Sally Broadway, Sep. 7, 1813. John Broadway, BM.

John Foster & Elizabeth Rogers, Sep. 21, 1813. John Doak, BM.

Anderson Freeman & Delila Yearnel, Dec. 22, 1813, by Ransom Rwyn, J.P., Dec. 23, 1813. Cater Freeman, BM.

William George & Calliney Hunt, July 19, 1813. Hardy Hunt, BM.

William Hall & Polly Hall, Sep. 22, 1813. James Ramsey, BM.

Furges G. Harris & Nancy Rather, March 22, 1813, by Thos. Calhoon, V.D.M., March 31, 1813.

Richard Hudson & Polly Smith, Sep. 17, 1813, by Isaac Winston, J.P., Sep. 23, 1813.

James Irwin & Elizabeth D. Robb, Dec. 15, 1813. Will Robb Junr, BM.

Robert Jennings & Polly Word, Sep. 21, 1813. John Jennings, BM.

William Jennings & Elizabeth Gibson, Sep. 24, 1813. John Hubbard, BM.

Burwell Kemp & Elizabeth Roveling (?), Nov. 3, 1813. James Dyer, BM.

John Knight & Nancy Knight, July 26, 1813, by James McAdow.

John Little & Betsey Reynolds (Rynols), Dec. 13, 1813. Warren Eatherly, BM.

William McNeely & Grace Shaw, Jan. 3, 1813. George Ross, BM.

James Meligan & Elizabeth Blanton, Nov. 13, 1813.
Westley Higgin, BM.
Obediah Merret & Priscilla Clemmons, Sep. 13, 1813.
Samuel Clemmons, BM.
Nicholas Myers & Elizabeth Baiter (Biter), July 24, 1813,
by Ransom Gwyn, J.P., July 26, 1813.
Simpson Organ & Sina Wilson, Oct. 4, 1813. Roley Organ,
BM.
John Pugh & Polly Donslon, Sep. 30, 1813. William M.
Richard, BM.
Fasiah Rogers & Patsey McElyea, Sep. 2, 1813. Levin
Mackey, BM.
Frances R. Smith & Sarah Morgan, Sep. 14, 1813. Joel
Lambeth, BM.
Neel Smith & Betsey Reese, March 10, 1813. Richard
Smith, BM.
James Stewart & Mary Allen, Sep. 20, 1813, by Isaac
Winston, J.P., Sep. 29, 1813. Walter Cloptom, BM.
Ali Allen & Elizabeth Lasater, Feb. 26, 1814, by J.
Winston, J.P., March 4, 1814.
William Anglin & Elizabeth Sheppard, Dec. 21, 1814.
Aaron Anglin, BM.
Andrew Baird & Patsey Hunt, Jan. 8, 1814, by Ransom
Gwyn, J.P., Jan. 13, 1814. David Baird, BM.
James Bates & Sally Stephenson, March 14, 1813. James
Bradberry, BM.
William Bennett & Ely Tippet, Jan. 31, 1814. John C.
Johnson, BM.
Morris Brewer & Sally Shannon, Dec. 6, 1814. James
Braden, BM.
Brinkley Bridges & Nicey McWhirter, Dec. 28, 1814.
William Young, BM.
John Cloyd & Lettis Alexander, May 13, 1814. Samuel
Meredith, BM.
Green Cooke & Polly Nicholson, April 11, 1814. Thos.
Bradley, BM.
Samuel Crutchfield & Nancy Mcholand (Meholand?), Aug. 29,
1814. John Cartwright, BM.
Solomon Deloach & Rachel Searcy, Sep. 12, 1814. Clai-
borne Whitworth, BM.
Bradford Edwards & Jenny Bond, Aug. 29, 1814. Thos.
Bond, BM.
James Ewing & Nancy Smith, March 7, 1814. A.G. Wasson,
BM.
James Griffin & Sally Woodward, Oct. 10, 1814, by J.
Winston, J.P., Oct. 13, 1814. Boswell Pearcy, BM.
Isaac Griffen & Ibby Wiley, Nov. 16, 1814. David Wiley,
BM.
Isaac Griffen & Ibby Wiley, Nov. 16, 1814. David
Wiley, BM.
William Gleeves (Gleaves) & Polly Wilson, Aug. 22, 1814.
William F. Harris, BM.
William Green & Polly Hooker, Nov. 23, 1814. William
Dunlap, BM.

Joseph Greenwood & Elizabeth Anderson, Dec. 20, 1814.
Arthur Harris, BM.
William Hall & Martha Willard, Dec. 19, 1814, by James
Meadow, J.P. James Willard, BM.
William Handsbrough & Elizabeth Marshall, Nov. 17, 1814.
Robert Marshall, BM.
Robert Hight & Betsey Harris, March 18, 1814. John
Bartlett, BM.
Elisha Hodges & Milley Ward, July 23, 1814. Josiah
Hodges, BM.
Anthony Huddleston & Elizabeth Lewis, Aug. 15, 1814, by
Winston, J.P., Aug. 18, 1814. Isaac Winston, BM.
Samuel Kelly & Polly Cross, Dec. 22, 1814. Elijah
Cross, BM.
Lewis Lands & Nancy Bethune, Dec. 28, 1814. Richard
Rogersdale (Ragsdale), BM.
John Langley & Sally Christy, Nov. 17, 1814. Samuel
Underhill, BM.
Joseph Laswell & Selah Hanby, Oct. 11, 1814. Wm.
Baskin, BM.
Thomas Lock & Polly Beasley, April 25, 1814. Thomas
Bonner, BM.
William McElyea & Jenney Sutton, May 10, 1814. Stephen
Barton, BM.
Richard Lewis McKnight & Permala Woodward, Aug. 9, 1814.
John Thomas, BM.
John Medley & Sarah Lasiter, Dec. 28, 1814. Jacob
Lasiter, BM.
James Miller & Nancy McPeak, March 14, 1814. William
McPeak, BM.
Britton Odum & Radley Blurton, Sep. 12, 1814. Jubel
Bobbet, BM.
Nathanial Parker & Polly Thomas, April 20, 1814. Willis
Bryson, BM.
James Quesenberry & Elizabeth Edwards, Nov. 14, 1814,
by J. Winston, J.P., Nov. 17, 1814.
John Quesenberry & Patsey Major, Aug. 15, 1814, by
J. Winston, J.P., Aug. 18, 1814.
William Reese & Lavina Scoby, Sep. 10, 1814, by Thos.
Calhoon, V.D.M., Sep. 11, 1814. James Turner, BM.
Murfree Reese & Rebecca Rowland, May 11, 1814. John
Little, BM.
John Rice & Drucilla Parker, Oct. 29, 1814. Benjamin
Estes, BM.
William Roach & Ann Sparrow, Sep. 3, 1814, by David
_____, V.D.M., Sep. 15, 1814. James Drennon, BM.
Josiah Rogers & Peggy McElyea, Sep. 12, 1814. John
McElyea, BM.
John Ross & Lucy Barnes, Sep. 10, 1814. Joshua Barnes,
BM.
Lewis Sheppard & Elizabeth Parrish, April 11, 1814.
William Parrish, BM.
James Smith & Patsey Johnston, Nov. 9, 1814. James
Braden, BM.

William Smith & Betsey Givin, Oct. 7, 1814. John
Roach, BM.
Edward Sims & Dolly Grubbs, Sep. 1, 1814. John H.
Dickerson, BM.
Jeremiah Stevins & Polly Hallum, March 16, 1814. Noah
Walker, BM.
Holland Sullivan & Polly Osment, Sep. 12, 1814. James
Ozment, BM.
Jesse Sullivan & Ann Rice, April 9, 1814, by Jacob
Sullivan, April 16, 1814. Holland Sullivan, BM.
Robert Telford & Nancy Chowning, March 1814, by David
Foster, V.D.M., March 15, 1814.
Melly (Nolly) Talbott & Rebecca Owens, Nov. 8, 1814.
Jeremiah Owens.
Noah Walker & Payseu Davis, March 22, 1814. Jeremiah
Stephens, BM.
John Williams & Elizabeth Browning, Feb. 28, 1814.
Elijah Jones, BM.
Levi Wood & Polly Pearcy, Oct. 1, 1814. Algen Pearcy,
BM.
Hezekiah Wright & Charlotte Hunt, March 14, 1814, by
Ransom Gwyn, J.P., March 15, 1814.
Henry Akins & Sally Stell, Feb. 23, 1814. Geo. W.
Steel, BM.
Jimerson Bandy & Elizabeth Taylor, July 8, 1815. Silas
Freeman, BM.
James Basford & Mary Bradshaw, Oct. 7, 1815. Robert
McCerary (McCreary), BM.
Jacob Bennet & Ceta Bonds, Sep. 7, 1815. James Bennet,
BM.
Thomas Bennet & Elizabeth Bond, Dec. 21, 1815. Truman
Modglin, BM.
Solomon Bond & Francis Alsup, Oct. 9, 1815. Asop
Alsup, BM.
John Boon & Sally Garrison, Feb. 8, 1815. William
Oakley, BM.
William Boyd & Faethy Lawrence, Oct. 9, 1815. Allen J.
Dearing, BM.
Samuel Braley & Peggy McSpadden, Dec. 20, 1815, by Thos.
Calhoon, M.G., Dec. 21, 1815. Samuel McSpadden, BM.
Josiah Birchun (Brichun) & Sally Organ, Jan. 21, 1815.
James Brichun, BM.
William Buchanan & Nancy Wortham, Oct. 11, 1815. B.W.
McWhirter, BM.
George H. Bullard & Elizabeth Spradlin, March 2, 1815.
John Harpole, BM.
Richard Cartwright & Ann Waters, Nov. 6, 1815. Wilson T.
Waters, BM.
John Cross & Elizabeth West, July 31, 1815. Joshua
Anderson, BM.
Aaron B. Curd & Nancy Wooldridge, Jan. 7, 1815. John
Cottle, BM.
Zachariah Davis & Elizabeth Hill, Nov. 30, 1815. James
Johnson, BM.

Stephen Dewry & Elizabeth Allen, Aug. 4, 1815, by Isaac
  Winston, J.P., Aug. 6, 1815. Frederick Walkins
  (Watkins ?), BM.
Edward Edwards & Nancy Clemmons, Dec. 19, 1815, by Isaac
  Winston, J.P., Dec. 28, 1815. Nicholas Edwards, BM.
Edward Estes & Nancy Lewis, Aug. 19, 1815. Martin
  Franklin, BM.
Richard Fields & Polly Edwards, Oct. 8, 1815, by Jacob
  Sullivan, Oct 9, 1815.
Andrew Finney & Nancy Phillips, Jan. 15, 1815. Armstrong
  Herd, BM.
Arthur Forbus & Rachel Carruth, June 9, 1815. Alexander
  Carruth, BM.
Aqualla Greer & Elizabeth Welch, March 21, 1815, John
  Johnson, BM.
Thos. Grisom & Margery Robinson, Dec. 30, 1815. Henning
  Peace, BM.
Seth Hackney & Fanny Edwards, April 22, 1815, by Isaac
  Winston, J.P., April 25, 1815. Jacob Lasater, BM.
John Harpole & Elizabeth Swingley, Jan. 26, 1815.
  George Harpole, BM.
Eli Harris & Cinthea Moore, April 26, 1815. Samuel
  Harris, BM.
Harrison Harris & Priscilla Brown, Oct. 9, 1815. William
  Bettis, BM.
Philip Haas & Gracy McNeely, Dec. 20, 1815, by James
  Henderson, J.P., Jan. 10, 1816. Christopher Cooper, BM.
Isaac Imperson & _____ ___, N.D. John Imperson, BM.
Jeremiah Jadwin & Elsey Rogers, June 24, 1815, by Edwin
  Crutcher. David Williams, BM.
Joel Jennings & Cinthea Gibson, Sep. 16, 1815. Levi H.
  Sims, BM.
Lot Joiner & Polly Jones, Dec. 7, 1815, by John Jarratt.
  John W. Lumpkin, BM.
Micajah Joiner & Patsey Wood, Aug. 4, 1815. Cornlius
  Joiner, BM.
John Johnson & Nancy Young, June 7, 1815. Littleton
  Medlin, BM.
Abraham Jones & Cela Rogers, May 18, 1815. Jedethan
  Rogers, BM.
Thos. Kirkpatrick & Susannah B. Curry, Jan. 31, 1815, by
  D. Foster, V.D.M., Feb. 16, 1815.
William Lawrence & Elizabeth Neel, Feb. 28, 1815. Samuel
  C. Roane, BM.
C.N. Lewis & Polly Figures, Jan. 12, 1815. Edward Dab,
  BM.
Smedley Lynch & Elizabeth Robertson, July 22, 1815.
  Hezekiah Rhode, BM.
Littleberry Madlock & Pheba Tharp, April 25, 1815.
  William Thomas, BM.
George Marlow & Elizabeth Terry, June 1, 1815. William
  Terry, BM.
Henry B. March & Peggy Taylor, Feb. 14, 1815. James
  Davis, BM.

Arthur McFarlin & Hallen Brinson, Oct. 7, 1815. John McFerlin, BM.

Thos. C. McSpedden & Jane Baker, Dec. 18, 1815, by Thos. Calhoon, M.G., Dec. 19, 1815. Robert Baker, BM.

John McFarlin & Sally Belbrew, June 17, 1815. John McFarlin, BM.

Samuel McDaniel & Jane McKnight, Oct. 21, 1815. Samuel Braden, BM.

Andrew McDaniel & Nancy Harris, April 20, 1815. James McDaniel, BM.

Alexander McNeely & Fanny Hamilton, Dec. 28, 1815, by David Foster, M.G., Jan. 2, 1816. W. Woodward, BM.

James Miller & Peggy Henderson, Nov. 4, 1815. Preston Henderson, BM.

John Mills & Elizabeth Hooker, Nov. 28, 1815, by Ransom Gwyn, J.P., Nov. 38, 1815. Joseph Swingley, BM.

Mason Moore & Cealy Caplinger, Dec. 5, 1815. Wilson Jenkins, BM.

Geo. Moore & Fanny Fuller, Dec. 29, 1815. William Draper, BM.

Warren Moon & Cleary Babb, Oct. 10, 1815. George W. Stell, BM.

William P. Morris & Lucy Maddock, July 8, 1815. Isham Morris, BM.

John Motheral & Cinthea Farr, Dec. 2, 1815. Allen Smith, BM.

John B. Parker & Ellender Tipton, Oct. 7, 1815. Edmun W. Vaughn, BM.

Richard Phelps & Patsey Akin, Dec. 11, 1815. Isham Palmer, BM.

William Pugh & Jenny Donelson, Feb. 14, 1815. David Pugh, BM.

Owen Quinley & Polly Sullivan, Aug. 3, 1815, by Jacob Sullivan, Aug. 4, 1815. Stephen W. Byrn, BM.

Henry Radford & Caty Crook, Nov. 21, 1815. James Crook, BM.

Riahcrd Ragsdale & Margret Mark, July 27, 1815. Kennard Bethoon, BM.

Henry Rice & Nancy Cawthon, Dec. 19, 1815, by John Hannah, Dec. 21, 1815. John Hannah, BM.

Reuben (Rewben?) Rider, & Martha Leech, May 3, 1815. James Luck, BM.

John Roach & Polly Kirkpatrick, Aug. 19, 1815, by David Foster, M.G., Aug. 24, 1815. Thomas Kirkpatrick, BM.

Jeremiah Russle & Elizabeth Hazelwood, Aug. 21, 1815. Thos. Hazelwood, BM.

Allen Ross & Susanah Proctor, Aug. 7, 1815. Edmund Procter, BM.

Julius Sanders & Penny Fields, Feb. 28, 1815. Richard Fields, BM.

Beverly Scurlock & Marrey Elizabeth Harpole, March 13, 1815. George Harpole, BM.

James Seal & Rebecca Foley, Jan. 31, 1815. John Cornegg, BM.

Archibald Shannon & Matilda Allin, July 25, 1815. Joseph Swingley, BM.

George Small & Philphena Jarman, Sep. 27, 1815. Robert Jarman, BM.

Joseph Smart & Polly Bennett, July 25, 1815. Thomas Rhodes, BM.

Richard Smith & Polly Merrett, April 7, 1815. Absolom Smith, BM.

Henry Smith & Polly Ashford, June 13, 1815. Graham Jackson, BM.

William L. Smith & Fanny Wooldridge, Aug. 16, 1815. John Barnard, BM.

George W. Still & Polly L. Wynne, Nov. 9, 1815, by John Jarratt, M.G. Sam'l L. Wynne, BM.

Joseph Stuart & Biddy Gibson, March 11, 1815, by Ransom Gwyn, March 12, 1815. James Brinson, BM.

Lewis Sutton & Nicey Kenneday, Oct. 12, 1815. James Allcorn, BM.

Peter Sullivan & Sally Avery, July 31, 1815, by Jacob Sullivan

Geo. Summers & Polly Jennings, July 22, 1815. Joel Jennings, BM.

James P. Thompson & Mary Givin, July 19, 1815. H. L. Douglass, BM.

Thomas Tune & Betsey Hickman, Oct. 4, 1815. Joseph Turnham, BM.

Elijah Wamock & Elizabeth Patterson, Oct. 4, 1815. John Campbell, BM.

Abner Wasson & Elizabeth Quarles, March 6, 1815. A. Dale, BM.

Richard Watkins & Catharine Jones, Jan. 11, 1815. Sam'l Wright, BM.

Ansel Whitefield & Janey Tesdale, March 8, 1815. Thos. Blair, BM.

John Whitlock & Nancy West, July 8, 1815. James Whitlock, BM.

Abel Williams & Peggy Massey, Dec. 16, 1815. Wm. Phillips, BM.

Thos. Williams & Elizabeth Williams, April 1, 1815, by Henry Smith, J.P. Thomas Williams, BM.

William Wisenir & Nancy Hopson, April 8, 1815. Wm. Tarver, BM.

George Williamson & Hannah Crutchfield, Jan. 6, 1815. Thomas Williamson.

Robertson Wright & Sally Goldston, Oct. 18, 1815. Stephen Sypert, BM.

Francis Wynne & Susannah Caves, Dec. 2, 1815, by John Williamson, J.P., Jan. 11, 1816. Thos. Bradley, BM.

Gidian Alexander & Elizabeth Borum, Dec. 14, 1816, by Wm. Steele, J.P., Dec. 15, 1816. David Barton, BM.

Houston Alexander & Abby Connata, Feb. 22, 1816, by Abner W. Bone, J.P., Feb. 23, 1816. Elijah Parsons, BM.

Hardy Ames & Polly Ridgeway, June 19, 1816, by Abner Hill, M.G.,June 20, 1816. Stephen Sypert, BM.

Banister Anderson & Betsey Anderson, July 10, 1816, by
Joseph T. Williams, J.P., July 11, 1816. Patrick
Anderson, BM.
Butler Arnold & Rachael Hudson, Nov. 7, 1816, by William
Gray, J.P. George Ross, BM.
David Arnold & Susanah Bryson, May 14, 1816, by John
McMinn, J.P., May 16, 1816. Wilson L. Parmer.
John Arnold & Judy Brown, Aug. 15, 1816, by John McMinn,
J.P., Aug. 20, 1816. David Arnold, BM.
Moses Barnet & Rebecca Fisher, May 8, 1816, by Ransom
Gwyn, J.P., May 9, 1816. Jeremiah Fisger, BM.
William Barton & Rebecca Marshall, Feb. 8, 1816. Smith
Hansborough, BM.
James Bradberry & Elizabeth Golston, Aug. 14, 1816, by
Abner Hill, Aug. 16, 1816. Elisha Cole, BM.
Jno. Bradley & Polley Gray, Nov. 6, 1816, by William
Gray, J.P., Nov. 7, 1816. Willie Turner, BM.
David Bradshaw & Terrissa Carson, Dec. 23, 1816, by
Abner Caruth, J.P., Dec. 29, 1816. Alexander C.
Caruth, BM.
Hinton Blurton & Susanah Howell, Feb. 28, 1816, by James
Foster, J.P. John Willis, BM.
Josiah Brinson & Betsey Modglin, April 6, 1816, by Abner
Hill, M.G., April 7, 1816. James Brinson, BM.
Abraham Britton & Mary Anne Crutcher, Oct. 28, 1816, by
Abadiah C. Finley, J.P. Harvey Douglass, BM.
Stephen Brown & Polly Crawford, Jan. 31, 1816. Sterling
Bryant, BM.
William Bryson & Lydia Stanley, Aug. 24, 1816. Andrew
Kirkpatrick, BM.
Hugh Campbell & Sally Horn (Hern?), May 24, 1816, by
A. W. Hone, J.P., May 28, 1816. Woodson Webb, BM.
John Campbell & Mary Dodd, Nov. 18, 1816, by John W.
Payton, J.P., Nov. 21, 1816. Simon Camper, BM.
Nathaniel G. Carter & Keseah H. Johnson, Jan. 9, 1816,
By James Foster, J.P., Jan. 11, 1816. Elijah Brien,
BM.
James Caruth & Polly Donnell, Aug. 29, 1816, by Samuel
Donnell, V.D.M. Josiah Donnell, BM.
Elijah Carr & Britan Decabor, May 10, 1816, by Abner
Hill, M.G., May 11, 1816. Walter Carr, BM.
Thomas Cawthon & Susan Daniel, July 17, 1816. James
Cawthon, BM.
Parkes Chandler & Louisia Allen, May 1, 1816. Ryland
Chamdler, BM.
Banjemine Chapman & Abigale Haris, June 30, 1816. James
Eason, BM.
Harry Clifton & Sarah Michie, March 11, 1816, by Chris-
topher Cooper, J.P., March 13, 1816. William Michie,
BM.
Benjamin Cox & Nancy Hearn, March 13, 1816, by Joseph T.
Williams, J.P., March 14, 1816. Harry L. Douglas, BM.
William Craddock & Polly Wortham, Sep. 24, 1816. George
Glegly (?), BM.

Moses Cunningham & Polly Cropper, July 19, 1816, by John
W. Payton, J.P., July 25, 1816. Robert Seat, BM.

James Crooms & Charity Tait, March 27, 1816, by John
Williamson, J.P., March 28, 1816. Hugh Harris, BM.

John Davidson & Rachel Carson, July 3, 1816, by Thos.
Calhoon, M.G., July 4, 1816. David Billings, BM.

David Devault & Ann McCrory, Sep. 2, 1816, by John
Hannah, J.P., Sep. 5, 1816. Stephen Byrn, BM.

Nathaniel Dews & Patsey Bumpass, March 26, 1816, by
Wm. Bumpass, D.D., March 26, 1816. Thomas Bradley, BM.

Elisha Dismukes & Fanny Petty, Dec. 8, 1816, by Jas.
Johnson, J.P. Thomas Stone, BM.

Howard Edwards & Diza Bennett, Feb. 19, 1816, by Jacob
Silivan (Sullivan), Feb. 20, 1816. Bradford Howard, BM.

David Estes & Hannah Jackson, Oct. 4, 1816, by James
McAdoo, J.P. John Franklin, BM.

William Fosher & Jenney Fisher, April 13, 1816, by Jos.
T. Williams, J.P., April 25, 1816. Benjamin Fisher, BM.

John Fields & Elizabeth Taylor, Oct. 7, 1816, by Edward
Harris, Oct. 8, 1816. David Fields, BM.

Richard Fields & Polly Edwards, Oct. 8, 1816. Howard
Edwards, BM.

John Flowers & Rachel Deloach, Jan. 27, 1816, by Abner
Stevenson, J.P., Feb. 7, 1816. Benjamin Morris, BM.

Amos Gibson & Jemimah Collins, July 3, 1816, by Edmund
Crutcher, J.P. Alexander Chambers, BM.

Solomon Gibson & Tempa Modglin, Dec. 7, 1816, by Abner
Hill, M.G., Dec. 8, 1816. Thomas Marrington, BM.

Eli Goldston & Elizabeth Bennett, Dec. 24, 1816.
William Moss, BM.

Parks Goodall & Elizabeth Palmer, Nov. 19, 1816. Frances
Palmer, BM.

Bachelor Graves & Nancy Ferrington, June 2, 1816. James
Bradon, BM.

James Grissom & Elizabeth Mosse, Nov. 20, 1816. Baker
Wrather, BM.

John Gunthrie & Cloe Babb, Jan. 16, 1816, by John
Jarratt, Jan. 17, 1816. Mathew Horn, BM.

Drury Hall & Sally Thrower, Dec. 3, 1815, by A. Harris,
J.P., Jan. 4, 1816. John Thrower, BM.

Smith Hansberry & Sally Marshall, March 5, 1816. Thomas
Bradley, BM.

Obediah Hardin & Polly Hall (Hull), Dec. 5, 1816, by
William Gray, J.P., Dec. 30, 1816. Ebenezer Gilbert,
BM.

George Harpole & Levina Johnson, Jan. 13, 1816, by R.
King, J.P.,

James Harris & Nancy Ames, Oct. 26, 1816, by Abner Hill,
M.G., Oct. 27, 1816. William Bettie, BM.

Thomas Harris & Mary Hern, June 18, 1816. Ebenezer
Hern, BM.

Charles Harrington & Nicey Johnson, Feb. 6, 1816, by
Abner Hill, M.G., Feb. 8, 1816. William Sypert, BM.

James Haw & Polly _____, March 13, 1816. William Eaken,
BM.

Thomas Hays & Sally Drake, Nov. 26, 1816, by J. F. Davis, J.P., Nov. 27, 1816. Robert Marshall, BM.

Ebenezer Hearn & Betsy Foster, Nov. 28, 1816, by Sam'l Canon, J.P., Nov. 28, 1816. James Hearn, BM.

Preston Henderson & Polly Teague, Sep. 10, 1816. James Miller, BM.

William Hickman & Polly Willeford, May 1, 1816, by Abner Hill, M.G., May 7, 1816. John Hickman, BM.

James Howard & Elizabeth Collings, July 22, 1816, by Joshua Lester, V.D.M., July 25, 1816. Wm. B. Smith, BM.

Abel Hunt & Elizabeth F. Bell, Aug. 28, 1816, by James Richard, J.P., Sep. 5, 1816. James Bell, BM.

John Hunt & Jane Moore, Oct. 3, 1816. Overton Harlow, BM.

William Jackson & Susanah Lewis, May 14, 1816, by James McAdow, J.P. William Jackson, BM.

Jesse Jennings & Nancy Craddock, Oct. 8, 1816. Edward Williams, BM.

John Jennings & Susannah Ward, Oct. 3, 1816, by James Cross, J.P., Nov. 7, 1816. John Hubbard, BM.

Sam'l Jennings & Matilda Biggers, Oct. 29, 1816, by Sam'l Donnell, V.D.M. Nathan Sparks, BM.

Enoch Kennedy & Nancy Bittis, Nov. 1, 1816, by Abner Hill, M.G., Nov. 3, 1816. Carter Crutcher, BM.

Samuel Kimberland & Polly Bartlett, Jan. 10, 1816. Jeremiah Johnson, BM.

Ransom King & Addy Rogers, April 8, 1816, by H. Shelby, J.P., April 9, 1816. Jeremiah Tucker, BM.

Abraham Knight & Elizabeth Martin, April 18, 1816. William Jones, BM.

Nathaniel Knight & Sarah Holland, Aug. 21, 1816. John Knight, BM.

Eli Lansdon & Elizabeth Bone, March 7, 1816, by Wm. Bumpass, D.D., March 21, 1816. William Cross, BM.

Absalom Lasater & Elizabeth Ramsey, March 21, 1816, by Isaac Winston, J.P., March 28, 1816. Jacob B. Lasater, BM.

Joseph Lawrence & Polly Neel, June 22, 1816, by Thomas Durham, M.G., June 27, 1816. Charles Neel, BM.

James Lewis & Martha Figures, Sep. 12, 1816. Abraham Britton, BM.

Wlater (Walter?) Lewis & Rachel Luffer, Nov. 26, 1816, by Jas. McAdow. William Jackson, BM.

Richard Locke & Francis Pool, Sep. 25, 1816. Jones Locke, BM.

John P. Maddox & Polly Jones, March 26, 1816, by Elijah Maddox, M.G., March 28, 1816. Willie Jones, BM.

James Marlow & Polly May, Jan. 27, 1816. Hezekiah Marlow, BM.

George Marrich & Rebecca Ferrett, April 22, 1816, by Hugh Roane, J.P., April 25, 1816. Rolly Organ, BM.

Abraham McBride & Sally Bartlett, Nov. 6, 1816. James Whitworth, BM.

William McCulla & Tabitha Mullings, March 22, 1816.
Frances Wynne, BM.
John F. McDaniel & Polly Thomas, Jan. 13, 1816. Moses
Owen, BM.
Jacob McDermet & Reely Trusty, Feb. 24, 1816, by Elijah
Maddox, Feb. 25, 1816. Jeremiah McWhirter, BM.
Daniel McWhirter & Sally McWhirter, July 15, 1816. Wm.
Leawell, Aaron McWhirter, BM.
Henry McGyre & Elvin Bay, Jan. 31, 1816, by Moore
Stevenson. John P. Harpole, Sam'l Doak, Robert
Anderson, BMS.
William Melton & Martha G. P'Pool, March 8, 1816, by
Am. Algood, March 12, 1816. John M. Jackson, BM.
Taywell Mitchell & Sally Stuart, Dec. 7, 1816, by John
Bonner, J.P., Jan. 16, 1817. Jones Mitchell, BM.
George Mitchell & Judith Flood, June 1, 1816, by James
McAdow, J.P. H. L. Douglass, BM.
William Modglin & Neely Dukes, Nov. 27, 1816, by Abner
Hill, M.G. Hidgon Harrington, BM.
Denton Modglin & Patsey Haily, Feb. 24, 1816, by Abner
Hill, M.G., Feb. 27, 1816. Stephen Sypert, BM.
George Moore & Fanny Fuller, Dec. 29, 1816, by John W.
Rayton, J.P.
John Masheras (?) & Cyntha Farr, Dec. 2, 1816, by Thos.
Calhoon, M.G., Dec. 5, 1816.
Mercer Morris & Rebecca Wright, Oct. 4, 1816, by Abner
Hill, M.G., Oct. 10, 1816. Gabriel Higdon, BM.
Henry Moser & Elizabeth Oneal, June 25, 1816, by Abner
Hill, M.G., June 25, 1816. John Conger, BM.
Benjamin S. Motley & Patsey Doak, Jan. 22, 1816, by
Sam'l Donnell, V.D.M. William Foster, BM.
Joseph Moxley & Levina Clemmons, March 13, 1816, by
Edward Harris, J.P., April 16, 1816. Dawson Hannah,
BM.
Allen Mulligan & Susanah Fuston, Aug. 7, 1816, by C.
Cooper, J.P., Aug. 9, 1816. John Fuston, BM.
John W. Nichols & Nancy Anderson, Nov. 11, 1816, by
Ransom Gwyne, J.P., Nov. 12, 1816. Joseph Swingley,
BM.
Charles Nicholson & Susan Johnson, July 10, 1816, by Wm.
Steele, J.P., July 12, 1816. Daniel Cherry, BM.
John Oakley & Sally Phillips, July 1, 1816. William
Phillips, BM.
William Oakley & Elizabeth Oakley, Dec. 9, 1816. David
Phillips, BM.
Moses Oldham & Christina Tarpley, Sep. 16, 1816. William
Draper, BM.
Cornelius Organ & Catherine Benthall, Nov. 9, 1816, by
Sam'l Cannon, J.P., Dec. 10, 1816. Elijah Cross, BM.
Cristes O'Neal & Polly Brooks, May 30, 1816, by James
Davidson, June 6, 1816. Jeremiah Brooks, BM.
Moses Owen & Jenney Reeves, Jan. 13, 1816, by James McAdow,
J.P. John F. McDaniel, BM.
Isham Patterson & Peggy Hill (late P. Bradley), May 29,
1816, by Isham Winston, J.P., May 30, 1816. Edmund

Crutcher, BM.

Isham Patterson Jr. & Polly Harlow, May 29, 1816.
Isham Patterson Sr.

Elijah Parsons & Polly Turner, April 13, 1816, by James
McAdow, J.P. Thos. H. Alexander, BM.

John Phillips & Sally Carlin, March 13, 1816, by Thos.
B. Reese, J.P., March 14, 1816. Benjamin Davidson, BM.

Joseph Phillips & Ann Wheeler, Aug. 31, 1816. Edward
Wheeler, BM.

Andrew Picket & Elizabeth Campbell, July 1, 1816. Hugh
Campbell, BM.

Armstead Pool & Judith W. McGahee, Aug. 21, 1816. Robert
W. Pool, BM.

Benjamin Prichard & Polly Campbell, July 15, 1816, by
Abner W. Bone, J.P., July 19, 1816. Hugh Campbell.

Edmund Proctor & Judith Hill March 12, 1816, by John
Jarratt, March 14, 1816. Thomas Proctor, BM.

Moses Purser & Mossy Arnet, Feb. 15, 1816, Stephen
Wetherford, BM.

Archibald Ray & Lieu Ellen Th ompson, Dec. 20, 1816, by
William Gray, J.P. David Glenn, BM.

Hezekiah Rhody & Sarah Cummings, Nov. 30, 1816. John
Charters, BM.

Nathaniel Rice & Polly Ellis, Sep. 27, 1816. John Ellis,
BM.

John Ridgway & Elizabeth Aims, March 4, 1816, by Abner
Hill, M.G., April 12, 1816. Hardy Amis, BM.

William Sadler & Susan Pemberton, Nov. 20, 1816, by
James McAdow. John McAdow, BM.

George Sands & Casey Green, March 4, 1816, by Joseph T.
Williams, J.P., March 14, 1816. Beverly Williams, BM.

James Shannon & Polly Shannon, Dec. 31, 1816. Thomas
Richmond, BM.

Leonard H. Sims & Elizabeth Washington, Sep. 22, 1816,
by Moore Stephenson, M.G. Thos. Bradley, BM.

William Simpson & Ann McCrary, Oct. 7, 1816, by Isaac
Winston, J.P. Samuel Vance, BM.

Neil Smith & Nancy McDougal, Feb. 21, 1816. H. L.
Douglas, BM.

William Smith & Elenor Woodward, Sep. 9, 1816, by A.
Harris, Sep. 10, 1816. Daniel Baker, BM.

John Stanford & Martha Woodcock, Aug. 28, 1816, by Wm.
Algood, Aug. 29, 1816. Sam'l Meredith, BM.

Elijah Stutlesworth & Francis Jones, May 2, 1816, by
James Richmond, J.P. Absalom Knight, BM.

Holland Sullivan & Polly Osment, Sep. 12, 1816, by J.
Sullivan, Sep. 14, 1816.

Simeon Sullivan & Nancy Sullivan, Jan. 17, 1816. William
Greer, BM.

Joseph Sweat & Susannah Goodall, Sep. 30, 1816. Parks
Goodall, BM.

Pleasant Tarpley & Mary Goddy (Gaddy?), Oct. 30, 1816.
David Phillips, BM.

Ira Tatum & Patsey Tatum, Jan. 21, 1816, by James Henderson, J.P., Jan. 24, 1816. Eli Creswell, BM.

James P. Thompson & Mary Owinn, July 19, 1816, by David
Foster, M.G., July 25, 1816.
Valentine Vanhoover & Sally Rowland, Dec. 14, 1816, by
Joseph T. Williams, J.P., Dec. 15, 1816. David
Upchurch, BM.
Lewis Vick & Jane David, Dec. 17, 1816. James Dark, BM.
Wilson T. Waters & Polly Lawrence, Aug. 3, 1816, by Thomas
Durham, M.G., Aug. 7, 1816. John A. Taylor, BM.
Wilson Webb & Frances Ann Tarpley, Nov. 18, 1816, by John
Page, Nov. 21, 1816. Richard Ramsey, BM.
Mark Whiting & Elizabeth Walker, Dec. 5, 1816, by Ransom
Gwyn, J.P. William Avery, BM.
William H. Whitson & Elizabeth Brinson, Nov. 22, 1816.
Josiah Brinson, BM.
Ridley Wynne & Fanny Miles, Sep. 2, 1816, by John
Hannah, J.P., Sep. 5, 1816. Johnie Hooker, BM.
Archibald Young & Polly Knight, April 27, 1816. William
Campbell, BM.
William Adklnson & Araminta Reed, N.D. (about 1816).
J. A. Johnson, BM.
William Allman & Susanah R. Mitchell, Dec. 8, 1817. John
H. Paskel, BM.
Thomas Ames & Elizabeth Aust, Jan. 27, 1817, by Abner
Hill, M.G., Jan. 29, 1817. Elijah Ruttledge, BM.
James M. Armstrong & Polley Payne, Sep. 12, 1817. Joseph
Patton, BM.
George Aspey & Lucrecy Brown, June 12, 1817. David
Brown, BM.
Daniel Astan & Jane D. Bell, Aug. 5, 1817, by Thos.
Calhoon, M.G., Aug. 6, 1817. James Slate, BM.
William Avery & Permelia Sperry, Dec. 16, 1817, by Jacob
Brown, J.P., Dec. 17, 1817. Peter Sullivan.
Allen Avery & Polly Wynne, Dec. 29, 1817. John Smith, BM.
Bennet Babb & Abegal Gunthrie, Jan. 21, 1817, by John
Jarratt, Jan. 22, 1817. Mathew Horn, BM.
William Baskin & Rebecca Belt (Balt), Feb. 22, 1817, by
Presley Lester, V.D.M., Feb. 23, 1817. Aaron Gibson,
BM.
William Belbro & Margaret McFarlin, Sep. 3, 1817, by
James Whitsite, Sep. 11, 1817. Jno. McFarlin, BM.
Sutton Belcher & Abehale Ellis, Sep. 16, 1817. James
Ellis, BM.
John Bradberry & Barsheba Golston, Nov. 2, 1817, by Abner
Hill, M.G. Thomas Arrington, BM.
John F. Brown & Margaret F. Seawell, Sep. 16, 1817, by
John Payne. Mathew Dew, BM.
James Braden & Betsey M. Merrett, April 12, 1817, by
James Foster, J.P., April 17, 1817. Alexander Braden,
BM.
James Bunton & Sindy H. Thomas, Jan. 9, 1817, by Abner
W. Bone. James Thomas, BM.
Peterson Burge & Elizabeth Palmer, Feb. 26, 1817. James
Slate, BM.
Miller Carter & Pheby Philips, June 2, 1817, by O. G.
Finley, June 21, 1817. Benjamin Phulips, BM.

Joseph Caskey & Caty Scobey, Jan. 15, 1817, by J. I.
Johnson, J.P., Jan. 16, 1817. Joseph Weir, BM.
Isaac Carver & Mary Hughley (Mrs. Mary Hughley), Oct. 11,
1817, by John Williamson, J.P., Oct. 12, 1817. William
Carver, BM.
Jordan Chandler & Elizabeth Avery, Dec. 16, 1817. William
Avery, BM.
William Chism & Patsey Griffin, July 21, 1817, by John W.
Payton, J.P., July 22, 1817. John Griffin, BM.
William Chumney & Elizabeth Fossey, Dec. 12, 1817, by
Abner W. Bone, J.P., Dec. 23, 1817. Richard Chimney, BM.
Benjamin Clayton & Lockey Quarles, March 26, 1817, by
Joshua Lester, V.D.M., March 27, 1817. Edward Clayton,
BM.
Joseph Cloyd & Caty Alexander, May 12, 1817, by Jesse
Alexander, V.B.D., M.A., May 15, 1817. W. I. Alexander,
BM.
Adam Cluck & Marinda Howel, March 17, 1817. William
Alsup, BM.
Mathias B. Click & Nancy Moss, May 6, 1817. William
Moss, BM.
William Coats & Patsey Tracy, April 12, 1817, by James
Davidson, April 15, 1817. J.B. Taylor, BM.
John Cooke (or Cocke) Senr & Elizabeth H. Williams,
Feb. 25, 1817, by Joshua Lester, V.D.M. William C.
Collings, BM.
Joseph Cocke & Sarah W. Winston, Dec. 16, 1817. William
C. Collings, BM.
William C. Sollins & Sarah Wortham, July 2, 1817.
Joseph Cocke, BM.
Adam Conger & Kizziah Davis, Dec. 29, 1817, by Elijah
Maddox, M.G., Dec. 30, 1817. Abner Harpole, BM.
Benjamin M. Davis & Casander Taylor, Aug. 16, 1817, by
Wm. B. Elgin, E.M.E.C., Aug. 19, 1817. William H.
Moore, BM.
John Davidson & Elizabeth Brown, Oct. 11, 1817, by John
W. Payton, J.P. Henry H. Howel, BM.
Thomas Davis & Elizabeth Robertson, Nov. 25, 1817, by
John Williamson, J.P. John Porter, BM.
Hardy Davenport & Martha Bryson, N.D. Abram Cooper, BM.
Jesse Donnell & Sally Cropper, April 12, 1817, by Sam'l
Cannon, J.P., April 15, 1817. John Donnell, BM.
H. L. Douglas & Zuritha Allcorn, Aug. 19, 1817. Harry
Cage, BM.
Ira E. Eason & Dolly Vaughn, Jan. 9, 1817. James A.
Hunter, BM.
Joseph Eddings & Parthena Henderson, Jan. 18, 1817.
Benjamin Tucker, BM.
Eli Edwards & Milly Hancock, June 17, 1817, by Edward
Harris, J.P., June 19, 1817. Jonathan Doke, BM.
Hiram Edwards & Sally Bond, April 28, 1817, by Edward
Willis, V.D.M., April 29, 1817. Bradford Edwards, BM.
John Ellis & Mary Sandiford, Jan. 18, 1817, by John
Williamson, J.P., Jan. 19, 1817. John Campbell, BM.

David Fields & Rhody Ferrington, April 26, 1817, by
Sam'l Cannon, J.P., April 29, 1817. Ivey Gibson, BM.
Green Flowers & Mary Sypert, Feb. 26, 1817. James T.
Coats, BM.
Allen Fuller & Nancy Harris, Oct. 28, 1817, by John W.
Payton, J.P., Nov. 13, 1817. Duke H. Harris, BM.
William Gallagly & Sarah Cummings, March 1, 1817, by
James Richmond, J.P., March 2, 1817. George Callagly,
BM.
James Godfrey & Frances Rogers, June 29, 1817, by John
Lester, V.D.M., July 12, 1817. Josiah Rogers, BM.
Boswell Goodman & Mary Bumpas, Aug. 30, 1817. Robert
Smith, BM.
James Goodrich & Patsey Taylor, Aug. 30, 1817, by
Thomas Durham, M.G., Sep. 2, 1817. John A. Taylor, BM.
John M. Greer & Rachel Thomas, March 19, 1817, by Abner
W. Bone, J.P., April 10, 1817. Samuel Y. Thomas, BM.
Joseph Hall & Rebeccah Archer, Feb. 11, 1817.
John W. Payton, J.P., Prescot Nickins, BM.
Samuel Hancock & Ann Avery, Jan. 8, 1817, by Ransom
Owyn, J.P., Jan. 22, 1817. William Hancock, BM.
Ephram G. Harris & Isabella H. Miller, July 21, 1817,
by Thos. Calhoon, M.G., July 22, 1817. Andrew Foster,
BM.
Enoch P. Hannes & Elizabeth Phillips, Jan. 21, 1817.
Elijah Cros, BM.
Sterling Harrison & Elizabeth Jones, Dec. 1, 1817, by
John Dew, M.G., Dec. 3, 1817. Thomas Edwards, BM.
Wright Hickman & Sarah Tucker, Nov. 20, 1817. Abner
Hill, M.G., Benjamin Tucker, BM.
Thomas L. Hill & Anna Lansden, Sep. 6, 1817, by Abner
W. Bone, J.P., Sep. 9, 1817. Abner W. Lansden, BM.
John Hazelwood & Rhody Pemberton, Aug. 5, 1817. Richard
Pemberton, BM.
John Hearn & Drucilla Bonner, Sep. 22, 1817. G.D.
Moore, BM.
Jacob Hollingsworth & Lydia Fuston, Jan. 28, 1817, by
C. Cooper, J.P., Feb. 29, 1817. James Hollingsworth,
BM.
Henry Horn & Elizabeth Brien, Dec. 6, 1817. Edmund
Crutcher, J.P., Richard Hight, BM.
Mathew Horn & Martha T. Babb, Sep. 11, 1817. John Jarratt,
William Babb, BM.
James M. Hurt & Martyha (Martha) Marshall, March 26,
1817. Samuel Meredith, BM.
John Irby & Nancy Harris, Aug. 30, 1817. Elijah
Maddox, M.G., William Steele, BM.
Daniel Jackson & Sally Jackson, Sep. 24, 1817. James
Slate, BM.
Bard Jacobs & Nancy Jennings, Aug. 23, 1817, by Jas.
Cross, J.P., Aug. 28, 1817. Archibald Campbell, BM.
Elijah Jennings & Elizabeth Rogers, M.D. Jonathan
Williams, BM.
James Johnson & Polly E. Erwin, Dec. 3, 1817, by Thos.
Calhoon, M.G., Dec. 4, 1817. Samuel Calhoon, BM.

WILSON COUNTY MARRIAGES

Edmund Jones & Elizabeth Stapleton, June 13, 1817, by
Wm. Seawell, June 14, 1817. Emanuel Scot, BM.

John C. Jones & Elizabeth Lane, March 24, 1817, by James
Richmond, J.P., March 25, 1817. Edward Jones, BM.

William Jones & Polly Dlorady (Dolrady?), Nov. 21, 1817.
Benjamin Pyland, BM.

William Jones & Lucy Wormack, Sep. 23, 1817. George
Bullard, BM.

George W. Jones & Christina G. Dance, Dec. 8, 1817, by
Jacob Sullivan, Dec. 9, 1817.

Wiley Jones & Pheby Saterfield, Aug. 5, 1817, by Elijah
Maddox, M.G., Aug. 7, 1817. John P. Maddox, BM.

Philip Koonee & Polly Fields, Dec. 22, 1817, by Edward
Harris, J.P., Dec. 23, 1817. David Fields, BM.

Levi Knotts & Elvy Young, Nov. 29, 1817. Booth Malone,
BM.

William A. Langstone & Rebeccah Sutton, Dec. 30, 1817.
Rowland Sutton.

Jesse Jennings & Nancy Craddock, June 1, 1817, by Joshua
Lester, V.D.M., Oct. 8, 1817.

John McAdow & Patsey Leech, July 25, 1817, by McMinn,
J.P., July 31, 1817.

John McAffrey & Patsey Hunt, March 21, 1817. Wm. Seawell,
Harvey H. Seawell, BM.

James L. McConnell & Anne L. Moore, Dec. 30, 1817, by
Thos. Calhoon, V.D.M., Dec. 31, 1817. Gabriel Barton,
BM.

John McMillen & Reesey Adamson, March 25, 1817. Jas.
Cross, J.P., Joseph Adamson, BM.

William Melton & Lucinda Wilmoth, Feb. 5, 1817. Archibus
Melton, BM.

John Merrett & Nancy Bonds, Dec. 26, 1817, by Edward
Willis, M.G., Dec. 30, 1817. Willie Caraway, BM.

William Michie & Betsey Flood, Feb. 4, 1817. James
McAdow, J.P., John McAdow, BM.

Moses Mitchell & Elenor Hodge, Feb. 24, 1817. George
Hodge, BM.

Sion H. Mitchell & Elizabeth Cook, Feb. 22, 1817, by
William Gray, J.P., Feb. 25, 1817. William Babb, BM.

George D. Moore & Priscilla Hern, Sep. 22, 1817. John
Hern, BM.

Haynes Moore & Mary Davis, May 29, 1817. Joseph Bell,
J.P., Solomon Moore, BM.

Isareal Moore & Sally Roach, June 16, 1817, by William
Gray, J.P., June 19, 1817. William Moore, BM.

Joseph Moore & Lyndia Odum, May 13, 1817, by O. F.
Finley, J.P., May 15, 1817. Elijah Cross, BM.

Daniel Mosely & Nancy Corder, May 31, 1817, by Joseph T.
Bell, J.P., June 3, 1817. William Talbot, BM.

Robert Motheral & Jane Kirkpatrick, Sep. 9, 1817, by
William Gray, J.P., Sep. 11, 1817. Samuel Motheral,
BM.

William S. New & Sally Hancock, Nov. 29, 1817, by Jesse
Alexander, J.P., Nov. 30, 1817. William Shanks, BM.

James Oneal & Elizabeth Caplinger, Jan. 20, 1817. John
W. Carter, BM.
James Osment & Elizabeth Eddings, July 14, 1817. Wm. M.
Smith, BM.
Samuel Parker & Mabel Shaw, Feb. 12, 1817, by Joseph T.
Bell, J.P., Feb. 20, 1817. Abner Shaw, BM.
John Patton & Elizabeth Shores, April 26, 1817, by Geo.
Clark, J.P., May 3, 1817. William Maxwell.
Joseph Patton & Ann Pattersons, Sep. 30, 1817. Andrew
Thompson, BM.
William Patterson & Lively Hight, Aug. 6, 1817. Frank
Puckett, BM.
Richard Pemberton & Chinea Gillespie, Nov. 15, 1817.
Elijah Cross, BM.
Turner Perry & Rhody Goodman, March 17, 1817. Jacob
Browning, M.G., William Goodman, BM.
John F. Porter & Isaphana Whitworth, Dec. 24, 1817, by
John Williamson, J.P., Dec. 28, 1817. John Bernard,
BM.
Richard Ramsey & Harriet New, Nov. _0, 1817. Robert C.
Davis, BM.
Elijah Rice & Joley Ann Brown, June 19, 1817. Stephen
Brown, BM.
Zachariah Ricketts & Sally May, Jan. 22, 1817, by John
Williamson, J.P., Jan. 23, 1817. Lanslot Vivett, BM.
Robert B. Roberts & Mary Ann Miller, Jan. 27, 1817, by
Wm. Steele, J.P., Jan. 28, 1817. Thos. Bradley, BM.
Aaron Romine & Polly Conger, Oct. 8, 1817, by Abner
Hill, M.G., Oct. 9, 1817. Robert Scypert, BM.
Levin Roper & Naoma Alsup, May 7, 1817. Samuel
Merredith, BM.
Alvis Sellers & Jane Cummings, Oct. 29,1817, by Edward
Willism, A.M.G., Oct. 30, 1817. George Cummings, BM.
William W. Setter & Sally Ray, Jan. 22, 1817, by William
Gray, J.P., Jan. 27, 1817. Willis Wray, BM.
James Shannon & Polly Shannon, Dec. 31, 1816, by James
Richmond, Jan. 2, 1817.
Philip Shores & Jane Creighton, Oct. 4, 1817, by Geo.
Clark, Oct. 9, 1817. Elijah Wommock, BM.
Nathan Simpson & Polly S. Mitchell, Oct. 16, 1817. Henry
B. McDonald, BM.
Elisha Sims & Ann Clopton, Oct. 13, 1817. Joseph
Cocke, BM.
James Slate & Elizabeth Hallum, Feb. 13, 1817. John
Hallum, BM.
Absolom Smith & Lydia Beard, Sep. 27, 1817, by John
Williamson, J.P., Oct. 2, 1817. James H. Young, BM.
W.B. Smith & Sarah Randolph, July 26, 1817. George B.
Smith, BM.
Philip Smart & Abejah Wright, Aug. 29, 1817. James
Somers, BM.
Samuel Speed & Patsey Archer, Sep. 24, 1817. Jacob
Archer, BM.
Moses Starns & Mary Chandler, March 12, 1817. Pitts
Chandler, BM.

WILSON COUNTY MARRIAGES

John Starnes & Elizabeth Chandler, Oct. 11, 1817. Joseph
  Swingley, BM.
Alexander Stewart & Chastain Evens, Feb. 27, 1817. Joseph
  T. Bell, J.P., Joseph Stewart, BM.
Thomas C. Stone & Sally Justice, Dec. 18, 1817. Isaac
  Easley, BM.
Bazil Summers & Tobinah Jacobs, Jan. 7, 1817. Jacob
  Sullivan, Thomas Bell, BM.
Ezekiel A. Sharp & Jane Lansdon, Aug. 23, 1817. Abner
  W. Bone, J.P., Abner Lansden, BM.
David M. Tait & Elizabeth Alampitt (Clampett), Aug. 28,
  1817. John Williamson, J.P., Nathan Clampett, BM.
Zedekiah Tate & Ellen Jones, Dec. 16, 1817, by D. Foster,
  M.G., Jan. 8, 1818. Moses T. Brooks, BM.
James Tarver & Keziah Hunter, Sep. 9, 1817. W. H. Peace,
  Thos. Bradley, BM.
Thomas Taylor & Anna Ramsey, Nov. 27, 1817. James
  Bowman, BM.
John Telford & Sally Gwin, March 18, 1817, by David
  Foster, M.G., March 20, 1817. Hugh Telford, BM.
David Todd & Margaret Luck, Sep. 2, 1817, by John
  McMinn, J.P., Sep. 12, 1817. O. G. Finley, BM.
John E. Warren & Sally Jennings, Sep. 2, 1817. Samuel
  H. Porterfield, BM.
George Webb & Nancy Cross, May 7, 1817, by Joshua Lester,
  V.D.M., May 13, 1817. Woodson Webb, BM.
Elisha Winters & Rhody Campbell, Jan. 30, 1817. William
  Phillips, BM.
Jonathan Wiley & Ruth M. Brown, March 10, 1817. Samuel
  Donnell, V.D.M., John Brown, BM.
Nathan Williams & Polly Arnold, April 2, 1817. Abner
  Hill, M.G., John Congers, BM.
William Willis & Rhody Sperry, Sep. 6, 1817. Elijah
  Maddox, M.G., Geo. Martin, BM.
Ezekerl C. Witty & Mary Allison, June 10, 1817, by
  Jacob Silivan (Sullivan), M.G., June 12, 1817. Ezekirl
  A. Sharp, BM.
Mills Woods & Elizabeth Telford, Oct. 11, 1817, by
  David Foster, M.G., Nov. 4, 1817. Elijah Curry, BM.
Willis Ray & Ann Wright, Jan. 9, 1817, by William Gray,
  J.P., Jan. 16, 1817. Isaac Wright, BM.
Edmund York & Nancy Bass, March 7, 1817. J.F. Davis,
  J.P., James Yogk, BM.
William Adams & Dorothy Richardson, July 7, 1818. B.
  Casilman, J.P., Elisha Dismukes, BM.
William Adkinson & Araminta Reed, Dec. 27,1818, by
  Jas. Johnson, Dec. 28, 1818.
Archibald Allen & Matilda Lambert, Aug. 29, 1818, by John
  W. Payton, J.P., Aug. 30, 1818. Wm. Hartsfield, BM.
Hezekiah Archer & Patsey Mitchell, Sep. 19, 1818. James
  Nickens, BM.
Jasper E. Ashworth & Casandra Berry, Aug. 8, 1818, by
  Jas. Johnson, J.P., Aug. 10, 1818.
___iam Bailey & Sally Tally, Nov. 14, 1818, by Jas.
  Cross, J.P., Nov. 19, 1818.

Delphan Bass & Frances Gaddy, Oct. 23, 1818. Thomas
Phillips.
Littleton Benthall & Susannah Stanley, April 9, 1818.
John W. Payton, Benjamin Stanley, BM.
Robert Boothe & Minerva Payne, Nov. 2, 1818, by Edward
Willis, M.G., Nov. 5, 1818.
James Bowman & Elizabeth Taylor, Feb. 14, 1818. Thomas
Taylor, BM.
Elisha Brien & Elizabeth Johnson, Sep. 20- 1818, by Wm.
Steele, J.P., Sep. 27, 1818. O. G. Finley, BM.
Milton P. Brittle & Winney Spring, Dec. 21, 1818. Geo.
L. Swan, BM.
Isaac W. Brooks & Martha Huddleston, Feb. 2, 1818, by
Joshua Lester, V.D.M., Feb. 5, 1818.
Stephen Frooks & Maria Swiney, Sep. 30, 1818. Jeremiah
Brooks, BM.
Jeremiah Brooks & Rachel Spring, Feb. 2, 1818. George
Swan, BM.
Thomas Breedlove & Sally Travillion, March 24, 1818, by
Elijah Maddox, M.G., March 26, 1818. Drury Bettis, BM.
Elisha Bryson & Polly Ward, Dec. 8, 1818, by John McMinn,
J.P., Dec. 10, 1818. John Leech, BM.
Nathan Bundy & Absilla Johnson, June 18, 1818. John
Dew, M.G., Elijah Jones, BM.
John Campbell & Judah A. Lambert, Oct. 23, 1818. John
Morros, BM.
Nobles Cannon & Annis Chandler, July 11, 1818, by Joseph
T. Williams, J.P., July 12, 1818. Byrd Guille, BM.
William Carlin & Sarah Johnson, Oct. 13, 1818. John
Cox, BM.
Willis Caraway & Susanna Clemmons, Sep. 25, 1818, by
Edward Harris, Oct. 1, 1818. Harrod Merrett, BM.
Humphrey Chappell & Charity Johnson, Nov. 13, 1818. John
Coe, BM.
John Cocke & Elizabeth Harris, Feb. 17, 1818. Joshua
Lester, V.D.M., Leonard H. Sims, BM.
George Cooper & Martha Dillard, May 26, 1818, by John
Page, May 28, 1818. James Browning, BM.
John Cox & Elizabeth Palmer, Oct. 13, 1818, by John W.
Payton, Oct. 20, 1818. William Carlin, BM.
William Cox & Evalina Reese, May 16, 1818, by Wm. Steele,
J.P., May 21, 1818. James Turner, BM.
Solomon Corder & Martha Brown, Feb. 12, 1818, by John
Bonner, J.P., Feb. 15, 1818. Jesse Shaw, BM.
Benjamin Davis & Nancy Mitchell, Sep. 1, 1818. Jesse
Lysles, BM.
James Davis & Penelope Drake, Oct. 10, 1818. J.T. Davis,
Thomas Soudder, BM.
Jose C. Dew & Nancy Hunter, Oct. 20, 1818, by John Dew,
M.G., Oct. 22, 1818. Mathew Dew, BM.
Ruben Dial & Zilphy Medlin, Aug. 1, 1818, by Jas. T.
Williams, Aug. 2, 1818. B. Bridges, BM.
Samuel Dickings & Ann Enoch, Dec. 21, 1818, by Elijah
Maddox, M.G., Dec. 22, 1818. James Dickings, BM.

William Dillard & Elizabeth Corder, June 15, 1818.
James Browning, BM.
Jesse Eagan & Narcisa Rieff, Jan. 29, 1818. William
Grey, J.P., Henry Howell, BM.
James Ellis & Rebecca Belcher, Jan. 5, 1818. Martin
Tally, BM.
Thomas W. Allis & Caroline Clanton, May 23, 1818, by
William Grey, J.P., May 25, 1818. Richard Byrd, BM.
George A. Evans & Thussey Higarty, Nov. 17, 1818. Wm.
Steele, J.P., Edward Burk, BM.
James Frazer & Hannah Shelby, Nov. 17, 1818, by Thos.
Calhoon, V.D.M., Nov. 18, 1818. Jno. L. Wynne, BM.
Miles Fuller & Charity Seals, July 26, 1818, by Robert
Branch, J.P., July 29, 1818. James Moore, BM.
Jonathan Fuston & Rebecca Stanly, July 15, 1818, by J.
McMinn, M.G., July 20, 1818. Joseph Fuston, BM.
John Garrett & Ann McWhirter, Sep. 9, 1818. J. L. Davis,
William Garrett, BM.
Isaac Green & Elizabeth Eagan, April 28, 1818. William
Gray, George Briggs, BM.
Zachariah Griffith & Elizabeth Baird, March 5, 1818, by
John Williams, J.P., March 5, 1818.
Stephen Hampton & Elizabeth Williams, Oct. 20, 1818.
William Tackett, BM.
Michial Harris & Nancy Tally, Dec. 22, 1818. Jesse
Tally, BM.
Moses Harris & Sally Dillard, Jan. 17, 1818. Abner
Hill, M.G., John Impson, BM.
Peter Harville & Sally Watkins, May 11, 1818, by William
Lawrence, J.P., May 14, 1818. Turner M. Lawrence, BM.
Thomas Horn & Louisa Woolard, March 30, 1818. Wm. Steele,
J.P., Alligood Woolard, BM.
John Hornberry (Hornsberry) & Elizabeth Martin, Nov. 27,
1818. Jos. T. Williams, Goodrich Andrews, BM.
Hyram Howard & Cinthia Bennett, Oct. 10, 1818, by Ben-
jamin Casilman, J.P., Oct. 19, 1818. Howard Edwards,
BM.
Robert Irwin & Rachel Bogle, April 13, 1818, by Christo-
pher Cooper, April 15, 1818.
Elijah Jennings & Elizabeth Jennings, Jan. 6, 1818, by
Joshua Lester, V.D.M., Jan. 7, 1818.
Robert Jennings & Hannah Ward, Dec. 18, 1818, by Jas.
Cros, J.P., Dec. 20, 1818. Bazel Jacob, BM.
Charles Johnson & _____ Barrow, Oct. 31, 1818, by
James Gray, J.P., Nov. 1818. Hardy C. Willis.
Mark Joplin & Malonie Maxwell, Nov. 21, 1818. James
Foster, J.P., John Howard, BM.
William A. Langstone & Rebecca Sutton, Dec. 30, 1817, by
Elijah Maddox, J.P., Jan. 1, 1818.
James H. Liggon & Elizabeth Thompson, July 28, 1818, by
Joseph T. Williams, July 30, 1818. Osborn Thompson,
BM.
James M. Lisk & Nancy Blair, Aug. 25, 1818. James Gray,
J.P., Hugh Blair, BM.

Thomas Marlow & Lucy Hull, April 7, 1818, by Jeremiah
Hendrick, J.P., May 3, 1818. Payton Marlow, BM.
Samuel McCorkle & Polly Priestly, April 8, 1818, by Thos.
Calhoun, V.D.M., April 9, 1818. H. L. Douglas, BM.
Andrew McDaniel & Sealy Grubbs, May 1, 1818. Stephen
McDaniel, BM.
Josiah McGehee & Scotty Mitchell, Feb. 24, 1818. Alex
C. Carruth, J.P., Armstrong P. Pool, BM.
William E. McSpadden & Margaret W. Miller, Sep. 16, 1818.
Thos. Calhoun, V.D.M., John McSapdden, BM.
Wilson Medley & Sally Sands, March 19, 1818, by Jos. T.
Williams, March 19, 1818. Bar Freeman, BM.
Jones Mitchell & Susan Owen, Sep. 29, 1818. Richard
Locke, BM.
Samuel Mosley & Mary Mosely, March 21, 1818, by Wm.
Nunn, V.D.M., March 26, 1818. Peter Mosely, BM.
James Moore & Margaret Roach, March 24, 1818. John Wm.
Payton, J.P., John White, BM.
John Owens & Dolsey Waters, March 19, 1818. Wm. Steele,
J.P., Nolley Talbut, BM.
Jesse Pendergrass & Polly Garrett, Aug. 27, 1818, by
Edward Williss, M.G., Aug. 28, 1818. John Garratt, BM.
Joshua Pedigo & Nancy Michie, Dec. 26, 1818, by James
McAdow, Dec. 28, 1818. Jeremiah Reaves, BM.
Jesse Pemberton & Ruth Drewry, May 5, 1818. Elijah
Cross, BM.
Thomas Proctor & Anne Dickins, Dec. 26, 1818. Jesse
Lisle, BM.
Patrick R. Puckett & Martha Cocke, Dec. 23, 1818. John
Bond, BM.
Richard Ramsey & Eliza Miles, May 13, 1818. James
Rice, BM.
Hiram Russell & Zilphy Midget, July 7, 1818. Nathan
Owin, BM.
James Seat & Sally Jones, Oct. 24, 1818. Jesse Tally,
BM.
James Scott & Fanny Coe, Nov. 5, 1818. Jesse Tally, BM.
Euben Sillivan & Polly Climer Feb. 7, 1818, by Jacob
Sullivan, Feb. 8, 1818. Barnard Sillivan, BM.
Allen Smith & Elizabeth Motheral, Oct. 19, 1818. Henry
Hobson, BM.
Andon Somers & Sally Walker, Sep. 12, 1818. R. King,
J.P., Thomas Bradly, BM.
William Stafford & Martha Cartwright, May 26, 1818, by
John W. Payton, J.P., May 28, 1818. John Jones, BM.
Benjamin F. Stevenson & Elizabeth Rutland, May 28, 1818,
by Jacob Browning, May 30, 1818. Rutherford Rutland,
BM.
James Stewart & Sarah Smith, Dec. 21, 1818. Jeremiah
Hendrick, J.P., William Gray, BM.
William Thomas & Elizabeth Hasty, June 9, 1818. Edward
Jones, BM.
Anderson Trice & Elizabeth Hickman, July 7, 1818, by
Abner Hill, M.G., July 9, 1818. Samuel Hickman, BM.

Green Tucker & Priscilla Williams, Jan. 12, 1818, by Jas.
Johnson, J.P., Jan. 13, 1818. Jesse Dew, BM.
Kendred Tucker & Darchus King, Nov. 25, 1818, by Elijah
Maddox, M.G., Nov. 26, 1818. Joseph Irby, BM.
Anthony Tittle (Little?) & Nancy Higgins, April 27, 1818.
George Tittle, BM.
Hansel Trusty & Nancy Welch, Jan. 27, 1818. Thomas
Mitchell, BM.
Joseph Underwood & Elizabeth Adamson, Nov. 10, 1818, by
Jas. Cross, J.P., Nov. 12, 1818. Jesse Adamson, BM.
George Waters & Polly Clark, Aug. 4, 1818, by Thomas
Durham, M.G., Aug. 6, 1818. Thomas Phillips, BM.
Edward B. Wheeler & Elizabeth Young, Sep. 22, 1818.
James Young, BM.
Kader White & Betsey Ligon, Sep. 3, 1818. Hooker
Reeves, BM.
Archibald Wilson & Elizabeth Cannon, April 6, 1818.
William Wilson, BM.
Benjamin Wilson & Charlotte Adamson, Aug. 6, 1818. Jesse
Adamson, BM.
Anthony Winston & Nancy Harris, Feb. 18, 1818. George
A. Huddleston, BM.
William G. Wood & Polly Davis, June 4, 1818. William
Searcy, BM.
Moses Woollen & Elizabeth Stokes, Feb. 17, 1818, by James
Gray, J.P., Feb. 22, 1818. Joshua Woolen, BM.
Redding Wright & Harty Patterson, Feb. 11, 1818. Thomas
Harrington, BM.
James Young & Nancy Branch, Oct. 12, 1818. David
Philips, BM.
Thomas Adkinson & Elizabeth Lambert, Oct. 9, 1819, by
Jeremiah Hendrick, J.P., Oct. 11, 1819. Allen Smith,
BM.
John Atherly & Polly Williams, Feb. 22, 1819, by Jos. T.
Williams, Feb. 25, 1819. James Atherly, BM.
William Allen & Eliza Marshall, July 19, 1819. Obadiah
Finly, BM.
Aaron Anglin & Hannah McGee, Jan. 26, 1819. Zachariah
Hutchings, BM.
James Anderson & Elizabeth McDaniel, Jan. 29, 1819.
Robert Sims, BM.
John Aytes & Elizabeth Tally, Sep. 16, 1819. Wyatt
Beckham, BM.
Thomas Babb & Polly Powell, April 27, 1819, by John
Jarratt, April 29, 1819. Thomas Guthrie, BM.
William Babb & Nancy Ross, March 6, 1819, by John
Jarratt, March 11, 1819. William Hartsfield, BM.
James Baird & Elizabeth Richmond, April 20, 1819, by
Edward Harris, J.P., April 22, 1819. Thomas Richmond,
BM.
William Baily & Peyton Tally, Nov. 14, 1819. Peyton
Tally, BM.
Josiah Beasley & Elizabeth Tarpley, Dec. 7, 1819. Stith
T. Tarpley, BM.

Ira Barber & Nancy Leith, Dec. 10, 1819, by J. A. Browning, M.G., Dec. 17, 1819. John Barber, BM.

Gabriel Barton & Jane Johnson, Dec. 28, 1819, by Thos. Calhoon, V.D.M., Dec. 29, 1819. Samuel Calhoon, BM.

Benjamin Barkley & Lydia Reeder, Dec. 23, 1819. John W. Payton, J.P., William Morgan, BM.

Solomon Bearden & Rebecca Woodrun, June 12, 1819, by John Bonner, J.P., June 17, 1819. John Riggs, BM.

Benny Beasley & Mary Jackson, Sep. 13, 1819, by Joseph T. Bell, J.P., Sep. 16, 1819. Edmond Jackson, BM.

Benjamin T. Bell & Cahrlotte Goodall, Jan. 30, 1819, by John T. Bell, J.P., Feb. 4, 1819. Thomas Cartwright.

James Berry & Mary Ann Taylor, Feb. 2, 1819. E. Burk, BM.

James Nettles & Temsy Bettis, Oct. 7, 1819. Alfred Bettis, BM.

Edward Burk & Allis Hegarty, April 20, 1819. William Hartsfield, BM.

David Bond & Lydia Jones, March 26, 1819. John Fakes, J.P., Claiborne H. Rhodes, BM.

Robert Bone & Polly S. Gun, Nov. 24, 1819. Abner W. Lansden, BM.

Robert Boothe & Minerva Payne, Nov. 2, 1819. William Payne, BM.

Ishmel Bradshaw & Levicy McWhirter, July 20, 1819, by Jos. T. Williams, J.P., July 21, 1819. Thomas Mitchell, BM.

John H. Briant & Elizabeth Puckett, Dec. 28, 1819. Leonard H. Sims, BM.

Isaac W. Brook & Martha Buddleston, Feb. 2, 1818. Zedekiah Tatem, BM.

William Brown & Mary Johnson, Aug. 12, 1819. James Thomas, BM.

William Brown & Delila Pate, Feb. 11, 1819, by John W. Payton, J.P., Feb. 20, 1819. Sam'l Meredith, BM.

Meshack Carrol & Martha Carrol, Sep. 7, 1819, by Isaac Linsley, Sep. 9, 1819. John Cooper, BM.

Hugh Carlin & Patsey Pemberton, May 4, 1819. John Pemberton, BM.

Thomas Cartwright & Patsey Davidson, Nov. 1, 1819, by Wm. Steele, J.P., Nov. 4, 1819. Alexander Braden, BM.

Stephen Cauley & Patsey Tally, Dec. 8, 1819. Woodson Layne, FM.

Vincen Cawthon & Rosanah Irwin, Feb. 1, 1819. Thomas Cawthon, BM.

William Chandler & Rachel Shannon, Dec. 28, 1819. Tobias Henderson, BM.

John Clampet & Sally Carey, May 22, 1819, by John Williamson, J.P., June 10, 1819. John R. Wilson, BM.

Jesse Clifton & Sally Smith, Jan. 4, 1819. James B. Guthrie, BM.

David Cloyd & Nancy Wilson, May 22, 1819. Osburn Thompson, BM.

William Cobb & Catharine Jackson, Dec. 21, 1819.
Harrison Irby, BM.
Edmond Collins & Delpha Drennon, Jan. 13, 1819. Henry
Belote, BM.
John C. Collings & Mahaly Wortham, March 20, 1819. James
Howard, BM.
John Conger & Susanah Spradling, Oct. 30, 1819, by
Abner Hill, M.G., Nov. 5, 1819. Cornemus Buck, BM.
Azariah Corder & Viney Shaw, Feb. 24, 1819, by Joseph
T. Bell, J.P., Feb. 25, 1819. Hugh Park, BM.
Anderson Cox & Sally Palmer, June 17, 1819. Thomas
Cos, BM.
William Davidson & Susan Cartwright, Nov. 1, 1819, by
Wm. Steele, J.P., Nov. 2, 1819. George Swann, BM.
Mathew T. Dew & Jane Bradley, Feb. 23, 1819. Thomas
Calhoon, V.D.M., John L. Wynne, BM.
Robert Dixon & Nancy Adams, Aug. 7, 1819, by James Gray,
J.P., Aug. 8, 1819. William Roberts, BM.
Bradford Edwards & Nancy Carraway, May 24, 1819, by
James Gray, J.P., June 3, 1819. John Carraway, BM.
John Edwards & Mary Richmond, Jan. 25, 1819, by Benjamin
Cassilman, J.P., Jan. 28, 1819. Bradford Howard, BM.
James Edward & Sally Jones Aug. 3, 1819. Petter Rag-
land, BM.
Elijah Foster & Polly Taylor, July 9, 1819, by Jas.
Cross, J.P., July 10, 1819. Littleberry Belcher, BM.
Silas Freeman & Sally Cooke (Cocke?), Feb. 17, 1819.
John Jarratt, William Babb, BM.
Thomas Ganis & Lundy Smith, Feb. 15, 1819. Michel Mc-
Dermint, BM.
Giles H. Glen & Phoeby Coe, Nov. 17, 1819, by John
Payton, J.P., Nov. 23, 1819. Thompson Glen, BM.
Jesse Goldman & Susannah Sullivan, Dec. 21, 1819, by
Jacob Sullivan, Dec. 23, 1819. Simion Sullivan, BM.
William Goodall & Elizabeth Phelps, Jan. 22, 1819.
William Cox, BM.
John Goodall & Elizabeth Akin, Jan. 7, 1819. Thomas
Cartwright, BM.
William Green & Polly Pickrell, April 24, 1819, by
Jeremiah Hendricks, J.P., April 28, 1819. Hansel
Trusty, BM.
John Green & Elizabeth Griffin, Feb. 1, 1819. Robert
Branch, J.P., John Wheeler, BM.
John Green & Malinda Bryant, March 20, 1819. John
Bryant, BM.
James Guthrie & Teracy McElroy, Oct. 26, 1819, by John
Jarratt, Oct. 27, 1819. Thomas Guthrie, BM.
Leonard Hathaway & Barthena West, June 17, 1819, by
Jas. Cross, J.P., June 18, 1819. Joseph Adamson, BM.
Stealey Hagor & Polly Whitley, Sep. 6, 1819, by John
McMinn, J.P., Sep. 7, 1819. William C. Odum, BM.
Moody P. Hains & Susanah Caplinger, Aug. 6, 1819. Henry
Chandler, BM
Bennerr W. Hall & Matilda Brashers, Sep. 7, 1819, by Jas.
Cross, J.P., Sep. 8, 1819. Corn Lewis, BM.

41

Mathew Hancock & Elizabeth Mills, March 13, 1819.
Jacob Sullivan, J.P., A. J. Crawford, BM.
Skein Hancock & Nancy Hearn, Dec. 20, 1819. B. Branch,
J.P., Martin Hancock, BM.
James Henry & Rebecca Mitchell, Oct. 13, 1819. James
Mitchell, BM.
William Horn (Hern) & Susannah Turner, Aug. 6, 1819.
James Hearn, BM.
Benjamin Hobson & Elizabeth Murry, Aug. 2, 1819. Thomas
Bradley, BM.
Elliott Holloman & Rachel Williams, Feb. 26, 1819. Abner
Hill, M.G., James Nickins, BM.
Charles Horn & Rachel Swindle, July 23, 1819. William
Horn, BM.
Howel Horn & Rebecca Stone, June 22, 1819. William
Horn, BM.
Robert Hughs & Sally Harpole, May 6, 1819, by B. King,
J.P., May 7, 1819. Adam Harpole, BM.
Robert Irvin & Rachel Bogle, April 13, 1819. John
Leech, BM.
Mark Jackson & Mary Ramsey, Nov. 20, 1819, by Joseph T.
Bell, J.P., Nov. 25, 1819. Peterson Burge, BM.
Atkinson Johnson & Sally Martin, May 31, 1819, by Wm.
Steele, J.P., June 2, 1819. James Johnson, BM.
Drury Joiner & Polly Wood, Feb. 9, 1819, by Jos. T.
Williams, Feb. 11, 1819. Cornellus Joiner, BM.
Richard Jones & Mary Martin, June 24, 1819. James Gray,
J.P., Henry Hunt, BM.
William Jones & Polly Jennings, June 5, 1819. E. Maddox,
M.G., John Maddox, BM.
Samuel Justice & Hannah Cartwright, Aug. 30, 1819.
Michell Yerger, BM.
Solomon Kemp & Hollon Ray, Jan. 19, 1819, by Jos. T.
Williams, Jan. 21, 1819. Jacob McDermat, BM.
Josiah Kirkpatrick & Nancy Telford, April 27, 1819, by
Jacob Browning, J.P., April 29, 1819.
John Liggon & Charity Alford, Feb. 12, 1819. John Thomp-
son, BM.
Geraldas Lynch & Sally Harrison, Sep. 2, 1819, by John
Page, Sep. 21, 1819. Norval Douglas, BM.
Hugh Martin & Elizabeth Lankford, Jan. 11, 1819, by J. T.
Johnson, J.P., Jan. 14, 1819. William Lankford, BM.
Elihu Maxey & Eveline Taylor, Aug. 10, 1819. Thos.
Calhoon, V.D.M., James Bowman, BM.
William Mayo & Sally Mayo, May 19, 1819. E. Maddox,
M.G., Sam'l McAdams, BM.
Thomas McGriff & Sally Mitchell, Aug. 5, 1819. R.W.
Grissim, BM.
David McKnight & Patsey M. McWhirter, Nov. 20, 1819, by
Jesse Alexander, V.D.M., Dec. 10, 1819. Leonard H.
Sims, BM.
George Miller & Mary Sellars, Nov. 1, 1819. John Lester,
V.D.M., Alford Miller, BM.
Henry Mitchell & Nancy Graves, Dec. 22, 1819. Benjamin
Davis, BM.

Daniel H. Mobiers & Sally Williams, April 24, 1819, by
Hugh Roane, J.P., April 27, 1819. James Weir, BM.
James Modglin & Lucinda Kenedy, Jan. 3, 1819, by Jos. T.
Williams, Feb. 4, 1819. Edward Birk, BM.
Whiteford Moore & Catharine Meredith, Dec. 27, 1819.
Mathew Dew, BM.
William Morton & Nancy Walker, July 5, 1819, by Isham
F. Davis, July 7, 1819. Richard Echoes, BM.
Zadock Mulinax & Polly Talley, Nov. 11, 1819, by Jas.
Cross, J.P., Nov. 12, 1819. Paton Talley, BM.
James Murry & Casa Yarnell, Dec. 28, 1819. Dandridge
Moss, BM.
Joseph Neal & Sally Smith, March 2, 1819, by J. F.
Davis, J.P., March 4, 1819. Murphy Reese.
James Nellum & Nancy Crooker, Feb. 25, 1819. Thomas
Mitchell.
James Nettles & Temsy Battie (Bettie), Oct. 7, 1819, by
Abner Hill, M.G., Oct. 9, 1819.
Henry Hichols & Elizabeth Hallum, Dec. 2, 1819. L.W.
Moore, BM.
William Norman & Elizabeth Pursley, Jan. 1, 1819. Thomas
Knights, BM.
William C. Odum & Charlotte Ward, Sep. 28, 1819, by
Jos. W. McMinn, J.P., Sep. 30, 1819. Jordan Ward, BM.
Shadrack Owens & Olive Dillard, March 27, 1819, by Abner
Hill, M.G., March 31, 1819. Henry Jacobs, BM.
William Owens & Rebecca Franklin, Jan. 2, 1819, by Thos.
Calhoon, V.D.M., Jan. 3, 1819. O. G. Finley, BM.
Thomas Partlow & Cloe Hooker, Aug. 3, 1819. Jacob
Sullivan, John Chandler, BM.
Andrew Patton & Elizabeth Firbus, Dec. 18, 1819. Joseph
Patton, BM.
John Potts & Cynthia Jones, Oct. 7, 1819. James Gray,
J.P., David Bond, BM.
Allen Powell & Anne T. Hutchings, Oct. 20, 1819, by
Joshua Lester, V.D.M., Oct. 27, 1819. Stephen T.
Hutchings, BM.
William Prim & Ann Johnson, Aug. 28, 1819, by Jos. T.
Williams, J.P., Sep. 2, 1819. Richard Jarratt, BM.
James Payne & Elizabeth Williams, March 19, 1819. James
Thompson, BM.
Thomas Phillips & Sally Lawrence, Aug. 28, 1819. Elijah
Bros, BM.
William Phillips & Nancy Waters, Aug. 10, 1819. Elijah
Cros, BM.
Abram Prim & Nancy Cook, Feb. 19, 1819, by John Jarratt,
Feb. 25, 1819.
William Reed & Rachel Penticost, Dec, 28, 1819, by
Edward Harris, J.P., Dec. 30, 1819. Absolum Harris, BM.
Nathaniel Rice & Nancy Rice, Jan. 22, 1819. Jos. T.
Williams, Willshire Bandy, BM.
Benjamin Rice & Elizabeth Climer, May 15, 1819. Geraldus
Bolton, BM.
Lemuel Robbins & Mary Brown, Nov. 16, 1819. Benjamin
Casilman, J.P., William Hickman, BM.

William Roberts & Sally Adams, Aug. 7, 1819, by James
Gray, J.P., Aug. 8, 1819. Robert Dixon, BM.
Richard Rowland & Polley Neal, Jan. 14, 1819, by Jos. T.
Williams, Jan. 28, 1819. Valentine Vanhozer, BM.
Reddick Rutland & Melberry Rutland, Dec. 12, 1819, by
J. A. Browning, M.G., Dec. 16, 1819.
Robert Scott & Nancy Bone, July 24, 1819. John Morrow,
BM.
Anderson Seat & Micy Mick, Aug. 24, 1819, by John W.
Payton, J.P., Aug. 26, 1819. Jesse Tally, BM.
Charles Seay & Mary Beard, Nov. 1, 1819, by John W.
Payton, J.P., Nov. 2, 1819. Matthew Dew, BM.
John Shaw & Nancy Drennon, Aug. 14, 1819, by Ransom Gwyn,
J.P., Aug. 25, 1819. Thos. Partlow, BM.
Jessee Shaw & Mary Park, Nov. 20, 1819, by Joseph T.
Bell, Nov. 30, 1819. Charles Irwin, BM.
William Shaw & Mary Shaw, May 4, 1819, by James Gray,
J.P., May 21, 1819. William Cummings, BM.
William Shanks & Patsey Wommack, July 10, 1819. David
Phillips, BM.
Archibal Sherrill & Agnes Moss, Dec. 7, 1819. Samuel
W. Sherrill, BM.
John Smith & Michie Hutcherson, Nov. 13, 1819. James
Smith, BM.
John Smith & Lettice Brown, Jan. 22, 1819, by John W.
Payton, J.P., Jan. 23, 1819. Edward Birk, BM.
James Smith & Delia Glanton, April 7, 1819, by William
Gray, J.P., April 18, 1819. John Comer, BM.
Robert Smith & Elizabeth Law, June 10, 1819, by David
Foster, M.G., June 15, 1819. Thos. T. Law, BM.
Robert Smith & Mary Smith, Nov. 8, 1819. Jesse Alexander,
V.D.M., Bernard Brown, BM.
John H. Southern & Polly Seat, Aug. 3, 1819. Thomas
Williams, BM.
Enoch Stiles & Caty McCoy, July 6, 1819, by J. Lester,
V.D.M., July 8, 1819. Samuel Alsup, BM.
Toliver Sutton & Ann Melton, June 3, 1819. R. King,
J.P., Benjamin Chapman, BM.
Robert Sweat & Elizabeth Glenn, Oct. 9, 1819. Alexander
Carruth, J.P., Edward Sweat, BM.
James Thomson & Matilda H. Scoby, Nov. 22, 1819, by
Wm. Steel, J.P., Nov. 25, 1819. Coleman Stone
James Thompson & Peggy Williams, Jan. 9, 1819. Isaac
Williams, BM.
Ozment Thompson & Polly Ann Curd, Sep. 20, 1819. George
Williams, BM.
Isaac Turnage & Patsey Bell, Oct. 9, 1819, by Joseph T.
Bell, J.P., Oct. 17, 1819. John J. Bell, BM.
David Upchurch & Sally Johnson, July 20, 1819, by
Alexander Carruth, J.P., July 21, 1819. Saml. N.
Moore, BM.
Seaburn Weaks & Nancy Johnson, Nov. 23, 1819. John
Wright, BM.
John F. West & Polly Lawrence, March 1, 1819, by Thomas
Durham, M.G., March 4, 1819. John F. West, BM.

WILSON COUNTY MARRIAGES

John Weir & Rebecca Rye, April 7, 1819, by Wm. Steele,
J.P., April 8, 1819. James Weir, BM.
John Weir & Elizabeth Chandler, Aug. 12, 1819. Wm. Steele,
J.P., Hansford Anderson, BM.
James Wilson & Polly Joyner, Jan. 20, 1819. Drewery
Joyner, BM.
John White & Anne Moore, July 20, 1819, by John Bonner,
J.P., July 22, 1819. Jeremiah Moore, BM.
Henry Whitlaw & Lucy McHaney, June 4, 1819, by John
Lester, V.D.M., June 8, 1819. James S. Lester, BM.
Daniel Wilkerson & Rebecca Masey, Sep. 25, 1819, by
Joseph T. Bell, Sep. 29, 1819. Littleberry Williamson,
BM.
James Williamson & Lucy Smith, Nov. 20, 1819, by John
Williamson, J.P., Dec. 7, 1819. George Williamson, BM.
William Williams & Jane Quarles, Oct. 28, 1819, by
Joshua Lester, V.D.M., Nov. 4, 1819. William Quarles,
BM.
James Woods & Elizabeth Morris, Nov. 2, 1819. Evan
Tracy, BM.
Isham Woods & Christina Motsinger, Dec. 6, 1819, by
Joseph T. Bell, Dec. 9, 1819. Thomas Turnage, BM.
John Woolard & Levina Meazler, March 2, 1819, by Wm.
Steele, J.P., March 4, 1819. Simeon Woolard, BM.
Joseph Wray & Elizabeth Moore, Feb. 12, 1819. William
T. Webb, BM.
Redding Wright & Harty Patterson, Feb. 11, 1819.
Henry Wrye & Sally Trant, Nov. 2, 1819, by John Borum,
Nov. 3, 1819. Thomas Edwards, BM.
James H. Young & Pheby Wooldridge, Nov. 24, 1819, by
Jos. T. Williams, J.P., Nov. 25, 1819. Jesse Wright, BM.
William Alsup & Polly Lane, Oct. 25, 1820, by Joshua
Lester, V.D.M., Dec. 22, 1820. Alsup Alsup, BM.
Joseph Barbee & Rachel Compton, Aug. 7, 1820. Archamal
Bass, BM.
Jesse Berry & Milly Shanks, Feb. 18, 1820, by Joshua
Lester, V.D.M., Feb. 24, 1820. George Donnell, BM.
Wiley Bodine & Nancy Rutchledge, Aug. 20, 1820. John
Stuart, BM.
William Buckley & Rebecca Johnson, Aug. 21, 1820, by
Joshua _____, V.D.M., Aug. 22, 1820. Oliver Johnson,
BM.
Midget Brooks & Rebecca Oneal, Aug. 24, 1820. Jeremiah
Brooks, BM.
Alfred Bryant & Nancy Hickman, March 30, 1820, by Wm.
Steele, J.P., March 31, 1820. Bryant T. Motley, BM.
Hazel Butt & Cynthia Hunt, Nov. 1, 1820. Ruben Webb, BM.
James Burton & Nancy Edwards, Dec. 29, 1820, by James
Gray, J.P., Dec. 31, 1820. Edward D. Burton.
Paskel Callico & Janny Wheeler, Oct. 17, 1820. John
Walton, BM.
John P. Campbell & Elizabeth Ann Lambut, Oct. 17, 1820,
by Geo. Clark, J.P., Oct. 19, 1820. John Campbell, BM.
William Campbell & Frances Arnold, Dec. 4, 1820, by Geo.
L. Smith, J.P., Dec. 20, 1820. Richard Harrison, BM,

45

WILSON COUNTY MARRIAGES

Ebenzer Carlock & Nancy Pemberton, Sep. 5, 1820. George Donnell, BM.

John Caraway & Narcissa Allen Rogers, Oct. 10, 1820. Tyloames Merritt, BM.

James C. Carruth & Mildred C. DAvis, Aug. 14, 1820, by Wm. Steele, J.P., Aug. 16, 1820. Foster G. Crutcher.

John H. Carthon & Nancy Rece, Aug. 9, 1820, by Ransom Gwyn, J.P., Aug. 10, 1820. James H. Cawthon, BM.

Joseph B. Chance & Nancy Braden, Nov. 13, 1820, by Edward Harris, J.P., Nov. 14, 1820. Elijah Chance, BM.

William Chapple & Elizabeth Walker, March 1, 1820, by J. F. Davis, March 2, 1820. Solomon Walker, BM.

William Chapple & Elizabeth Redding, May 5, 1820, by James Gray, J.P., May 7, 1820. Nathan Redding, BM.

James Chance & Mary Nichols, Nov. 18, 1820, by Thomas S. Green, J.P., Nov. 21, 1820. Henry C. Nichols, BM.

John Conrod & Caty Morris, April 22, 1820. Bazil Davis, BM.

John Cook & Annis S. Metheny, Dec. 4, 1820, by James Gray, J.P., Dec. 20, 1820. Job Metheny, BM.

Frances Cooper & Ann Thomas, Oct. 31, 1820, by John McMinn, J.P., Nov. 5, 1820. James Reed, BM.

L. D. Crabtree & Winney Medling, April 3, 1820. Harbird Young, BM.

Robertson Crook & Seleny Eatheridge, April 5, 1820. Charles Nicholson, BM.

John A. Creswell & Martha Mays, June 13, 1820, by William Gray, J.P., June 13, 1820. Alexander Kirk-Patrick, BM.

Martin Cartmell & Margaret E. Neil, Oct. 20, 1820, by Jemiah Hendrick, J.P., Oct. 23, 1820.

William Chester & Sophia M. Hogg, Feb. 12, 1820. John Wiseman.

Reubin Davenport & Susan Richardson, June 13, 1820, by John McMinn, J.P., June 15, 1820. Frances Cooper, BM.

William Davis & Elizabeth Webb, Oct. 17, 1820. Joshua Lester, V.D.M.

John Dillard & Sarah Jacobs, July 18, 1820, by Abner Hill, M.G., July 19, 1820. Shadrack Owens, BM.

Jonathan Doak & Isabel Donnell, Jan. 25, 1820. Josiah Donnell, BM.

Ebenezer Donelson & Elizabeth Davis, Dec. 7, 1820. Isham F. DAvis, BM.

John Dorch & Cynthia Walker, July 31, 1820, by W. H. Race, Aug. 6, 1820. Lewis Sutton, BM.

Martin Douglas & Nancy Masey, Aug. 3, 1820. John Springs, BM.

William Drennon & Hetty Eddins, Dec. 14, 1820. Lewis Wright, BM.

James Dunmore & Delilah Cowen, Sep. 21, 1820, by Geo. Clark, J.P., Sep. 22, 1820. Shadrack Gowen, BM.

James Dyer & Lucy Horn, Dec. 6, 1820, by Wm. Johnson, Dec. 10, 1820. James Little, BM.

Reese Eagan & Peggy Tipton, Feb. 2, 1820, by Jeremiah Hendrick, J.P., Feb. 3, 1820. Abraham Green, BM.

46

Richard A. Echols & Abigail M. Brown, Oct. 16, 1820, by
John Jarratt, Oct. 17, 1820. Mathew Drw, BM.
Marvin Edwards & Polly Whitlaw, Nov. 13, 1820. Joseph
Stacy, BM.
Presley Edwards & Mary Sims, Nov. 15, 1820. John
Atkinson, V.D.M., Thomas Edwards, BM.
Robert Ellis & Prudence Belcher, Feb. 19, 1820. James
Ellis, BM.
Zachariah Evans & Cynthia Sweat, March 6, 1820, by John
Bonner, J.P., March 19, 1820. Alexander Stuart, BM.
Alexander Foster & Martha Doak, April 4, 1820, by James
Foster, J.P., April 6, 1820. James Foster, BM.
John L. Foster & Elizabeth Cox, Dec. 23, 1820, by John
Green, Dec. 28, 1820. John Cox, BM.
Littleberry Freeman & Elizabeth Young, Jan. 26, 1820.
Isaiah Paschal, BM.
James Guston & Elizabeth Adams, Feb. 3, 1820, by Abner
W. Bone, J.P., Feb. 6, 1820. John Adams, BM.
Anthony Ganes & Temple Scott, Sep. 20, 1820, by James
Henderson, Sep. 28, 1820. Thomas Ganes, BM.
James Gates & Elizabeth Bellow, Dec. 18, 1820, by Geo.
L. Smith, J.P., Dec. 1820. James Doak, BM.
Ivy Gibson & Sally Aytes, Jan. 15, 1820, by Edward
Harris, J.P., Jan. 20, 1820. Harvey Robertson, BM.
Robert Goodman, Jr. & Martha Richardson, Feb. 20, 1820.
Thos. S. Green, J.P., Robert Goodman Senr.
Jubal Grant & Nancy Hightower, Oct. 28, 1820, by B.
Wiley Bridges, Nov. 4, 1820. James Arnold, BM.
Robert Gunthrie & Aseneth Motheral, Oct. 13, 1820, by
Hugh Kirkpatrick, M.G., Oct. 19, 1820. Allen Smith, BM.
William Gray & Mary Motheral, April 14, 1820, by J.
McClain, J.P., April 15, 1820.
Philip Grisim & Sally Spring, Jan. 14, 1820. Rowland W.
Grisim, BM.
Charles Hancock & Nancy Ramsey, April 18, 1820. William
Lawrence, J.P., John Ramsey, BM.
William Hankins & Fanny Abanather, Sep. 9, 1820. Mark
Abanather, BM.
Charles Hardin & Jane Alexander, June 14, 1820, by Jesse
Alexander, V.D.M., June 22, 1820. William L. Alexander,
BM.
William Hartsfield & Frances H. Anderson, _____ 18, 1820.
Levi Anderson.
Thomas Hill & Elizabeth Johnson, Feb. 10, 1820. B.
Casilman, J.P., Lawrence Sypert, BM.
Josiah W. Hings & Charlotte Heiflim, June 3, 1820. John
Manning, BM.
James W. Hodges & Polly Pucket, March 8, 1820, by J.
Lester, V.D.M., March 9, 1820. William Hartsfield, BM.
Thomas Hodges & Elizabeth Pucket, Feb. 7, 1820. J.
Lester, V.D.M., John A. Smith, BM.
Thomas C. Hoskins & Jane Simpson, Dec. 12, 1820. Joshua
Lester, Robert Marshall, BM.
William Hudson & Sally Tracy, Nov. 10, 1820. Albin
Dearing, BM.

William Hutcherson & Jenney Williams, March 18, 1820.
James Smith, BM.
Mark Hollerman & Hannah Glen, Jan. 22, 1820. Benjamin
Glen, BM.
Asal Jennings & Sopha Craddock, Jan. 21, 1820. Joshua
Lester, V.D.M.
Austin Johnson & Ann Elizabeth Corley, Sep. 4, 1820, by
John Page, Sep. 6, 1820.
Oliver C. Johnson & Haney H. Buckley, May 17, 1820.
Joshua Lester, V.D.M., William Cummings, BM.
William A. Johnson & Lucretia Aspy, Oct. 10, 1820.
Edward Harris, J.P., James Allcorn, BM.
Abram Keeton & Jane Hughes Hall, Sep. 2, 1820, by
Christopher Cooper, J.P., Sep. 4, 1820. John N. Hall,
BM.
Zachariah Keeton & Margaret Walker, March 8, 1820, by
James McAdow, J.P., March 9, 1820. Henry Dillon, BM.
Taylor Kelly & Cynthia Davis, Nov. 28, 1820, by James
McAdow, J.P., Dec. 7, 1820. William Whiteside, BM.
Sampson Knight & Nancy Robertson, Jan. 25, 1820, by
James Gray, J.P., Jan. 27, 1820. Thomas Knight, BM.
Jacob Keeton & Lucinda Fewston, Aug. 2, 1820. Jeremiah
Turner, BM.
Hezekiah King & Nancy Hunt, Feb. 8, 1820. Hardy Hunt,
BM.
John Lasiter & Lucy Edward, Jan. 15, 1820, by James
Gray, J.P., Jan. 17, 1820. Eli Edwards, BM.
John Leech & Betsy Cooper, Dec. 16, 1820, by John McMinn,
J.P., Dec. 19, 1820. Jeremiah Brys, BM.
Henry Leeman & Kesiah Warren, Oct. 4, 1820, by Joshua
Lester, V.D.M., Oct. 5, 1820. A. Winston, BM.
Payton Marlow & Elizabeth Smith, Feb. 25, 1820, by
Jeremiah Hendirck, J.P., Feb. 29, 1820. Richard Marlow,
BM.
Garret Mansfield & Lydia Sullivan, Dec. 14, 1820. W. H.
Reece, J.P., Reuben Webb, BM.
Alfred McClain & Harriet F. Robinson, Feb. 10, 1820-
Martin Cartmell, BM.
Andrew McHaney & Oney Johnson, Aug. 9, 1820. Joshua
Lester, V.D.M., Theophilus W. Short, BM.
Alexander McKnight & Anne Greer, Feb. 17, 1820. Samuel
Grier, BM.
William Miles & Martha Gwyn, Jan. 31, 1820, by John
Bonner, J.P., Feb. 2, 1820. John Mesingall, BM.
Aston Morgan & Ann Edwards, Jan. 19, 1820. A. Croneer,
V.D.M., Eaton Edwards, BM.
William McKnight & Elizabeth McWhiter (Whirter), Feb. 24,
1820. Milus McCorkle, BM.
Robert McKee & Elizabeth Turner, Oct. 22, 1820, by Jas.
Cross, J.P., Oct. 24, 1820.
William Moore & Elizabeth Brothers, July 15, 1825 (?),
by Geo. Clark, J.P., July 21, 1825 (?).
Abram Murray & Polly Hotton (Hutton), Aug. 31, 1820.
John Murray, BM.

James Murray & Casa Yarnall, Dec. 28, 1819, by Ransom
Gwyn, J.P., Jan. 5, 1820.
John Neely & Jane Brown, July 26, 1820. E. Maddox, M.G.,
Paul Sullivan, BM.
Lemuel Nicholson & Levina Young, Nov. 25, 1820, by
Brinkley Bridges, J.P., Nov. 25, 1820. Robert Young,
BM.
Lemuel Nickings & Martha Holton, Dec. 19, 1820, by Abner
Hill, M.G., Dec. 25, 1820. O. G. Finley, BM.
Williamson Nipper & Nancy Moore, July 17, 1820, by James
Gray, J.P., July 20, 1820.
James Osment & Levina Osment, Nov. 4, 1820, by Benjamin
Castleman, J.P., Nov. 9, 1820. William M. Swan, BM.
John D. Otts & Martha Andrews, March 6, 1820, by Thos. S.
Green, J.P., March 9, 1820. William Walker, BM.
Robert Owen & Elizabeth Micks, Aug. 8, 1820, by Wm.
Steele, J.P., Aug. 10, 1820. Joseph L. Wilson, BM.
Alexander Perryman & Sally Basken, July 17, 1820, by
James Cross, J.P., July 20, 1820. Allen Perryman, BM.
John Perryman & Polly Arnold, July 20, 1820. Phillip
Perriman, BM.
Isaac Perriman & Nancy Patterson, April 19, 1820. John
Perriman, BM.
Phillip Perriman & Hannah C. Fouch, July 15, 1820, by
Joshua Lester, V.D.M., July 17, 1820. John Perryman,
BM.
David Phillips & Polly Waters, Dec. 11, 1820, by Thomas
Durham, M.G., Dec. 14, 1820. Archamack Bass, BM.
Goldman Pucket & Elizabeth Ellison, Nov. 22, 1820. John
H. Bryan, BM.
John Ricketts & Sarah Alsup, March 6, 1820. B. Castilman,
J.P., Jacob Castleman, BM.
William Saterfield & Ann Tally, Jan. 29, 1820. Thomas
Delapp, BM.
John Sauls & Fanny Davenport, Aug. 2, 1820. Willie
Davenport, BM.
John Scroggins & Wincy Pearcy, Jan. 20, 1820. John Reggs,
BM.
Thos. C. Scott & Polly Burton, Aug. 26, 1820, by James
Gray, J.P., Aug. 31, 1820. Nathan Reding, BM.
Joseph W. Seawell & Indianna Seawell, Oct. 23, 1820, by
John Jarratt, Oct. 26, 1820. John L. Wynne, BM.
Alfred Sherrill & Peggy Sherrill, Oct. 12, 1820. Z.
Tatum, BM.
Allen Smith & Frances Wood, Dec. 4, 1820, by William
Gray, J.P., Dec. 6, 1820. James W. Wispin (Winston),
BM.
Hugh Smith & Betsey Roach, Nov. 23, 1820. Thos. McSpaddin,
BM.
John A. Smith & Nancy McHaney, April 1, 1820, by Joshua
Lester, V.D.M., April 6, 1820. James S. Lester, BM.
John Smith & Mary Cloyd, March 24, 1820, by David Foster,
M.G., March 30, 1820. John Wilson, BM.
Shadrick Smith & Noma Howard, Oct. 15, 1820, by Joshua
Lester, V.D.M., Oct. 23, 1820.

James Somers & Anne McFarland, Dec. 19, 1820, by Edward
Willis, M.G., Dec. 21, 1820. Mathew Dew, BM.
David Spring & Lavicy Jones, Dec. 7, 1820. Abner Hill,
M.G., Lot Joiner, BM.
Thomas Stanley & Mary Ann Huggins, Dec. 19, 1820, by
James McAdow, J.P., Dec. 21, 1820. Joshua Pedigo, BM.
John Stephenson & Nancy Tristy (Trusty ?), Oct. 17,
1820. Jeremiah McWhorter, BM.
Solomon Suggs & Iva Jacobs, Jan. 2, 1820. Samuel
Booker, BM.
Jesse Sullivan & Elizabeth Carter, July 13, 1820.
Ramson Gwyn, Owen Quinby, BM.
William Sutherland & Polly Hobbs, Dec. 1, 1820. Jno.
Bowman, Presley Simpson, BM.
Isiah Swindle & Juliann Hickman, Feb. 6, 1820. Wm.
Steele, J.P.
Jesse Tally & Margaret Wynne, June 10, 1820, by John W.
Payton, J.P., June 19, 1820. Benjamin T. Jones, BM.
Jabez Tims & Elizabeth Tims, Sep. 8, 1820. Allen McVey,
BM.
Wayne Thomas & Anne Barton, Nov. 13, 1820. John Blackburn,
BM.
William Todd & Elizabeth Steele, Nov. 23, 1820. E.
Maddox, M.G., George Steele, BM.
Zachariah Toliver & Rebecca Sherrill, Jan. 9, 1820.
Norval Douglas, BM.
Edward Trice & Lilly Smith, Dec. 1, 1820. John Hickman,
BM.
John Travilion & Polly Allison, Oct. 23, 1820. J. John-
son, J.P., David Bradshaw, BM.
Jeremah Turner & Nancy Hancock, Feb. 15, 1820. Wm.
Lawerence, Robert McPete, BM.
Mellkijah Vaughn & Sarah R. Vaughn, Jan. 5, 1820, by
William Gray, J.P., Jan. 6, 1820. William Tisdale, BM.
Andrew Ward & Sally Ward, Dec. 1, 1820. Jacob Browning,
M.G., Turner Perry, BM.
Shelah Waters & Sarah Clark, Jan. 12, 1820, by Thomas
Durham, M.G., Jan. 13, 1820. David Philips, BM.
William Whitsett & Nancy Kelly, Dec. 26, 1820, by James
McAdow, J.P., Dec. 28, 1820. Isham Keaton, BM.
Joseph Williams & Jinney Patterson, July 13, 1820.
Joseph Patton, BM.
Julius Williams & Margaret Cason, Feb. 19, 1820. Joseph
Stacy, BM.
Drennon Wheeler & Caty Reeder, April 8, 1820. Joseph
Phillips, BM.
James Witherspoon & Elizabeth Cowen, Aug. 9, 1820, by
John McMinn, J.P., Aug. 10, 1820.
Alleggood Woolard & Ellender Jones, Sep. 30, 1820, by
Benjamin Casilman, J.P., Oct. 5, 1820. William Sypert,
BM.
John Womach & Milley Webster, Aug. 25, 1820, by Geo.
Clark, J.P., Sep. 6, 1820. John Campbell.
Ransom Ward & Patsey Rogers, Oct. 3, 1820, by Benjamin
Casilman, J.P., Nov. 3, 1820. Jesse Gibbs, BM.

Byrd Wall & Fanny Johnson, Nov. 13, 1820. John Akinson, V.D.M., Benjamin Wall, BM.

Silas M. Williams & Franky Shaw, Sep. 5, 1820. William Flowers, Sr., James B. Hankins, BM.

Jesse Woodcock & Elizabeth M. Williams, June 8, 1820. Burchel Douglas, Abraham Woodcock, BM.

Willie Wray & Eliza Catter, July 16, 1820. Joshua Gibbs, BM.

Jesse Wright & Mary Young, March 13, 1820. James W. Young, BM.

William Adams & Mary Lewis, May 29, 1821. Geo. L. Smith, J.P.

Royal Atkinson & Rebecca Doak, Dec. 20, 1821. Wm. Seawell, James Johnson, BM.

Thomas Babb & Hicksey Hunt, April 2, 1821, by John Jarratt, April 3, 1821. Henry B. Babb, BM.

Lumford Bagwell & Rispa Truet, April 14, 1820, by John Bond, V.D.M., March 19, 1821. William Trevell, BM.

Jonathan Baker & Sally Eagan, May 26, 1821. Wilaon Hearn, J.P., Jesse Shaw, BM.

Samuel Bell & Eliza McCleary Beard, Oct. 10, 1821, by Wilson Hearn, M.G., Oct. 11, 1821. James Mitchell, BM.

Pernell Bennett & Arnis Williams, Oct. 9, 1820, by John Bond, V.D.M., Oct. 11, 1820. Ang. Lamb, BM.

Samuel Bickers & Elizabeth Morris, Aug. 22, 1821, by John W. Payton, J.P., Aug. 23, 1821. Levi Donnell, BM.

William Blackburn & Lucy Clark, Aug. 14, 1821, by E. Willis, M.G., Aug. 16, 1821. Lewis Blackburn, BM.

Azor Bone & Hulda W. Sherrill, Dec. 18, 1821. John Provine, M.G., Geo. K. Smith, BM.

Thomas Bradley & Catharine Caplinger, March 10, 1821, by Wm. Steele, March 11, 1821. William Robinson, BM.

Joshua Bradberry & Susan Brinson, April 10, 1821, by Thomas S. Green, J.P., April 26, 1821. Joseph Bradley, BM.

George J. Cain & Christiana G. Jones, Sep. 22, 1821, by Joshua Lester, V.D.M., Sep. 25, 1821. George Smith, Jr., BM.

Wallace Caldwell & Abigail Nicholson, April 11, 1821, by Wm. Gray, J.P., April 13, 1821. William T. Webb, BM.

George Cato & Euphenia Rife, Dec. 31, 1821. John R. Rutherford, BM.

Solomon Caplinger & Martha Mosey (Masey), Sep. 18, 1821. Douglas, BM.

Walter Carr & Sarah McDaniel, Oct. 11, 1821. E. Maddox, M.G.

Willis Cofired & Maria McDonald, Oct. 10, 1821. Stephen McDonald, BM.

George Collings & Nancy Renshaw, Sep. 15, 1821. Jeremiah Collings, BM.

Charles Collings & Elizabeth Sanders, March 10, 1821. Elisha Collings, BM.

David Cole & Diley Pike, Feb. 21, 1821. Tobias Henderson, BM.

John Conger & Meecy Hill, April 3, 1821. Wm. Peace, J.P., Walter Carr, BM.

Sampson Conner & Sally Knight, May 9, 1821, by James McAdow, J.P., May 20, 1821. James Hollingsworth, BM.

William Corder & Martha Stone, Nov. 10, 1821, by Abner Hill, M.G., Nov. 11, 1821. James Stone, BM.

William Cox & Holland Greer, July 25, 1821. Britton Drake, BM.

Halem Creswell & Elizabeth Johnson, Aug. 29, 1821. E. Maddox, M.G., David Brown, BM.

Robert Crudupe & Polly Gwyll, June 19, 1821, by J. F. David, June 23, 1821. Samuel Sperry, BM.

Isham F. Davis & Sally Curd, July 2, 1821. William McGrigor, BM.

Owen C. Dennis & Deborah Green, June 20, 1821, by William Gray, J.P., June 22, 1821. Isaac Green, BM.

Edward Denton & Rebeccah Dillard, April 2, 1821. Thomas Denton, BM.

Arther W. Dew & Nancy Hallum, July 4, 1821, by John Dew, V.D.M., July 6, 1821. Anderson Cook, BM.

Willie Dockins & Fanny Goodall, March 14, 1821. Benajah Cartwright, BM.

Ruben Dockins & Rhody Hankins, March 11, 1821. Jonathan Baker, BM.

Levi Donnell & Cynthia Donnell, _____, 1821. John F. Doak, BM.

Ennis Douglas & Matilda Corley, Nov. 14, 1821. Richard Johnson, James Browning, BM.

Daniel Dyer & Elizabeth Cropper Aug. 8, 1821. Jesse Donnell, BM.

Green B. Edwards & Martha Howard, July 21, 1821. James Bond, V.D.M., Benjamin Casulman, BM.

Warren Edwards & Polly Whitlaw, Nov. 13, 1821, by Joshua Lester, V.D.M., Nov. 15, 1821.

Absolom Ellis & Elender L. Jones, March 17, 1821, by Brinkley Bridges, J.P., May 7, 1821. Redding B. Jones, BM.

Thomas W. Ellis & Sally Wright, Sep. 10, 1821, by William Gray, J.P., Sep. 13, 1821. John Blurton, BM.

Josiah Elly & Jane Lawrence, June 2, 1821, by John Gray, June 7, 1821. Oliver Oneal, BM.

John H. Evans & Catharine Davis, July 14 1821, by Elijah Maddox, July 19, 1821. Gros. Scruggs, BM.

Anderson Evans & Mily Stuart, April 8, 1821. Alexander Stuart, BM.

Robert Ferguson & Polly Farr, Aug. 3, 1821, by J. Bonner, J.P., Aug. 4, 1821. Edward Jackson, BM.

Miles Fuller & Nancy Clifton, Sep. 12, 1821, by John W. Payton, J.P., Sep. 13, 1821. Anderson Loyd, BM.

John Furguson & Barbary Harpole, Oct. 24, 1821. Edward Willis, Sion Duke, BM.

Martha Gibson & Mary Jarman, Jan. 10, 1821. Joshua Lester, V.D.M., John Wilson, BM.

James Goddy (Gaddy) & Elizabeth Bass, June 8, 1821. Archa Mebas, BM.

Andrew Gwyn & Esther Rice, Aug. 25, 1821, by David Foster, M.G., Aug. 30, 1821. Hugh Gwyn, BM.

John N. Hall & Lewereasy Murphy, July 10, 1821, by James McAdow, J.P., July 12, 1821.

Joseph Heflin & Emassy Ward, June 11, 1821. John Neil, BM.

Enoch Henry & Jane Masey, Feb. 14, 1821. Joseph Cutrell, BM.

William Hickman, Jr. & Equilla Swingle, Feb. 15, 1821. Wm. Steele, J.P., William Hickman Senr., BM.

Lemuel Hickman Jr. & Susanna H. Trice, July 11, 1821, by Abner Hill, M.G., July 12, 1821. Lemuel Hickman Senr., BM.

Snoden Hickman & Milly Richardson, March 29, 1821. Wm. Steele, J.P., William Hickman, BM.

Peter Hollingsworth & Polly Miller, March 19, 1821, by James Bond, V.D.M., March 22, 1821. James Knight, BM.

William Hill & Rebecca Hill, Dec. 26, 1821, by Edward Willis, Dec. 30, 1821.

Phillip Howell & Cynthia Willis, Oct. 22, 1821, by Peter Fehey, Oct. 23, 1821. Phillip Howell, BM.

William Horn & Celia Woolard, Jan. 27, 1821, by Wm. Steele, J.P., Feb. 1, 1821. Simeon Woolard, BM.

Mathew Hunt & Elizabeth Moore, May 31, 1821. William Gray, J.P., James Moore, BM.

Wm. Hunter & Elizabeth Drake, Aug. 27, 1821, by Wm. Steele, Aug. 29, 1821.

John Jennings & Sally Harris, Aug. 26, 1821 (?), by William Gray, J.P., Aug. 29, 1821. William Jones, BM.

Daniel Johnson & Sally Gwyn, April 19, _____. Thomas Calhoon, V.D.M., Mathew Dew, BM.

Dennis Kelly & Drucilla Donnell, _____, 1821. Levi Donnell, BM.

Murphy Kemp & Ann Baird, Jan. 1, 1821, by Brinkley Bridges, J.P., Jan. 3, 1821. Daniel Smith, BM.

Thomas Lankford & Lucy Martin, June 14, 1821. Wm. Steele, J.P., Littleberry Stephens, BM.

Herod Lasiter & Polly Patterson, Aug. 25, 1821, by Geo. L. Smith, J.P., Sep. 10, 1821. Joseph McGee, BM.

Jacob B. Lasiter & Levina McMinn, Aug. 7, 1821, by James Bonds, V.D.M., J__ 21, 1821. Elihu McMinn, BM.

Turner M. Lawrence & Ann Barbee, April 4, 1821, by Thomas Durham, M.G., April 19, 1821. Silas Taver (Tarver), BM.

Prior Lawrence & Rebecca Hopkins, Jan. 7, 1821. Jesse Pugh.

Jesse Lilse & Patsey Gilbert, Oct. 23, 1821. W. H. Leon, James Arnold, BMS.

James Lowery & Sally Wetherly, Nov. 5, 1821. John Ozment, BM.

Lemuel Lloyd & Harriet Jones, Dec. 29, 1821, by John Dew, V.D.M., Jan. ___, 1822. Andrew Loyd, BM.

Pleasant Markham & Sally Carlton, Aug. 11, 1821, by William Grey, Aug. 13, 1821. John Irby, BM.

Garrett Masey & Levi Cropper, Sep. 19, 1821. Job Swan,
BM.
David Martin & Martha Weir, April 12, 1821, by Wm.
Steele, J.P., April 12, 1821. John Chandler, BM.
Robert Martin & Fanny Coe, July 2, 1821. Hugh Chandler,
BM.
Stephen McDaniel & Jane Williams, July 14, 1821. Richard
Johnston, Alex. McDaniel, BM.
Simon McLindon & Frances Overby, Nov. 5, 1821. B. Bridges.
Richard Melton & Polly Burdine, Dec. 4, 1821, by John
Bonner, J.P., Dec. 6, 1821. Lewis Button, BM.
Sherrof Merrit & Tobitha Edwards, June 12, 1821, by
James Bonds, V.D.M., June 19, 1821. John Merret, BM.
Allem Mitchell & Patsey Glasgow, Sep. 13, 1821. John
Bonner, J.P., Jones W. Locke, BM.
Thomas Merrit & Tempy Bennett, Oct. 1, 1821. Howell
Ward, BM.
James Mitchell & Eliza Reese, Dec. 12, 1821, by Wilson
Hearn, M.G., Dec. 13, 1821. John Beard, BM.
John C. Miller & Peggy Harland, Aug. 1, 1821. John W.
Payton, J.P., R. H. Hight, BM.
Marmaduke Mitchener & Barbary Boon, Oct. 13, 1821. David
Beard, BM.
James Moore & Rebecca Cooper, Oct. 6, 1821, by William
Gray, J.P., Oct. 8, 1821. Mothern Hunt, BM.
Shadrack Moore & Nanny Sweney, Dec. 26, 1821. Robert
Dallas, BM.
Dandridge Moss & Sally Richmond, Sep. 22, 1821. Aaron
Churn, BM.
Alfred Mount & Mary Thomas, Sep. 18, 1821. William
Thomas, BM.
John Nichols & Sally Harris, Feb. 24 1821, by Nelson
Hearn, M.G., March 1, 1821. John Springs, BM.
Richard Ozment & Rebecca Eddins, June 5, 1821, by Ben-
jamin Casilman, J.P., June 7, 1821. Stephen Clemmons,
BM.
James Pane & Anne Campbell, Feb. 20, 1821, by Geo. L.
Smith, J.P., Feb. 22, 1821. James M. Armstrong, BM.
Lewis Patterson & Sally Jennings, March 1, 1821, by
Joshua Lester, V.D.M., March 13, 1821. John Hubbard,
BM.
George Pemberton & Celah Patterson, June 6, 1821, by
Joshua Lester, V.D.M., June 10, 1821. Epenitus Car-
lock, BM.
Samuel Patterson & Jane Smith, Jan. 19, 1821. David
Smith, BM.
William Peak & Ruth Jones, Feb. 18, 1821. Sion Duke,
BM.
William Phepps & Elizabeth Cummings, May 22, 1821.
Joshua Lester, V.D.M., Moses Williams, BM.
Kinney Prim & Polly Johnson, July 13, 1821, by B. Bridges,
J.P., Aug. 6, 1821. Allen Hill, BM.
William Redden & Priscilla Knight, Dec. 22, 1821, by
James Bond, J.P., Dec. 27, 1821. Hermon Rose, BM.

Hughy Reyland & Rhoda Jackson, July 9, 1821. Benjamin
Edwards, BM.
Lewis Richard & Sally Delay, Jan. 9, 1821, by Geo. L.
Smith, J.P., Jan. 11, 1821. Jacob Mishark, BM.
Isaac H. Rutland & Emily Rutland, Aug. 28, 1821. James
Whitside, Rutherford Rutland, BM.
David Scoby & Eliza Heflin, March 3, 1821, by Wm. Steele,
J.P., March 29, 1821. Joseph Caskey, BM.
Isiah Swindle & Julian Hickman, Feb. 6, 1821. Pledge
Swindle, BM.
John Southern & Polly David, Oct. 4, 1821, by John W.
Payton, J.P., Oct. 11, 1821. James Reed, BM.
Benjamin Stanley & Patsey Carter, Jan. 18, 1821. Wilson
Hearn, M.G., Littleton Benthal, BM.
David Stanley & Nancy Sherrill, Dec. 8, 1821, by Jacob
Sullivan, Dec. 9, 1821.
James Stevins & Polly Allen, Oct. 7, 1821. Ruben Webb
BM.
Littleberry Stevens & Saley Chambers, Sep. 12, 1821, by
Wm. Steele, Sep. 13, 1821. Archibald Wilson, BM.
Solomon Suggs & Iva Jacobs, Jan. 2, 1821. Wikson Hearn,
M.G.
Uriah Sweat & Finetta Phillips, Feb. 24, 1821, by John W.
Payton, J.P., Feb. 27, 1821. William Phillips, BM.
Jonas Swingley & Martha Curd, Dec. 18, 1821, by Elijah
Maddox, M.G., Dec. 20, 1821. Jonas Hale, BM.
Pledge Swingle & Nancy Hickan, March 17, 1821, by Jno.
Borum, March 18, 1821. Herrod Seat, BM.
Jacob Sullivan & Celey Barton, June 9, 1821, by Edward
Willis, M.G., June 10, 1821. Isaac Craver, BM.
Peter Sullivan & Polly Tarver, July 24, 1821, by Jacob
Sullivan, July 25, 1821. Jacob Sullivan, BM.
Paton Tally & Rachel Cross, March 21, 1821, by Joshua
Lester, V.D.M., March 22, 1821. Richard Tally, BM.
Thomas Taylor & Polly Garner, Dec. 18, 1821, by Geo.
Clark, J.P., Dec. 25, 1821. Jno. Garner, BM.
Joseph Teppet & Ann Ragsdale, Jan. 3, 1821, by Wilson
Hearn, M.G., Jan. 4, 1821. Isaac Moore, BM.
Alexander Thorn & Elizabeth Harrington, July 4, 1821,
by Abner Hill, M.G., July 7, 1821. Samuel Conger, BM.
James Thrift & Elizabeth Sanderson, Nov. 19, 1821, by
Isaac Lindsay, M.G., Nov. 22, 1821.
John S. Topp & Elizabeth Crutcher, Aug. 30, 1821, by
Thos. Calhoon, V.D.M., Aug. 31, 1821. Albert H.
Wynne, BM.
James L. Tally & Betsey Butler, June 29, 1821, by John W.
Payton, J.P., July 30, 1821. Spencer W. Tally, BM.
Pryor Tyrell & Elizabeth Collins, Jan. 10, 1821, by
James Gray, J.P., Jan. 11, 1821. Jerimiah Collins, BM.
John Upchurch & Caty Johnson, Aug. 17, 1821, by Jno.
Bonner, M.G., Aug. 24, 1821. Jordon Johnson.
James L. Vance & Tabitha Scott, May 16, 1821. John
Benson, BM.
Bird Wall & Christian Kidwell, Jan. 8, 1821, by Abner
Hill, M.G., Jan. 8, 1821. Robert Johnson, BM.

Burrell Wall & Sally M. Johnson, Jan. 19, 1821. Abner Hill, M.G., Benjamin Wall, BM.

John Walden & Susa Tally, Feb. 26, 1821, by Sterling C. Brown, March 7, 1821. Fulton Tally, BM.

John Ward Jr. & Elizabeth Hodges, Aug. 21, 1821, by Jno. Lester, V.D.M., Aug. 25, 1821. John Ward Sr., BM.

Anderson Webb &·Susanah Lester, Nov. 5, 1821, by Joshua Lester, V.D.M., Nov. 8, 1821. Henry D. Lester, BM.

William Webb & Bestey Hull, Feb. 3, 1821, by Brinkley Bridges, J.P., March 10, 1821. James Driver, BM.

Joseph Weir & Lydia Allen, Feb. 10, 1821, by Jno. Borum, Feb. 14, 1821. James Weir, BM.

Edward White & Rachael Williamson, March 30, 1821, by James Foster, J.P., April 3, 1821. Littleberry White, BM.

William Willeford & Allis Chamberlain, May 5, 1821, by Wilson Hearn, M.G., May 10, 1821. Jeremiah Johnson, BM.

Archibald Wilson & Cinthia Johnson, Sep. 12, 1821, by Alex C. Carruth, J.P., Sep. 13, 1821. Littleberry Stevens, BM.

John Wilson & Nancy Koonce, May 22, 1821. John H. Johnson, BM.

William Wilkerson & Peggy Kickpatrick, June 12, 1821. Robert Campbell, BM.

Jacob Woodram & Nancy Miles, Dec. 18, 1821, by David Foster, M.G., Dec. 20, 1821. John H. Prestly, BM.

John Word & Polly Simpson, Nov. 5, 1821, by Joshua Lester, V.D.M., Nov. 16, 1821.

John Wright & Rebecca Rickets, Nov. 30, 1821, by Benjamin Casilman, J.P., Dec. 6, 1821. Benjamin Casilman, BM.

Lewis Wright & Temperance Eddings, Jan. 13, 1821, by John Dew, V.D.M., Feb. 7, 1821. John Drenon, BM.

Hardy Youbanks & Nancy Arnold, March 19, 1821. Thomas Arnold, BM.

Elijah Adamson & Susanah Hathaway, April 24, 1822. Jesse Pugh, BM.

Daniel Alexander & Rachel Scott, June 9, 1822. James Martin, BM.

Pleasnt Arnold & Sythea Barns, May 6, 1822, by James McDonnal, V.D.M., May 7, 1822. Thos. Arnold, BM.

Walter W. Asher & Lydia Blackburn, Oct. 29, 1822. Edward Willis.

George S. Avery & Judy Chandler, March 9, 1822. Edings Chandler, BM.

Clinton Baird & Patsey Harris, Aug. 7, 1822, by Edward Barris, J.P., Aug. 8, 1822.

Isham Baker & Sally Caldwell, March 2, 1822. Isaac Lawernce, BM.

Franklin Barlett & Polly Micks, April 13, 1822. George L. Smith, BM.

Archmack Bass & Rachael Phillips, June 18, 1822. Sion Bass, BM.

Alford Bettis (Bettie?) & Margaret Conger, March 3, 1822,
by Abner Hill, M.G., March 5, 1822. William Bettis,
BM.
George Blaze & Elizabeth Loyd, Jan. 17, 1822   Abner
Hill, M.G., Lemusl Loyd, BM.
William Boaz & Harriet Simpson, April 20, 1822, by
William Flowers Sr., May 4, 1822   Presly Simpson, BM.
John Bone & Lavina McMinn, Sep. 7, 1822, by Thos.
Calhoun, V.D.M.
Bennett Bowden & Polly Haily, Oct. 22, 1822, by G. Mirtle,
J.P., Oct. 24, 1822.
David Brine & Susannah Haleman, July 15, 1822, by G. H.
Bullard, J. P., July 27, 1822.
Samuel Brown & Lucy Chandler, Dec. 12, 1822. G. H.
Buzzard, J.P.
William Brown & Elizabeth Brown, July 22, 1822, by Elijah
Maddox, M.G., July 23, 1822.
William Bryson & Elizabeth Nicholson, Aug. 20, 1822.
Samuel C. Odom, BM.
Thomas Burk & Fanny Robertson, Feb. 26, 1822.   Thos.
McKnight, BM.
Benja. Canahan & Rebecca McMinn, June 19, 1822.   Wesley
Walker, M.G.
Thomas Cannon & Elizabeth Garrett, June 25, 1822, by
Edward Willis, June 26, 1822.
Benjamin Carver & Nancy Lumpkin, Feb. 6, 1822. J. F.
Davis, J.P., Jas. C. Drake, BM.
James Cason & Jane McKnight, Feb. 6, 1822, by Jas. Bond,
V.D.M., Feb. 14, 1822. Albert Wynne, BM.
George Cato & Euphama Rife, Dec. 31, 1821, by Brinkley
Bridges, J.P., March 28, 1822.
Henry Chandler & Elizabeth Dew, June 20, 1822. Wm.
Steele.
James Clemmons & Elizabeth Lee, Feb. 26, 1822, by James
Bond, V.D.M., March 6, 1822. William Clemmons, BM.
Jarratt Cocke & Martha Simpson, Nov. 18, 1822, by Joshua
Lester, V.D.M., Nov. 21, 1822.
Flute Cook (Cock) & Nancy Harris, Dec. 27, 1822. Joshua
Lester, V.D.M.
William Coonrood & Patsey Rogers, April 2, 1822. James
Grisim, BM.
Samuel Conger & Elizabeth Kenedy, April 20, 1822, by
Abner Hill, M.G., April 25, 1822. John Conger, BM.
Zach H. Carlin & Sally Hill, Nov. 9, 1822, by Elijah
Maddox, M.G., Nov. 12, 1822.
Alex Davis & Polly Tipton, Feb. 21, 1822. William Gray,
J.P., Edward Burk, BM.
John Davis & Sally Crosland, Dec. 14, 1822, by Elijah
Maddox, M.G., Dec. 19, 1822.
Allen R. Dillard & Emma B. Taylor, Jan. 3, 1822. John
Provine, M.G., Harry Jackson, BM.
John Foster & Elizabeth Hunter, Jan. 10, 1822. Wm. Steele,
J.P., Foster Crutcher, BM.
Robert Dalton & Lucinda Harris, Oct. 18, 1822, by G. H.
Bussard, J.P.

Lewis Dwyer & Elizabeth Warren, Oct. 19, 1822, by John
Bonner, J.P., Nov. 4, 1822.
Elias Edwards & Nancy Mansfield, July 6, 1822, by John
Jarratt, July 9, 1822.
Hugh Edwards & Judy Hill, Nov. 9, 1822, by Elijah
Maddox, M.G., Nov. 12, 1822.
John Estes & Synthia McDaniel, April 25, 1822. Burwell
Reeves, BM.
Hobson Ferrell & Martha Parrish, Dec. 10, 1822, by Daniel
Moser, Dec. 12, 1822.
Jeremiah Fisher & Sally Drennon, Feb. 25, 1822, by Jas.
Browning, D.D., March 13, 1822. Green B. Lannom, BM.
Pearson Garrison & Eleander Baker, Oct. 3, 1822. John
Scoby, BM.
Enis Harper & Polly Davis, Dec. 10, 1822, by Elijah
Maddox, M.G., Dec. 11, 1822.
John Harrel & Sally Hutson, May 7, 1822. James Gray,
J.P., Hutson, BM.
Whitmell Harrington & Syrena Brown, March 12, 1822. Abner
Hill, M.G., Benton Modglin, BM.
Thomas Hicks & Rebecca Tucker, Aug. 19, 1822, by John W.
Payton, J.P., Aug. 22, 1822.
Ambros Holland & Rhoda Winters, March 16, 1822, by Wilson
Hearn, M.G., March 20, 1822. Woodson Layne, BM.
William Howard & Rebecca Edwards, Feb. 2, 1822, by James
Bond, V.D.M., Feb. 7, 1822. Nathaniel Edwards, BM.
Enoch Hugle & Polly Walker, Feb. 14, 1822, by Jacob
Sullivan, Feb. 16, 1822. Samuel Hugle, BM.
Reuben Jackson & Levina Miller, Feb. 11, 1822. Dudley
Scurlock, BM.
Real James & Mary Cook, June 22, 1822, by Edward Willis,
June 25, 1822.
Phillip Johnson & Nancy Carr, May 11, 1822, by John W.
Payton, J.P., May 14, 1822. John W. Payton, BM.
Fredeick Jolly & Nicey Ames, April 20, 1822, by John
Dew, V.D.M., April 25, 1822. Cornelius Buck, BM.
David King & Lucy Pennul (Penuel?), March 30, 1822.
J. Laster, M.G., Ransom Perriman, BM.
James Knight & Merrell, Feb. 19, 1822, by John Bond,
V.D.M., Feb. 22, 1822. John Merrell, BM.
Thomas Kirkpatrick & Angeline Roach, June 25, 1822, by
David Foster, M.G., Aug. 7, 1822.
Alexander Lackey & Elenor Garmany, May 6, 1822, by
Jesse Alexznder, V.D.M., May 9, 1822. William Garmany,
BM.
Theophilus Lambert & Charlotte Reynolds, Feb. 26, 1822,
by Jesse Alexander, V.D.M., May 9, 1822. John Alex-
ander, BM.
Prior Lawrence & Rebecca Hopkins, Jan. 7, 1822, by
William Lawrence, J.P., Jan. 9, 1822.
James Mainier & Patsey Irby, Feb. 11, 1822, by John W.
Payton, Feb. 28, 1822. Tobias Henderson, BM.
James Mason & Ollive Pety, May 2, 1822, by James Gray,
J.P., May 3, 1822. James Moore, BM.

Samuel Mathews & Mary Arnold, April 3, 1822. Abraham Lasiter, BM.

Alex F. McClain & Nancy Young, Aug. 24, 1822, by Wm. Johnson, Aug. 27, 1822.

Jesse McDerment & Anne Duke, Feb. 1, 1822. Sion Duke, BM.

Ephraim McEwing & Polly Ross, Sep. 17, 1822, by John Jarratt, BM.

Samuel M. McCorkle & Nancy Cahoun (Calhoun), Oct. 24, 1822, by Thos. Calhoon, V.D.M.

John Medlin & Fanny Sands, March 20, 1822, by Brinkley Bridges, J.P., March 25, 1822. Robert Anderson, BM.

Israel Moore & Susannah Hunt, March 26, 1822, by Hardy Hunt, J.P., March 29, 1822. James Moore, BM.

John Moss & Susan Murray, July 8, 1822, by Jacob Sullivan, July 23, 1822.

William Nipper & Epsly Gibson, Oct. 29, 1822, by James Gray, J.P., Nov. ___, 1822.

William Nuner (Numor) & Nancy Laughlin, Jan. 30, 1822. John Cox, BM.

Oliver Oniel & Elizabeth Taylor, Feb. 11, 1822. David Baird, BM.

Fountain Owen & Alaminta Hancock, Nov. 19, 1822. Samuel Odom, BM.

Anderson Pearcy & Caty Lasiter, Sep. 28, 1822. Jacob Martin, J.P.

John Pemberton & Lockey Johnson, Jan. 9, 1822. Jesse Pemberton, BM.

John Penticost & Jane Parrish, Oct. 10, 1822. Richard Johnston.

Perrigrin Taylor & Mary Williams, Feb. 7, 1822. John Apflock, BM.

Isaac Perryman & Patsey Seawell, July 19, 1822.

Algermon Pericy & Lucy Lewis, Feb. 9, 1822. Joshua Lester, V.D.M., Drewry Dantz, BM.

George Phillips & Lucinda Turner, March 29, 1822, by William Lawrence, J.P., March 31, 1822. Jere Turner, BM.

Peter Phillips & Ruth Adams, Sep. 10, 1820, by Abner W. Bone, J.P., Sep. 12, 1822.

James Porterfield & Polly Jennings, May 14, 1822. Samuel H. Porterfield, BM.

Daniel Pound & Malinda Jennings, Sep. 24, 1822.

John B. Puckett & Rebecca W. Rice, Aug. 31, 1822, by Jacob Browning, D.D., Sep. 10, 1822.

William Ray & Martha P. Willis, Oct. 26, 1822, by Peter Fuqua, M.G., Oct. 29, 1822.

James Reed & Elizabeth Bryson, Oct. 4, 1822, by John McMinn, J.P., Oct. 10, 1822.

James Rice & Ann Harrison, Nov. 25, 1822, by Ransom Gwynn, J.P., Nov. 28, 1822.

Higdon Robertson & Elizabeth Allen, March 13, 1822. Pleasant Irby, BM.

Westly Roberts & Nancy Reese, Nov. 1, 1822, by Abner Hill, M.G., Nov. 2, 1822.

George Rochell & Polly Climer, Oct. 2, 1822, by Edward
Harris, J.P., Oct. 3, 1822.
Nathaniel Sanders & Naomi Sumers, Feb. 2, 1822, by Benj.
Casilman, J.P., Feb. 6, 1822. John Somers, BM.
Abner Shaw & Susannah Park, Feb. 7, 1822, by John Borum,
March 11, 1822.
John Shepherd & Frances Graves, Oct. 23, 1822, by J. T.
Davis, J.P., Jan. 2, 1823.
Robert Sheppard & Susan Guill, June 1, 1822, by Elijah
Maddox, June 6, 1822. Jno. Shepherd, BM.
George K. Smith & Fanny Dillon, Nov. 1, 1822.
George Charing (Chowning?), BM.
Henry H. Smith & Sally Belote, Oct. 1, 1822, by G. H.
Bussard, J.P., Oct. 19, 1822.
Abraham Sneed & Martha Brown, March 11, 1822, by James
McAdow, J.P., March 14, 1822. John McAdow, BM.
Levy Stites & Mary Adamson, May 5, 1822, by William
Lawrence, J.P., May 9, 1822. Jesse Pugh, BM.
Noah A. Suggs & Nancy Tarver, March 18, 1822. Howel
Tarver, BM.
Howell Tarver & Sally Richmond, Jan. 19, 1822, by Jacob
Sullivan, Jan. 20, 1822. Peter Sullivan.
James Thomas & Isbel Doak, Sep. 14, 1822, by Thos.
Calhoon, V.D.M.
Eli Thompson & Abegale Godfrey, Aug. 6, 1820, by Joshua
Lester, V.D.M., Aug. 8, 1820.
Eli Thrower & Rebecca Wall, Feb. 22, 1822, by Abner
Hill, M.G., Feb. 23, 1822. John Hickman, BM.
John Ward & Elizabeth Glas, Nov. 15, 1822. John Mc
Caffrey, BM.
Bennett Webb & Patsey Hull, Feb. 13, 1822, by William
Gray, J.P., Feb. 14, 1822. James Driver BM.
Reubin Webb & Mary Allen, June 5, 1822. W. H. Pean,
J.P., Gray Webb, BM.
Abner Wetherly & Mary Edmiston, March 24, 1822   Sam'l
Donnell, BM.
John Whitson & Susannah Green, Feb. 4, 1822 (?).
William Nray, J.P., Owen Dennis, BM.
Allen Wilkinson & Mary Dickings, Dec. 16, 1822, by Elijah
Maddox, M.G., Dec. 17, 1822.
Robert Wilson & Elizabeth Rich, June 24, 1822, by Wilie
Walk, Nov. 16, 1822.
Benton Wood & Lucy Patterson, Aug. 7, 1822, by Joshua
Lester, V.D.M.
Edmund Wood & Menath Smith, Feb. 3, 1822. James L.
Lester, BM.
James Wright & Rebecca Kirkpatrick, Feb. 11, 1822, by
William Gray, J.P., Feb. 13, 1822. Obediah G. Finley.
Richard Akers & Anne Bickings, Feb. 27, 1823. Abner
Hill, M.G.
John Adnerson & Jane Roane, Oct. 23, 1823. John Provine,
M.G., Andrew Roane, BM.
Knox Armstrong & Nancy Greer, Aug. 16, 1823. Samuel
Armstrong, BM.

WILSON COUNTY MARRIAGES

Etheldred Bass & Nancy Barter, Nov. 29, 1823. John Bass, BM.
Sion Bass & Sally Phillips, Aug. 2, 1823. John Bass, BM.
William G. Barr & Chany Lane, Feb. 6, 1823, by R. Gwyn, J.P., Feb. 11, 1823.
Jefferson Bodine & Peggy Furgason, Dec. 22, 1823, by John Bonner, J.P., Dec. 26, 1823. Thomas L. Bonner, BM.
Bastly Bowers & Marge Mahafy, N.D. Jeremiah Bonner, BM.
Benjamin Branch & Sarah Moore, Jan. 25, 1823, by Robert Williams, M.G., Jan. 30, 1823. George Brison, BM.
Henry Brown & Rebecca Mitchell, Aug. 7, 1823, by John Bonner, J.P., Aug. 12, 1823. Taswell Mitchell, BM.
William Bryant & Ceyley Higdon, Aug. 27, 1823. James Allcorn, BM.
James Bundy & Rebecca Williford, Feb. 11, 1823, by Wilson Hearn, M.G., Feb. 13, 1823.
Nathan Byrd & Prudence Smith, Feb. 25, 1823, by Abner Hill, M.G., Feb. 26, 1823.
Thos. Byrd & Budy Kemp, April 1, 1823. B. Bridges.
William Byrd & Nancy Waters, Feb. 25, 1823, by Abner Hill, M.G., Feb. 26, 1823.
Hezekiah Cartwright & Mary Brown, Jan. 7, 1823, by John Bass, J.P., Jan. 8, 1823.
James York & Nancy Blurton, Aug. 22, 1822, by James Gray, J.P., Oct. 24, 1822. Moses Odum.
John Casilman & Martha Bell, Aug. 15, 1823. John J. Bell, BM.
Allen Clemmons & Jimey Young, Oct. 14, 1823, by Joshua Woolard, M.G., Oct. 16, 1823. William Russell.
Joseph G. Clendenon & Hannah Kitkpatrick, June 11, 1823, by William Gray, J.P., June 12, 1823. William Mackentire, BM.
Benjamin Clifton & Hannah Clifton, June 30, 1823, by Howard Harris, J.P., July 1, 1823. Lawrence Sypcert, BM.
William Colewick & Margarette Steele, Aug. 7, 1823. B. Taylor, BM.
Thos. Conger & Sally Aust, July 5, 1823, by G. H. Bussard, J.P., Aug. 20, 1823. John Conger, BM.
John Craddock & Ruth E. Hicks, June 14, 1823. Josua Lester, V.D.M., Jesse Jennings, BM.
Joseph Cuthrel & Margaret Spring, Sep. 12, 1823. Milton W. Grissom, BM.
James N. Davis & Elizabeth McAdow, Jan. 3, 1823. Abner W. Bond, J.P.
Robert Donelson & Elizabeth Rutherford, Feb. 24, 1823, by Elijah Maddox, M.G., Feb. 27, 1823.
Willie Davenport & Lucinda Ward, Sep. 8, 1823, by John McMinn, J.P., Sep. 9, 1823. John Sauls, BM.
Robert S. Donnell & Anne B. McAdow, April 1, 1823.
Richard Dortch & Susan Hunt, Sep. 16, 1823. Thomas Scurlock, BM.

Sion Duke & Saly Bradshaw, Dec. 12, 1823, by Elijah
Maddox, M.G., Dec. 18, 1823. James Drake, BM.
Greenberry Eaton & Jensey McKinney, Aug. 24, 1823, by
John Green, Aug. 25, 1823. John Womach, BM.
David Ackols & Lytsy Bradshaw, Aug. 8, 1823. John
Foster, BM.
Anderson Evans & Lucy Stuart, Sep. 19, 1823. John
Drennon, John Smith, BM.
William Ferrell & Elizabeth Wilson, Aug. 22, 1823. John
Provine, M.G., Ewing Wilson, BM.
Levy Fuston & Pstaey Adams, June 24, 1823. Sam'l
Little, BM.
Henry Fite & Mary Grandstaff, Oct. 7, 1823, by Cantrell
Bethell, M.G., Oct. 9, 1823. John Grandstaff BM.
Gideon Fox & Unis Bennett, Dec. 25, 1823. Solomon
Warren, BM.
William Garret & Sarah Welch, Jan. 22, 1822, by James
Drennon, J.P., Jan. 24, 1822. Michael McDearmon.
Archibald Gibson & Fanny Mosely, Nov. 27, 1823, by
Edward Willis, Nov. 30, 1825. Hardy H. Seawell.
Aaron Gibson & Elizabeth Patterson, March 3, 1823. James
Bonds, V.D.M.
John C. Gibson & Sally Ratterce, July 16, 1823, by Wm.
Steele, J.P., July 17, 1823. George Campbell, BM.
Edmund Gillum & Lucinda Merrit, Feb. 24, 1823, by James
Foster, J.P., Feb. 25, 1823.
James Godfrey & Nancy Whitlock, Sep. 22, 1823. James
Thompson, BM.
Thomas Griffin & Thankful Ozment, Feb. 18, 1823, by
Benj. Casilman, Feb. 20, 1823.
William Green & Elizabeth Douglas, Dec. 8, 1823, by Eze-
kiel Cloyd, M.G., Dec. 9, 1823. Robert Anderson, BM.
Alexander Hamilton & Jane East, June 12, 1823, by Jacob
Sullibam, July 16, 1823.
Hope Hancock & Patsey Rogers, Oct. 13, 1823, by Edward
Harris, J.P., Nov. 6, 1823. Eli Edwards.
Henry Hancock & Priscilla Hancock, Aug. 23, 1823, by
Edward Harris, J.P., Aug. 25, 1823. Nelson Hancock.
John Harlin & Elizabeth S. Bradly, June 7, 1823. John
Borum.
William H. Hern & Susan H. Turner, Aug. 6, 1819, by
Wilson Hearn, M.G., Feb. 13, 1823.
Henry Hobson & Lucy L. Tarver, Oct. 2, 1823, by John
Jarratt, Oct. 7, 1823. John H. Dew, BM.
George S. Hooper & Elizabeth Winston, Feb. 26, 1823.
Joshua Lester, V.D.M.
Geo. W. Hughly & Rachel Drennon, Dec. 18, 1823. John
Drennon, J.P., Joseph Drennon, BM.
Henry Hulme (Hull) and Lucy Wright, Sep. 2, 1823, by
William Gray, J.P., Sep. 11, 1823. Jesse Lisle, BM.
Benjamin Hunt & Lucy Maro, Dec. 11, 1823, by Hardy Hunt,
J.P., Dec. 23, 1823. John B. Harris, BM.
Jesse Jackson & Temperance Altern, June 8, 1823, by Geo.
Clark, J.P., June 11, 1823.

WILSON COUNTY MARRIAGES

William Jackson & Eunice Chandler, Feb. 4, 1823, by John
Williamson, J.P., Feb. 12, 1823.
Watkins Johnson & Patsey Edwards, Dec. 10, 1823.
Anderson Loyd, BM.
Richard Jones & Elizabeth Norman, April 4, 1823, by John
McMinn, J.P., April 5, 1823.
Michael Jones & Hannah Dallas, Aug. 7, 1823, by John
Borm, Aug. 14, 1823. Alpa Philips, BM.
Richard Jones & Jane Graves, Oct. 2, 1823. Bartly
Graves, BM.
Larkin Keeton & Mary Willard, Dec. 8, 1823 (1825?).
John W. Hall, BM.
William E. Leetle (Leeth) & Aline Fields, Dec. 22, 1823,
by J. Gray, J.P., Dec. 25, 1823. John Barber, BM.
Nathaniel P. Lewis & Eleanor A. McKee, April 21, 1823.
Joshua Lester, V.D.M.
Henry Ligon & Martha Shepherd, Aug. 7, 1823. G.W. Buzzard,
J.P., Elisha Crupup, BM.
Henry D. Luster & Matilda Jones, Dec. 31, 1822, by
Joshua Lester, V.D.M., Jan. 10, 1823.
Grasty Mansfield & Fanny Edward, April 1, 1823. John
Jarratt.
James McCowan & Mary Clifton, Dec. 22, 1823, by Edward
Harris, J.P., March 22, 1824.
Enodh McNeely & Elizabeth McSpadden, Feb. 19, 1823.
John Provine, M.G.
Charles McWhiter (McWhirter) & Nancy Griffin, Dec. 10,
1823. Hugh B. McWhirter.
Sylvanus Merritt & Priscilla Bennett, Aug. 19, 1823, by
James Bond, V.D.M., Aug. 22, 1823. Howard Edward, BM.
Dandridge Moss & Catharine Avains (Evins), Oct. 2, 1823.
John Murray, BM.
Peter Myers & Diana Carter, Dec. 22, 1823, by David
Foster, M.G., Dec. 24, 1823. Thomas Kirkpatrick, BM.
Ashley Neal & Elizabeth Waters, Oct. 26, 1822. Joseph
B. Lawrence, BM.
Benjamin Nickols & Polly G. Sherrill, Jan. 7, 1823, by
Jacob Sullivan, Jan. 8, 1823.
Robert Nickols & Lucy Nickols, Jan. 9, 1823. Benj.
Casilman, J.P.
Perry Oddle & Elizabeth Joiner, Oct. 22, 1823, by J. L.
McClain, J.P., Oct. 24, 1823. John Clampett, BM.
Richard Ozment & Susannah Rice, Jan. 1, 1823. Jacob
Sullivan
Eli Ozment & Sally Ozment, Jan. 29, 1823, by Benj.
Casilman, J.P., Feb. 2, 1823.
Samuel Ozment & Nancy Waddle, Jan. 10, 1823. Benj.
Casilman, BM.
Watkins Owens & Peggy Kias, Oct. 18, 1823, by Wm. Flowers
Sr., Oct. 23, 1823. Robert Pully, BM.
Lewis Patterson & Polly Edwards, Aug. 13, 1823, by James
Bonds, V.D.M., Aug. 14, 1823. Samuel G. Barrett, BM.
William Paterson & Happy Edwards, Feb. 15, 1823, by
James Bond, V.D.M., Feb. 20, 1823. Rubert Baskin, BM.

Isaac Paynter & Nancy Edwards, March 12, 1823, by G. H. Bussard, J.P., March 13, 1823.

Thomas Pemberton & Polly McHeney, June 30, 1823. Joshua Lester, V.D.M., Henry D. Lester, BM.

Jacob Berriman & Nancy Ward, March 10, 1823, by John McMinn, J.P., March 13, 1823.

Ramon (Ransom) Perriman & Nancy Ward, Nov. 7, 1823.

Nathaniel Puckett & Elizabeth Rice, Jan. 5, 1823, by R. Gwyn, J.P., Jan. 8, 1823.

Isaiah Pugh & Mahala Cansby, Jan. 23, 1823. William Lawrence, J.P.

Wyatt Pickman (Rickman?) & Patsey Sims, Sep. 12, 1823. Wilaon Hearn, M.G., Benjamin Standley, BM.

John Pully & Reba Franklin, Dec. 4, 1823. William Owens, BM.

Hiram Pursley & Elly Jones, Oct. 22, 1823, by John McMinn, J.P., Oct. 23, 1823. Joel Hunter, BM.

Edward Radford & Sally Thompson, April 1, 1823, by John Williamson, J.P., April 4, 1823.

Peyton W. Randolph & Margary Tucker, March 15, 1823, by Thos. Calhoon, V.D.M., March 16, 1823.

Burnell Roives & Maria Wilson, July 11, 1823. Joseph Fite, J.P., JOhn H. Stoneman.

Thomas Robertson & Hannah Tally, Feb. 13, 1823, by Wilson Hearn, M.G., March 3, 1823.

Robert Sanders & Elizabeth House, March 5, 1823. Wm. Steele, J.P.

Ephraim Sherrill & Polly Bell, Sep. 23, 1823, by John W. Peyton, J.P., Sep. 25, 1823. Samuel Y. Thomas.

John Simpson & Polly Ann Teague, Dec. 27, 1823, by James Bond, V.D.M., Dec. 28, 1823. Abner Teague, BM.

William W. Sims & Margaret Bone, Feb. 18, 1823, by James McDonnal, V.D.M., Feb. 20, 1823.

James Smith & Gilley Stewart, July 26, 1826 (1823?), by John Bonner, J.P., Aug. 3, 1823.

Elijah Spencer & Nancy Nelson, March 24, 1823, by Joshua Woollen, M.G., March 25, 1823.

James Stephens & Elizabeth Chambers, Dec. 1, 1823. John Provine, M.G., John Afflack, BM.

Charles Sullivan & Elizabeth Huddleston, June 17, 1823. Jacob Sullivan, BM.

Robert Sypert & Priscilla Davis, Dec. 4, 1823. Elijah Maddox, M.G., Thomas Sypert, BM.

Asa Tatum & Charlotte Harris, Sep. 22, 1823. Thomas Smith, BM.

Bryant Tipton & Elizabeth Douglas, March 24, 1823. Will Spicard (?), BM.

James Travillion & Elizabeth Mattox, March 22, 1823, by Elijah Maddox, M.G., March 27, 1823.

Jacob Vantrease & Nancy Bass, July 31, 1823, by Robert B. Williams, M.G., July 31, 1823. John Bass, BM.

Johnson Vaughn & Sally Byter, Aug. 23, 1823, by Jas Gray, J.P., Aug. 24, 1823. William Hickman, BM.

Radford Walker & Mary Hunter, Feb. 13, 1823, by G. H. Bussard, J.P., Feb. 14, 1823.

James Warmack (Warrick) & Geney P. Payton, Nov. 12, 1823.
Hugh Gwyn, BM.
Solomon Watkins & Nancy Kirkpatrick, March 4, 1823.
Joshua Woollen, M.G.
Jonathan W. Weaver & Elizabeth B. Jones, July 7, 1823.
Thomas Broughton, BM.
James C. Wier & Mary Wier, Nov. 6, 1823. John Provine,
M.G., James Wier, BM.
John R. Wilson & Mary Donelson, May 20, 1823, by
Ezekiel Cloyd, J.P., May 22, 1823.
Richard Winsor & Elizabeth A. Miles, Jan. 9, 1823.
Jacob Sullivan.
John Wood & Haley Robertson, Jan. 2, 1823. Jas. Johnson,
J.P.
John Word & Polly Simpson, Nov. 5, 1823. John Jennings,
BM.
Elijah Williams & Polly Clifton, Dec. 28, 1823, by
Edward Harris, J.P., Dec. 29, 1823. Thomas Crutcher,
BM.
James T. Williams & Polly Henry Pamar (Palmer or Parmer),
June 4, 1823. Geo. A. Lucas, J.P.
Robert Williams & Jane Williams, July 2, 1823. Walter
Carruth, J.P., William McIntyre, BM.
John Winn & Peggy Kennedy, April 12, 1823, by Jere_____,
April 13, 1823.
Littleberry Wright & Elizabeth Kirkpatrick, Oct. 14, 1823,
by Danl. Moser, J.P., Oct. 30, 1823. W. Walker, BM.
Solomon Allman & Elizabeth Puckett, July 28, 1824.
Thomas Allman, BM.
Thomas Almond & Margaret Ellison, Sep. 28, 1824, by
Nan Overall, M.G., Sep. 30, 1824. Thomas Almond, BM.
Willis Allen & Elizabeth Joyner, Aug. 12, 1824. John
Bond, Yancey Masey, BM.
Goodrich Andrews & Aley B. Tarver, July 20, 1824. G.B.
Andrews, BM.
James Arnold & Sarah T. Mitchell, Dec. 22, 1824, by
Hardy Hunt, J.P., Dec. 23, 1824. John Gay, BM.
John W. Avory & Malinda Ann Tarver, Jan. 23, 1824. Wm.
Murray, BM.
Batt Baird & Elizabeth Askew, Sep. 27, 1823, by John
Bond, V.D.M., Oct. 15, 1824. James Baird.
David Baird & Polly Avery, Feb. 14, 1824, by J. Gray,
J.P., Feb. 19, 1824. William Wynne, BM.
John Baird & Elener Bell, Oct. 19, 1824. David Baird,
BM.
Jonathan Baker & Lucy Ann Foster, Nov. 24, 1824, by
Burchell Douglas, J.P., Dec. 2, 1824. James Allcorn,
BM.
James Baker & Levina Donnell, Oct. 4, 1824. James B.
Murry, BM.
Richard Bass & Emily Duke, Dec. 28, 1824. Isaac Jenkins,
BM.
Orang D. Bearden & Margaret Woodvill, April 30, 1824.
John Bonner, J.P., Henry Woodvill, BM.

Jefferson Bell & Leathy Johnson, Oct. 11, 1824, by Wilson
Hearn, Oct. 24, 1824. James Johnson, BM.
John Bettis & Milly Jolly, July 13, 1824. William
Bettis, BM.
Jesse Bloodworth & Celia Tucker, Feb. 14, 1824, by John
W. Payton, J.P., Feb. 17, 1824. Benjamin Tucker, BM.
Willie Booker & Sally Joplin, April 15, 1824. James
Foster, J.P., William Alexander, BM.
James C. Bone & Mary W. Smith, Nov. 26, 1824, by William
Williams, J.P., Dec. 1, 1824. David K. Donnell, BM.
Elisha Bonds & Elizabeth Truett, Feb. 18, 1824, by John
Bond, V.D.M., Feb. 19, 1824. Henry Truett, BM.
James Bond & Sarah Clemmons, Dec. 28, 1824. Joshua
Lester, BM.
Charles Bradberry & Nancy Fields, Oct. 24, 1824. Henry
Robertson, BM.
James C. Bradshaw & Charlotte Organ, March 1, 1824.
Ewing Wilson, BM.
Wilson Bradshaw & Polly Spickard, March 2, 1824. Sion
Duke, BM.
Hezekiah Brown & Betsy Collings (a woman of Color),
June 30, 1824, by James Drennon, J.P., July 1, 1824.
Anderson Evans, BM.
Robert Bondurant & Pemila Mosely, Nov. 10, 1824, E.A.
White, BM.
Samuel Calhoun & Martha H. Figures, July 15, 1824, by
John John Jarratt, July 20, 1824. Thomas Bradley, BM.
William Campbell & Polly Warren, Aug. 10, 1824, by
Joshua Lester, V.D.M., Aug. 11, 1824. Solomon Suggs,
BM.
Elisha Cato & Jency Anderson, May 25, 1824, by Hardy
Hunt, J.P., May 29, 1824. James H. Hunt, BM.
Robert Cato & Frances J. Waters, June 20, 1824, by Hardy
Hunt, J.P., July 2, 1824. James Allcorn, BM.
Green Chandler & Betsy Lumpkin, Jan. 6, 1824. William
Chandler, BM.
Robert Chandler & Margaret Calhoon, Dec. 27, 1824. John
Dew, BM.
William Chester & Sophia M. Hogg, Feb. 12, 1824. R.M.
Burton, BM.
John Cluck & Mary Martin, Feb. 24, 1824. Thomas Martin,
BM.
Elijah Cloe & Patsey Lane, Dec. 28, 1824. Patrick
Buckley, BM.
Newton Cloyd & Elizabeth Williamson, Jan. 7, 1824, by
John Williamson, J.P., Jan. 8, 1824. John Williamson,
BM.
Jeremiah Collings & Gilly Evans, Aug. 26, 1824. James
Drennon, J.P., Lemuel Nickings, BM.
Thomas Copeland & Elizabeth Mount, July 16, 1824. Joshua
Copeland, BM.
Benjamin B. Cooper & Rebecca Owen, Dec. 4, 1824. Warren
Davenport, BM.
Robert Cos & Rebecca Rowton, March 20, 1824, by John
Grary, J.P., March 23, 1824. Andrew Cox, BM.

William Cock & Elizabeth Hubbard, Dec. 27, 1824, Solomon Thomas, BM.

Nathaniel Corley & Nancy Turner, July 30, 1824, by Geo. Clark, J.P., Sep. 9, 1824. Michael Yerger, BM.

John Cox & Betsy Edwards, Aug. 26, 1824. Alexander Rutledge, BM.

John Craddock & Lucretia Arnold, Jan. 12, 1824. Robert Bumpas, BM.

James Cropper & Rhoda HOlland, Dec. 28, 1824. Reed A. Holland, BM.

William M. Crook & Rebecca Pasiter, Nov. 23, 1824, Isaac Shark, BM.

Hezekiah Davis & Nancy Wilson, Oct. 23, 1824 Millner Walker, BM.

Sam'l Dock & Nancy Word, Nov. 7, 1824. Joshua A. Lester, V.D.M., Valentine Ligon, BM.

Eden Donnell & Eliza Garmony, Jan. 19, 1824, by Jesse Alexander, V.D.M., Jan. 29, 1824. Lea Donnell, BM.

Ila Douglas & Elizabeth Harris, Jan. 5, 1824, by William Algood, Jan. 8, 1824. F.G. Crutcher, BM.

Joseph Drennon & Lucinda Drennon, June 28, 1824. James Drennon, J.P., James Drennon, BM.

William Eatherly & Elizabeth Bernard, Sep. 24, 1824, by David Foster, M.G., Sep. 30, 1824. James Williams, BM.

Jacob Furgerson & Mary Furgerson, Dec. 28, 1824, by Wm. H. White, M.G., Dec. 29, 1824. Lemuel Furgerson, BM.

Thomas W. Forbus & Nancy Clifton, April 5, 1824. Hugh Wiley, BM.

Obediah Freeman & Elizabeth Hancock, Feb. 12, 1824, by John Rice, Feb. 18, 1824. Joseph Freeman, BM.

Robert Furgerson & Nancy Organ, Jan. 9, 1824, by Wilson Hearn, M.G., Jan. 14, 1824. John Coe, BM.

Jeremiah Garner & Fanny Tracy, June 30, 1824. Edward Moore, BM.

Henry Gosset & Polly Dill, Nov. 29, 1824, by Joshua McMinn, J.P., Dec. 9, 1824. John Gosset, BM.

Peter Goard & Dice Smith, Dec. 1, 1824. William Williams, J.P., Achilles Smith, BM.

Asa Graves & Sally Jones, Sep. 22, 1824, by Edward Harris, J.P., Sep. 23, 1824. Richard Jones, BM.

Ezekiel Greer & Jane Leech, Nov. 7, 1824, by John McMinn, J.P., Nov. 25, 1824. Amos M. Bone, BM.

William Green & Polly Cox, Dec. 20, 1821 (?). Thomas Cook, BM.

James G. Grubbs & Elizabeth Grubbs, Jan. 22, 1824, by William Algood, E.M.EC. Jan. 25, 1824. Edmund Sims, BM.

Thomas Guill & Polly Rice, Sep. 28, 1824. James Drennon, J.P., Jonathan Drennon, BM.

Robert Hallum & Ann T. Dew, Jan. 22, 1824. Elijah Maddox, M.G., Norval Douglas, BM.

Lesley Hancock & Nancy Smith, June 27, (1824?). Lee Anderson, BM.

James W. Harris & Catsey Smith, Aug. 30, 1824, by William Gray, J.P., Aug. 31, 1824. Isaac Ragan, BM.

James Hays & Polly Thomas, Dec. 15, 1824. Thomas Owen, BM.

Hugh Hays & Sally Dark, Nov. 15, 1824. James Hay, BM.

Thomas Hearn & Elizabeth Nettles, Nov. 29, 1824. Benjamin Nettles, BM.

Young L. Herndon & Sally Kelly, Dec. 8, 1824. John S. Kennedy, BM.

Benjamin Hooker & Martha Clemmons, Oct. 11, 1824. J. Sullivan, Thomas Partlow, BM.

George A. Huddleston & Harriet Cummings, Feb. 23, 1824. Joshua Lester, M.G., William Cummings, BM.

Jesse Hunt & Martha Baker, Aug. 2, 1824. Geo. M. Pirtle, J.P., Israel Moore, BM.

James H. Hunt & Rebecca Adkinson, April 3, 1824, by Hardy Hunt, April 5, 1824. Israel Moore, BM.

Baily Hutcherson & Betsey Harvey, Oct. 25, 1824. Ruf Chumly, BM.

John Hutcherson & Nancy Harvey, Oct. 25, 1824. Richard Dhumly, BM.

Joseph Jenkins & Mary Vantrease, Sep. 18, 1824. William Vantrease, BM.

Setphen Jennings & Nancy Glanton, Dec. 22, 1823, by William Gray, J.P., Jan. 4, 1824.

William Johns & Mary Major, Nov. 1, 1824, by James Foster, J.P., Nov. 24, 1824. William Major, BM.

Isham Johnson & Susan Smith, June 8, 1824, by Wm. Johnson, J.P., June 10, 1824. Peter Johnson, BM.

Watkins Johnson & Patsy Edwards, Dec. 10, 1824, by Wilson Hearn, Dec. 11, 1824 (?)

Ansel B. Jolley & Patsey Wright, Feb. 2, 1824, by John Bond, V.D.M., Dec. 8, 1824. Philip Sharp, BM.

Abel Jones & Sally Bateman, Sep. 13, 1824, by Joshua Woollen, M.G., Sep. 16, 1824. John S. Woollen, BM.

Erasmus Jones & Christiana Bond, Oct. 4, 1824, by John McMinn, J.P., Oct. 7, 1824. John Sweatt (Seatt), BM.

Aaron F. Jones & Nansey T. Buchler, Jan. 16, 1824. Benjamin Evans, BM.

Richard Jones & Jane Graves, Oct. 2, 1824, by Wm. Seawell, Oct. 5, 1824.

Samuel Jones & Lucy Winston, Jan. 31, 1824. Joshua Lester, V.D.M., John Winston, BM.

Talbot Jones & Anny Saterfield, Jan. 19, 1824, by Wm. Steele, J.P., Jan. 29, 1824. John Seat, BM.

Thomas Jones & Elizabeth Compton, Aug. 5, 1824. Joseph L. Green, BM.

Alexander Kirkpatrick & Lucy Smith, Feb. 19, 1824, by William Gray, J.P., Feb. 24, 1824. Thomas Bradley, BM.

William Knight & Lavina Redding, May 3, 1824. Joshua Woollen, M.G., James Knight, BM.

John Lacky & Jane White, Oct. 11, 1824. Saml. T. White, BM.

Thornton Lane & Fanny Haralson, March 2, 1824, by Jacob Sullivan, March 3, 1824. Vincent Haralson, BM.

Abram Lasiter & Nancy Puckett, Oct. 8, 1824. Joshua Lester, V.D.M., John Arnold, BM.

Jonathan Lasiter & Nancy Davis, Nov. 11, 1824, by Jacob
Martin, J.P., Nov. 13, 1824. James Allcorn, BM.
William Lawness & Nancy Curd, Feb. 24, 1824, by E.
Maddox, M.G., March 4, 1824. Jacob Lawness, BM.
James M. Lively & Mary Ann Herrod, Dec. 29, 1824. Thomas
D. Lansden, J.P., John M. Greer, BM.
Jones M. Locke & Lucy D. Honner, July 8, 1824. Bartholomew
Figures, BM.
James Ligon & Priscilla Harris, May 31, 1824. John White,
BM.
Teynear H. Mason & Elizabeth, N.D. Henry Mason, BM.
Thomas Mason & Nancy Johndon, Aug. 25, 1824. Sam Brown,
BM.
Eli Massey & Mary David, Feb. 20, 1824. Simon Donnell,
BM.
William I. Mayo & Sally Eagan, Sep. 7, 1824, by Hardy
Hunt, J.P., Sep. 8, 1824. Benjamin Hunt, BM.
Thomas H. McCrairy & Jane Harlow (Harlaw), Dec. 21, 1824,
by William Williams, J.P., March 25, 1825. James Bas-
ford, BM.
William McDonald & Polly Chandler, Sep. 29, 1824.
Beverly Chumly, BM.
Robert Miligan & Mary Blanton, June 11, 1824. James
Milligan, BM.
Thomas P. Moore & Tempy Jones, Sep. 28, 1824. Michael
Jones, BM.
William Nosely & Jemima Turner, April 7, 1824. Robert
N. Coles, BM.
Gardner Morgan & Polly Chaven, Feb. 23, 1824. Randolph
Morgan, BM.
James Neal & Nancy Hearn, Feb. 18, 1824, by Edward Harris,
J.P., Feb. 19, 1824. Geo. D. Moore, Geo. Dillard, BMS.
George Neil & Martha Branch, Oct. 9, 1824. Joseph B.
Drennon, BM.
John Nettles & Penny (Pemmy) Cartwright, May 15, 1824.
Jas. Dodd, BM.
James S. Odom & Mary Francis, Sep. 14, 1824, by John
McMinn, J.P., Sep. 16, 1824. Saml. C. Odom, BM.
Laban Oneil & Matilda Baker, Sep. 11, 1824. Jeremiah
Brooks, BM.
Cheatham Olnant & Ann Wright, April 1, 1824. Jas.
Johnson, J.P.
Nelson Owen & Peggy Duggan, Sep. 7, 1824, by John McMinn,
J.P., Sep. 9, 1824. James Duggan, BM.
William Parker & Mary Cloudas, Feb. 8, 1824. William
Gray, BM.
Alexander Penny & Kitty Harrison, Sep. 20, 1824, by John
Borum, Sep. 25, 1824. Jesse Wade, BM.
James Pemberton & Harky Bradley, Oct. 16, 1824. Thomas
P. Moore, BM.
Josiah Phillips & Polly Bass, March 22, 1824, by Geo.
Clark, J.P., March 25, 1824. Richard Bass, BM.
Jessey Pue & Rhody Hathaway, Sep. 20, 1824. John
Adamson, BM.

Samuel Quarles & Parthena Hines, Jan. 14, 1824. Joshua Lester, V.D.M., Zachariah Wortham, BM.

John Rains & Lucinda Cartwright, Aug. 23, 1824, by John Smith, M.G., Sep. 10, 1824. William Maholland, BM.

Robert D. Reed & Sally Reed, Dec. 8, 1824, by Edward Harris, J.P., Dec. 9, 1824. Samuel Donnell, BM.

William Reese & Martha Taylor, March 2, 1824, by Abner Hill, March 24, 1824. Thomas Cox, BM.

Jordan Robert & Mary Peacock, Nov. 3, 1824, by Joshua Woollen, M.G., Nov. 4, 1824. Sterling Edwards, BM.

John Rogers & Lucy Goard, Sep. 14, 1824, Thomas Copeland, BM.

Frederick Rotrambee (?) & Celia Maddoxk, Dec. 4, 1824, by E. Maddox, M.G., Feb. 5, 1824. John B. Harris, BM.

John Seat & Abslay Bond, Sep. 4, 1824. Jordan Johnson, BM.

Jonathan Shore & Jenny Pane, N.D. James M. Armstrong, BM.

John Sims & Elizabeth Caplinger, Aug. 4, 1824. Robert Corley, BM.

William H. Smith & Lucy W. Pearcy, June 4, 1824, by Jacob Martin, J.P., July 1, 1824. Drury Dance.

Isaac Spark & Orpah Thompson, Sep. 27, 1824 James Foster, J.P., John Major, BM.

Isaac Stephenson & Minerva Norris, Dec. 21, 1824, by P. Fuqua, M.G., Dec. 23, 1824. B.F. Stevenson, BM.

James Spradlin & Margaret Spradlin, Dec. 20, 1824. Nathan H. Allen, BM.

Cyrus Stewart & Elizabeth Roach, Oct. 5, 1824. James T. Tompkins, M.G., Robert Hallum, BM.

Benjamin Sullivan & Polly Sullivan, March 1, 1824, by Edward Willis, March 3, 1824. William M. Swain, BM.

Harry Taylor & Mary Biles, Oct. 7, 1824. Joshua V. Taylor, BM.

Anderson Thorn & Mahala Lemons, May 1, 1824, by J. Gray, J.P., May 6, 1824.

Moses Thompson & Lucinda Donnell, Dec. 4, 1824, by James Foster, J.P., Dec. 11, 1824. James P. Henry, BM.

Washington Thomas & Plly New, Sep. 13, 1824. Robert Thomas, BM.

Adam Trout & Sally Dallas, Oct. 25, 1824. Henry Morge, BM.

Jonathan Turner & Nancy Sneed, Dec. 15, 1824, by Joseph Foster, J.P., Dec. 23, 1824. John Sneed, BM.

Anderson Turpin & Carline Buck, July 15, 1824. Elijah Maddox, M.G., W. Lamberth, BM.

Elijah Vanderpool & Hannah Fuston, June 4, 1824, by John McMinn, J.P., June 10, 1824. John Standly, BM.

David Vincade & Sally McWhirter, Feb. 24, 1824, by Hardy Hunt, J.P., Feb. 27, 1824. John Vincade, BM.

Henry Vivrette & Polly Hickman, July 28, 1824, by Abner Hill, M.G., July 29, 1824. John Hickman, BM.

Charles Wade & Frances Harrison, Aug. 13, 1824, by Abner Hill, M.G., Aug. 25, 1824. Henry M. Hancock, BM.

Martin Wadkins & Sally Hopkins, Feb. 14, 1824. Martin Wadkin, Obediah Rich, BM.

Granville Wammack & Rachel Crooper, June 17, 1824. Mansfield Massey, BM.

Baker Woodward & Martha Pearcy, Nov. 3, 1824. George Woodward, BM.

Peter S. Wood & Sarah Seal, Nov. 27, 1824. William Wood, BM.

Zachariah Wortham & Sally Gun, Nov. 10, 1824. John Puckett, BM.

Greenberry Adams & Sally Periman, June 23, 1825. Benjamin Periman, BM.

John Adamson & Polly David, Oct. 3, 1824. Jesse Pugh, BM.

William Askins & Mahala Stiblefield, Oct. 13, 1825. Benjamin Spring, BM.

Thomas Alexander & Nancy Jennigs, Jan. 10, 1825, by James Foster, J.P., Jan. 18, 1825. William S. Alexander, BM.

John Allen & Frany Adams, Aug. 19, 1825, by Joseph Fite, J.P., Aug. 20, 1825. Zechariah Sommers, BM.

Thomas Ames & Sally Ray, March 18, 1825. Harch Ames, BM.

William Ames & Ann Eagan, Sep. 24, 1825. Hardy Sypert, BM.

Malone Hinderson & Mary A. McMurry, Nov. 10, 1825. Joseph Kirkpatrick, BM.

Frederick Aust & Matilda Allen, April 6, 1825. John Conger, BM.

Hardy H. Baird & Nancy Baird, Sep. 30, 1825. Jas. Sullivan, Bartholomew Baird, BM.

William Baird & Lucinda Baird, Aug. 22, 1825, by John Bond, V.D.M., Sep. 8, 1825. Seldon Baird, BM.

James H. Barr & Eliza Miller, Sep. 1825. David Foster, M.G., Samuel W. Barr, BM.

John Bass & Elizabeth G. McDermont, Feb. 1, 1825, by Geo. Clark, J.P., Feb. 10, 1825. William Naird, BM.

Samuel Baxter & Frances Irby, Aug. 27, 1825, by John W. Peyton- J.P., Sep. 1, 1825. Jacob Wilhelms (Williams ?), BM.

Benjamin Bell & Polly Spring, Nov. 22, 1825. Benjamin Spring, BM.

George Benthall & Sally Brown, March 8, 1825. Littleton Burchat, BM.

Horation Bernard & Jane Atherly, April 11, 1825. Evans Mabry, BM.

William B. Blackburn & Sarah Fletcher, June 16, 1825, by B. Graves, J.P., June 19, 1825. Bird Gwil, BM.

Julius Blalock & Truce Bell, Dec. 22, 1825. Thos. S. Green, J.P., George W. Horn, BM.

Wiley Bodine & Nancy Rutledge, Aug. 20, 1825. John Bonner, J.P.

Elisha Bonds & Patsey Bennett, Jan. 18, 1825, by James Bonds, V.D.M., Jan. 20, 1825. John Merrett, BM.

James Bond & Sarah Clemmons, Dec. 28, 1825, by Joshua Lester, M.G., Jan. ____, 1825. William Bond, BM.

Charles Bradley & Polly Bradley, Nov. 28, 1825. William Jenkins, BM.
David Briant & Mary Lane, March 1, 1825. Richard Hight.
George Brison & Easter Reed, July 21, 1825, by John McMinn, J.P., Aug. 2, 1825. Levy Reed, BM.
Samuel Brison & Isbel Bogel, March 15, 1825. John McMinn, J.P., George Brison, BM.
William Brison & Sally Davinport, July 21, 1825, by John McMinn, J.P., July 24, 1825.
James M. Brown & Celia Roach, July 28, 1825, by David Foster, M.G., Aug. 4, 1825. James H. Barr, BM.
John Brown & Beedy Wright, Dec. 29, 1825, by B. Bridges, J.P., March 27, 1826. James B. Cole, BM.
John Brown & Sarah Williams, April 4, 1825. George Benthall, BM.
John G. Brown & Sarah Scott, March 23, 1826. Moses Brown, BM.
Moses Brown & Tabitha Gardner, Feb. 14, 1825, by Ezekiel Cloyd, M.G., Feb. 17, 1825. Anderson Evans, BM.
Hiram Bryant & Mary Wray, Jan. 3, 1825, by Jas. T. Tompkins, M.G., Jan. 5, 1825. Elisha Vaughn, BM.
Brooking J. Burnett & Lethi Moss, March 10, 1825. Reynear H. Mason, BM.
Isham Butterworth & Elizabeth Ross, Jan. 1, 1825, by Isaac Lindsey, E.M.G., Jan. 6, 1825. William W. Babb, BM.
Jarris Campbell & Sarenia Hambleton, Feb. 8, 1825, by John Bonner, J.P., Feb. 9, 1825.
James Campbell & Polly Prichard, March 7, 1825. Benjamin Prichard, BM.
John Campbell & Malinda Bone, Sep. 6, 1825. Hugh Campbell, GM.
Gideon Carter & Martha Devault, March 28, 1825, by James Drennon, J.P., March 31, 1825. Abraham Carter, BM.
James T. Carruth & Nancy Williams, Jan. 26, 1825, by Walter Everett, J.P., Jan. 27, 1825. Thomas Guthrie, BM.
Lovet Caraway & Peggy Shannon, March 13, 1825. Merit Caraway, BM.
William Carruth & Elizabeth Davis, April 21, 1825. Jesse Jackson, BM.
Alford Clemmons & Elizabeth Young, Nov. 23, 1825, by Jacob Sullivan, Nov. 25, 1825. Allen Clemmons, BM.
James Clemmons & Mavis Parton, April 10, 1825, by Edward Harris, J.P., May 7, 1825. Etheldred Clemmons, BM.
Thomas Clifton & Nancy Seat, Sep. 7, 1825. Spencer W. Tally, BM.
Ezekiel Cloyd & Nancy White, July 18, 1825, by David Foster, M.G., July 21, 1825. Edward White, BM.
John Cluck & Mary Martin, Feb. 24, 1825, by Jacob Martin, J.P., Feb. 27, 1825.
John Coe & Patsey Parmer, Dec. 27, 1825, by William Sypert, J.P., Dec. 29, 1825. Alfred H. Harris, BM.
Flemming Cocke & Martha Williams, March 23, 1825, by J.S. McCall, J.P., March 24, 1825. William Gray, BM.

WILSON COUNTY MARRIAGES

Stephen H. Coleman & Nancy P. Harrison, Aug. 29, 1825, by James T. Tompkins, D.D., Sep. 1, 1825. Joshua Harrison, BM.

Charles Cox & Martha Palmer, June 20, 1825, by Jas. Johnson, J.P., June 24, 1825. John Cox, BM.

George Cummings & Martha D. Foster, April 13, 1825. John Provine, M.G., John Hearn, BM.

John Cunningham & Sally WArren, July 30, 1825. Moses Cunningham, BM.

James Cunningham & Elizabeth Patterson, Aug. 31, 1825. Joshua Lester, V.D.M., William F. Alexander, BM.

John DAvis & Mary Bryant, Sep. 17, 1825, by James T. Tompkins, D.D., Sep. 19, 1825.

Benjamin H. Dinnes & Rhoda Sanders, Sep. 22, 1825, by James Drennon, J.P., Oct. 13, 1825. Johnson Vaughn, BM.

James Davenport & Nancy Mobias, Oct. 5, 1825. John Provine, M.G., James M. Irwin, BM.

Warren Davenport & Susey Whitlock, Feb. 25, 1825, by John McMinn, J.P., Feb. 26, 1825. James S. Leech, BM.

Jonathan Drennon & Lucy G. Liggon, Nov. 14, 1825, by Jas. Drennon, J.P., Nov. 18, 1825. Josiah Ligon, BM.

Redding Fields & Polly Ferrington, Dec. 31, 1825, by James Bond, N.D.M., Jan. 3, 1826. David Fields, BM.

Epaphroditus Francis & Nancy Cropper, Feb. 21, 1825, by John McMinn, J.P., Feb. 24, 1825. James S. Leech, BM.

Joel Frazer & Mary Gilbert, June 15, 1825, by Dnl Moser, June 16, 1825. Alexander Rutledge, BM.

Hugh George & Polly Gains, Jan. 4, 1825. Anthony Gains, BM.

Jesse Gibson & Susan Holland, Jan. 15, 1825, by Danl. Moser, Feb. 8, 1825. Robert Bell, BM.

David Gillispie & Indiana Seawell, Nov. 16, 1825, by Wm. Hume, V.D.M., Nov. 17, 1825. Jno. L. Wynne, BM.

Allen W. Goodwin & Mary Cummings, Dec. 13, 1825, by James Gray, J.P., Dec. 14, 1825.

Obediah Gordon & Frances R.B. Drake, April 1, 1825. Samuel C. McWhirter, BM.

Berry Greer & Catherine Myres, Sep. 27, 1825, by Jacob Sullivan, Sep. 29, 1825. Aquilla Greer, BM.

Daniel J. Guthrie & Mary White, Dec. 20, 1825, by John W. Payton, J.P., Dec. 30, 1825. Thomas Guthrie, BM.

Ezekiel Holloway & Jane Shannon, March 23, 1825, by Abner Hill, M.G., March 24, 1826. James Ozment, BM.

Stephen Haily & Ann Gregor, Jan. 6, 1825 (1845?). Benny B. Beasly, BM.

Gilpin Hallum & Parthena Graves, Aug. 17, 1825, by B. Graves, J.P., Aug. 18, 1825. Norval Douglas, BM.

William Hamilton & Elizabeth Christopher, Sep. 2, 1825, by Robert Baker, M.G., Oct. 28, 1825. John McNeely, BM.

John Hankkns & Elizabeth Roatin, July 7, 1825. James Powell, BM.

Thomas Harrington & Lydia Anglin, Jan. 27, 1825. David Foster, M.G., Peter Mires, BM.

Zara Harrison & Margaret Hessy, Oct. 18, 1825, by Jacob Sullivan, Oct. 19, 1825. John Murray, BM.

James Hays & Mallnda Night, Feb. 23, 1825 (?). Joseph Fite, J.P., Wingate Truit, BM.

John Hayworth & Lucy Wynne, Dec. 10, 1825, by Hardy Hunt, J.P., Dec. 15, 1825. Micajah Hayworth, BM.

Silas Hedgepath & Rebecca Rice, Dec. 10, 1825. Leven Woollen & bondsman.

Mabry Heflon & Isabel Brungton, March 21, 1825, by Joseph Fite, J.P., March 31, 1825.

Alexander Henry & Sarah Carruth, Feb. 5, 1825, by Walter Carruth, J.P., Feb. 6, 1825. David Walsh, BM.

Alfred M. Hill & Mary Lasiter, Aug. 31, 1825, by Jacob Martin, J.P., Sep. 1, 1825. William Lasiter, BM.

Allen Hill & Sarah Peace, April 25, 1825. James Allcorn, BM.

Joel B. Holbert & Tursey Sherrill, May 3, 1825, by James Foster, J.P., May 5, 1825. Zachariah Tolliver, BM.

Isaac Hollingstowth & Alliminta Fustin, Feb. 12, 1825. William Hollingsworth, BM.

Simeon Horse & Sally Sneeds, May 9, 1825. Ransom Perriman, BM.

Caleb Howell & Margaret Clanton, March 1, 1825, by William Gray, J.P., March 10, 1825. Ransom Howell, BM.

James Farveal & Sally Farveal, Dec. 2, 1825. William Cooper, BM.

James Irby & Sarah Kinrid, Sep. 30, 1825 Thomas Kindred, BM.

Jesse Jackson & Nancy Bonner, May 5, 1825. James Slate, BM.

Jorden Johnson & Sally Bartlett, Oct. 11, 1825. Alpha Philips, BM.

Isham Joiner & Rachael Echols, Sep. 21, 1825. Edmund Jones, BM.

Josiah Joiner & Cairy Allen, June 30, 1825. Willis Allen, BM.

William Joiner & Polly Coe, Jan. 11, 1825. Harmon Lash, BM.

William Jolly & Martha Golston, April 12, 1825. Elijah Maddox, M.G., Warren Lambott, BM.

Edward Jones & Lucy Lea, Sep. 5, 1825, by James Foster, J.P., Oct. 6, 1825. Henry H. Harris, BM.

Larken Keeton & Mary Willard, Dec. 8, 1825. Chrostopher Cooper, M.G.

Zachariah Keeton & Nancy Pedigo, Aug. 5, 1825. Joseph Fite, J.P., Joseph Fite, BM.

Absolum Knight & Penilla Dodd, Dec. 10, 1825, by Joshua Woollen, M.G., Dec. 11, 1825. Samuel Ozment, BM.

David Lane & Lucy E. Lane, Dec. 3, 1825, by Jacob Sullivan, Dec. 4, 1825. John Lane, BM.

Mark Leeke & Elizabeth Lewis, July 29, 1825, by John McMinn, J.P., July 30, 1825. William Leeke, BM.

Thomas Lewis & Elizabeth Hays, Aug. 1, 1825. James A. Strong, BM.

Isaac Lindsey & Cynthea Peeder, Oct. 1, 1825, by
Edward Willis, M.G., Oct. 2, 1825.
Logan Linch & Elizabeth Wier, March 21, 1825. William
Joiner, BM.
Thomas Lyon & Susannah Swan, Aug. 15, 1825. James
Swan, BM.
William Maddox & Sally C. Hancock, Aug. 22, 1825, by
Obediah Freeman, Sep. 1, 1825. Henry Hancock, BM.
James Manning & Louisa Bobbett, July 13, 1825. Brittain
Odom, BM.
Robert Manning & Nancy Lannum, Nov. 11, 1825, by William
Lawrence, J.P., Nov. 13, 1825. William Searcy, BM.
Granville Mansfield & Francis Scurlock, Feb. 15, 1825,
by A. Harpole, Feb. 17, 1825. James Allcorn, BM.
Abram Marlow & Rebecca Hanes, Oct. 20, 1825. William
Algood, M.G., John Bell, BM.
James Martin & Mary Eason, March 15, 1825. Patrick
Higerty, BM.
Martin Marrs & Mary Morrison, Jan. 5, 1825, by James
Foster, J.P., Dec. 27, 1825. Alexander Marrs, BM.
Thomas Martin & Thursey Richardson, June 3, 1825. Ewing
Wilson, BM.
Daniel McBride & Molly Benthal, Aug. 13, 1825. Daniel
Moser, BM.
Aaron McCrary & Mary Oliver, May 23, 1825, by Wm.
Williams, M.G., May 26, 1825. James Basford, BM.
Moses McCrary & Elizabeth Weatherly, May 23, 1825, by
Wm. Williams, M.G., May 26, 1825. James Basford, BM.
Enos McKnight & Sally M. Greer, Nov. 5, 1825, by John
McMinn, J.P., Nov. 10, 1825. Wimphrey Witherspoon, BM.
Simon McLenoon & Frances Overby, N.D. George A. Evans,
BM.
Joseph Mingle & Sally Bonds, June 1, 1825. Thomas
Nawlen, BM.
Thomas Moore & Elizabeth Tarver, Sep. 10, 1825, by
Jacob Sullivan, Sep. 11, 1825. Joseph T. Bell, BM.
William Moore & Elizabeth Brothers, July 15, 1825.
Mathew Hearn, BM.
John Mosely & Martha Holbrook, Aug. 18, 1825. James O.
Lambert, BM.
Samuel Mosely & Elizabeth Dill, Oct. 19, 1825. William
Allen, BM.
John Murray & Amy Hessey, Oct. 18, 1825, by Jacob
Sullivan, Oct. 19, 1825. Zara Harrison, BM.
Norfleet Nelms & Lydia Dickins, Dec. 30, 1825, by James
T. Tompkins, D.D., Jan. 1, 1826. Jesse Cook, BM.
Benjamin Nettles & Priscilla Mosley, Sep. 9, 1825.
Richard Compton, BM.
James New & Ann Chanler, Dec. 28, 1825, by John Bonner,
J.P., Dec. 29, 1825. Josiah Beasley, BM.
William C. New & Ivy Hamilton, July 26, 1825. Henry
Jackson, BM.
Whaland Newby & Elizabeth Cooksey, March 28, 1825, by
William Lawrence, J.P., April 14, 1825. James Cooksey,
BM.

Robert N. Nichols & Mary T. Chance, Nov. 24, 1825. Thos.
S. Green, J.P., Jesse M. Wade, BM.

Moses Odom & Lucy Lawrence, Aug. 4, 1825. Thomas
Barbee, BM.

Armstrong Ozment & Martha Hudson, Oct. 14, 1825, by
James Bond, V.D.M., Oct. 17, 1825. Absolom Knight, BM.

James Ozment & Martha Holloway, May 25, 1825, by Abner
Hill, M.G., May 26, 1825. James R. Allen, BM.

John Palner & Margaret Reese, Aug. 22, 1825, by John
Green, Aug. 25, _____. John Cox, BM.

John S. Patterson & Harruet Reynolds. Oct. 1,1825.
William Thompson, BM.

Jonathan Patton & Ruth Godfrey, May 3, 1825, by Jesse
Alexander, V.D.M., May 5, 1825. James Thompson.

Samuel F. Patterson & Lucy Waters, Sep. 20, 1825.
Nelson G. Alexander, BM.

Thos. Patton & Rebecca Patterons, Aug. 30, 1825, by
Jesse Alexander, V.D.M., Sep. 1, 1825. William Thompson.

John Prim & Inde Mattox, Aug. 4, 1825. Elijah Maddox,
M.G., Frederick Rotramel, BM.

Jesey Pue & Rody Hathaway, Sep. 20, 1825. Joseph Fite,
J.P.

Levin Ragsdale & Rebecca Merrit, Sep. 3, 1825. James
Bond, V.D.M., Asa Ragsdale, BM.

Elum Reed & Elizabeth Penticost, June 1, 1825, by Edward
Harris, J.P., June 2, 1825. Henry Reed, BM.

Henry Reed & Agnes M. Carruth, July 27, 1825, by Wm.
Steelem, J.P., July 28, 1825. Robert Reed, BM.

James P. Roach & Nelly McNeely, Aug. 13, 1825, by David
Foster, M.G., Aug. 16, 1825. James H. Barr, BM.

Washington Robertson & Barshaba Williford, Dec. 31, 1825.
Thomas Davis, BM.

Lewis Seay & Margaret Ann Rollman, Nov. 23, 1825, by
Thomas D. Lansden, Nov. 28, 1825. Thomas Wilson, BM.

Drew Shoecraft & Nancy Nickings, May 5, 1825. Mark
Nickings, BM.

Gabriel Shaw & Locky Organ, March 17, 1825. Willis
Allen, BM.

Jacob Smith & Mary Compton, Dec. 17, 1825, by Jno.
Rains, M.G., Dec. 19, 1825. Thomas Barbee, BM.

John Scurlock (Spurlock?) & Sinthy McAdoo, Jan. 21, 1825.
John Swan, BM.

Thomas Scurlocm & Jane Compton, Jan. 11, 1825, by Due
Moser, Jan. 13, 1825. Granwell Manfield, BM.

Benjamin Stephenson & Elizabeth Willis, April 5, 1825.
Wm. Steele, M.G., Stephen Moss, BM.

John H. Stoneman & Feby Moore, July 14, 1825. John
McMinn, J.P., B. Moore, BM.

William Stobey & Margaret Ray, Sep. 24, 1825. John
Clampett, BM.

William Stuart & Mary Tooly, May 13, 1825. Samuel
Mosey (Masey), BM.

John Tarpley & Sarah Davis, June 15, 1825, by Wnl. Moser,
June 15, _____. William New, BM.

John Taylor & Mariah Edward, Jan. 20, 1825, by Geo. Clark, J.P., Feb. 1, 1825.

John D. Taylor & Nancy Williams, Aug. 31, 1825, by W. Johnson, Sep. 1, 1825. Henry Young, BM.

William Taylor & Polly Brown, July 5, 1825, by John W. Payton, J.P., July 7, 1825. Joel Watkins, BM.

Abner Teague & Rhody McKnight, Jan. 3, 1825, by Joel Martin, J.P., Jan. 4, 1825. Stephen Golgly, BM.

James Thrift & Elizabeth Shannon, M.D. Edward White, BM.

James T. Tims & Martha Puckett, Nov. 19, 1825, by Thomas D. Lansden, J.P., Nov. 28, 1825. Leo Donnell, BM.

John Trout & Mary Ann Tomlinson, Dec. 15, 1825. Zealous Johnson, BM.

James Viverett & Sally Hill, April 6, 1825, by _____ Bridges, June 29, 1825. Henry F. Smith, BM.

Jesse Warren & Sally Farmer, Dec. 6, 1825. John Provine, M.G., Perigrin Taylor, BM.

Robert Whitten & Elizabeth Cook, Nov. 19, 1825. William C. Collins, BM.

William Williams & Rebecca Jackson, Dec. 15, 1825. F. G. Crutcher, BM.

Thomas Willis & Malvina Rieff, Aug. 30, 1825. Edward Willis, Thomas Baget, BM.

Joseph L. Wilson & Margret Barton, July 5, 1825. Joseph Johnson, BM.

Samuel R. Wilson & Nancy Golston, May 18, 1825, by John W. Payton, June, 1825. Anderson Cook, BM.

Alygood Woolard & Elizabeth Hutcherson, Nov. 12, 1825, by Thos. S. Green, J.P., Nov. 13, 1825. William Sypert, BM.

Levin Woollen & Nancy Peacock, Dec. 20, 1825, by Joshua Woollen, M.G., Dec. 28, 1825. John L. Woollen, BM.

Lemuel Wright & Sarah Drennon, June 28, 1825, by James Drennon, J.P., June 30, 1825. Thomas Drennon, BM.

John L. Wynne & Minerva Allcorn, Nov. 8, 1825. H. L. Douglas, BM.

John Yandal & Elizabeth Jones, Feb. 21, 1825, by David Foster, M.G., Feb. 22, 1825. James P. Roach, BM.

Lewis D. Tarnell & Ann Arnold, Jan. 18, 1825, D.H. Baird, BM.

Samuel Yerger & Hannah Johnson, June 16, 1825. Benjamin S. Litton, BM.

Edmund York & Ann Carrall, Sep. 14, 1825, by Isaac Lindy, E.M.A., Sep. 15, 1825. Alsey Garret, BM.

John Young & Nancy Vowell, March 17, 1825. James Foster, J.P., James L. Vowel, BM.

William Alsup & Morning Hill, Nov. 26 (?), 1826, by Jacob Martin, J.P., Nov. 29, 1826. Solomon Bond, BM.

Thomas Ames & Salley Ray, March 18, 1826, by Edward Willis, M.G., March 19, 1826.

John W. Avery & Malinda Ann Tarver, Jan. 23, 1826. Jacob Sullivan.

James S. Bailey & Lucy Puckett, Dec. 4, 1826, Joshua Lester, V.D.M., Stanlope Sharpe, BM.

Thomas Bewbanks & Ann Riddle, May 23, 1826. Millner (Milton?) Walker BM.

Noah Barefood & Patsey Cook, April 1, 1826. Benja Goodwin, BM.

Thomas L. Taylor & Hester Taylor, Dec. 4, 1826. Joseph Barbee, BM.

Isaac Barnett & Nancy Long, May 13, 1826, by John Bond, V.D.M., May 14, 1826. James H. Long, BM.

James W. Beauchamp & May Wilson, Sep. 12, 1826. Wm. Steele, J.P., James Cloyd, BM.

Joseph Bell & Jane Donnell, Aug. 24, 1826. Wm. Swain, J.P., Jesse M. Wade, BM.

Nathaniel Bell & Lucinda Smith, Feb. 4, 1826, by Jacob Sullivan, Feb. 5, 1826. E. Sherrill, BM.

Robert D. Bell & Elizabeth Roane, Dec. 13, 1826, by Thos. Calhoon, V.D.M., Dec. 14, 1826. James Astoce, BM.

Simpson Bennett & Nancy Jackson, Aug. 26, 1826, by Stephen McDonald, J.P., Dec. 14, 1826. Randal McDonald, BM.

Horatio Bernard & Margaret M. Williamson, Oct. 11, 1826. B. Graves, J.P., Henry F. Smith, BM.

Charles Blalock & Patsey Tucker, Jan. 5, 1826. John W. Payton, J.P., James Mays, BM.

William Bond & Lovely Simmons, _____ 16, 1826. John Bond, V.D.M.

Enos Bone & Lucy Hern, May 27, 1826, by James Foster, J.P., June 1, 1826. James P. Henry, BM.

Samuel Bryson & Mary Milligan, Feb. 3, 1826, by Christopher Cooper, M.G., Feb. 4, 1826. David Milligan, BM.

Henry Burnett & Parthenea Moss, Jan. 9, 1826. Jacob Sullivan, Reynor H. Mason, BM.

Harris Campbell & Sarena Hamilton, Feb. 8, 1826. William O. Neal, BM.

William Cason & Mary McKnight, Sep. 2, 1826, by James Bond, V.D.M., Sep. 7, 1826. George Smith, BM.

Leven Clifton & Hannah Skeen, Nov. 8, 1826. Obadiah Freeman, M.G., George Tucker, BM.

John Cloyd & Elizabeth Griffet, Sep. 11, 1826, by John Williams, J.P., Sep. 13, 1826. John Nunner, BM.

Valentine Coker & Thiny Lee, June 24, 1826, by Abner Hill, M.G., June 26, 1826. Joseph T. Bell, BM.

James B. Cole & Jacout (?) Bridges, July 27, 1826, by B. Bridges, J.P., July 30, 1826. Aaron Britton, BM.

James Cowen & Nancy Walker, Jan. 12, 1826. Elijah Maddox, M.G., Mathew Horn, BM.

William M. Cowen & Mary M. Mosely, Sep. 20, 1826. James Allcorn, BM.

Henry R. Cox & Purlena Shorter, Nov. 11, 1826. William Cos, BM.

James Cox & Lucy Cox, Nov. 11, 1826. William Cox, BM.

James Daniel & Elisa Smith, June 17, 1826, by Josiah S. McClain, J.P., June 22, 1826. Josiah McClain, BM.

Francis P. Davidson & Sarah Hearn, Dec. 18, 1826. Thomas Cox, BM.

WILSON COUNTY MARRIAGES

Ellis Davis & Mary Minor, Jan. 14, 1826, by J. B. Lasater, J.P., Dec. 29, 1826.

Edward Dillard & Martha S. Gold, Dec. 11, 1826. A. W. Wynne, BM.

Nathan Dillon & Sarah Green, Dec. 9, 1826. William Nipper, BM.

William M. Dillard & Elizabeth F. Corley, Sep. 3, 1826, by William Algood, Sep. 5, 1826. Robert Corley, BM.

Alanson F. Doak & Adaline Donnell, July 11, 1826, by James Foster, J.P., July 18, 1826. T. S. Donnell, BM.

Joseph Eaton & Mary P. Underhill, April 6, 1826, by John McMinn, J.P., April 30, 1826.

Elan Edge & Mary Barbee, Sep. 27, 1826. Jno. Rains, M.G., Thomas Barbee, BM.

William England & Seluda Ferguson, Feb. 10, 1826, by Brittain Drake, J.P., Feb. 26, 1826. James Irby, BM.

Edward Freeman & Charlott Everrett, Aug. 26, 1826. Brinkley Bridges, BM.

John Gay & Mariah A. Clay, May 4, 1826. G. Baker, Hardy Hunt, BM.

Thompson Glenn & Julia Scurlock, Nov. 21, 1826. Jas. L. Wilson, BM.

William B. Gleaves & Harriet Simpkins, Nov. 20, 1826. William McNeel, BM.

Hardin & Polly Scoby (Scobey), July 29, 1826. Thomas B. Rees, BM.

John Gossett & Frankey Ones (Owens?), March 4, 1826, by John McMinn, J.P., March 9, 1826.

James W. Green & Lucy Ann Bonner, March 28, 1826, by Wilson Hearn, M.G., March 31, 1826. James Allcorn, BM.

David Grindstaff & Margaret Phillips, July 22, 1826. Mitchell Hearn, BM.

John Gun & Polly Sims, Feb. 10, 1826, by Thomas D. Lansden, J.P., Feb. 20, 1826 Caswell S. Sims, BM.

Leeman Hancock & Caty Moxley, April 1, 1826, by Obadiah Freeman, April 13, 1826. Nelson Hancock, BM.

Samuel Harlin & Susanna Bradley, Aug. 24, 1826. Wm. Hodges, BM.

McGee Harris & Polly Givins, Dec. 28, 1826, by Wm. Steele, J.P., Dec. 29, 1826. Forgust S. Harris, BM.

Stephen Hearn & Polly G. Hankins, June 29, 1826. William H. Hearn, BM.

Charles Hicks & Claresa Webb, Oct. 28, 1826. Willie Dockings, BM.

David Hodges & Mary Rolls, Nov. 18, 1826, by Wm. Swain, J.P., Nov. 19, 1826. John Rawls, BM.

Charles Ferris & Susannah Mason, Sep. 5, 1826, by J. B. Lasiter, J.P., Sep. 6, 1826. John Mason, BM.

Micajah Horn & Sarah Harper, Nov. 20, 1826. Byrd Molen, BM.

Merritt Hubbard & Dolly Cawthon, Aug. 22, 1826, by B. Graves, J.P., Aug. 23, 1826.

Paschal P. Hudson & Alliphair Hearn, Aug. 26, 1826, by Thomas Smith, M.G., Aug. 31, 1826. L.S. Donnell, BM.

WILSON COUNTY MARRIAGES

Thomas C. Hudson & Cintha McLeroy, Jan. 3, 1826, by
Thomas Smith, M.G., Jan. 5, 1826. Jas. Guthrie, BM.
Jesse Johnson & Rebecca Stuart, Dec. 22, 1826. John
Willimson, J.P., Jones M. Johnson, BM.
Phillip Johnson & Elenor Harrison, Dec. 11, 1826. Robt.
Johnson, BM.
Turner M. Johnson & Elizabeth Taylor, Feb. 15, 1826.
Geo. Clark, J.P., Willis Dowell, BM.
Allen Jones & Michie Hutcherson, Feb. 10, 1826, by Wm.
L. Sypert, J.P., Feb. 12, 1826. William L. Sypter, BM.
Geo. W. Jones & Chrisina G. Dance, Dec. 8, 1826. Elisha
Sims, BM.
Michael Jones & Margaret Bond, March 8, 1826. Jediah
McMinn, M.G.
Lemuel Koonce & Drufiney Odom, Jan. 2, 1826, by John
McMinn, J.P., Jan. 20, 1826.
John Lane & Nancy Arnold, July 11, 1826. Nathan Williams,
BM.
Hugh Lansden & Ann Marshall, Feb. 4, 1826. Leon Donnell,
BM.
Hyram Lea & Elizabeth Lea, Sep. 21, 1826. Abner Hill,
M.G., Samuel R. Comer, BM.
Josiah Ligon & Mary M. Fletcher, July 11, 1826, by B.
Graves, J.P., July 12, 1826. John Wm. Hugheley.
Richard Lyon & Ann Swain, Nov. 14, 1826. Marshall H.
Ward, BM.
Richard Maddox & Elizabeth Johnson, Sep. 5, 1826. Larkin
Spradlin, BM.
Requear H. Mason & Elizabeth Moss, Jan. 9, 1826, by
Jacob Sullivan, Jan. 10, 1826.
Alfred Mathew & Jeney Hollingsworth, Sep. 30, 1826.
Nathan C. Mathews, BM.
Henry Mathew & Sally Seat, Dec. 2, 1826. Tolbert Jones,
BM.
Drury Mays & Susan M. Williams, May 17, 1826, by B. Bridges
J.P., May 18, 1826. John Brown, BM.
Edwin A. McCorkle & Jane M. Thomas, Nov. 25, 1826, by
Wm. Steele, J.P., Nov. 28, 1826. Wm. Thomas, BM.
William McGregor (McGerggor) & Frances H. Graves, N.D.
Wm. Walker, BM.
David D. McCully & Sarah Drolingder, Aug. 7, 1826, by
John Williams, J.P., Aug. 10, 1826. William Drolingder,
BM.
James Melton & Nancy Palmer, Dec. 20, 1826. Henry
Southern, BM.
David Milligan & Anney Standley, Aug. 2, 1826, by John
McMinn, J.P., Aug. 21, 1826.
James Mitchell & Susan Owen, Sep. 29, 1826. John
Honner, J.P.
John C. Moncline & Maria Youree, Jan. 12, 1826. Benjamin
Chapman, BM.
Alston Morgan & Ann Edwards, Jan. 19, 1826, by James
Bond, V.D.M., Jan. 22, 1826.
Henry Morris & Easter Hearn, Aug. 19, 1826, by Wm. Swain,
J.P., Sep. 7, 1826. Micajah Rogers, BM.

80

WILSON COUNTY MARRIAGES

John C. Mosley & Sally Jones, April 10, 1826. Asa
Mosely, BM.
Moore S. Moss & Dianniah Hughley, March 10, 1826, by B,
Graves, J.P., March 14, 1826.
John H. Paisley & Martha Thrower, March 13, 1826. David
Foster, M.G., James Jackson, BM.
John K. Parker & Elizabeth Tipton, Feb. 1, 1826, by John
W. Payton, J.P., Feb. 2, 1826. Flemming Cocke, BM.
Alphy Philips & Alizabeth Edwards, Sep. 23, 1826.
Hez. Cartwright, BM.
Montgomery Pitner & Jane Wray, Aug. 21, 1826. Edward
Willis, M.G., William Pitner, BM.
William B. Pursley & Harriott Johnson, Aug. 5, 1826.
Robertson Johnson, BM.
Asa Ragsdale & Rhoda Ragsdale, Nov. 1, 1826, by James
Bond, V.D.M., Nov. 2, 1826. Leaven Ragsdale, BM.
Elisha L. Rhodes & Sally Moseley, Oct. 2, 1826, by Edward
Willis, Oct. 3, 1826. J. R. Ashworth, BM.
William Richard & Maryon McCoy, June 6, 1826 by Geo. L.
Smith, J.P., June 13, 1826.
Fountain Robertson & Sarah Cason, July 24, 1826, by
James Bond, V.D.M., July 27, 1826. Thos. McKnight, BM.
Samuel Rogers & Martha Ward, Dec. 2, 1826, by Thos. S.
Green, J.P., Dec. 7, 1826.
Edmund Rucker & Louisia Winchester, Oct. 26, 1826, by
Wm. Sypert, J.P., Nov. 26, 1826. John W. Rucker, BM.
Washington Sanders & Polly Sanders, Dec. 25, 1826, by
Joshua Woollen, M.G., Dec. 26, 1826.
James Sands & Susan Moser, Aug. 4, 1826, by Stephen
McDonald, J.P., Aug. 7, 1826. Alex Carruth, BM.
Tompthy Seat & Elizabeth Clifton, May 3, 1826. Pledge
Swindell, BM.
Joseph Seay & Elizabeth Barker, Sep. 14, 1826, by Thomas
D. Lansden, J.P., Sep. 25, 1826. Robert Buster, BM.
Henry Shannon & Margaret Clemmons, June 19, 1826, by
Wm. Smith, J.P., June 22, 1826. William M. Swain, BM.
William Shepheard & Rachel Caroline Youree, Nov. 18, 1826,
by Stephen McDonald, J.P., Nov. 19, 1826.
Thomas Sherring & Sally Baxter, Feb. 7, 1826. Jeremiah
Murry, BM.
William T. Sherrell & Elenor M. Thomas, Dec. 20, 1826.
J. Provine, M.G., Murfree Long, BM.
Thomas Short & Elizabeth Pemberton, April 7, 1826. Jesse
Pemberton, BM.
Caswell S. Sims & Nancy Carter, March 13, 1826. Thomas
Cox, BM.
Edmund Simpson & Rachael Whitton, Sep. 18, 1826, by
Joshua Lester, V.D.M., Sep. 21, 1826. Stanhope
Sharpe, BM.
Samuel Smith & Catharine _____, Jan. 13, 1826, by
Josiah S. McClain, Jan. 19, 1826. Thomas Bradley, BM.
William H. Smith & Jane Smith, May 1, 1826. Geo.
Donnell, V.D.M., Joshua Smith, BM.
Benjamin Spring & Catarine Spring, Oct. 30, 1826. Jas.
Hearn, BM.

Barna Stewart & Jane Morris, Dec. 30, 1826, by John
Williamson, J.P., Jan. 30, 1827. Thomas Gains, BM.
Cyrus Stuart & Mary S. Gleaves, Aug. 8, 1826. David
Foster, M.G., Robert Campbell, BM.
Valentine Stull & Susan Rice, Oct. 21, 1826. James
Drennon, BM.
Henry Suthern & Bathelela Melton, Oct. 26, 1826. William
Williams, BM.
Thomas D. Tarver & Sarah Hallum, Sep. 7, 1826. John W.
Payton, J.P., John T. Hail, BM.
Richard B. Tate & Rebeckah Alexander, Jan. 30, 1826.
Ezekiel Cloyd, J.P., James Wilson, BM.
John Talor & Mariah Edwards, Jan. 20, 1826. John Gaddy,
BM.
John N. Taylor & Cary Ann Sheppard, Nov. 20, 1826. John
Provine, M.G., Philander Davis, BM.
Richard Terrell & Sally Holloway, July 19, 1826, by
Abner Hill, M.G., July 21, 1826. William Comer, BM.
Reddin Tidwell & Mary Enoch, Dec. 7, 1826. John Sullivan,
BM.
Christopher Tims & Elizabeth Malsinger, May 16, 1826.
Edward Tims, BM.
William Trusty & Aley Mitchell, Feb. 14, 1826. Hardy
Hunt, J.P., Ishmiel Bradshaw, BM.
William Vantrease & Ann Lawrence, Jan. 28, 1826. Davie
Granstaff, BM.
Samuel Vinson & Christina Stuart, Nov. 12, 1826. Jonathan
L. Farr, BM.
Anderson Walker & Elizabeth Bradley, Oct. 21, 1826, by
Wm. Flowers, J.P., Oct. 26, 1826. John H. Swindle, BM.
Henry Walker & Elizabeth Denton, Dec. 14, 1826. German
Baker, Hubbard Frerll, BM.
Samuel Walker & Johannah Graves, Aug. 22, 1826. B.
Graves, J.P.
William Walker & Polly Fletcher, Jan. 19, 1826. B.
Graves, J.P.
Wyatt Walker & Jane Petty, Sep. 5, 1826, by Joshua
Coollen, M.G., Sep. 8, 1826. John Mason, BM.
Solomon Warren & Nancy Howard, Feb. 14, 1826, by Jas.
Gray, J.P., Feb. 16, 1826. Absalom Knight, BM.
John Webber & Elizabeth Atherly, Sep. 30, 1826, by John
Williamson, J.P., Oct. 10, 1826. F. P. Wood, BM.
Nathan Wheeler & Catharine Grindstaff, April 1, 1826.
Thomas Tracy, BM.
Isaac Whitehead & Sarah Mosley, Oct. 3, 1826, by William
Flowers, J.P., Oct. 10, 1826. John Mosley, BM.
Medy White & Sarah Campbell, Aug. 10, 1826, by Wm.
Steele, J.P., Aug. 13, 1826. John C. Gibson, BM.
Thomas P. Williams & Mary Henry, Nov. 13, 1826. Edward
G. Jacobs, BM.
Edmund Word & Aseneth Smith, Feb. 3, 1826. Joshua
Lester, V.D.M.
William Young & Martha Lumsford, July 18, 1826. B.
Meador, J.P.

WILSON COUNTY MARRIAGES

Malekyah Zachary & Polly Peak, Aug. 28, 1826, by Wm.
  White, M.G., Aug. 30, 1826. John Peak, BM.
Thomas B. Afflack & Martha D. Warren, Dec. 28, 1827.
  Lewis H. Dwyer, BM.
James R. Allen & Lusinda Smart, March 13, 1827. Wm.
  M. Swain, J.P., Abraham Wright.
John Allison & Margaret Bond, March 16, 1827. John
  Bond, BM.
Sam'l Allison & Malinda Florida, Nov. 20, 1827, by
  Jeremiah McMinn, Nov. 27, 1827. John Bond, BM.
Benjamin Andrews & Polly Parker, May 22, 1827. James
  Naylor, BM.
George Apperson & Elisa Cole, May 9, 1826, by Dal. Moser,
  J.P., May 10, 1826. Edward White, BM.
Syrus Armstrong & Jane Maxwell, Dec. 20, 1827. Joseph
  P. Wharton, BM.
Joseph S. Atkinson & Mary Guthrie, July 25, 1827, by
  John Powell, J.P., July 26, 1826 (?)
Cornelius Baily & Rebeccah Patterson, Jan. 9, 1827.
  Joshua Lester, V.D.M.
Cornelius W. Bailey & Rebeccah Patterson, Jan. 9, 1827.
  Pater Patterson, BM.
Lindley Baird & Lewarken Medley, Nov. 3, 1727, by Wm.
  Willis, J.P., Nov. 7, 1827. Henry Codey, BM.
Claibourne Baily & Francis Philips, Dec. 27, 1827.
  Robert Wilson, BM.
George Barufield & Polly Williams, Feb. 24, 1827. William
  M. Justice, BM.
David Bass & Harriet Harris, Aug. 27, 1826. Thomas Cox,
  BM.
William Barnett & Peggy Gunn, Jan. 9, 1827. Thomas D.
  Lansden, J.P., Robert Raymay, BM.
William Batey & Sarah Grissum, Sep. 3, 1827, by Thomas
  S. Green, J.P., Sep. 4, 1827. Henry Partin, BM.
John Beard & Margaret Cloid, Aug. 27, 1827, by David
  Foster, M.G., Aug. 30, 1827. David Cloid, BM.
James Belcher & Rebeckey Tally, July 20, 1826. David
  Phillips, BM.
Thomas Belcher & Delily Adamson, April 27, 1827. Zeddock
  Mullinall, BM.
Benjamin Belt & Polly Reed, Aug. 20, 1827, by Walter
  Carruth, J.P., Aug. 30, 1827. Edward Campbell, BM.
William Billbro & Elizabeth Johnson, Sep. 3, 1827. J. B.
  White, BM.
Jesse Bledworth & Jane Tucker, June 28, 1826. Wm.
  Bloodworth, BM.
John Bond & Bidsey Calliss, Feb. 15, 1826. John Bond,
  V.D.M.
Jesse Bond & Sarah Sypert, March 15, 1827. John Bond,
  V.D.M., Drury Dance, BM.
Robert Foster & Margaret Rea, June 26, 1827. David
  Foster, BM.
Samuel Bond & Elizabeth Melton, July 24, 1827. Elisha
  Bond, BM.

Samuel Booth & Sarah Ealey, June 15, 1827. David Bass, BM.

Samuel Boothe & Louisa Graves, April 14, 1827, by B. Graves, April 19, 1827. Samuel Walker, BM.

Thomas Branch & Jane Moon, Oct. 13, 1827. George Neal, BM.

Allen H. Bridges & Sarah Hancock, Nov. 28, 1827, by Josiah S. McClain, Nov. 29, 1827. Joseph Freeman, BM.

William W. Brooks & Lousara Huddleston, M.D. Isaac W. Brooks, BM.

Joseph Bryson & Jane Bryson, Aug. 1, 1827. John McMinn, J.P., William Bryson, BM.

Arnold Burke & Margaret Smith, May 18, 1827. Thos. Burk, BM.

Edmund Burton & Amanda, June 30, 1827. Josiah L. McClain, BM.

Edward Campbell & Seanath Maxwell, Dec. 21, 1827. Edward Campbell, BM.

Samuel Caplinger & Rebecca March, Oct. 29, 1827. John Swan, BM.

Conrad Carpenter & Aliza Ann Quarles, March 5, 1827. Joshua Lester, V.D.M., J. L. Lester, BM.

Walter Carruth & Nancy Keath, Jan. 10, 1827, by Stephen MdDonald, J.P., Jan. 11, 1827. Thomas Dean, BM.

Richard Carr & Jemimah Glenn, Jan. 27, 1827, by Elijah Maddox, M.G., Jan. 28, 1827. Wm. Steele, BM.

John P. Carter & Mary Lackey, April 28, 1827. Jesse Medley, BM.

Hezekiah Cartwright & Sally Mchollan, Oct. 16, 1827, by German Baker, Oct. 17, 1827. William Davidson, BM.

Archills Chandler & Cloe Dow, July 31, 1827, by Wm. Steele, J.P., Aug. 2, 1827. Thomas Cox, BM.

Joshua Clark & Nancy Bowers, Jan. 31, 1827. William Hartsfield, BM.

Henry Cooly & Malinda Lunce, Dec. 22, 1827. B. Bridges, J.P., Gray Medling, BM.

Alexander J. Compton & Martha Wood, Sep. 4, 1827. Mathew Compton, BM.

Samuel Creswell & Sarah Mays, Sep. 5, 1827, by J. Kirkpatrick, J.P., Sep. 6, 1827. James Edding, BM.

David Crowder & Elizabeth Pugh, March 14, 1827. Lewis Vick, BM.

Elisha B. Crudupe & Lousina Alford, April 14, 1827, by John Williamson, J.P., April 16, 1827. Lamuel Booth, BM.

George Crutchfield & Amy Hancock, Jan. 9, 1827. Obadiah Freeman, James Allcorn, BM.

Lemuel Cutchen & Jane Drennon, April 2, 1827, by James Drennon, J.P., April 4, 1827. Thomas Drennon, BM.

Thomas Davis & Jane Donnell, Dec. 15, 1827, by Amzi Bradshaw, Dec. 20, 1827. Calvin Donnell, BM.

Henry K. Dice & Elizabeth Springs, Dec. 5, 1827. Daniel Bennett, BM.

John F. Doak & Coloe Harrison, April 4, 1827, by Amzi Bradshaw, April 5, 1827. Leo. Donald, BM.

George Donnell & Elizabeth McMurry, June 11, 1827. F. G.
Crutcher, BM.
Isaac Dortch & Martha Allen, April 25, 1827. Abram
Harpole, BM.
Elisha Dowell & Elizabeth Barbee, Feb. 5, 1827. Mathew
Cartwright, BM.
Edward L. Douglas & Delia Douglas, Jan. 26, 1827. Thos.
Calhoun, V.D.M.
James Eddins & Pathena Brown, Aug. 29, 1827. James H.
Davis, J.P., Samuel Creswell, BM.
Sterling Edwards & Mahala Pucket, Dec. 24, 1827. James
B. Guthrie, BM.
Hicks Ellis & Lucy Jones, Sep. 25, 1827, by A. Provine,
Oct. 25, 1827. Michael Jones, BM.
Isaac Ellis & Nancy Jennings, Oct. 31, 1827, by James T.
Tompkins, Nov. 2, 1827. Jesse B. White, BM.
John Escue & Sarah Lumpkins, March 7, 1827. Samuel
Roberts, BM.
Russie Eskew & Margaret Brown, Sep. 24, 1827. Thomas
Kirkpatrick, BM.
Robert Foster & Margaret Reay, June 26, 1827, by Francis
Johnston, M.G., June 28, 1827.
Daniel Freeman & Polly Ann Cunningham, Nov. 13, 1827.
John Bonner, J.P., Jefferson Hamilton, BM.
Joel Fusten & Ranny Hollingsworth, Aug. 6, 1827. Isaac
Hollingsworth, BM.
Thomas Furgerson & Rebeccah Furgerson, Jan. 16, 1827.
Wm. H. White, M.G., L. Ferguson, BM.
George Gaddy & Leoy (Bucy) Bass, Sep. 22, 1827. Thomas
Branch, BM.
Henry Gilliam & Fanny Shaw, July 28, 1827. Henry Mitchell,
BM.
Jesse Grimes & Tempsey Murry, Sep. 3, 1827. Cader Bass,
BM.
Jefferson Hamilton & Rody Cunningham, June 30, 1827.
John Bonner, J.P., Josiah Beasley, BM.
Abner Harris & Mary Alexander, Feb. 14, 1827. Joseph
Johnson, BM.
Thomas W. Harvey & Cinthia Bass, March 5, 1827. J.
Provine, M.G., Robert D. McDpaden, BM.
Harvey Hawkins & Mary Bugg, Jan. 18, 1827. J. Kirkpatrick,
J.P., James L. Hawkins, BM.
James Hays & Sally Night, Dec. 16, 1827. Thomas Hays,
BM.
Preston Hays & Ann Searcy, Aug. 14, 1827. Hugh Hays, BM.
Thomas Hearn & Sarah Sillaman, Dec. 1, 1827, by Walter
Carruth, J.P., Dec. 3, 1827. John Hearn, BM.
Joab Heflin & Margaret Moore, May 21, 1827, by James B.
Taylor, J.P., May 31, 1827. James Moore, BM.
Bracton Hill & Polly Tarpley, Dec. 11, 1827, by John
Bonner, J.P., Dec. 13, 1827. James McDaniel, BM.
Jonathan Hooker & Margaret Gwyn, March 26, 1827. Joshua
Hooker, BM.
John Hollingsworth & Nancey Dill, Aug. 8, 1827. John
Gossett, BM.

William Houston & Mary Mann, June 18, 1827. Brittain Drake, BM.

Allen Hunt & Rebeccah Sanders, Aug. 1, 1827. Allen Wilkerson, BM.

George Hunter & Jane Winset, Aug. 22, 1827, by R. W. Morris, M.G. (?), Aug. 23, 1827. James Winset, BM.

William Hunter & Elizabeth Drake, Aug. 27, 1827. James Allcorn, BM.

Joseph Ingram & Susan Bates, April 23, 1827. B. Bridges, J.P., Joseph Bloodworth, BM.

James M. Irwin & Jane C. Bullard, May 31, 1827. John Provine, M.G., Leo Donnell, BM.

Mayfield Johnson & Mandane Rutland, Nov. 24, 1827, by John Williamson, J.P., Dec. 2, 1827. Gregory D. Johnson.

John P. Johnson & Eliza Mitchell, Sep. 15, 1827, by German Baker, Sep. 18, 1827.

Lot Johnson & Matilda Eason, Nov. 17, 1827, by Abner Hill, M.G., Nov. 22, 1827. Isaac Hill, BM.

William Johnson & Mary Rice, March 7, 1827, by German Baker, March 21, 1827. W. Pitner, BM.

Jesse Joiner & Cinthy Tally, July 13, 1827. G. W. Bussard, J.P.

Jacob Keeton & Sally Painter, Jan. 5, 1827. James A. Strong, BM.

Dennis King & Elizabeth Beadle, Sep. 9, 1827. Dennis King, BM.

Josiah Kirkpatrick & Nancy Tilford, April 27, 1827. John H. Kirkpatrick, BM.

Robert Laid & Ann Telford, Nov. 26, 1827. Hugh Telford, BM.

Merritt Lyon & Nancy Aster, Aug. 29, 1827. E. A. White, BM.

Isaac Mahafy & Mary Watson, March 27, 1827. Elijah Maddox, M.G.

William Maholland & Sally Hopson, Dec. 20, 1827. Dnl. Moser, J.P., Hezekiah Cartwright, BM.

Hardy Manning & Lisa Robertson, Oct. 5, 1827. James Manning, BM.

James M. Martin & Mary E. Holland, Oct. 17, 1827. A. Wynne, BM.

Robert Y. Martin & Martha Ann Chappell Jones, Dec. 31, 1827, by D. Lansden, J.P., Aaron F. Jones, BM.

William Martin & Emily Alcorn, Sep. 3, 1827. B. Hubbard, BM.

Abram Massey & Tabitha Hearn, Dec. 11, 1827. Thomas Davis, BM.

Yoncy Massey & Nancy Galaspa, Oct. 1, 1827. John Dice, BM.

John Maxwell & Catharine Williams, March 29, 1827, by William Phillips, J.P., M. Claswell, BM.

Briant McDearmon & Elizabeth McDearmon, Feb. 1, 1827. Henry Rutland, BM.

Daniel McKee & Sarah Thomas, Aug. 22, 1827. Henry Thomas, BM.

WILSON COUNTY MARRIAGES

James Merret & Sally Ferringlow, April 4, 1827, by James Bond, V.D.M., April 10, 1827 (1821?). Sherrod Merret, BM.

Jacob Mick & Mary Lott, Jan. 29, 1829. Henry Robertson, BM.

Beverly Miller & Beludar Stovall, April 25, 1827, by G. H. Bussard, BM, Isaac Hunter, BM.

Henry Mitchell & Henrietta Jackson, Nov. 20, 1827, by John Bonner, J.P., Nov. 28, 1827. Theophilus T. Gray, BM.

John Mitchell & Elizabeth Crocker, Oct. 31, 1827, by E. P. Horn, J.P., Nov. 1, 1827. Butler Arnold, BM.

John R. Moody & Casander F. Allison, Sep. 18, 1827. Thos. Allman, BM.

John W. Morris & Mary Morris, Feb. 7, 1827, bv B. Graves, J.P., Edmund Jones, BM.

Peterson Morris & Catherine Wiley, Feb. 7, 1827, by Amzi Bradshaw, Feb. 9, 1827. Thomas Davis, BM.

Jeremiah Murry & Rhewry Hessy, Dec. 12, 1827. William Murry, BM.

Clayburn Neal & Amy Moore, March 28, 1827. Isaac Neal, BM.

John Nickings & Sally Nicking, N.D. Preston Bicking, BM.

Stephen Norton & Polly McDaniel, Dec. 12, 1827. James Wlatton (Patton?), BM.

John A. Nunner & Martha Baird, June 16, 1827, by Wm. Willis, J.P., June 17, 1827. L. Bass, BM.

Washington Oneal & Isabella Biles, Aug. 7, 1827. Wm. S. Swan, BM.

David Patterson & Malinda Etheridge, July 2, 1827. Shadrack C. Smith, BM.

Beverly Seay & Mary Bowers, Jan. 29, 1827. Hezekiah Woodward, BM.

John Perkins & Renanna Sherrill, Feb. 8, 1827. Alanson Sherrill, BM.

Thomas Pettyjohn & Martha M. Davis, Sep. 27, 1827. Paulin Anderson, BM.

Green Proctor & Margaret Kitrall, Dec. 18, 1827, by E. P. Horn, J.P., Dec. 20, 1827. Wilbon R. Winter, BM.

Washington J. Pucket & Frances Pucket, Oct. 11, 1827, by _____, Uriah Jennings, BM.

William Pucket & Mahala Franklin, Dec. 17, 1827. Benjamin Motley, BM.

George R. Pugh & Mary Hopkins, Aug. 20, 1827. Isaiah Pugh, BM.

Wyatt Ramsey & Peggy Rice, Jan. 4, 1827, by James Drennon, J.P., Jan. 8, 1827. William G. Barr, BM.

John Reynolds & Abigail Baskins, March 15, 1827, by Thomas D. Lansden, J.P., April 2, 1827. George Smith, BM.

David C. Richards & Elizabeth S. Parrish, Aug. 9, 1827, by German Baker, Warren Moore, BM.

William Ricketts & Sally Porterfield, May 7, 1827. James Ricketts, BM.

Martin Rogers & Tempy Warren, July 3, 1827, by Jas. B.
Taylor, J.P., July 5, 1827. Nathan Midgett, BM.
John R. Rutherford & Mary Hightower, July 10, 1827, B.
Bridges, J.P., July 15, 1827. Robert Donaldson, BM.
Joseph Rutland & Margaret Thompson, Dec. 5, 1827, by
B. Graves, J.P., Albert McGrigon, BM.
William Russel & Pertheny Chandler, Nov. 19, 1827.
William Chandler, BM.
James P. Scott & Jane C. Carruth, Nov. 27, 1827, by
Amzi Bradshaw, Nov. 28, 1827. William Scott, BM.
Edward Scruggs & Alitha Martin, Oct. 29, 1827, by B.
Graves, J.P., John H. Drake, BM.
Jesse Shaw & Polly McHensy (McHaney), March 3, 1827.
David Biles, BM.
Mekins Ship & Marry Warren, July 21, 1827. Benton Ship,
BM.
Elias Sinclair & Sally McDermit, Dec. 15, 1827. by B.
Graves, J.P., Thomas Jones, BM.
Edward Sims & Martha Mayho, June 5, 1827, by Geo. F.
Whirter, J.P., June 28, 1827. John Ferguson, BM.
George Smith & Narsissa Davis, Jan. 8, 1827, by James
Foster, J.P., Jan. 10, 1827. Jno. F. Doak, BM.
Harvey F. Smith & Missouri Gleaves, March 5, 1827, by
Thos. Calhoon, V.D.M., March 6, 1827. Robert Topp, BM.
William Smith & Teddy Turner, March 15, 1827, by Dnl.
Moser, J.P., Saml. Stuart, BM.
Samuel Sperry & Mourning Wright, June 18, 1827, by Jas.
Drennon, J.P., June 25, 1827. John Sperry, BM.
John Summers & Elizabeth Leach, Oct. 10, 1827, by John
McMinn, J.P., Oct. 18, 1827. Abner Smith, BM.
Thomas W. Tarpley & Susannah Harvey, March 3, 1827.
George Gaddy, BM.
John W. Tate & Elizabeeh Cloyd, Oct. 7, 1827, by John
Beard, M.G., Oct. 11, 1827. Newton Cloyd, BM.
Richard Taylor & Liddy Baird, Aug. 3, 1827, by Jas. B.
Taylor, J.P., Aug. 9, 1827. John Waters, BM.
Joseph Thompson & Elizabeth Dodds, Oct. 23, 1827. John
A. Patterson, BM.
William Thompson & Mirandy Kelley, Oct. 29, 1827, by
Richard W. Morris, E.M.E.C., Nov. 4, 1827. Daniel
Kelly, BM.
William Threat & Sophy McKee, Dec. 4, 1827, by Joshua
Lester, V.D.M., P. W. Brient, BM.
Jacob Tilman & Julia McGrigor, May 2, 1827, by B. Graves,
J.P., May 10, 1827. Jno. Shepherd, BM.
Barna Tipton & Harriett Bridges, May 9, 1827, by James
H. Davis, J.P., May 11, 1827. John Vivrett, BM.
Richard Townsend & Sarah A. Phipps, April 23, 1827. C.
M. Jennings, BM.
Erasmus Tracy & Derusha Taylor, Jan. 3, 1827. Wiley
Garner, BM.
Thomas Tracy & Rutha Hearn, March 22, 1827, by John
Rains, M.G., Wiley Garner, BM.
George Tucker & Abagail Hartsfield, Oct. 10, 1827.
Josiah Smith, BM.

James Walton & Mary Mosier, Oct. 16, 1827. Stephen Wade,
  BM.
James A. Warpole & Nancy P. Tilman, Sep. 26, 1827, by
  B. Graves, J.P., Gregory G. Johnson, BM.
James Warren & Celia Organ, Oct. 23, 1827. James Seate,
  BM.
Right M. Weatherly & Ann Bryant, March 10, 1827, by
  Thomas D. Lansden, J.P., March 27, 1827. Daniel
  Williamson, BM.
Thomas White & Siny Putman, Nov. 29, 1827, by Thomas D.
  Lansden, J.P., Nov. 30, 1827.
William Wilkerson & Peggy Kirkpatrick, June 15, 1827,
  by William Gray, J.P., June 16, 1827.
Beverly B. Williams & Patsey Marlow, Aug. 8, 1827, by
  Josiah S. McClain, J.P., Meredith Marlow, BM.
Harry B. Williams & Nancy Copeland, Dec. 24, 1827.
  Washington Williamson, BM.
William Williamson & Nancy Crutchfield, Dec. 11, 1827,
  by Ezekiel Cloyd, Dec. 13, 1827. John A. Williamson,
  BM.
Allen Wilson & Elizabeth David, Nov. 21, 1821, by Jas.
  Fite, J.P., Oct. 1, 1827. James Strong, BM.
Hose Word & Milly Johnson, Nov. 10, 1826, by Joshua
  Lester, V.D.M., Edmund Lester, BM.
William H. Wortham & Lucy Harris, Jan. 23, 1827, by
  Joshua Lester, V.D.M., Wm. Craddock, BM.
Anderson Wright & Sina Eagan, Dec. 5, 1827. William
  Motheral, BM.
John Wriston (Winston) & Sina Edwards, June 20, 1827,
  by Jos. B. Taylor, J.P., June 20, 1827. Saml. Harb (?),
  BM.
Chistley Wynne & Martha Whitson, Nov. 17, 1827, by James
  T. Tompkins, Nov. 19, 1827. James Eagan, BM.
William Young & Martha Lunsford, July 18, 1827, by
  B. Bridges, J.P., July 20, 1827.
Patrick Youree & Sela Harris, Feb. 13, 1827. William
  Chapman, BM.
William Young & Nancy Huguley, Dec. 29, 1827, by B.
  Graves, J.P.
Allen Zachary & Margaret Woollard, March 17, 1827.
  Thomas Hamilton, BM.
Hartwell Zachary & Anny Willis, Dec. 11, 1827, by W. H.
  White, M.G., Dec. 12, 1827. William Wray, BM.
Nelson H. Alexander & Mary Patterson, May 13, 1828, by
  Amzi Bradshaw, May 13, 1828. James Carruth, BM.
William M. Andrews & Elizabeth Silliman, March 19, 1828,
  by Wilson Hearn, M.G., March 20, 1828. George D.
  Moore, BM.
Knox Armstrong & Nancy C. Greer, Aug. 16, 1828, by
  Thomas D. Lansden, J.P., Aug. 19, 1828.
John B. Arnold & Frances Young, July 31, (1827?), by
  Thomas D. Lansden, J.P., July 29, 1828 (?). William
  Young, BM.
Castor F. Ballentine & Nancy Taylor, Nov. 28, 1828, by
  Wm. W. Elis, J.P., Dec. 1, 1828. Caleb Taylor, BM.

Thomas Baskins & Susan Arnold, April 16, 1828, by Thomas
D. Lansden, J.P., April 19, 1828. Tilman Patterson.

Pleasant G. Belcher & Sally Belcher, March 19, 1828.
James Powell, BM.

Baxter Bennett & Elizabeth Chandler, June 3, 1828. Eli
Gladstone, BM.

Allen Blankenship & Elia J. Spinks, July 4, 1828. William
Mitchell, BM.

Michael Bond & Elizabeth King, Feb. 8, 1828, by James
Foster, J.P., Feb. 21, 1828. Thomas King, BM.

Alexander Michael & Eliza Powell, Dec. 11, 1828. Wilie
Powell, BM.

John Booker & Lucinda B. Griffis, Feb. 18, 1828, by
Thomas S. Green, J.P., Feb. 18, 1828. Green H. Hancock.

Mathews Brown & Elizabeth Walker July 30, 1828, by
T. Kirkpatrick, J.P., John H. Coles, BM.

Thomas Brown & Rebecca Boon, March 12, 1828. Granville
Edwards, BM.

Ruffin Cassel & Lucinda Eddins, June 13, 1828. Allen W.
Vicks, BM.

John Carr & Mary Riddle, Jan. 3, 1828, by John Jarratt
William Gentry, BM.

Gideon Carter & Lydia Case, March 10, 1828, by John
Beard, M.G., March 11, 1828. Snodon Hicmman, BM.

William W. Carter & Izabella Roan, Nov. 20, 1828. Wm.
M. Chapman, BM.

Hezekiah Cartwright & Delila Searcy, June 6, 1828, by
James B. Taylor, J.P., John Cox, BM.

John Cates & Alley Johnson, June 17, 1828. Thomas
Chamberland, BM.

Clabourn Clark & Sarah Neal, Aug. 2, 1828. Isaac Neal,
BM.

William Climer & Jane Lane, May 8, 1828, by Benjamin
Graves, J.P., May 9, 1828. Anderson Perry, BM.

Henry Cluck & Mary Robertson, July 19, 1828. Thomas
Burk, BM.

Samuel Coles & Calister (Colista) Walker, March 10, 1828,
by Dnl. Moses, J.P., March 11, 1828. John Davis.

Crofford Collins & Polly Collins, Sep. 20, 1828, by
Joshua Woollen, M.G., Sep. 27, 1828.

Jas. Comer & Sarah Ellison, Dec. 2, 1828. John L.
Allison, BM.

John Conrod & Matilda Wheeler, April 5, 1828. Enoch
Davis, BM.

Robert Corley & Maryan Adam, March 22, 1828. Samuel
Corley, BM.

Samuel Corn & Mary Moore, July 1, 1828, by John McMinn,
J.P.

Abner G. Craze & Mary Sullivan, Oct. 17, 1828, by Wm. M.
Swain, J.P., Oct. 24, 1828. Samuel Rutter, BM.

Charles W. Cummings & Eliza W. Foster, Nov. 19, 1828, by
J. Provine, M.G., Benj. T. Motley, BM.

Alfred Dakes & Nancy Bradshaw, Jan. 9, 1828. Joshua
Peak, BM.

William Davis & Sarah White, July 15, 1828, by James T.
Tompkins, M.G., July 17, 1828.
Lovick Dies & Matilda Johnson, April 2, 1828, by P.
Douglas, J.P., April 3, 1828.
John A. Dods & Margaret M. Thompson, March 7, 1828,
Joins B. Thompson, BM.
William Dotson & Elizabeth Hefley, July 9, 1828, by
James B. Taylor, J.P., July 10, 1828, Moses Harrison.
William B. Drake & Ann Robertson, Aug. 14, 1828 by
Ezekial Cloyd, M.G., Aug. 15, 1828. Thomas K. Wynne,
BM.
Edwin Duncan & Aley Cooper, April 16, 1828, John Gee,
BM.
Ozburn Eddings & Elizabeth Bone, Dec. 16, 1828. H. C.
Hubbard, BM.
William Eddins & Sarah Hooker, Aug. 10, 1828, Banj. T.
Tucker, BM.
William Edwards & Patsy Maning, Sep. 8, 1828. F. Brown
(?), BM.
William England & Candis Travilion, Aug. 11, 1828. James
Travilion, BM.
Thomas Estes & Eliza Edkinson (Adkinson), Dec. 31, 18__,
by _____ Tompkins, Donnell Freeman, BM.
David Fillops & Aney Francis, March 22, 1828, by Robert
McKee, J.P., March 23, 1828. David Fillips, BM.
Thomas Fillops & Cissey Jonston, Feb. 12, 1828, by
Joshua Lester, V.D.M., Benjamin Caleb, BM.
Albert Foster & Lucinda Major, Aug. 12, 1828, Saml.
Donnell, BM.
Pervires Fox & Narcissa Bennett, July 21, 1821. James
Baird, BM.
Robert Fullerton & Priscilla Clifton, Aug. 20, 1828.
David Berry, BM.
Charles George & Fosti Hughs, Jan. 10, 1828. George P.
Hugh, BM.
John G. Gleaves & Elizabeth Curd, Dec. 16, 1828. William
McNeill, BM.
William J. Goodwin & Mary McHenry, Oct. 22, 1828, by
James Gray, J.P., Oct. 27, 1828. Jesse A. Goodwin,
BM.
James Hallum & Rebecca Underhill, Oct. 18, 1828, by
Zedikiah McMinn, Edmund Goodman.
Nelson D. Hancock & Margaret Woodrum, Jan. 19, 1828, by
John Beard, M.G., Jan. 24, 1828. Henry M. Hancock, BM.
Samuel Hancock & Martha V. Donnell, May 30, 1828, by
Amzi Bradshaw, June 5, 1828.
Daniel Harpole & Jane Allen, Jan. 26, 1828, by Dnl.
Moser, J.P., Jan. 27, 1828. George Harpole, BM.
Sneed Harris & Fany Tilford, Dec. 17, 1828. Randal
McDonald, BM.
Edmund R. Harrison & Rebecca Hawkins, Nov. 11, 1828.
Alexr. Penny, BM.
Stith Harrison & Harriet Word, Sep. 3, 1828, by Joshua
Lester, V.D.M., Saml. Stone, BM.

Wilson Hearn & Elizabeth Winford, Dec. 22, 1828, by
John Jarratt, Dec. 23, 1828. John Hearn, BM.
Michael D. Henderson & Elizabeth Wiley, July 19, 1828,
by Jesse Alexander, V.D.M., July 24, 1828 (1824?).
David K. Thorn, BM.
Rollins Henderson & Minerva Kennedy, Feb. 18, 1828.
William H. Henderson, BM.
Isaac Hill & Polly Johnson, Jan. 11, 1828, by Abner
Hill, M.G., Jan. 16, 1828. Phil W. Harrington, BM.
Isaac W. Hill & Sarah Baird, Oct. 27, 1828, by James T.
Tompkins, M.G., Oct. 29, 1828. William Hill, BM.
Jacob Holderfield & Elizabeth Horn, May 3, 1838.
Richard Horn, BM.
John B. Holman & Lavina Randolph, Sep. 18, 1828, by G.
H. Bussard, J.P., Sep. 19, 1828. Jesse Gibson, BM.
Charles Sillivan, BM.
Alfred Hunt & Susan Gant, Dec. 8, 1828, by James T.
Tompkins, Dec. 11, 1828.
John Ingrum & Eliza Todd, Jan. 3, 1828, by Abner Hill,
M.G., Joshua Clark, BM.
Elijah Jacobs & Jane Bonner, June 12, 1828. Ethelbridge
Brantz, BM.
David C. Jackson & Mary Wood, Feb. 23, 1828, by John
Saunders, J.P., March 4, 1828. John M. Murraym, BM.
Abner Jennings & Cloey F. Lester, Oct. 13, 1828, by
Joshua Lester, V.D.M., Oct. 18, 1828. Rial C.
Jennings, BM.
Zealous Johnson & Delila Allen, Dec. 3, 1828, by William
Flowers.
Murfrey Kemp & Mary Howell, Oct. 10, 1828, by James T.
Tompkins, M.G., Oct. 12, 1828.
Samuel H. Lasater & Sally Barker, Feb. 23, 1828, by J.
B. Lasater, J.P., Feb 24, 1828. Ambrose Reynolds, BM.
William Lasater & Polly Hill, Dec. 22, 1828. Abner
Walker, BM.
James S. Leach & Elizabeth Burns, Nov. 11, 1828, by John
McMinn, J.P.
John T. Lea & Louiza Murry, July 20, 1828, by James T.
Tompkins, M.G., July 29, 1828. James N. Lee, BM.
John Little & Matilda Brown, Nov. 5, 1828, by James T.
Tompkins, M.G., Murphree Camp, BM.
Anderson Loyd & Lucy Johnson, Feb. 7, 1827 (?). John
Hearn, BM.
John Meak & Charlotte S. Morris, Nov. 14, 1828. Joshua
V. Taylor, BM.
Nathan McCullough & Elizabeth Lanom, Jan. 13, 1828.
Garratt Johnson, BM.
John McCaffrey & Lavina Ward, Oct. 23, 1828, by Joshua
Lester, V.D.M.
John McDaniel & Elizabeth Moore, July 29, 1828, by James
B. Taylor, J.P., Aug. 31, 1828. John Johnson, BM.
Randolph McDaniel & Jane Chambers, Jan. 28, 1828, by
Stephen McDonald, J.P., Feb. 3, 1828. John Chambers,
BM.

WILSON COUNTY MARRIAGES

Briant McDeamon & Elizabeth McDeamon, Feb. 1, 1828, by
  B. Graves, J.P.
Wiley McDermon & _____, Sep. 15, 1828. Mathew Dew, BM.
Edward McMillan & Elisa Donnell, April 17, 1828, by Amzi
  Bradshaw, V.D.M., May 17, 1828. John L. Sloan, BM.
Samuel C. McWhirter & Mary P. Cowen, May 28, 1828, by
  Amzi Bradshaw, V.D.M., F. G. Crutcher, BM.
Alexander Michaels & Elisa Powell, Dec. 11, 1828, by
  Wilson Hearn, M.G., Dec. 17, 1828.
Thomas Michell & Jane Southworth, Dec. 1, 1828, by
  Stephen McDonnel, J.P., Dec. 9, 1828. John Chambers,
  BM.
Joseph Moore & Susannah Wood, March 19, 1828, by John
  Williamson, J.P., March 20, 1828. R. P. Shelton, BM.
Ellison Morris & Tempy Johnson, Aug. 6, 1828. Joel
  Graves, BM.
Thomas B. Moss & Mourning Davis, April 2, 1828, by
  James T. Tompkins, M.G., April 3, 1828. William
  Chapman, BM.
Asa Mosley & Francis Snody, Feb. 19, 1828. Meida White,
  BM.
Elijah Harris & Lucy Motsinger, May 23, 1828, by Stephen
  McDonnell, J.P., May 28, 1828.
Gibson Murfrey & Mary Cooksey, Sep. 25, 1828, by James B.
  Taylor, J.P., Sep. 30, 1828. Joshua V. Taylor BM.
Allen Nelson & Sarah Pugh, Jan. 28, 1828, by James
  Drennon, J.P., Jan. 31, 18__. William Gibson, BM.
John Owen & Minervey Armstrong. June 10, 1828, by
  John McMinn, J.P.
Oliver Oneal & Nancy Clark, March 24, 1824. David Beard,
  BM.
Lewis Patterson & Martha Ward, Oct. 23, 1828, by Joshua
  Lester, V.D.M., Tillman Patterson, BM.
Peter Patterson & Sarah Edward, Nov. 29, 1828, by William
  Williamson, J.P., Benton Woods, BM.
William Patrick & Fibby Smith, Sep. 24, 1828, by Joshua
  Woollen, M.G., Sep. 27, 1828.
Samuel Patton & Elenor Compton, Sep. 23, 1828. Charlie
  Compton, BM.
John Pemberton & Emaline Massey, Nov. 8, 1828. Samuel
  Bland, BM.
Jesse Pemberton & Lucinda Bradley, Nov. 13, 1828.
  William Pemberton, BM.
Benjamin F. Phelps & Mary Devaught, July 18, 1828, by
  Jas. Drennon, J.P., July 22, 1828. Jno. Perkins, BM.
Josiah Phillips & Darkus K. Nettles, Oct. 15, 1828.
  Benjamin Philips, BM.
James Poe & Elizabeth Lantern, April 19, 1828, by
  Ezekiel Cloyd, April 20, 1828. Henry Davis, BM.
Charles Puckett & Eliza Lane, June 23, 1828, by Ezekiel
  Cloy, M.G., June 24, 1828. George K. Smith, BM.
Alsey Reese & Willey Medling, Oct. 2, 1828, by B. Bridges,
  Oct. 3, 1828. Richardson Rowland, BM.
John H. Reynolds & Jane Barrett, Oct. 15, 1828, by Abner
  Hill M.G., Oct. 17, 1828. Willis Caraway, BM.

Daniel Richmond & Mary Bond, June 26, 1828, by Joshua A. Lester, V.D.M., Charles M. Cummings, BM.

Kinchen Richard & Martha Murry, June 18, 1828, by James T. Tompkins, M.G.

Marcus Rieff & Eliza Hulm, June 25, 1828, by James T. Tompkins, M.G., Taurus Rief, BM.

Taurus Reif & Charlotte Hall, Sep. 4, 1828, by James H. David, J.P., Sep. 7, 1828.

Alexander Roach & Elizabeth Wright, July 1, 1828, John R. Wright, BM.

Obediah Roger & Sarah Underwood, June 14, 1828, James Wynne, BM.

John Sanders & Sarah Patterson, April 2, 1828. John Cummings, BM.

William S. Scott & Sally Sneed, Jan. 8, 1828. Thos. Cox, BM.

Joseph H. Sellers & Polly Guyn, March 3, 1828, by James Bond, V.D.M., March 6, 1828. Samuel McMinn, BM.

John A. Simmons & Elizabeth Tomlinson, N.D. John Trout, BM.

William N. Sinclair & Penelope B. Biter, Sep. 9, 1828, by J. Drennon, J.P., Sep. 11, 1828.

Daniel Smith & Amy Neal, Aug. 2, 1828. B. Clark, BM.

David B. Smith & Mary Lester, Oct. 27, 1828. John A. Smith, BM.

James Smith & Gilley Stewart, July 26, 1828. Wily Berdine, BM.

Macon Smith & Elizabeth Young, Feb. 22, 1828. J. S. Smith, BM.

William Smith & Jane Blurter, Feb. 9, 1828, by James T. Tompkins, M.G., Feb. 10, 1828. Wilborn Smith, BM.

John J. Sneed & Ann Leach, July 29, 1828, by John McMinn, J.P., July 31, 1828.

Sanford Somers & Jane Partin, Dec. 2, 1828, by Wm. M. Swain, J.P., Dec. 4, 1828.

Martin Sparks & Rachel Marrs, Dec. 3, 1828, by James Lester, J.P., Dec. 3, 1828. Samuel R. Comer, BM.

Byrd Spurlock & Elizabeth Hancock, May 5, 1828. George Michie, BM.

Henry R. Stembridge & Selina Smith, July 2, 1828, by Abner Hill, M.G., Josiah Smith, BM.

Sanders Stephens & Nelly Chambers, Jan. 8, 1828. Allen Tomlinson, BM.

John M. Stroud & Mary Jinnings, June 9, 1828, by H. W. Pickett, M.G., June 12, 1828.

William Stuart & Mary Tooly, May 3, 1828, by J. Johnson J.P., May 13, 1828.

Eclemuel Sullivan & Martha M. Stone, Dec. 12, 1828, by Wm. M. Swain, J.P., Dec. 18, 1828. N. Thompson, BM.

Zedekiah Tate & Zadia Hunt, Nov. 15, 1828. J. Perkinson, BM.

James H. Taylor & Martha Hunter, Feb. 21, 1828. John Afflack, BM.

James Thompson & Elizabeth Dodd, Sep. 12, 1828. Joseph Thorn, BM.

WILSON COUNTY MARRIAGES

William A. Thompson & Astamisea Thompson, July 4, 1828,
by William Williams, J.P., July 6, 1828. Jos. Brown,
BM.
Hansel Trusty & Catherine Biter, Oct. 28, 1828, by Jas.
Drennon, J.P., Nov. 15, 1828.
Samuel Turner & Rebecca Parrish, April 30, 1828, by
James S. Tompkins, M.G., May 1, 1828. Robert Coles, BM.
Toliver Turner & Elizabeth Grindstaff, Nov. 18, 1828.
John Grandstaff, BM.
Abner Upchurch & Nancy Pyland, March 24, 1828, by James
B. Lasater, J.P., William Babb, BM.
James Vaughn & Maria Martin, May 10, 1828. John Martin,
BM.
Pleasant Vic & Rebecca Tarver, Nov. 11, 1828. Nelson
Tarver, BM.
William A. Vowell & Caroline Campbell, March 18, 1828,
by James Foster, J.P., March 20, 1828. Albert Foster,
BM.
Jesse Walden & Martha Turner, Oct. 16, 1828, by Dnl.
Moser, J.P., Joel Dill, BM.
Strother B. Walker & Mariah Akin, Jan. 1, 1828. John
Ward, BM.
John Ward & Elizabeth Glass, Nov. 16, 1828, by Joshua
Lester, V.D.M.
Shelah Waters & Nancy Cannon, Aug. 8, 1828, by Amzi
Bradshaw, M.G., Aug. 11, 1828. William Phillips.
Abner Weatherly & Jane Sims, March 18, 1828, by Thomas
D. Lansden, J.P., March 20, 1828. Washington Williams,
BM.
Thomas V. Wier & Polly Morris, Sep. 15, 1828. John
Pemberton, BM.
Jonathan Whitton & Mary Mount, Sep. 3, 1828, by
Williamson Williams, J.P., J. Powers (?), BM.
William Wilkinson & Elizabeth Lane, Jan. 12, 1828, by
B. Graves, J.P., William C. Climer, BM.
Littleberry E. Williamson & Rebecca E. Powell, Oct. 18,
1828, by Wilson Bearn, M.G., Oct. 22, 1828. B. Figures,
BM.
Washington Williams & Minerva Doak, Nov. 22, 1828, by
Amzi Bradshaw, M.G., Nov. 27, 1828. John Hearn, BM.
Hall J. Winsett & Elizabeth Jarman, Feb. 18, 1828.
Shadrack Jarman, BM.
Wilburn Winter & Mary Denton, April 21, 1828, by E. P.
Horn, J.P., April 24, 1828. Benjamin Tarver, BM.
John Word & Elizabeth Wasson, Dec. 3, 1828, by Joshua
Lester, V.D.M., Dec. 4, 1828. William Word, BM.
Charles Wright & Mary Ann Hessey, Aug. 16, 1828. Hollis
Wright, BM.
Hyram S. Wroe & Mary D. Hodges, Jan. 31, 1828, by Joshua
Lester, V.D.M., Ozburn Eddings, BM.
Stokes Zachary & Delila R. Peak, July 14, 1828, by Wm.
H. White, M.G., July 16, 1828. A. Zachary, BM.
Doak Young & Sarah Reeder April 30, 1828. Mathew Horn,
BM.

John Adamson & Rebecca Neighbours, Dec. 22, 1829. Thomas
Belcher, BM.
Absolum Allen & Abby Dill, March 12, 1829, by Dnl. Moser,
J.P., March 13, 1829. Saml. Johnson, BM.
Aaron Alexander & Susan Bradley, March 5, 1829. Anderson
Walker, BM.
Robert Anderson & Mailsy Jones, June 1, 1829. William
Young, BM.
Rowland G. Andrews & Polly M. Sullivan, Aug. 11, 1829,
by Wilson Hearn, M.G., Stephenson L. Hearn, BM.
Davis Arnold & Martha Puckett, Aug. 27, 1829, by
Williamson Williams, J.P., Aug. 28, 1829. Stith
Harrison, BM.
John Arnold & Nancy Bond, Jan. 12, 1829, by John McMinn,
J.P., Jan. 14, 1829.
Jesse Badgett & Sarah Routon, Aug. 4, 1829. H. R. Cox,
BM.
John Badgett & Elizabeth Green, Jan. 31, 1829. William
Cox, BM.
Robert Beasley & Sarah Cunningham, July 2, 1829, by
Stephen McDonald, Ira Lynch, BM.
Samuel Bell & Milly Moor, May 9, 1829. A. Brogan, BM.
Wiley W. Bell & Susan J. Crags, May 9, 1829, by Wm. M.
Swain, J.P., May 10, 1829. Jesse L. Moore, BM.
Joseph Bennett & Orina Harlow, Aug. 3, 1829, by Joshua
Lester, V.D.M., Robert Simpson, BM.
Washington Blackburn & Lavina Sullivan, Jan. 29, 1829,
by Edward Willis, M.G., Thomas Ames, BM.
Joseph H. Bogel & Mary Summers, Sep. 14, 1829, by H. W.
Pickett, V.D.M., Sep. 17, 1829.
James C. Bone & Nancy Bone, Jan. 28, 1829, by Williamson
Williams, J.P., Jan. 29, 1829. James Scott, BM.
James Borum & Martha Ann Borum, Oct. 27, 1829. Francis
Eubanks, BM.
Thomas Bradley & Susan Harpole, March 7, 1829. James
McDaniel, BM.
Wilson Bradshaw & Nancy D. Mitchell, May 2, 1829, by E.
P. Horn, J.P., Thomas Mitchell, BM.
Alexander Bridges & Elizabeth Rolls, Aug. 17, 1829, by
John Beard, M.G., Aug. 18, 1829. Taylor Lindsay, BM.
Armstead Brogan & Jane Moor, May 9, 1829. Samuel Bell,
BM.
George W. Thomas & Julia B. Brewer, Nov. 2, 1829.
William McGriger, BM.
John Bryson & Nancy Fuston, Oct. 15, 1829. George Bogle,
BM.
Moses P. Calahan & Sarah R. Hearn, March 7, 1829. Wm. L.
Sypert, BM.
William T. Cannada & Susan Dwyer, Feb. 18, 1829. Jas.
Riddle, BM.
Walter Carr & Sarah Daniel, Oct. 11, 1828. H. L. Douglass,
BM.
Ruffins Capel & Lucinda Eddins, Jan. 13, 1829, by Geo.
F. McWhirter, J.P., Jan. 14, 1829.

John Casey & Elow Melton, June 17, 1829. Thos. Bradley, BM.

Thomas Chappell & Nancy Jones, Jan. 6, 1829. Jos. Davenport, BM.

Joshus Clark & Sarah Allen, Aug. 17, 1829. Wm. M. Chapman, BM.

Elisha Clower & Martha Tucker, Dec. 24, 1829. Geo. H. Bussard, BM.

James M. Cloyd & Margaret C. Sharpe, Oct. 18, 1829, by Jesse Alexander, V.D.M., Oct. 20, 1829.

Wilson Coapland & Milly Rhea June 17, 1829, by Williamson Williams, J.P., June 18, 1829. Henry Williams, BM.

Christopher Cobb & Sally Underhill, April 21, 1829. John Langley, BM.

Jesse Collins & Irin Wynne (?), Sep. 30, 1829. George Thomas, BM.

John H. B. Coles & Elizabeth White, Oct. 17, 1829. George Apperson, BM.

John Collins & Nancy Drew, April 2, 1829, by Joshua Woollen, M.G., April 3, 1829. William Patrick, BM.

Crafford Collins & Polly Collins, Sep. 26, 1829. James Nickens, BM.

Jesse Cook & Mary Clay, July 29, 1829. Joseph Freeman, BM.

James M. Coppedge & Elizabeth Miller, Feb. 3, 1829, by E. P. Horn, J.P., Feb. 5, 1829. John O'Neal, BM.

Samuel Corley & Esther Priestly, July 13, 1829. Hallum Priestly; BM.

John Cox & Zeda Edwards, June 20, 1829, by J. B. Taylor, J.P., Thomas Taylor, BM.

L. D. Crabtree & Winney Medling, April 3, 1829, by Wm. Willis, J.P., April 16, 1829.

Edmant Crawford & Elizabeth Smith, Dec. 16, 1829, by John Beard, M.G., Dec. 17, 1829. Gilbert Yojng, BM.

Jesse Crocker & Jane Kirkpatrick, June 23, 1829, by John Jarratt, M.G., John O'Neal, BM.

James Curd & Susan Everett, Nov. 26, 1829. William Curd, BM.

Ferrell Davis & Frances J. Joplin, Nov. 2, 1829, by Williamson Williams, J.P., Nov. 3, 1829. John Favid, John J. Joplin, BM.

Francis Davidson & Jane M. Cartwright, Sep. 23, 1829, by A. Provine, March 22, 1830. W. P. Davidson, BM.

James H. Dickens & Lydia Pitner, Sep. 19, 1829. Norfleet B. Nelms, BM.

Joseph R. Dickson & Catherine L. Alexander, Aug. 31, 1829, by Jesse Alexander, V.D.M., Sep. 1, 1829. James M. Cloyd, BM.

John H. Dortch (Dorch) & Winny Todd, Dec. 30, 1829. P. H. Buckley, BM.

William Doughty & Betsy Springs, Sep. 8, 1829. David Sckols, BM.

John Driver & Mary Campbell, Dec. 17, 1829, by Wilson Hearn, Fisher Cloucess, BM.

Woodson Dudley & City (Caty) Hearn, March 24, 1829. Rolley Organ, BM.

William Dunn & Sealy Jones, May 11, 1829. William Chumly, BM.

Barnaba Eagan & Sarah Cooper, Dec. 19, 1829. John R. Wight, BM.

Robertson Eatherly & Ameda Bond, March 24, 1829. Malcomb Smith, BM.

Joseph Eckols & Margaret Coonrad, May 27, 1829. John Smith, BM.

Robert H. Edwards & Minerva Robertson, Jan. 24, 1829. John T. Lee, BM.

Robert Elliott & Elizabeth Curry, Sep. 18, 1824 (1829?), by John Beard, M.G., Sep. 22, 1829. Adam Elliot, BM.

Albert Goodman & Loury Ragsdale, Sep. 28, 1829, by Wm. M. Swain, J.P., Oct. 1, 1829. Caleb M. Swain, BM.

Edmond Goodman & Rachel Watts, March 26, 1829, by Thomas D. Lansden, J.P., James Word, BM.

Jesse A. Goodwin & Rebecca L. Ozment, March 11, 1829. Pickward Holloway, BM.

Balem Graves & Elizabeth Gilbert, Sep. 26, 1829. John O'Neal, BM.

Lorenso Graves & Jane Alexander, March 9, 1829. Alexander Braden, BM.

Samuel Gray & Elizabeth Williams, April 2, 1829, by James H. Davis, J.P., April 7, 1829. Simpson Ray, BM.

Anderson Green & Martha Harris, Dec. 15, 1829. H. T. Turner, BM.

Joseph Grissom & Martha R. Spring, Dec. 12, 1829. Benjamin Spring, BM.

Joseph Bailey & Nancy Estes, Dec. 3, 1824 (?), by Geo. McWhirter, J.P., Davett Freeman, BM.

Thomas Hammons & Rachel Green, Sep. 9, 1829, by Jas. T. Tompkins, Reece Tipton, BM.

Samuel Hancock & Martha Donnell, May 30, 1829. Green H. Hancock, BM.

Theophilus Hanks & Jane Tilford, Dec. 5, 1829, by John Beard, M.G., Feb. 19, 1830. Wm. G. Hanks, BM.

Mathew C. Hankins & Martha P. Grissim, Oct. 12, 1829, by John Seay, M.G., Oct. 15, 1829. Mathew Hawkins, Mathew Cartwright, BM.

Hugh Harper & Mary Watson, Aug. 18, 1829, by T. Kirk-patrick, J.P., Hugh Taylor, BM.

Birdsong Herring & Easter Johnson, Feb. 11, 1829. Henry F. Johnson, BM.

Jesse Harris & Elizabeth Seatt, June 9, 1829. Zachariah Davis, BM.

William Hastings & Frances Hawkins, July 15, 1829, by Wilson Hearn, Thomas Vaughn, BM.

Snoden Hickman & Frankey Vanhook, Jan. 20, 1829, by Obadiah Freeman, Wright Hickman, BM.

Lewis C. Hill & Daritha Rieff, Sep. 22, 1829, by James T. Tompkins, Abner Hill, BM.

Joseph C. Hobbs & Joannah Jenkins, Dec. 14, 1829. T. Swan, BM.

Joseph Hobson & Margaret Clay, July 7, 1829, by R. Gwyn, J.P., July 16, 1829. Sma'l. Sherrill, BM.
Robert M. Holman & Elizabeth Ann Jackson, Dec. 2, 1829. Jesse Gibson, BM.
John Holland & Susan Booker, Oct. 14, 1829. William P. Morris, BM.
Mathew H. Hooker & Nancy Cloyd, Sep. 15, 1829, by Ezekiel Cloyd, M.G., Sep. 17, 1829. H. J. Thomas, BM.
Peter Hubbard & Minerva M. Cage, June 30, 1829, John Wiseman BM.
Stephen Jennings & Nancy Clanton, Dec. 22, 1829. Eli Joyner, BM.
William M. Johns & Jane Garmany, Dec. 17, 1829. James M. Armstrong, BM.
Henry F. Johnson & Minerva Sypert, Sep. 16, 1829, by Dn'l. Moser, J.P., David T. Berry, BM.
Littleberry Johnson & Marinda Clifton, Jan. 13, 1829. William Sweat, BM.
Rollings H. Johnson & Catharine _____, Jan. 21, 1829, by G. Donnell, M.G., Jan. 22, 1829. Allen W. Vick, BM.
Samuel G. Johnson & Nancy W. Cooper, Dec. 9, 1829, by T. Kirkpatrick, J.P., Dec. 10, 1829. Charlie W. Cooper, BM.
Dennis Jonson & Menthey Stoude (Troude), Dec. 14, 1829, by H. W. Picket, M.G.
William F. Lain & Elizabeth Hugly, July 29, 1829, George W. Hugly, BM.
Edmund V. Lester & Elizabeth Jennings, Dec. 11, 1829. Joseph Biddle, BM.
Josiah B. Lindsay & Malinda Donnell, March 23, 1829, by Amzi Bradshaw, March 24, 1829. James Carruth, BM.
Wm. W. Maddox & Anny Cidwell, Nov. 19, 1829. Frederick F. Rotranate, BM.
James Mark & Nancy Spring, Sep. 7, 1829. M. Cutrell, BM.
Anthony Marler & Casander Williams, Feb. 23, 1829, by Zadoo McMillen, J.P., March 1, 1829.
Levi Manly & Malinda Nickens, April 1, 1829, by Abner Hill, M.G., Lemuel Nickens, BM.
Josiah S. McClain & Martha H. Johnson, Aug. 22, 1829. P. Anderson, BM.
Sampson McDowan & Parthena Prior, April 27, 1829. Alison Brader, BM.
Elias McDaniel & Lucinda Furlong, Oct. 16, 1820, by William Algood, M.E.C., Oct. 22, 1829. William Corley, BM.
Marvin McDoogle & Pollt Mathis, March 4, 1829. Alfred Mathas, BM.
Thomas McKnight & Jane Fare, Sep. 28, 1829, by Joshua Woollen, M.G., Sep. 30, 1829. Etheldred Bass, BM.
John Milton & Patsy Brown, March 26, 1829, by Stephen McDonald, April 2, 1829. Jacob Hunter, BM.
Robert R. Moore & Elizabeth Hutchings, Dec. 19, 1829. Allen Powell, BM.
Benjamin L. Mosely & Eliza Thomas, July 12, 1829, by Thos. Joplin, J.P., July 17, 1829. Wm. Standerson, BM.

Mathias Mount & Tabitha Whitten, June 13, 1829. Hiram
Percie, BM.
William Mount & Frances Williams, Sep. 24, 1829, by
Williamson Williams, J.P., Sep. 25, 1829. Theos.
Mount, BM.
Moore L. Moss & Diannah Huguley, ___. 10, ____. Albert
McGregor BM.
William Moss & Sara Carr, March 19, 1829. Wm. H. Chapman,
BM.
Sam'l. J. Nesbitt & Martha Walker, Dec. 22, 1829. Jno.
W. White, BM.
Burwell Nattles & Irecy Vaughanville, Aug. 31, 1829, by
William Phillips, J.P., Sep. 1, 1829. Edward G. Jacobs,
BM.
Rowland Newby & Lucy Cooksey, Oct. 26, 1829. James B.
Cooksey, BM.
Andrew Nickins & Angelina Nickens, Feb. 25, 1829. Calvin
Nickins, BM.
William Nunnerly & Elizabeth Lawrence, Nov. 12, 1829.
John Barbee, BM.
James Oliver & Margaret Patterson, Feb. 12, 1829, by
Joshua Woolen, M.G.
Chrostopher Owen & Purmela Brison, Sep. 21, 1829, by
John McMinn, J.P., Sep. 23, 1829.
Camrin Ozment & Sally Kelly, March 31, 1829. J. A.
Doowin, BM.
Thomas K. Palmer & Sarah Jackson, Nov. 11, 1829. Thos.
R. Jackson, BM.
James Peace & Morthel Bils, Nov. 30, 1829.
Isaac Perryman & Nancy Patterson, April 19, 1829, by
Joshua Lester, V.D.M., April 20, 1829.
Joshua Peak & Elizabeth Kemp, Nov. 4, 1829. John Duke,
BM.
Joseph Phillips & Rachel Reeder, July 17, 1829. Harris
Reeder, BM.
Henry Phillips & Sally Sweatt, March 7, 1829. Robt.
Owen, BM.
Robert Phelps & Robb Phelps, Aug. 21, 1829. Joab
Goodman, BM.
John B. Pittman & Rebecca Moore, Nov. 17, 1829. John
Campsey, BM.
Thos. W. Porterfield & Elizabeth Jackson, Sep. 29, 1829,
by H. W. Pickett, Oct. 1, 1829.
James Powell & Elizabeth Vaughan, Nov. 24, 1829, by
Wilson Hearn, Nov. 25, 1829. Jas. Cato (Gate), BM.
Abram Prim & Nancy Cook, Feb. 19, 1829. William Harts-
field, BM.
Martin B. Ray & Sally Jones, Nov. 10, 1829. John Stear,
BM.
Samuel Ray & Rachel Jennings, Jan. 8, 1829, by James H.
Davis, J.P., Jan. 11, 1829. Samuel Ray, BM.
John Russel & Mary B. Chappel, Oct. 21, 1829, Benj. T.
Mabry, Oct. 21, 1829. Littleton Rogers, BM.
James Rice & Patriser Baird, Aug. 22, 1829. James M.
Swain, BM.

WILSON COUNTY MARRIAGES

Ellis G. Right & Jane Atherly, Feb. 20, 1829, by John
Williams, J.P., Feb. 22, 1829. James Atherly, BM.
Joseph Roach & Polly D. Barton, Dec. 1, 1829, by John
Beard, M.G., Feb. 19, 1830. James B. Roach, BM.
Lewis Robertson & Louisa King, Feb. 21, 1829, by John
Powell, J.P., Feb. 26, 1829.
James Sampson & Jane Martin, April 14, 1829. Thos. Martin,
BM.
Martin Seat & Milly Organ, Nov. 30, 1829. William Sweatt,
BM.
Abner Shaw & Susannah Park, Feb. 6, 1829. Gabriel Shaw,
BM.
Morgan Shearn & Mary Wood, April 20, 1829. Luke Wood,
BM.
Hugh Sherrill & Jane Scoby, Feb. 10, 1829, by Wm. Steele,
J.P., Feb. 17, 1829.
Hugh Smith & Betsey Roach, Nov. 23, 1829, by Ransom Gwyn,
J.P., Nov. 28, 1829.
Thomas Spain & Polly Melton, Dec. 14, 1829. Soloan Spain,
BM.
Lewis Spears & Amanda Donnell, Dec. 7, 1829, by Amzi
Bradshaw, Dec. 10, 1829. Alfred E. Donnell, BM.
Andrew B. Spradley & Agnes Spradley (Spraklin), Sep. 10,
1829. James Spradley, BM.
Alijah Stewart & _____ Loyd, June 24, 1829. John Gunter,
BM.
Spencer W. Tulley & Araminta Eddings, Jan. 1, 1829, by
Joshua Lester, V.D.M., Jan. 29, 1829. James S. Lester,
BM.
Peterson Tallor (Taylor) & Susan Campton, Aug. 29, 1829.
James McWhirter, BM.
William W. Talley & Emily B. Holland, Aug. 3, 1829.
Michael Harris, BM.
Richard Tate & Polly Alexander, Aug. 13, 1829, by B.
Graves, J.P., Hugh Haus, BM.
Andrew Thompson & Milly Ricketts, Sep. 29, 1829, by H.
W. Puckett, M.G., Oct. 6, 1829. Thos. Porterfield, BM.
George W. Thomas & Julia B. Brwer (Brewer), Oct. 2, 1829,
by B. Graves, J.P.
John W. Tucker & Elizabeth Bonds, Jan. 28, 1829.
Benjamin Tucker, BM.
Hamilton Violette (Vivrette) & Margaret Springs, July
21, 1829. Moses Harrison, BM.
Micajah Vivrett & Elizabeth Wall, Dec. 22, 1829, by Abner
Hill, M.G., Dec. 23, 1829. Henry Vivrette, BM.
James D. Walker & Ceala L. Hamilton, Aug. 1, 1829, by
Dn'l. Moses, J.P., Aug. 3, 1829. Robert Lawrence, BM.
Milner Walker & Nancy Jarrott, Oct. 28, 1829, by Wilson
Hearn, Jas. McDaniel, BM.
Benjamin Wall & Priscilla Tidwell, April 6, 1829, by
Abner Hill, M.G., Eli Thrower, BM.
Cantrell Warren & Sarah Ann Williams, Feb. 21, 1829, by
Williamson Williams, J.P., Feb. 22, 1829.
William Watkins & Katharine Smith, Sep. 7, 1829, by Lena
A. Durham, Sep. 12, 1829. Andrew Clark, BM.

George W. Watkins & Sarah T. Etherly, Nov. 27, 1829.
Thos. W. Barksdale, BM.

John Webber & Margaret Eatherly, April 20, 1829, by
Ezekiel Cloyd, M.G., April 21, 1829.

Allen Webster & Mary Green, Oct. 21, 1829. Sam'l Green,
BM.

James Whitehead & Tellia White, Aug. 7, 1829. George
White, BM.

Lewis Williams & Elizabeth Brite, Dec. 17, 1829. Hiram
F. Persell, BM.

Wm. Wilbourn & Nancy Johnson, Dec. 22, 1829. Peter
Risen, BM.

Robert Wilson & Sarah Hodge, Sep. 15, 1829, by Amzi
Bradshaw, William Donnell, BM.

Alexander S. Winford & Wilzabeth R. Moss, Dec. 21, 1829,
by Wilson Hearn, Dec. 23, 1829. William Winford, BM.

William Woodrum & Martha Harris, July 27, 1829, by
Obadiah Freeman, July 30, 1829. Joseph B. Chance, BM.

Isham Word & Elizabeth Hays (Bays), Feb. 10, 1829, by
T. Tompkins, Jefferson Motsinger, BM.

James N. Wright & Martha M. Tate, Nov. 21, 1829. Thomas
Wright, BM.

John R. Wright & Sarah Mayo, Oct. 4, 1820 (1829?).
Barnebus Eagan, BM.

James Wynne & Ruth Hancock, Nov. 14, ____. Robert Gwyn,
BM.

Joseph Young & Harriet Smith, Nov. 11, 1829. Joseph
Freeman, BM.

William Young & Nancy Hughley, Dec. 29, 1829. Alexander
Z. Holland, BM.

Allen Zachary & Margaret Woollard, March 17, 1829, by
Jas. Drennon, J.P., March 20, 1829.

Wiley Allen & Susan Whitehad, Sep. 16, 1830. Joseph
Ligon, BM.

Ebenezer Andrews & Syntha C. Clifton, Dec. 20, 1830, by
Wilson Hearn, M.G., Dec. 22, 1830. Simpson Organ, BM.

Pernel H. Andrews & Susan Spears, March 16, 1830, by
John Seay, M.G., March 17, 1830. G. A. Wilson, BM.

Robert Barkley & Sarah Goalston, July 21, 1830. Frances
Anderson, BM.

Hickerson Barksdale & Harriet Lowe, June 23, 1830. Asa
B. Douglas, BM.

Ezekiel Bass & Maria Barbee, Aug. 17, 1830. Elias Bass,
BM.

Henry Bass & Sinah Phillips, Oct. 29, 1830. Archinack
Bass, BM.

Solomon Bass & Elizabeth Parten, Dec. 27, 1830. Cader
Bass, BM.

Wm. F. Braswell & Malissa Eddings, Dec. 27, 1830. J. S.
Lester, BM.

Jefferson Baxter & Rebecca Wynn, Sep. 27, 1830. Robert
Gray, BM.

Ewin Bell & Elizabeth G. Swan, Dec. 20, 1830, by Wikson
Hearn, M.G., Dec. 23, 1830. John Swan, BM.

Robert Bell & Polly Hooker, Jan. 14, 1830. Alexander
Simmons, BM.
James Blair & Anne S. McWhirter, Oct. 11, 1830, by
Ambrose F. Mizkell, M.G., James W. Moses, BM.
Alexander Blythe & Eliza Kiely, Nov. 2, 1830. John S.
Kennedy, BM.
Adney Bone & Martha A. McMinn, Feb. 6, 1830, by J. Provine,
M.G., Wm. B. Merritt, BM.
James M. Boyd & Martha Thomas, Sep. 11, 1830. David N.
Berry, BM.
Josel Bridges & Lucy Eskew, Jan. 26, 1830. C. Neal, BM.
Jacob C. Brown & Nancy Miller, Jan. 2, 1830. L. Miller,
BM.
Irwin Brown & Minerva Booker, Aug. 12, 1830, G. W. Bussard,
Lemuel Loyd, BM.
John Brown & Margarett Gilliam, Nov. 20, 1830, by Joshua
Lester, V.D.M., William Gilliam, BM.
Jordan Brown & Sarah N. Hill, Sep. 1, 1830, by John M.
Holland, Sep. 28, 1830. A. W. Hicks, BM.
Jefferson Bryan & Fany Locke, Feb. 21, 1830, by James B.
Taylor, J.P.
William Bryson & Sophia Matthews, Sep. 8, 1830. James
Wilson, BM.
Elisha G. Cain & Mary Ann Sherrill, May 20, 1830, by F.
E. Pitts, M.G.
Moses P. Callahan & Sarah R. Hearn, March 7, 1830, by
J. B. Lasiter, J.P., March 12, 1830.
Merritt Caroway & Nancy Sherrell, Nov. 17, 1830, by James
Somers, J.P., Nov. 25, 1830. Silas Ragsdale, BM.
John Carroll & Rebecca Baker, Aug. 5, 1830. Edmund York,
BM.
John Carter & Narcissa Gibson, Jan. 31, 1830, by Joshua
Woollen, M.G., Feb. 1, 1830.
John Chambers & Edney Johnson, Dec. 15, 1830. Thi. T.
Gray, BM.
Charles C. Chamberlain & Jane Clifton, Jan. 13, 1830.
Robert McKee, BM.
Joshua Clark & Sarah Allen, Aug. 13, 1829, by Banja.
Maddox, M.G., Aug. 30, 1829.
James Clary & Penny Stephens, Nov. 25, 1830, by B. S.
Mattlas (Maddox), J.P., Loyd Richmond, BM.
John Clopton & Matilda Drake, March 25, 1830, by Ezekiel
Cloyd, April 3, 1830. Jno. Bussard, BM.
Elijah Clower & Nicy Sutton, Oct. 4, 1830. Mathew Dew,
BM.
Jesse Collins & Julia Collins, Dec. 1, 1830. William
Patrick, BM.
Henry Collis & Elizabeth Farrington, Sep. 23, 1830, by
James Foster, J.P., William Dollner, BM.
Sam'l. R. Comer & Mahala Marrs, Oct. 12, 1830, by Jno. F.
Doak, J.P.
Henry R. Cox & Maria Clifton, March 26, 1830, by Jas. C.
Willford, J.P., March 31, 1830. E. D. Foster, BM.
William Coppage & Mary T. Davis, Dec. 1, 1830. Charles
Coppage, BM.

Richard Craddock & Polly Alsup, Sep. 16, 1830, by J.
Lester, V.D.M., James Adams, BM.
Midget Cutrall & Fanny Swan, Oct. 16, 1830.   John Swan,
BM.
William Davis & Lucy Stewart, Sep. 7, 1830.   John Webb,
BM.
Henry Devault & Susan Jackson, May 1, 1830.   Snoden
Hickman, BM.
Samuel Dickens & Nancy Chandler, June 16, 1830, by Wm.
White, M.G., June 17, 1830.
Thomas Dillon & Harriet Roane, Oct. 18, 1830.   Andrew
Roane, BM.
Thomas Drennon & Evalina Miles, N.D.   John W. Hugueley,
BM.
Nelson Doak & Jane Smith, Jan. 20, 1830.   Sam'l C. Smith,
BM.
Josiah Donnell & Nancy P. Thompson, May 17, 1830, by
Amzi Bradshaw, May 18, 1830.   Thomas W. Brigson, BM.
Robert Donnell & Cleopatry Hearn, Dec. 2, 1830, by
Obadiah Freeman, Robert McKee, BM.
William H. Donnell & Susannah Benthal, June 11, 1830, by
Wilson Hearn, M.G., June 17, 1830.   David Standley, BM.
George Dooley & Emily Jackson, Aug. 11, 1830.   Sam
Golladay, BM.
Littleton C. Duke & Milany Scott, Oct. 6, 1830, by James
Foster, J.P., Oct. 7, 1830.   John H. Vowell, BM.
Joseph Eckols & Margaret Coonard, May 27, 1830, by James
B. Taylor, J.P.
Josiah Aley (Elsy) & Martha W. Boothe, Sep. 21, 1830.
John S. Booth, BM.
Addison Eakins & Caroline Harrison, April 2, 1830.   John
Barbee, BM.
Francis Eubanks & Fanny Harland, Aug. 17, 1830.   Davis
Standley, BM.
William Exum & Sarah E. Jackson, Feb. 9, 1830, by
Stephen McDonald, J.P., Feb. 10, 1830.
Edward P. Faulkner & Rebecca New, June 4, 1830.
John B. Forester & Elizabeth Hall, June 17, 1830.   Jno.
Brown, BM.
Darrell Freeman & Elizabeth E. Estes, Jan. 27, 1830.
Joseph Freeman, BM.
Littleberry Freeman & Elizabeth Young, Jan. 26, 1830,
by J. T. Williams, J.P., Jan. 27, 1830.
James Gibson & Rachel Bowers, May 17, 1830, by Wm. Steele,
J.P., May 18, 1830.   Samuel Stone, BM.
William Gibson & Levicy Nelson, Feb. 23, 1830, by J.
Gray, J.P., Feb. 24, 1830.   William Nelson, BM.
Levi S. Gilliam & Eliza Hodges, Feb. 9, 1830.
Stanhope Sharpe, BM.
Don'l. Glenn & Lucy Dowry, Oct. 25, 1830.   Josiah Wood,
BM.
James B. Goodwin & Mildred Powell, Dec. 18, 1830.   George
N. Martin, BM.
Benjamin Graves & Harriet Young, Dec. 29, 1830, by John
Shane, J.P., Samuel Walker, BM.

WILSON COUNTY MARRIAGES

Abram Green & Mary Ann Ballard, May 1, 1830. Charles
Wilkerson, BM.
Samuel Green & Anne Osborn, March 31, 1830. Spencer W.
Williams, BM.
Barnett Guill & Sarah B. Fletcher, Dec. 3, 1830. Jas.
Ligon, BM.
John H. Guill & Nancy Burton, Jan. 11, 1830. John S.
Hubane, BM.
Robt. Gwynn & Judith Wynne, Feb. 5, 1830. Mathew H.
Hooker, BM.
William Harrington & Mary Johnson, Sep. 22, 1830.
Birdsong Harrington, BM.
Henry R. Harris & Rebeccah Dillard, Nov. 16, 1830.
Theophilus T. Gray, BM.
George Harris & Alinera Cloe, May 6, 1830. John Irby,
BM.
William Harris & Nancy Travilian, Oct. 23, 1830. A. L.
Tombs, BM.
Winston Hart & Agnes B. Bilbo, July 7, 1830. John W.
White, BM.
William J. Hays & Mary P. Allford, Nov. 12, 1830. Hugh
Hays, BM.
Edmund Hearn & Elizabeth Dwyer, Sep. 16, 1830. Wm.
Halbrook, BM.
Jonathan Hendrison & Clarissa Lemons, May 1, 1830.
Benjamin Spring, BM.
James Hessy & Martha Thompson, July 31, 1830, by Ezekiel
Cloyd, M.G., Aug. 3, 1830.
Lemuel Hickman & Elenor Blurter, July 28, 1830, by Wm.
Willis, J.P., July 29, 1830.
Joseph W. Hight & Sarah Mount, Jan. 11, 1830. John S.
Hight, BM.
James B. Hobbs & Fanny Stone, Oct. 12, 1830. John C.
Lash, BM.
James Holt & Mary Pane, Jan. 21, 1830. Noah Walker, BM.
Joshua Jarrell & Mary Dill, March 9, 1830, by H. Holmes,
J.P., March 10, 1830. Fontain Jarrell, BM.
Drury Jones & Bijah Cannon, May 7, 1830, by John Shane,
J.P., Oct. 27, 1830. Eclemuel Sullivan, BM.
David M. Johnson & Elizabeth Davidson, Sep. 7, 1830.
Robert C. Davis, BM.
Philip Johnson & Michie P. Tilman, Jan. 23, 1830, by B.
Graves, J.P., G. L. Johnson, BM.
Isham Jones & Susannah Lea, Dec. 4, 1830. Henry F.
Johnson, BM.
John Jones & Mariah Woolard, Aug. 25, 1830, by G. H.
Bussard, Lemuel Loyd, BM.
Henry Kean & Mary Gains, Aug. 17, 1830. John Scott, BM.
James L. Lanwinset & Syntha Joins, Feb. 18, 1830. Thos.
J. Meeritt, BM.
Stanford Lasater & Leah Fouch, Aug. 7, 1830. John S.
Hight, BM.
William Lasater & Polly Hill, Dec. 22, 1830, by J. B.
Lasater, J.P.

Joseph Lash & Elizabeth Benthal, Oct. 13, 1830. P. Anderson, BM.

Daniel W. Lester & Lurana Jones, Aug. 27, 1830, by Joshua Lester, V.D.M., Lemuel Loyd, BM.

Joseph Ligon & Mary Mariah Penington, Oct. 3, 1830, by Wm. Steele, J.P., Oct. 9, 1830. Asa Mosley, BM.

John Major & Jane C. Donnell, Dec. 21, 1830. Sam'l. Donnell, BM.

Clark D. Mannin & Sarah Patterson, July 24, 1830, by J. Lester, V.D.M.

Jacob Mayo & Polly Driver, June 10, 1830. John Webb, BM.

Eli Merritt & Sarah Merritt, Nov. 22, 1830. Benjamin Goodwin, BM.

Henry McPeak & Nancy Fane, June 28, 1830, by G. A. Huddleston, J.P., June 30, 1830. John Lemons, BM.

David Moore & Emeline Bond, Dec. 6, 1830. James Wilson, BM.

David B. Moore & Elizabeth Donnell, Nov. 3, 1830, by J. Provine, M.G., Robt. Donnell, BM.

McCoy Moore & Ovalina Williams, Dec. 18, 1830. Wm. Standley, BM.

Thomas Moore & Nancy Odom, Oct. 16, 1830. Joab Griffin, BM.

William W. Moore & Susan Vaughn, Nov. 16, 1830, by G. H. Bussard, J.P., Mathew Vaughn, BM.

Mathew Morgan & Jane Morriss, March 5, 1830, by James Drennon, J.P., Gardiner Morgan, BM.

William Morris & Nancy Smith, Feb. 14, 1830. Hugh George, BM.

William Murry & Alethia S. Matlock, Oct. 9, 1830, by Ezekiel Cloyd, M.G., Oct. 12, 1830.

Benjamin Nettle & Frances Talley, Oct. 9, 1830. Wm. Wady, BM.

Jas. Nickins & Jinsey Trammwell, Dec. 29, 1830. Calvin Nickins, BM.

John O'Meal & Cherry F. Hunt, Aug. 10, 1830. James M. Hunt, BM.

Rayley Organ & Sidney Williams, July 3, 1830, Benjamin Mabry, M.G., Samuel Stone, BM.

Ezekiel S. Patterson & Elizabeth Payne, July 16, 1830, by R. W. Morris, E.A.C.C., Aug. 11, 1830. Joseph Williams, BM.

Alfred Patton & Lucinda Ray, Sep. 2, 1830, by S. Kirk-patrick, J.P., William P. Allin, BM.

William Pea & Mady M. Tilman, Jan. 12, 1830, by B. Graves, J.P.

Williamson Pearcy & Easther Brother, April 12, 1830, by Tis. J. Elliott, M.G.

William Pemberton & Martha Brooks, Nov. 3, 1830. Thos. W. Barksdale, BM.

Thomas Picket & Salina Jackson, Sep. 21, 1830. John Rice, BM.

William A. Provinces & Nancy Bowers, Jan. 4, 1830. Samuel F. Provine, BM.

Thomas Pulley & Fanny Franklin, Sep. 4, 1830. Simpson Organ, BM.

Alexander C. Ramsey & Martha Ann Smith, Dec. 6, 1830. James Wilson, BM.

Alfred A. Reader & Nancy Avery, March 4, 1830, by Thos. J. Elliott, M.G., J. Moray, BM.

Shelby Reynolds & Elizabeth Barrett, Oct. 5, ____ (1830?). Williamson Meritt, BM.

Andrew Richmond & Nancy Phipps, Dec. 12, 1830. Daniel Richmond, BM.

Peter Rizen & Roxalana Sypert, Sep. 2, 1830. John Canpsey, BM.

Henry Rutland & James B. Thompson, April 10, 1830, by B. Graves, J.P.

John M. Scott & Jane Boswell, Feb. 21, 1830, by Wm. Johnson, J.P., Feb. 23, 1830.

William Searcy & Nancy Ridinngs, March 13, 1830. John Cox, BM.

Sard Sellars & Elizabeth Goodwin, June 16, 1830. Higdon Harrington, BM.

John A. Simons & Elizabeth Tomlinson, March 22, 1830, by A. Privine.

Alexander Smith & Elizabeth Lasater, Dec. 8, 1830. James Mitchell, BM.

Lebourn Spane & Martha Bond, June 25, 1830. Sam'l. Bond, BM.

Francis Spurlock & Sarah Ashford, Aug. 27, 1830. Jesse Dillon, BM.

John Swain & Martha Rogers, May 6, 1830, by Thomas S. Green, J.P., May 7, 1830.

William Tanner & Jane McCown, Feb. 5, 1830, by Wilson Hearn, M.G.

Peter G. Terry & Martha W. Eakin, May 20, 1830. Addison Reese, BM.

John Todd & Mary Romines, Aug. 18, 1830. John Ingram.

Milton Underwood & Nancy Petway, Oct. 16, 1830. Dan'l. Underwood, BM.

John Ventrease & Hester McMillan, April 20, 1830, by H. W. Pickett, V.M.G., April 22, 1830.

Thomas Vic & Elizabeth Richmond, Aug. 4, 1830. Joseph Michell, BM.

Samuel Wallace & Nancy Sellas, Sep. 18, 1830. Prichard F. Wasson, BM.

Baker Walsh & Jane T. Robertson, Feb. 4, 1830. Sam Hawkins, BM.

B. Warren & Mary Warren, April 12, 1830. Pleasant Martin, BM.

Hollis Wright & Elizabeth Liggon, June 19, 1830, by B. Graves, J.P.

Mortimore Waters & Ethalinda Askin, Jan. 18, 1830. Joseph Gore, BM.

Rodger Williams & Priscilla King, Nov. 18, 1830. Samuel Stone, BM.

Turner Williams & Elizabeth Webb, Feb. 11, 1830. Thomas Wright, BM.

Frederick Winter & Mary Dickerson, Jan. 11, 1830. J. S. McClain, BM.

James Winter & Sarah Rice, N.D. Silas Hedgpath, BM.

Jas. Wilson & Syntha Byrn, Dec. 5, 1830. L. B. Moore, BM.

Mathew Wilson & Mary Rich, Aug. 25, 1830. George Rich, BM.

Allison Wray & Fathey Alexander, Nov. 8, 1830, by Wm. Neigh Liowe, M.G., Nov. 11, 1830. Abraham Green, BM.

Abraham Wright & Martha Smart, Aug. 18, 1830, by James Somers, J.P., Aug. 19, 1830. John Lemon, BM.

Lemuel Wright & Susan Stull, Aug. 21, 1830, by James Drennon, J.P., Aug. 22, 1830.

David Young & Mary C. Calhoon, Dec. 25, 1830. Samuel C. Harrison, BM.

Gilbert Young & Rebecca Tucker, Jan. 20, 1830.

John Adams & Nancy Jones, Dec. 1, 1831, by Wm. Neigh Jiowrs, M.G., William Dunn, BM.

Brittain D. Alford & Martha Graves, Aug. 6, 1831, by B. Graves, J.P., Solomon D. Wright, BM.

Edmund Anderson & Sarah Gleaves, June 18, 1831. William P. McClain, BM.

William Arbuckle & Mary E. Harris, Aug. 6, 1831. D. N. Berry, BM.

Edward P. Baker & Elizabeth G. Crowley, Oct. 27, 1831. Caleb C. Cummings, BM.

John P. Barton & Martha Johnson, Dec. 14, 1831. Joshua Pemberton, BM.

William Baily & Elizabeth Puckett, June 1, 1831, by Joshua Lester, V.D.M., James S. Baily, BM.

Thomas Barns & Polly Nickins, Jan. 15, 1831. James Nickins, BM.

John M. Bartlett & Martha Foust, Nov. 8, 1831. M. H. Biles, BM.

Simpson Bennett & Mary Ann Jackson, Nov. 12, 1831, by Stephen McDonald, J.P., Dec. 1, 1831. Robert Jackson, BM.

John A. Bingham & Margaret Sims, July 11, 1831, by Amzi Bradshaw, M.G., July 13, 1831. Benjamin L. Massey, BM.

Albert G. Blakemore & Edna B. Sanders, July 10, 1831. J. J. Finley, BM.

Charles Bradley & Agnis Calhoun, Aug. 13, 1831. Wm. Martin, BM.

Thomas Bradshaw & Martha Thompkins, Aug. 31, 1831. William Pitner, BM.

Joseph F. Brown & Susan Bass, Aug. 1, 1831, by B. Bridges, J.P., Aug.3, 1831. William Brown, BM.

Richard Brown, & Elizabeth P. Scruggs, Oct. 8, 1831. W. P. McClain, BM.

William Brown & May Curry, Nov. 18, 1831, by James Drennon, J.P., William Jones, BM.

George Byrum & Susan Harris, July 28, 1831. John D. Harris, BM.

John Campsey & Elizabeth D. Peace, Aug. 11, 1831.

Hugh L. Campbell & Mary Tracy, Sep. 16, 1831. by William
Phillips, J.P., Sep. 27, 1831. John H. Vowell, BM.
Spencer Carlin & Manerva Hogan, Feb. 26, 1831, by James
C. Willifort, J.P., Feb. 28, 1831.
John Carter & Narcissa Gibson, Jan. 31, 1831. Thos.
Weber, BM.
John M. Chandler & Mary Ann Belcher, Feb. 26, 1831, by
H. W. Pickett, V.D.M., March 3, 1831.
Andrew Clark & Mary Taylor, July 16, 1831. James Taylor,
BM.
John Clay & Harriet Andrews, Sep. 26, 1831. Samuel N.
Ross, BM.
John Clay & Martha Davis, Oct. 10, 1831, by Henry Hobson,
J.P., Ebenezer Gilbert, BM.
John A. Clopton & Elizabeth Ann Hurd, Nov. 10, 1831.
Isaac Barnett, BM.
William J. Cocke & Manerva Bloodworth, Nov. 7, 1831.
Jonathan Tipton, BM.
Charles Compton & Nancy Hancock, July 9, 1831, by William
Philips, J.P., Aug. 23, 1831. Northern Nooner, BM.
William Compton & Elisa Coe, Aug. 29, 1831. John Barbee,
BM.
Robert Criswell & Rebecca Thomas, July 12, 1831, by B.
Bridges, J.P., July 13, 1831. David Thomas, BM.
Edward Denton & Susan Smith, Oct. 13, 1831, by Silas
Tarver, J.P., Joseph Simmons, BM.
Samuel W. Donnell & Martha W. Hearn, June 1, 1831, by
Obadiah Freeman, M.G., June 2, 1831. Henry Major BM.
Lorenza Doughty & Sarah Cooksey, Aug. 3, 1831. James
A. Doughty, BM.
Jonathan Dukes & Holly Dobson, Oct. 29, 1831, by Geo.
Clark, J.P., Oct. 31, 1831. James Edwards, BM.
John Dwyn & Rebecca Hearn, Dec. 14, 1831, by Thos. P.
Holman, J.P., Dec. 22, 1831. Edward Hearn, BM.
Barna B. Eagan & Deborah Whitson, July 23, 1831. William
Eagen, BM.
Alexander Eanes & Mary Ann New, July 2, 1831. Matt
Martin, BM.
James K. Eason & Jane H. Fisher, Sep. 7, 1831. L. C.
Shanklin, BM.
Michael Edwards & Sarah Bennett, Sep. 21, 1831, by S. A.
Huddleston, J.P., Sep. 22, 1831. Crafford Edwards, BM.
John Epperson & Eliza Gregory, Oct. 24, 1831. James H.
Brittain, BM.
Elensley D. Foster & Martha Ann Doak, Nov. 30, 1831, by
Geo. Donnell, M.G., Dec. 1, 1831. Samuel Stone, BM.
Thomas Frazer & Mahala Dickens, Oct. 17, 1831. Sam'l.
Dickens, BM.
Andrew Fulk & Jane Caplinger, July 30, 1831. Henry Bundy,
BM.
Thomas Grisham & Sarah Elizabeth Bell, Sep. 7, 1831, by
J. Kirkpatrick, J.P., Sep. 8, 1831. Noah W. Halbrook,
BM.
James Thomas Hale & Pennina Brown, Sep. 13, 1831, by
Stephen McDonald, J.P., James Primm, BM.

Thomas Hale & Polly Warren, April 12, 1831, by G. H. Huddleston, J.P., John Adamson, BM.

William A. Hamilton & Jane H. Hughley, Nov. 28, 1831. John W. Hughley, BM.

Lesley Hancock & Louisa Hobson, Dec. 26, 1831. P. Freeman, BM.

Alfred H. Harris & Elizabeth Woodrum, July 20, 1831, by John Beard, M.G., July 21, 1831. Joshua Harrison, BM.

Isaac Harrison & Elizabeth Telford, Oct. 24, 1831, by James Donnell, J.P., Oct. 28, 1831. Thomas Gibson, BM.

Nathan S. Harris & Tellitha Mount, Nov. 7, 1831. John R. Harris, BM.

William S. Harris & Hannah R. Harris, Oct. 5, 1831. N. T. Harris, BM.

John R. Herndon & Frances E. Tanner, Nov. 12, 1831, by Wilson Hearn, M.G., Nov. 16, 1831. Bailey Philips, BM.

James Holmes & Elizabeth Compton, May 13, 1831. William Compton, BM.

Matt. H. Hooker & Nancy B. Tate, June 7, 1831, by E. Cloyd, M.G., June 9, 1831. Alexander Posey, BM.

Albert Hoss & Louisa Patterson, Oct. 13, 1831. Thomas Dunn, BM.

Hurnard Holtzclaw & Mariah Leach, Oct. 6, 1831. George Apperson, BM.

William Hubbard & Nancy Whitlock, Sep. 24, 1831. Thomas Dunn, BM.

Robert Jackson & Rebecca R. Warren, Nov. 12, 1831. Coleman Jackson, BM.

Thomas Jackson & Margaret Parham, Sep. 23, 1831. James H. Parham, BM.

Fountain Jarrell & Elizabeth Jarrell, Jan. 6, 1831. George W. Pane, BM.

Boswell Jarrell & Nancy Murfrey, June 7, 1831, by E. P. Horn, J.P., Wm. Leach, BM.

Deverix Jarrett & Martha Ward, Nov. 28, 1831, by Saml. K. Davidson, M.G., Robt. L. Caruthers, BM.

Anthony Hogan & Elizabeth Carter, Jan. 16, 1831. William Buchanan, BM.

Robert Jennings & Chany Word, March 29, 1831, by Joshua Lester, V.D.M., March 31, 1831.

Clifton R. Jones & Frances F. Youree (Yourie), Oct. 17, 1831, by T. P. Holman, J.P., Oct. 21, 1831. Andrew W. Johnson, BM.

John W. Jones & Elizabeth Crawford, Jan. 13, 1831. John Yand (?), BM.

William Joplin & Mary Stone, July 23, 1831. Green Elliston, BM.

Burvid Joy & Frances Goodman, Dec. 19, 1831. Thomas Gunn, BM.

Henry Keen & Lucinda Gaines, a free woman of color, Dec. 5, 1831. John D. Scott, BM.

Armsted Lane & Nancy McCartney, Dec. 31, 1831, by James Somers, J.P., Jan. 5, 1831. Alfred Eakew, BM.

Green Summers & Frances Taylor, Sep. 27, 1831, by Silas Tarver, J.P., Sep. 29, 1831. Benjamin Tarver, BM.

Ranson Lockerd & Sarah Christopher, Au. 6, 1831, by Wm.
M. Swain, J.P., Aug. 7, 1831. Joseph Stewart, BM.
John P. Martin & Mary Ann Foster, Aug. 31, 1831, by Wm.
Steele, J.P., Aug. 4, 1831. J. W. Hawkins, BM.
John A. McClain & Minerva Rosse, May 6, 1831, by F. E.
Pitts, May 9, 1831. Rufus H. McClain, BM.
Thomas McKee & Margaret Donnell, Nov. 2, 1831, by Jno.
F. Doak, J.P., Nov. 3, 1831. Norman Walsh, BM.
Albert M. McKnight & Elisa Thomas, Sep. 12, 1831. Jacob
Thomas, BM.
Gregory Moore & Orey Ann Clark, Dec. 2, 1831, by J. B.
Taylor, J.P., Dec. 15, 1831. D. A. McCathon, BM.
John L. Moore & Sarah M. Gilliam, Dec. 31, 1831, by Joshua
Lester, V.D.M., J. L. Hill, BM.
Jesse L. Moore & Sarah Shannon, Dec. 28, 1831, by Wm.
M. Swain, J.P., Dec. 29, 1831. John A. Shannon, BM.
Levi Morrison & Martha Donnell, Oct. 27, 1831, by Jesse
Alexander, V.D.M., Oct. 28, 1831. Emsley D. Foster, BM.
Adam Moser & Elizabeth Caplinger, Feb. 17, 1831, by B. T.
Mathews, J.P., Jno. E. Eason, BM.
William Nelson & Elizabeth Bennett, Jan. 10, 1831, by G.
Huddleston, J.P., Jan. 11, 1831.
William S. New & Edy Sparks, July 13, 1831, by Wilson
Hearn, July 21, 1831. Hope Hancock, BM.
Nathan Nooner & Sarah Compton, July 9, 1831, by William
Philips, J.P., July 13, 1831. Charles Compton, BM.
Thomas Odum & Elizabeth Allen, May 14, 1831. John Waters,
BM.
John L. O'Neal & Martha Smith, Dec. 30, 1831, by E. P.
Horn, J.P., James M. Hunt, BM.
Richard Owen & Mary Ann Chias, Oct. 15, 1831, by F. S.
Harris, Nov. 4, 1831. Robt. Pulley, BM.
James H. Parham & Jane Alsum, Nov. 8, 1831. Thomas
Jackson, BM.
Frederick Pennel & Lucinda Jennings, Dec. 1, 1831, by
Joshua Lester, V.D.M., John B. Baird, BM.
John Pennell & Nancy Whotlock, Oct. 4, 1831. Sampson
Knight, BM.
James R. Petty & Vicy Russell, Sep, 29, 1831, by Benj.
S. Mabry, Wm. Russell, BM.
Alexander M. Provine & Mary Bradley, Dec. 17, 1831.
Samuel Stone, BM.
Robert Reed & Elizabeth Casselman, Dec. 31, 1831, by
Obadiah Freeman, Jan. 4, 1832. G. H. Hancock, BM.
Edwin A. Robinson & Sarah Ann Robinson, Oct. 1, 1831, by
Samuel R. Davison, M.G., Carter Irby, BM.
Henry Rotranel & Eliza Maddox, April 5, 1831. William
Winford, BM.
Daniel L. Rutledge & Malinda Johnson, Aug. 27, 1831, by
Jacob Ellinger, Sep. 1, 1831.
John W. Sanders & Selah Roach, May 17, 1831, by John
Beard, MG, June 21, 1831. John Sanders, BM.
George Simpson & Mary Sims, April 9, 1831. Benjamin
Philip, BM.

Dudley B. Sims & Elizabeth Lackey, May 7, 1831. Thomas
L. Gunn, BM.
Champ Smith & Martha W. Sullars, July 25, 1831, by
Williamson Williams, J.P., July 26, 1831. Samuel
Donnell, BM.
Grief A. Sneed & Mary Trout, Sep. 14, 1831, by Geo.
Donnell, M.G. Sep. 15, 1831. David Watkins, BM.
John P. Spain & Sally Bond, Dec. 10, 1831 by Jacob
Milton, V.D.M., Dec. 14, 1831. David Bone, BM.
Joseph Stewart & Mary Christopher, Nov. 5, 1831, by Wm.
M. Swain, J.P., Nov. 6, 1831. Jesse Christopher, BM.
William Stewart & Meniza Smith, Dec. 17, 1831, by Thos.
Somers, J.P., Calvin Bennett, BM.
Joseph Swindle & Polly Jones, Nov. 19, 1831, by Benj. S.
Mabry, M.G., Nov. 22, 1831. Joshua Pemberton, BM.
Laurince Tally & Jane Williams, April 29, 1831, by H. W.
Pickett, V.M.G., May 3, 1831. James Thompson, BM.
William Tanner & Jane McCown, Feb. 6, 1831. Jas. Powell,
BM.
Benjamin Tarver & Susan Robinson, Nov. 24, 1831, by E. P.
Horn J.P., S. E. Morris, BM.
James Taylor & Mary Dearing, July 16, 1831. Andrew Clark,
BM.
Julius Thomason & Elizabeth Donaldson, Oct. 12, 1831.
Samuel Walker, BM.
John N. Thompson & Esther Patterson, Oct. 10, 1831, by
Jesse Alexander, V.D.M., Oct. 20, 1831. Joseph Williams,
BM.
William Trolender & Elizabeth Bond, June 9, 1831, by John
F. Doak, J.P., Wm. J. Alexander, BM.
Thomas Turner & Penelope Cartwright, April 19, 1831, by
Wilson Hearn, April 28, 1831. Richard H. Johnson, BM.
Joel Underwood & Rebecca Pettaway, Sep. 24, 1831. Richard
Carr, BM.
James H. Vaden & Elizabeth Jackson, Dec. 1, 1831, by B.
T. Motley, J.P., Dec. 20, 1831. Howell Rucks.
Allen W. Vick & Martha R. Winter, Dec. 21, 1831, by Benj.
S. Mabry, M.G., J. J. Findley, BM.
William D. Vivrett & Nancy Hickman, Jan. 13, 1831, by
Obadiah Freeman, Henry Vivrett, BM.
Lytle Walker & Elizabeth Thompson, Nov. 12, 1831, by
Ezekiel Cloyd, M.G., Nov. 16, 1831. Samuel Walker, BM.
John M. Watson & Lockey S. Brown, March 31, 1831, by
German Baker, M.G., April 5, 1831.
Francis S. Anderson & Peggy Robinson, Dec. 21, 1831.
Joel West, BM.
William White & Hannah S. White, Aug. 17, 1831. George
White, BM.
William Willard & Lovey Duggan, Oct. 3, 1831. Larkin
Keeton, BM.
Argus Williams & Lydia Warren, April 16, 1831, by
Williamson Williams, J.P., April 17, 1831. Henry
Rogers, BM.
James Williams & Lucinda Campbell, July 18, 1831, by H.
W. Puckett, V.M.G., July 21, 1831. James Armstrong, BM.

WILSON COUNTY MARRIAGES

William Williams & Martha Hughs, Dec. 6, 1831, by B. H.
Billy, J.P., Dec. 8, 1831. Francis Anderson, BM.
James M. Willis & Syntha M. Mcfarland, Oct. 3, 1831.
William Petner, BM.
John Wilson & Charlotte Mathews, Dec. 2, 1831. R. W.
Baskins, BM.
Rolls P. Wilson & Priscilla C. Young, Nov. 16, 1831, by
John Parker, J.P., Nov. 17, 1831. Marcus W. Cage, BM.
John C. Wood & Sarah W. Drennon, Sep. 19, 1831, by
Francis Johnson, M.G., Sep. 21, 1831. William Rea, BM.
William Youngblood & Mariah Wilkerson, March 31, 1831,
by T. Kirkpatrick, J.P., March 31, 1831. Reuben
Johnson, BM.
Alexander Allison & Madaline S. Allcorn, June 5, 1832,
by George Donnell, Wm. Martin, BM.
Meede P. Anderson & Martha Bass, Feb. 4, 1832, by B.
Bridges, J.P., Feb. 6, 1832. W. P. McClain, BM.
Green Arnold & Eleanor Gossett, Dec. 10, 1832, by J. L.
Moore, J.P., Dec. 11, 1832. Richard Arnold, BM.
William Arnold & Sindi Franklin, Dec. 4, 1832, by E.
Stephens, J.P., Dec. 5, 1832. Isham Franklin, BM.
Alford Askew & Urania Lane, Feb. 14, 1832. Andrew
Ashew, BM.
Warren Bass & Mary Barbee, Dec. 27, 1832, by Levi A.
Durham, M.G., ___. 17, 1833. John Bass, BM.
William Bass & Nancy Phillips, Oct. 30, 1832. Benjamin
Phillips, BM.
John Bates & Polly Hill, April 2, 1832, by B. Bridges,
J.P., April 6, 1832. William S. Hill, BM.
Alfred Bass & Lucinda Mitchell, March 6, 1832. John
Gray, BM.
Alex Bass (a free man of Color) & Eleanor Scott (a free
woman of Color), June 7, 1832, by G. H. Bussard, J.P.,
Izecier Scott, BM.
Andrew Bogle & Sally Gibson, Sep. 18, 1832. Adam Tuttle,
BM.
James Bogle & Jane Milligan, Dec. 18, 1832, by John McMinn,
J.P., Dec. 20, 1832. William Milligan, BM.
Joseph Bogle & Sarah Harris, Feb. 10, 1832. William
Matthews, BM.
William R. Bogle & Julia Jones, May 26, 1832. Elin
Witherspoon, BM.
James B. Belcher & Katherine George, Dec. 3, 1832. Zedie
Mullin, BM.
John R. Belcher & Amerilla Swinney, Jan. 25, 1832, by
B. S. Mabry, Robt. M. Ellis, BM.
John Belt & Mary Bonfield, June 2, 1832, by Williamson
Williams, J.P., June 3, 1832. Thos. Campbell, BM.
Reason Belt & Elizabeth Williams, Nov. 24, 1832. John
Thompson, BM.
William Belt & Metilda Campbell, Dec. 3, 1832, by Thomas
Smith, M.G., Benjamin Belt, BM.
Burrell Bender & Elizabeth Smith, Aug. 10, 1832, by J. H.
Davis, J.P., Aug. 17, 1832. Turner Vaughn.

David N. Berry & Martha C. SMith, March 20, 1832, by P.
Y. Davis, M.G., March 27, 1832. H. S. Barry, BM.
ALfred Bloodworth & Lucinda Bloodworth, March 26, 1832.
C. Vinsor BM.
William Brannon & Susan Ring, July 25, 1832, by Thos. P.
Holman, J.P., John Kindreee, BM.
James Bright & Betsey Comer, July 5, 1832. William
Paty, BM.
William Brinkley & Lucy Ann Jones, March 18, 1832. Martin
Whitten, BM.
David H. Brittain & Utilda Porterfield, Aug. 29, 1832.
E. T. Loggins, BM.
John A. Brogan & Elizabeth Moore, May 4, 1832. E. W.
Cartwright, BM.
Bernard Brown & Martha Hoskins, Aug. 4, 1821 (?), by
Joshua Lester V.D.M., Aug. 25, 1821 (?).
Daniel Brown & Elizabeth Vivrette, Jan. 8, 1832. John B.
Vivrette, BM.
Edward Brown & Sarah Ann Roberts, July 24, 1832. Henry
Ligon, BM.
Clifton Browning & Jane Williamson, Dec. 10, 1832. Jno.
A. Williamson, BM.
Joseph Beadle & Patience Ann Wommack, Sep. 4, 1832.
Benjamin Phillips, BM.
Hugh Burton & Elizabeth Chandler, Feb. 10, 1832, by
Frances Jarratt, M.G., William D. Tarver, BM.
Fletcher Campbell & Alizabeth R. Gray, Dec. 11, 1832.
Joseph C. Johnson, BM.
William Caplinger & Harriet Nelson, Nov. 14, 1832, by
William Algood, M.G., Dec. 20, 1832. Christopher
Corley, BM.
John Carney & Mary Vess, Aug. 8, 1832. Sam Henderson, BM.
Sam'l. C. Carruth & Mary C. Lane, Dec. 3, 1832. John
Barnfield, BM.
Redman Carter & Mary Welch, July 4, 1832, by James Drennon,
J.P., July 5, 1832. Isaac Peake, BM.
Joseph Chandler & Vashtie Chandler, Jan. 7, 1832.
Christopher Lane, BM.
Jesse Christopher & Susan Shoemaker, July 31, 1831, by
Joshua Woollen, M.G., Aug. 9, 1832.
Thomas Climer & Sally Kemp, Dec. 18, 1832, by John Shane,
J.P., Dec. 20, 1832. James S. Swain, BM.
Robert Coggins & Priscilla Merritt, Dec. 24, 1832, by
J. Melton, Dec. 26, 1832.
Allen Compton & Mary Bettis, Jan. 6, 1832, by Henry
Hobson, J.P., Jan. 13, 1832. Allison Sypert, BM.
Vincent Compton & Mary Scurlock, Dec. 30, 1832, by Henry
Hobson, J.P., Thos. Sypert, BM.
Thomas Cook & Delila Belt, Dec. 11, 1832, by Thomas
Smith, M.G., Thomas Campbell, BM.
Edmund Corley & Clankey Beasley, Dec. 18, 1832. John
Ward, BM.
John Cason & Elmira Miles, Dec. 19, 1832. C. W. Cummings,
BM.

WILSON COUNTY MARRIAGES

George Courtney & Nancy Atwood, Dec. 4, 1832. William
Spring, BM.
Mathew Criswell & Jane Gray, Dec. 1, 1832. William Gray,
BM.
James P. Cropper & Malinda Bass, June 11, 1832. J. G.
Green, BM.
Tho. H. Cropper & Elizabeth Dellis, March 19, 1832, by
B. T. Mottley, J.P., March 20, 1832, Michael Jones, BM.
Arthur Cummings & Mary McFarland, Oct. 9, 1832. James
M. Willis, BM.
William Curd & Susan Davis, Nov. 21, 1832, by Ezekiel
Cloyd, M.G., Nov. 22, 1832. John Curd, BM.
Eli Davis & Mary Allen, July 3, 1832. Jonathan L. Fare,
BM.
Morgan Dellis & Elizabeth Allen, Jan. 14, 1832, by B. S.
Motley, M.G., Jefferson Bell, BM.
James H. Denton & Nancy Hillsman, May 10, 1832, by Silas
Tarver, J.P., Alexander W. Winter, BM.
James Dillon & Katharine Word July 30, 1832, by Joshua
Lester, V.D.M., Elisha G. Cain, BM.
James P. Donnell & Julet Waters, Aug. 22, 1832, by Levi
R. Morrison, V.D.M., Aug. 23, 1832. Calvin Donnell, BM.
William S. McDonald & Unice Baird, March 27, 1832. John
Baird, BM.
James C. Drake & Jane Ozment, Dec. 6, 1832, by Levi
Holloway, J.P., James Hancock, BM.
William H. Drennon & _____, May 3, 1832. Albert Jones,
BM.
Joel Echols & Nancy Compton, Dec. 27, 1832, by H. Hobson,
J.P., Allison Sypert, BM.
Samuel C. Edgar & Amanda Tollison, Aug. 24, 1832, by
Ennis Douglas, Aug. 26, 1832. E. P. Lowe, BM.
Eaton Edwards & Merrim Bennett, May 2, 1832. Stokes
Edwards, BM.
James Edwards & Levy Henry, March 3, 1832. J. H. Brittain,
BM.
Stokes Edwards & Sarah Lane, Jan. 9, 1832. Eaton Edward,
BM.
Alfred Eskew & Urania Lane, Feb. 14, 1832, by Wm. M.
Swain, J.P.
Jesse L. Finley & Amenda Yerger, Oct. 3, 1832, by A. F.
Drizkill, Richard H. Johnson, BM.
James P. Florida & Mary Upchurch, May 8, 1832. Samuel
Allison, BM.
Anthony Gaines & Nancy Stewart, April 17, 1832, by John
S. Shaw, J.P., Oct. 27, 1832. Henry Stewart, BM.
Ansel Goodman & Polly Walton, Dec. 22, 1832, by Thos. P.
Holland, Dec. 27, 1832. Price Lambert, BM.
Thos. B. Green & Betsy Robertson, Aug. 15, 1832, by W.
R. D. Phipps, J.P., Aug. 16, 1832. Thos. Burke, BM.
Hansel Gregory & Elizabeth Moore, Dec. 27, 1832, by
Elisha Vaughn, Warren M. Mays, BM.
James Griffin & Delphia Howell, Feb. 15, 1832. Robert
Young, BM.

Mathew Hammons (a free man of Color) & Polly Scott (a free woman of Color), June 11, 1832, by John Shane, J.P. Anthony Gains, BM.

John Hanks & Jane McBride, Dec. 27, 1832, by Jas. C. Wilford, J.P. A. C. Leech, BM.

John Hanks & Elizabeth Hankins, July 19, 1832, by B. S. Mabry, July 20, 1832. Edward T. Seay, BM.

John Harris & Laury Adams, Dec. 8, 1832, by William Allgood, Dec. 9, 1832. Samuel Stone, BM.

Thomas J. Harris & Coaley Arnold, Jan. 3, 1832. William Martin, BM.

William F. Harris & Margaret B. McNeely, June 6, 1832, by George Donnell, M.G., Samuel N. Provine, BM.

Sam'l. C. Harrison & Mary C. Powell, Jan. 22, 1832, by B. T. Mabry, Jan. 24, 1832. B. T. Motley, BM.

Sampson Harpole & Julia Gerguson, April 18, 1832, by Benj. Billups, John S. Robb, BM.

Alfred Huguley & Nancy Jenkins, July 31, 1832, by J. F. Graves, J.P., William Young, BM.

John Hughs & Polly Morgan, July 11, 1832. Uriah Morgan, BM.

Henry A. Hughuley & Elsa Ann Young, Dec. 10, 1832. John W. Huguley, BM.

Thomas G. Hughs & Elizabeth Bell, Jan. 27, 1832, by Ennis Douglass, Feb. 8, 1832. Joseph G. Bell, BM.

Henry Humphrey & Elizabeth Hagar, Nov. 20, 1832. John Green, BM.

Edward G. Jacob & Rutley Williams, May 7, 1832. John Belt, BM.

Charles Jarrell & Susan Russell, Jan. 12, 1832. John H. Johnes, BM.

Anderson Jennings & Verinda Hancock, April 27, 1832, by Obadiah Freeman, May 1, 1832.

Albert Jones & Benitha Donnell, Aug. 22, 1832, by Joshua Lester, V.D.M., Josiah Jones.

Edd Jones & Minerva Knight, March 24, 1832, by Williamson Williams, J.P., March 25, 1832. Hiram Pursell, BM.

Isaiah Jones & Susan Webb, Dec. 18, 1833, by J. Lester, V.D.M., Harrison Word, BM.

John Kelly & Lavinia Campbell, Jan. 26, 1833, by Simpson Sheptine, Jan. 27, 1833.

John Kirkpatrick & Caroline Gleaves, Dec. 10, 1832. James Wells, BM.

James H. Lampkin & Sally Dudly, Aug. 15, 1832, by Benjamin Billings, J.P., William Dudly, BM.

William Lavender & Elvira Moore, Feb. 29, 1832, by Thos. P. Holman, J.P., March 1, 1832. Thos. Travilion, BM.

William Lawrence & Faitha Ann Dearing, July 14, 1832. Thomas Kitching, BM.

William A. Leach & Cornelia Logue, Dec. 26, 1832, by Jas. Drennon, J.P., Dec. 28, 1832.

Albert Lea & Jane Rhea, Aug. 5, 1832, by Williamson Williams, J.P., Aug. 15, 1832. A. W. Booth, BM.

Vincent Lester & Elizabeth Duffer, Dec. 10, 1832. Morrison Lester, BM.

WILSON COUNTY MARRIAGES

William P. McClain & Sarah H. Shepherd, Nov. 21, 1832.
William Walker, BM.
Joseph McDearman & Sally Lewis, May 24, 1832, by G. A.
Huddleston, J.P., May 26, 1832. Edward Denton, BM.
Ira McFarland & Mahala Chandler, March 2, 1832. Samuel
N. Ross, BM.
James B. McMineway & Nancy E. Calhoun, April 10, 1832,
by George Donnell, M.G., April 11, 1832. Wm. W.
Searcy, BM.
G. W. McPeak & Elizabeth Sanders, March 15, 1832. John
Manneere, BM.
John Neily & Jane Clerk, Aug. 24, 1832. Henry Clerk, BM.
Nelson N. New & Matilda Foster, Oct. 26, 1832, by Wilson
Hearn, M.G., Nov. 28, 1832. Thos. Turner, BM.
George Nickings (a free man of Color) & Elizabeth Archer
(a free woman of Color), April 17, 1832, by Walter
Carruth, J.P., John Nickins, BM.
Woodford Organ & Jane Weir, Aug. 8, 1832, by Benj.
Billings, J.P., George Sanders, BM.
Francis Palmer & Martha Scoby, Dec. 3, 1832. James
Hankins, BM.
Albert Parish & Sarah Turner, Oct. 24, 1832, by Tho. Babb,
J.P., William Smith, BM.
Zachariah P. Peak & Evaline Dukes, May 9, 1832, by Wm.
Whitten, M.G., Isaac Peak, BM.
Joshua Pemberton & Harriet A. Cason, Jan. 14, 1832, by
B. T. Mabry, Jan. 18, 1832. Norman Walsh, BM.
William Pemberton & Jane Pemberton, Nov. 19, 1832.
William Pemberton, BM.
James H. Peyton & Nancy McFarland, Dec. 12, 1832. John
W. Peyton, BM.
Cornelius Philips & Mary Robertson, April 24, 1832.
Samuel Herrell, BM.
Zachariah Phillips & Polly Poland, Aug. 21, 1832. S. W.
Pennebaker, BM.
Charles Porterfield & Maria Buckley, March 15, 1832.
James Porterfield, BM.
Samuel Porterfield & Jane W. Patterson, Nov. 17, 1832,
by Jesse Alexander, V.D.M.
Samuel N. Provine & Emily B. Bowers, Aug. 28, 1832.
Samuel Stone, BM.
Joshua Prewett & Isabella O'Neal, Aug. 6, 1832, by John
Kelly, E.M.E.C., Aug. 7, 1832. H. Arrington, BM.
Samuel Puffer (Duffer) & Lucinda Caldwell, Oct. 13, 1832.
William Smith, BM.
John J. Pugh & Mary George, Feb. 1, 1832. George R.
Pugh, BM.
David Puryear & Nancy Young, March 7, 1832, by E. Douglas,
J.P., March 13, 1832. William W. Patton, BM.
Silas M. Rgasdale & Nancy Rice, Nov. 6, 1832, by Wm.
Swain, J.P., Nov. 11, 1832. S. W. Chandler, BM.
Addison Reese & Susan Palmer, Feb. 16, 1832. William
Turner, BM.
John Reese & Elizabeth Harlin, Sep. 28, 1832, by John
Borum, Oct. 2, 1832. Francis Palmer, BM.

Frederick L. Rhodes & Delpha Pentycost, Feb. 1, 1832.
James T. Penny, BM.

Anderson C. Rice & Elizabeth Hester, Feb. 18, 1832, by
James B. Bridges, Feb. 19, 1832. Robert Creswell, BM.

James P. Rice & Kasandany Hearn, May 5, 1832. Richard
Ozment, BM.

Thomas Riley & Jane Sinclair, Dec. 10, 1832, by James
Drennon, J.P. Dec. 11, 1832. Eli Sinclair, BM.

James Risen & Mary Ann Sypert, Dec. 4, 1832, by Jas. C.
Williford, J.P., Dec. 8, 1832. George W. Anderson, BM.

Stephen Robinson & Charlotte Hays, Oct. 26, 1832, by L.
Moore, J.P., L. Moore, BM.

Henry Rogers & Nancy Morris, March 29, 1832, W. D.
Phillips, J.P., Brinkley Rogers, BM.

John Rutledge & Lurana George, July 26, 1832. Calvin F.
Tarver, BM.

James H. Shanon & Isabella Braden, Dec. 18, 1832, by
Jno. F. Doak, J.P., Dec. 19, 1832. James Foster, BM.

Anderson Simpson & Eliza Hill, Dec. 22, 1832. William
S. Searcy, BM.

Eli Sinclair & Catharine Jones, Nov. 3, 1832, by James
Drennon, J.P., Nov. 4, 1832. Isaac N. Curry, BM.

Isaac Smith & Sarah Neal, Jan. 31, 1832, by Wm. Laurence,
J.P., Feb. 25, 1832. William Waters, BM.

George Smith & Elizabeth Dawson, Jan. 21, 1832, by
Williamson Williams, J.P., John Swain, BM.

Morgan Smith & Nancy Duvault, Dec. 7, 1832, by R. Gwyn,
J.P., Dec. 9, 1832. Hiram Dobson, BM.

Thompson C. Smith & Mary Smith, March 10, 1832. L. C.
Shankin, BM.

George L. Snell & Harriet Bettis, May 23, 1832, by Benj.
S. Mabry, M.G., May 25, 1832. William A. Wherry, BM.

Thomas Standley & Merrissa Milligan, Nov. 28, 1832, by
John McMinn J.P., Dec. __, 1832. Wm. W. Milligan, BM.

James Stephens & Frances Maddox, Dec. 27, 1832, by
Thomas Smith, M.G., Joshua Hall, BM.

Ira E. Stewart & Elizabeth Brown, Sep. 8, 1832, by
James Drennon, J.P., Sep. 9, 1832. Jesse Smith, BM.

James M. Studer & Sarah McDearman, Feb. 29, 1832. James
McDearman, BM.

Caleb W. Swain & Martha Climer, March 4, 1832. Silas M.
Ragsdale, BM.

James Swan & Susan Lands, Sep. 29, 1832, by Stephen
McDonald, Oct. 2, 1832. John W. Donnell, BM.

Clevers W. Swift & Martha D. McClain, Nov. 2, 1832.
Henry F. Johnson, BM.

John Swindle & Fanny Edwards, Feb. 7, 1832, by B. T.
Motley, J.P., Feb. 8, 1832. Gilliam Talley, BM.

Ephraim Tally & Wineford Stone, Feb. 11, 1832, by H.
Billings, J.P., Feb. 15, 1832. Norman Walsh, BM.

Isiah P. Taylor & Rebecca Williams, Jan. 31, 1832, by
Wm. Willis, J.P., Feb. 2, 1832. James Foster, BM.

Milton Taylor & Nancy Gray, Dec. 20, 1832, by Micajah
Estes, M.G., Joseph Freeman, BM.

WILSON COUNTY MARRIAGES

Nathaniel Thaxton & Elizabeth M. Fletcher, Aug. 1, 1832.
Jos. Ligon, BM.
Thomas Tiller & Mijorie Tipton, May 5, 1832. William
Eagan, BM.
Jefferson Todd & Elizabeth Sweat, Jan. 14, 1832.
William Sweat, BM.
Ambrose Tumblin & Betsey Kelly, Nov. 24, 1832, by J.
Kirkpatrick, J.P., Nov. 25, 1832. David Kirkpatrick,
BM.
William Turner & Judy S. Cheek, May 24, 1832, by Wilson
Hearn, M.G., June 7, 1832. Henry Turner, BM.
Abram Vaughn & Margaret S. Gold, April 30, 1832, by Thos.
Joplin, J.P., Pleasant Gold, BM.
Hardy C. Vinson & Eliza S. Stewart, Jan. 2, 1832. William
Gray, BM.
William B. Vivrett & Elizabeth C. Thompson, July 14, 1832,
by John Shaw, J.P., Oct. 21, 1832. Jonathan Atherly,
BM.
John Vowell & Harriet Duke, March 28, 1832, by James
Foster, J.P., April 4, 1832. Anthony Campbell, BM.
Nimrod Williams & Nancy Beadles, Nov. 24, 1832, by J.
Lester, V.D.M., Ira M. Johnson, BM.
James Williams & Jane Walden, Jan. 10, 1832, by F. A.
Jarratt, M.G., Patrick Youree, BM.
William Williams & Naomi Maxwell, Jan. 7, 1832, by S.
Hearn, M.G., Jan. 12, 1832. E. G. Campbell, BM.
Samuel Williams & Martha Williams, Dec. 22, 1832, by
A. F. Doak, J.P.
Stephen Wilson & Elizabeth Harrison, Sep. 18, 1832.
Adam Little, BM.
William Wilson & Polly Neighours, Dec. 22, 1832. Obadiah
Rich, BM.
John Winters & Melissa Anderson, Dec. 25, 1832, by John
Shane, J.P., Dec. 26, 1832. Washington Blackburn, BM.
Luke Wood & Polly Thornton, Oct. 20, 1832. Ephraim
Haralson, BM.
Allison Woollard & Sally Jones, Dec. 26, 1832. John W.
Wynne, BM.
William Wright & Emily Abanatha (Abanatay), June 9, 1832,
by Wilson Hearn, M.G., Robt. Stanfield, BM.
John Alexander & Sarah O'Neal, Nov. 29, 1833, by Jesse
Alexander, V.D.M., Dec. 5, 1833.
Isaac Alexander & Nancy Parsons, June 20, 1814 (?).
George Michie, BM.
William W. Andrews & Emily E. Summerhill, Aug. 24, 1833,
by Jacob S. Hearn, M.G., Aug. 26, 1833.
Eli Allen & Elizabeth Lasater, Feb. 25, 1814 (?).
Thomas Sypert, BM.
Levi Baird & Dicy Fox, Sep. 6, 1833, by G. A. Huddleston,
J.P.
Joseph Barbee & Hesther Taylor, March 21, 1833, by Wilson
Hearn, March 25, 1833.
Stephen Bateman & Malinda Knight, Dec. 26, 1833, by
Joshua Woollen, M.G., Cullen Sanders, BM.

Cader Bass & Lucy York, Aug. 22, 1833. Moses Odum, BM.

George W. Baster & Rebecca Ann Hooker, July 15, 1833. Wm. Donoho, BM.

Thomas Bay & Polly Eddings, Jan. 2, 1833. Robert Davis, BM.

William Buyford & Louisa Franklin, June 18, 1833, by Geo. S. Hooper, J.P., June 20, 1833.

James M. Bentley & Nancy Rutledge, Sep. 26, 1833. James R. Youree, BM.

Zebulon Blackburn & Polly Smith, Jan. 29, 1833, by S. Graves, J.P.

David Bloodworth & Matilda Tucker, Dec. 28, 1833, by Silas Tarver, J.P., Dec. 29, 1833.

William R. Bone & Elizabeth Phelps, Oct. 3, 1833, by R. P. Donnell, J.P.

William Borum & Eliza White, Feb. 16, 1833, by F. S. Harris, J.P., Feb. 21, 1833.

Daniel Bryson & Martha Reed Oct. 28, 1833, by John McMinn, J.P., Nov. 6, 1833.

Hiram Bryson & Jemima A. Alexander, Aug. 31, 1833, by John McMinn, J.P., Aug. __, 1833.

Robert Bryson & Sarah Stanley, Aug. 9, 1833, by John McMinn, J.P., Aug. 15, 1833.

Samuel Caplinger & Martha Carter, March 20, 1833, by A. J. McDonell, J.P., March 21, 1833.

Eli S. Carruth & Elizabeth Hunter, Sep. 25, 1833, by Stephen McDonald, J.P.

Edward W. Cartwright & Dicy H. Crutchfield, Feb. 19, 1833, by E. J. Allen, M.G., Feb. 27, 1833.

Walter Caruth & Sarah Prier, May 17, 1833, by F. Carter, J.P., May 27, 1833.

John R. Cawthorn & Ruth Alford, Nov. 18, 1833, by B. Graves, J.P.

John B. Scobey & Sarah Sweat, April 1, 1833, by F. G. Harris, J.P., April 10, 1833.

David Chandler & Nancy E. Pride, May 7, 1833, by R. S. Tate, M.G.

Albert G. Cherry & Eliza W. Bradley, Sep. 12, 1833.

John Clark & Sally Alsup, June 23, 1812 (?).

Charles Clay & Rebecca Douglass, July 3, 1833, by H. Hobson, J.P., James Rochelle, BM.

Edwin Clemmons & Sally Teague, Dec. 8, 1813 (?), James Clemmons, BM.

William Clemmons & Rachael Truett, Dec. 26, 1833. John Fields, BM.

Jesse Cloey & Elizabeth Aust, Jan. 9, 1833, by Henry Hobson, J.P., Jan. 10, 1833.

William A. Clopton & Elizabeth Medlin, Oct. 21, 1833, by Joshua Lester, V.D.M.

Washington Congill & Vilet Hager, Oct. 22, 1833, by John Beard, M.G., Oct. 23, 1833.

William Conger & Aggey Arrington, March 3, 1814 (?). Philip Bryan, BM.

John Cook & Martha Huddleston, Aug. 9, 1833, by Geo. S. Hooper, J.P.

Mathew Criswell & Jane Gray, Dec. 1, 1832, by Elisha
Vaughn.
Aaron B. Curd & Nancy Wooldrid, Jan. 7, 1815 (?).
Anderson Davis & Narciss Campbell, Feb. 2, 1860 (?).
J. S. Womack, BM.
Richard Davis & Lucy Lantern, May 11, 1833, by R. Gwyn,
J.P., May 12, 1833.
William Davis & Harriet Walker, July 5, 1833, by H.
Hobson, J.P., July 9, 1833. B. B. Sypert, BM.
David Demery & Sally Murry, June 23, 1814 (?). Mark
Murry, BM.
Bradford Dickens & Nancy Jarrell, Aug. 31, 1833, by E. P.
Horn, J.P., Sep. 5, 1833.
John B. Dill & Mary Jarrell, Aug. 25, 1833, by Thos. P.
Holman, J.P.
Henry Dillard & Rebecca Meholland, June 17, 1833. Joseph
Nasworthy, BM.
William Dillon & Dovey Jarman, Nov. 11, 1833, by J. Lester,
V.D.M.
Calvin Donnell & Milly Hancock, Oct. 19, 1833, by Levi
P. Morrison, Oct. 26, 1833.
Thomas B. Donnell & Isabella Jones, March 30, 1833, by
L. Moore, J.P., April 4, 1833.
John Drennon & Rebeccah A. Brown, July 31, 1830. William
Rice, BM.
Addison Duncan & Margaret Caruth, Dec. 9, 1833, by F. N.
Jarvett, M.G., Dec. 10, 1833.
John F. Dunn & Nancy W. Lester, April 17, 1833, by J.
Lester, V.D.M.
William W. Eagan & Melinda Tipton, Aug. 5, 1833, by J. H.
Davis, J.P., Aug. 8, 1833.
William Eagan & Mary B. Cooper, May 25, 1833, by Thos.
Burge, M.G.
William B. Elgin & Elizabeth Ann Morris, Nov. 1, 1833.
John Smith, BM.
Thomas W. Ellis & Martha Cook, May 21, 1833, by Thomas
Babb, J.P., O. M. Rice, BM.
William Fairstair & Nancy Wade, Sep. 22, 1833, by G. H.
Bussard, J.P.
William Foster & Elizabeth Turner, June 8, 1833. James
Braden, BM.
John Floyd & Sally Hunt, Dec. 10, 1833, by Wm. Lawrence,
J.P., Dec. 13, 1833.
Andrew Francis & Katherine Searcy, Sep. 3, 1833, by
Wilson Hearn, Sep. 4, 1833.
Joseph Freeman & Maria Dew, Nov. 30, 1833, by Geo. Donnell,
M.G., Dec. 1, 1833.
Isham Freeman & Rebeccah McElyea, Feb. 14, 1814 (?).
John McElyea, BM.
Henry M. Gibbs & Nancy Midget, Oct. 11, 1833, by J. B.
Taylor, J.P., Nov. 11, 1833.
James Gibson & Patience Puckett, May 9, 1814 (?),
Charles Puckett, BM.
Samuel Gilmore & Dolley Dwyer, Dec. 16, 1830. Wm. Miller,
BM.

John W. Golladay & Polly Bell, Aug. 10, 1833, by W. T.
   Waters, J.P., Aug. 14, 1833.
Francis M. Graves & Angelina Harris, Oct. 18, 1833, by
   R. P. Donnell, J.P.
Francis Graham & Charlotte Sims, July 17, 1833, Samuel
   Irwin, BM.
John G. Green & Trecy Bass, Jan. 22, 1833, Allen Donnell,
   BM.
William Grisham & Mary D. Smith, Jan. 22, 1833, by
   Joshya Lester, V.D.M.
Francis M. Grimes & Sallie Orren, Feb. 4, 1861 (?). J.
   B. Coleman, BM.
Thomas Guess & Rebecca Wammack, June 4, 1833, by John
   Bone, J.P., John Stacey, BM.
Hollis Hager & Polly Lane, Oct. 9, 1830. Hollis Wright,
   BM.
Thomas R. Hamilton & Manerva Brown, Jan. 3, 1833, by
   James Davis, J.P.
Grief B. Hawkins & Dorcas Neel, Nov. 1, 1833, by J. B.
   Taylor, J.P.
John Hankins & Katharine Edwards, July 23, 1833, by J. B.
   Taylor, J.P.
Jacob Harpole & Rebecca Devine, Feb. 2, 1833, by B. T.
   Motley, J.P., Feb. 15, 1833.
Richard Harrison & Polly Panter, May 8, 1833, by L. Moore,
   J.P., May 13, 1833.
Frederick Herron & Martha Dosier, Sep. 16, 1833, by F. S.
   Harris, J.P., Sep. 18, 1833.
John S. Height & Caoline Herd, Feb. 21, 1831. Thomas
   Harris, BM.
Israel M. Hill & Margaret Almon, Oct. 22, 1833, by
   George S. Hooper, J.P.
Samuel Hill & Mary Simpson, Sep. 24, 1833, by J. Lester,
   V.D.M.
John Hollaway & Mary Caraway, June 21, 1833.
Richard Holloway & Unice M. Shannon, July 9, 1833. John
   Hickman, BM.
George W. Howdystill & Rebecca Tipton, Sep. 10, 1833, by
   R. S. Tate, M.G.
Peter Hubbard & Martha Brigs, Feb. 7, 1833, by Silas
   Tarver, J.P.
John S. Hudson & Emeline Ozburn, June 26, 1833, by Wm.
   M. Swain, J.P., July 11, 1836 (?). John Edwards, BM.
Richard Hudson & Polly Smith, Sep. 17, 1813 (?). Jno.
   Queensberry, BM.
Simpson Hughs & Elizabeth Harpole, April 27, 1833, by
   B. T. Motley, J.P., April 28, 1833.
John W. Hulm & Charlotte E. Wright, Dec. 21, 1833, by
   Joseph B. Wynne.
Jacob Hunter & Sarah Furguson, Aug. 16, 1830. William
   Williams, BM.
Shadrack Jarman & Margaret Hardy, March 11, 1833.
Wesley Jarroll & Matilda Smith, Nov. 13, 1833, by E. P.
   Hern, J.P.

Robert Johns & Katharine Penticost, Sep. 3, 1833, by
Obadiah Freeman
Henry F. Johnson & May Hill, Feb. 3, 1833, by Henry
Hobson, J.P., Feb. 4, 1833.
Isaac Johnson & Winneby Jones, Oct. 10, 1833, by B. Graves,
J.P.
John Johnson & Elizabeth Bartlett, June 17, 1833. John
Organ, BM.
Jesse Jones & Mary Winston, Sep. 28, 1833. Isaac Winston,
BM.
Isham Jones & Susannah Lea, Dec. 4, 1833, by Jos. F. D.,
J.P., Dec. 9, 1833.
Thomas Jones & Hannah Peace, Nov. 2, 1833, by John Seay,
Nov. 4, 1833.
Allen G. Joplin & Susannah Bennett, Jan. 30, 1833, by
Wilson Hearn, M.G., Jan. 31, 1833.
William Kennedy & Drusella Hobson, Feb. 21, 1833. Edmund
Crutcher, BM
Braxton M. Key & Jane Ann Wilson, Oct. 1, 1833, by B. W.
Smith, J.P., Oct. 3, 1833.
Thomas Kirkpatrick & Susannah B. Curry, Jan. 31, 1833.
Elijah Cross, BM.
Squilla Knight & Anna Redding, Jan. 14, 1833. Charles
Warren, BM.
Sampson Knight & Elizabeth Ann James, Oct. 19, 1833, by
Geo. Donnell, M.G., Oct. 31, 1833.
Armstead Lain & Louisa Sheppard, Feb. 2, 1833, by B.
Graves, J.P.
William A. Lane & Ann Donalson, Nov. 23, 1813 (?). John
Marshall, BM.
Alexander J. W. Lands & Margaret B. Reed, May 2, 1833, by
Obadiah Freeman.
John Lasiter & Sally Bettis, Oct. 8, 1833. Lawrence
Sypert, BM.
Thomas L. Lasiter & Celia Copeland, Aug. 10, 1833, by
J. B. Lasater, J.P., Aug. 11, 1833.
William F. Ligon & Nancy Medlin, Dec. 23, 1833, by
Micajah Estes, M.G.
Charles Mackey & Evaline C. Fisher, Dec. 20, 1833, by
E. P. Horn, J.P.
Clark D. Manner & Sarah Patterson, July 24, 1830 (?).
Jarrett Cock, BM.
James Martain & Harriett Hagerty, Nov. 10, 1830 (?).
Thos. Sypert, BM.
Henry Mathew & Sally Seats, Dec. 2, 1833, by Josiah
McMinn, J.P., Dec. 3, 1826 (?).
William Mathews & Evilina Higgans, Aug. 17, 1833, by
John McMinn, J.P., Aug. 19, 1833.
John B. McCartney & Huldah Green, Dec. 14, 1833, by Wm.
M. Swain, J.P., Dec. 15, 1833.
Miles McCorkle & K. Ann Meniford, March 20, 1830. Hugh
Roberts, BM.
William A. McLin & Sally McKnight, March 3, 1833.
William McKnight, BM.

Henry Mitchell & Elizabeth Craig, July 27, 1833, by James
Thomas, Aug. 1, 1833.
Dunkin Moore & Dudema George, Nov. 6, 1833, by J. B.
Taylor, J.P.
Isaac Moore & Nancy Dillard, Oct. 17, 1814 (?). John C.
Tippett, BM.
William Moseley & Malinda Brown, May 28, 1833, by J.
Kirkpatrick, J.P., May 28, 1833. Z. David, BM.
Jefferson Motsinger & Elizabeth Pearson, May 14, 1833,
by Stephen McDonald, J.P., May 15, 1833.
Richard Mount & Nancy Edwards, Jan. 2, 1833, by James
Bond, V.D.M., Jan. 5, 1833. Martin Whittain, BM.
William Murray & Alethea Matlock, Oct. 9, 1830 (?). J.
B. White, BM.
Nathan Nelson & Sarah Ragsdale, Aug. 3, 1833, by G. A.
Huddleston, J.P., Aug. 4, 1833.
David Nowlen & Lucy Joplin, Sep. 9, 1833, by Thomas Holman
Sep. 9, 1833.
William C. Odum & Francis Cooper, Sep. 24, 1832. Sam'l.
Garrison, BM.
Edmund Oliver & Easther Paterson, Sep. 24, 1833, by W.
B. Phipps, J.P., Isham Jones, BM.
Madison Organ & Jane Brown, July 4, 1833, by B. S. Mabry,
J.P., July 5, 1833. C. W. Jackson, BM.
Thomas J. Ormand & Martha Crocker, Jan. 21, 1833, by
H. Hobson, J.P.
Jeremiah Oweing & Tealy Gibson, Jan. 20, 1815 (?).
Hooker Reeves.
Alfred Page & Rebecca Campbell, Nov. 6, 1833, by Robt.
Tate, M.G.
John Patterson & Caty Ragsdale, July 14, 1814 (?).
Richard Ragsdale.
William C. Patterson & Elizabeth W. Bland, May 28, 1833,
by W. T. Waters, J.P.
William Petty & Sally Cummings, March 11, 1833. Alvis
Sellars, BM.
Thomas Petway & Susan Evertt, Aug. 1, 1833, by John
Bonner, J.P., Dec. 17, 1833. William Grubbs, BM.
Samuel Perryman & Edy Kennedy, Sep. 7, 1833, by Jacob
Melton, Sep. 8, 1833.
Uriah Perry & Mary Ann Dellas, Nov. 18, 1833, by F. S.
Harris, J.P.
Irvis Porterfield & Mary Brown, Feb. 18, 1833, by John
Bone, J.P., Feb. 21, 1833.
Alexander Posey & Elizabeth Chapman, Jan. 16, 1833, by
J. Hooker, M.G.
Eeddin D. B. Price & Malinda Moser, Feb. 18, 1833, by B.
T. Mottley, J.P., Feb. 19, 1833.
William B. Pursley & Sophia Rutherford, Dec. 9, 1833,
John Seay, BM.
James Quesshenberry & Elizabeth Edwards, Nov. 14, 1814 (?)
Eli Eli Edwards, BM.
John Quesenberry & Patsy Mayor, Aug. 15, 1814 (?). John
Merritt, BM.

WILSON COUNTY MARRIAGES

James Rattern & Jane Chambers, Oct. 24, 1833. Ransom
Stroud, BM.
Eli Reed & Sally Pentecost, Nov. 18, 1833, by Obadiah
Freeman.
Adam Reeder & Polly Grindstaff, Nov. 27, 1833, by Jacob
S. Hearne, M.G., Nov. 28, 1833.
Samuel H. Riggan & Martha Ann Tarver, Feb. 7, 1833, by
Henry Hobson, J.P.
Thomas B. Reese & Polly Barbee, Sep. 30, 1833, by J. B.
Taylor, J.P., Oct. 1, 1833. Adison Askins, BM.
Archibald Rhea & Elizabeth Massey, Nov. 18, 1833.
Lewis Robertson & Martha Denton, Sep. 26, 1833, by Silas
Tarver, J.P.
Jonathan Rogers & Anna Rogers, Feb. 22, 1814 (?).
Jeptha Williams, BM.
David Rotranel & Frances Cole, Nov. 28, 1833, by Silas
Tarver, J.P.
Jesse Shaw & Tericy Rowland, July 13, 1833. Solomon R.
Shaw, BM.
Isaac R. Seaburn & Rachel M. Hayes, Nov. 20, 1833, by
R. S. Tate, M.G.
Daniel Searcy & Jane Pride, April 19, 1833, by E. Cloyd,
M.G.
Robert L. Shaw & Lavinia Dodd, July 6, 1833. Hiram Dodd,
BM.
John Smith & Polly Smith, Aug. 1, 1814. John Smith, Sr.,
BM.
Obaidah Smith & Malinda Booker, Nov. 14, 1833, by Thomas
Smith, M.G., Nov. 15, 1833.
Samuel Smith & Dicy B. White, Dec. 28, 1833, by Elisha
Vaughn, M.G., Jan. 1, 1834.
Sampson Smith & Harriet W. Reynolds, Sep. 10, 1833, by
Joshua Woolen, M.G., Sep. 12, 1833.
William Smith & Elizabeth Dillard, Feb. 22, 1833.
Nathaniel G. Carter, BM.
Jesse H. Sparks & Julia Marrs, Oct. 28, 1833, by Jno.
F. Doak, J.P., Oct. 29, 1835.
William Spears & Jane Cloyd, Jan. 16, 1833, by L. K.
Morrison, V.D.M., Jan. 17, 1833.
Charles Stewart & Nancy Simmons, Dec. 26, 1836, by
Isaac Hunter.
Benjamin H. Stone & Sarah Willis, March 12, 1833, by
John Shane, J.P., March 14, 1833.
James Swann & Elizabeth Fisher, Dec. 30, 1833, by
Solomon Caplinger, J.P., Jan. 2, 1834. William Swann,
BM.
Parker Sullivan & Mary E. Hamilton, Dec. 28, 1833, by
John Beard, M.G., Dec. 31, 1833.
George Tait & Rebecca Tait, Jan. 31, 1814. William
Clampit, BM.
Saxey Tarpley & Mary Hawkins, Oct. 14, 1833, by Thos.
Holman, J.P., Oct. 17, 1833.
Robert Telford & Nancy Chawning, March 11, 1814. Thomas
Telford, BM.

John P. Thomas & Calsey Maria Ensey (Linsey), Jan. 31, 1816. George Goodloe, BM.

Terry Thompson & Mary M. Springs, Aug. 10, 1833, by Solomon Caplinger, J.P., Feb. 26, 1834.

Jeremiah Tucker & Rutha Harris, Feb. 28, 1833, by G. H. Bussard, J.P., Jordan Brown, BM.

Joel W. Wammack & Mary Alexander, Oct. 19, 1833, by Jesse Alexander, V.D.M., Oct. 31, 1833.

Norman Walsh & Sarah Hearn, Jan. 22, 1833, by Wilson Hearn, M.G., Jan. 24, 1833.

Thomas Wherry & Manerva Caroline Smith, Jan. 9, 1833, by E. P. Horn, J.P., Jan. 10, 1833.

William A. Wherry & Narcissa G. Cain, Nov. 27, 1833. John Seay, BM.

Littleberry White & Rebecca Leach, Dec. 27, 1813. Levi Fawks, BM.

Robert R. Whitlock & Frances Beedles, Nov. 2, 1833, by Joshua Lester, V.D.M.

Amos Williams & Sally Leech, Dec. 18, 1810. James Leech, BM.

A. W. D. Williams & Sarah P. Foster, Nov. 6, 1833, by Wm. Bransford, M.G., Nov. 13, 1833.

Alexander G. Winford & Sarah C. Harris, Aug. 11, 1833, by E. J. Allen, M.G., Aug. 14, 1833. Ebenezer Hearn, BM.

William W. Winford & Susan Flowers, April 13, 1833, by Wilson Hearn, April 18, 1833.

Thomas Woods & Betsy Mobias, Sep. 21, 1833, by F. S. Harris, J.P., Oct. 8, 1833.

George W. Woolard & Amanda M. Allen, Aug. 1, 1833, by B. T. Mabry, Aug. 21, 1833.

Hezekiah Wright & Charlotte Hunt, March 14, 1814. Anderson Freeman, BM.

William Wright & Abigail Bird, Feb. 26, 1814. Phillip Bryan, BM.

Allen Azachary & Leviniah Woolen, March 14, 1831. Moses Woolen, BM.

William Adamson & Sarah Hatheway, June 20, 1834, by Wm. Laurence, J.P., June 22, 1834.

James Afflack & Nancy Warren, Jan. 2, 1834, by B. T. Mottley, J.P., George W. Anderson, BM.

Thompson Anderson & Mary S. Johnson, July 31, 1834. Geo. W. Smith, BM.

Thomas C. Anderson & Aseneth McMurry, June 18, 1834. Hugh B. Hill, BM.

George E. Alexander & Margaret W. Tate, March 6, 1834, by John Beard, M.G., March 21, 1834. Richard Tate, BM.

Larkin Allen & Jemima Chapman, Jan. 2, 1834. Isaac J. Dodson, BM.

George B. Baily & Eliza Scott, Nov. 27, ____, by James Foster, J.P., Nov. 27, 1834. Alfred E. Donnell, BM.

Apperson Bandy & Elizabeth Walker, Dec. 22, 1834, by Silas Tarver, Dec. 25, 1834. Answorth Harrison, BM.

Solomon Bass & Mahala Crisp, Feb. 5, 1829, by Thom. B. Bridges, J.P., Feb. 6, 1829.

WILSON COUNTY MARRIAGES

David Belcher & Elizabeth Whitehead, Feb. 12, 1836, by
Robert H. Ellis, M.G., Feb. 14, 1834. Field Tanner, BM.
Bernice Bender & Elizabeth Ann Smith, Feb. 24, 1834, by
Barton Brown, M.G., Feb. 25, 1834. William D. Smith,
BM.
Henry Blurton & Wealthy Williams, Jan. 29, 1834. Paton
Neel, BM.
Green Bond & Elizabeth Williams, Dec. 22, 1834, by
Williamson Williams, M.G., Dec. 23, 1834. Thomas
Williams, BM.
William Bond & Margaret M. Alexander, Dec. 11, 1834,
by John Beard, M.G., Henry Eewards, BM.
William Bonds & Elizabeth Stewart, May 13, 1834, by J.
Hooker, M.G., Cullen Carter, BM.
Thomas E. Bonner & Manerva M. Bonner, Sep. 11, 1834, by
John Seay, M.G., B. A. Latimer, BM.
Albert Bradley & Emily Devault, Jan. 7, 1834. Hamilton
Snead, BM.
Evret Bradley & Anna Bundy, May 17, 1834, by John Borum,
May 20, 1834. James Hankins, BM.
Thomas M. Brinson & Mary Ruff, Nov. 25, 1834, by E. P.
Horn, J.P., A. S. Winford BM.
Mathew Brooks & Margaret Eagan, Feb. 21, 1834, by Thos.
Babb, J.P., Feb. 30, 1834. J. C. Spillens.
Lytle Brown & Jane Conger, Aug. 19, 1936 (?), by Thos.
Babb, J.P., Aug. 20, 1834. Robert Lawrence, BM.
Samuel Brown & Nancy McDombs, Oct. 29, 1834, by John
Beard, M.G., Oct. 30, 1834. Owen Quenly, BM.
Charles Bruce & Sally Hawkins, Jan. 9, 1834, by B. L.
Mabry.
Samuel Briant & Harriet Mitchell, Feb. 12, 1834, by E. P.
Horn, J.P., Joseph C. Johnson, BM.
John Bundy & Nancy Williford, Jan. 21, 1834, by B. T.
Mabry, Jan. 23, 1834. John Obrian, BM.
Stephen L. Bush & Elizabeth Tate, Sep. 8, 1834. James
P. Hays, BM.
James Caldwell & Louisa Ballard, May 19, 1834, by John
Beard, M.G., May 22, 1834. Banister Tally, BM.
Andrew M. Calhoun & Seills Martin, Oct. 25, 1836, by
John Provine, M.G., W. H. Crenshaw, BM.
William Campbell & Polly Rhea, Oct. 28, 1834, by William-
son Williams, M.G., Oct. 30, 1834. G. Williams, BM.
John Carter & Nancy Silliman, Dec. 4, 1834, by Walter
Carruth, J.P., A. E. Donnell, BM.
Solomon Carter & Ann H. Stewart, Oct. 21, 1834, by R.
Gwyn, J.P., John Carter, BM.
Marshall Carter & Priscilla Clifton, Dec. 13, 1834. John
W. Wynne, BM.
Allen Carr & Polly Crocker, Aug. 27, 1834, by T. P. Holman,
J.P.
Richardson Carr & Joanna Dwyne (Gwyne), Oct. 27, 1834,
by Thos. P. Holman, J.P., Jan. 24, 1835. W. M. Carr
BM.
Hezekiah Cartwright & Nancy H. Grissim, Oct. 6, 1834,
T. C. Grissim, BM.

Samuel Carver & Pamelia Lumpkin, Feb. 7, 1834, by Ezekiel
Cloyd, M.G., Feb. 24, 1834. William T. Eatherly, BM.
Robert Casselman & Ardminta Reed, Nov. 26, 1834, by Levi
Holloway, J.P., Nov. 27, 1834. Thomas Pentecost, BM.
Edward Chambers & Eliza E. Hunter, Sep. 11, 1834, by
Stephen McDonald, J.P., Joseph Astor, BM.
Micholas Chambers & Elizabeth McDonald, June 25, 1834.
Joel Algood, BM.
William Chandler & Elizabeth Wadkins, Sep. 6, 1834, by
Robert H. Ellis, M.G., Sep. 17, 1834. Alexander
Belcher, BM.
Nathan A. Clampett & Amanda Ann Gillespie, June 14, 1834.
Josiah Strange, BM.
John Clay & Sally Davis, Dec. 24, 1834, William C. Ross,
BM.
William Climer & Elizabeth Wilkinson, Nov. 1, 1834, by
Thomas Somers, J.P., Nov. 7, 1834.
Robert Laine & Maria Blood, Sep. 13, 1834. William
Climer, BM.
Thornton H. Cook & Eleanor B. Clopton, June 5, 1834, by
William P. Smith, M.G., William A. Clopton, BM.
William C. Corder & Margaret Prichette, Jan. 23, 1834,
by M. T. Cartwright, Jan. 23, 1834. Benjamin Corder,
BM.
Thomas Cos & Nancy Baily, Dec. 22, 1834, by Moses Ellis,
J.P., Jan. 1, 1835. Sam'l. Yerger, BM.
James M. Crutchfield & Elizabeth B. (?) Lain, Oct. 8,
1834, by John Beard, M.G., Oct. 9, 1834. Albert G.
Williamson, BM.
James Davis & Susan Tippett, Sep. 4, 1834, by M. T.
Cartwright, J.P., Dabney Carr, BM.
Robert Davis & Mary Shorter, May 15, 1834, by B. Pyland,
M.G., Jesse Jackson, BM.
James B. Doherty & Sarah L. Alsup, July 23, 1834, by W.
R. D. Phipps, J.P., July 28, 1834.
William T. Dejarnet & Sarah Ann Pemberton, Oct. 6, 1834.
William B. Bandy, BM.
David S. Dew & Elizabeth Rutherford, March 3, 1834.
William B. Kerley, BM.
Thomas Dillon & Mary Arbuckle, Aug. 20, 1834, by J. Lester,
V.D.M., Aug. 20, 1834. Hall J. Winsett.
Samuel Dabbs & Elizabeth Martin, Jan. 7, 1834, by Ezekiel
Cloyd, M.G., Jan. 8, 1834. George W. Smith, BM.
Lodaway Dobbs & Pamelia Williams, Nov. 18, 1834, by H.
Hobson, J.P., Samuel Williams, BM.
Isaac J. Dodson & Octave Bullard, April 29, 1834, by
James Coffield Mitchell, M.G., James M. Trwin, BM.
William R. Donnell & Isabella Ann Foster, Sep. 4, 1834,
by Levi R. Morrison, V.D.M., Oct. 6, 1834. Thomas
Pentecost, BM.
James Drennon & Cynthia Davis, Sep. 12, 1834, by John
Beard, M.G., Sep. 18, 1834. Thomas Partlow, BM.
Jordan Driver & Patsey Williams, March 24, 1834, by
Micajah Estes, M.G., Sep. 18, 1834. James Driver, BM.

Joseph Earheart & Nancy Thompsom, Jan. 8, 1834, by Ezekiel Cloyd, M.G., Jan. 9, 1834. James Rutland, BM.
John K. Edwards & Elizabeth E. Billings, Nov. 8, 1834. James Hankins, BM.
Alfred Enoch & Malissa Hancock, Dec. 25, 1834. Geo. D. Cummings, BM.
Richard Eskridge & Maria Goodman, Sep. 10, 1834. G. W. Hill, BM.
William Fakes & Elizabeth Moser, July 12, 1834. Hugh Edwards, BM.
John Fields & Nancy Truett, Feb. 24, 1834. Reddin Fields, BM.
Bathlomew Figures & Caroline Matilda Davis, June 9, 1834. William H. Crenshaw.
Grant A. Flippin & Anna Taylor, Jan. 15, 1834, by Wilson Hearn, M.G., James B. Taylor, BM.
George E. Frazer & Elizabeth Ann Cage, Jan. 27, 1834. Robt. Hallum, BM.
James Gallagly & Dovey McPeak, March 7, 1834. James S. Graan, BM.
James Green & Amanda Carter, April 2, 1834, by B. Graves, J.P., Isham S. Green, BM.
John Gates & Eliza Hunt, Nov. 1, 1834, by Wm. Lawrence, J.P., Nov. 3, 1834. Valentine Gates, BM.
Pleasant Giddins & Elizabeth Lanceford, April 28, 1834. William Young, BM.
John F. Gilbert & Sarah Davis, Aug. 14, 1834, by Thos. Babb, J.P., Jesse Holt, BM.
Joseph D. Graves & Frances Carter, Aug. 10, 1834, by John Shane, J.P., Aug. 17, 1834. Jno. N. Radcliffe, BM.
William Graves & Winneford Lanceford, Jan. 29, 1834. Pleasant Gideon, BM.
Nathaniel Green & Jane Robinson, July 19, 1834. Robert Green, BM.
James A. Guill & Mary Ann Shepherd, Dec. 27, 1834, by D. Alford, J.P., Dec. 30, 1834. John Cawthorn, BM.
John E. Hager & Nancy Rice, Jan. 15, 1834. Silas Hedgpath, BM.
Joseph Hale & Polly Howard, Jan. 21, 1834, by W. R. V. Phipps, J.P., July 22, 1834. Solomon Warren, BM.
Green H. Hancock & Prudence Doak, Aug. 18, 1834, by Levi Holloway, J.P., G. W. Hill, BM.
John Harkreader & Caroline Steele, Aug. 6, 1834. Ashworth Harrison, BM.
George F. Harris & Levina Gray, March 6, 1834, by Elisha Vaughn, M.G., March 11, 1834. Jordan Driver, BM.
James P. Hays & Sarah Blurton, Oct. 6, 1834, by S. L. Bush, M.G., Oct. 7, 1834. John H. Seaborn, BM.
Joseph M. Hearn & Sedision Edwards, Oct. 28, 1834, by Jacob S. Hearn, M.G., Oct. 29, 1834. Joseph P. Moseley, BM.
Purnel Hearn & Julia Ann Cartwright, Jan. 4, 1834. G. W. Hill, BM.
Samuel Hester & Sally Griffin, July 7, 1834, by M. Estes, M.G., July 8, 1834. Hardy B. Griddin, BM.

John Hessy & Mary Murry, (i.e., John Huguley Hessy & Mary Elizabeth Murray), Dec. 17, 1836. Rev. William Murry, BM (bride's father).

Isaac Hill & Nancy Searcy, Oct. 3, 1834. Anderson Lumpkin, BM.

Lewis Hill & Ibby Whitson, Oct. 17, 1834. James T. Tompkins (Thompkins), BM.

Luke Hill & Susan Bridges, Dec. 25, 1834, by Ezekiel Cloyd, M.G., Dec. 26, 1834. Anderson Lumpkin, BM.

James E. Hollis & Amy Pigg, June 12, 1834. James T. Tompkins, BM.

Thomas Howell & Quinney Griffin, June 7, 1834, by Micjah Estes, June 11, 1834. Handy B. Griffin, BM.

Wiley M. Hubbard & Elizabeth Ann Jennings, Oct. 13, 1834. Lea Hubbard, BM.

James W. Huguley & Nancy M. Cawthon, Feb. 3, 1834, by John Shane, J.P., Feb. 4, 1834. Josiah Wright, BM.

Alford M. Hunt & Nancy Province, Sep. 6, 1834; Samuel M. Hunt & Penelope Bridges, Oct. 27, 1834, both by Wm. White, M.G., Oct. 30, 1834. Samuel W. Ross, BM.

Allen Ingram & Nancy Todd, July 28, 1834. Henry Chambliss, BM.

Wm. P. Jackson & Adaline Martin, Oct. 20, 1834. Saml. C. Anderson, BM.

Austin C. Jacobs & Martha L. Williams, Sep. 15, 1834, by _____, Sep. 16, 1834. Jeremiah Belt, BM.

William R. James & Isabel Willard, Feb. 12, 1834. William W. Milligan, BM.

Rial C. Jennings & Drucilla Smith, Dec. 9, 1834, by J. Lester, V.D.M., E. W. Lester, Wm. P. Jennings, BM.

Thomas Joplin & Charlotte Powell, Oct. 27, 1834. Seymore Powell, BM.

James Johnson & Alesy McAffy, Aug. 13, 1834. Hosea Ward, BM.

Thomas J. Kidwell & Susan Wood, Dec. 23, 1834, by Wm. Laurence, J.P., Dec. 25, 1834. Joseph Neal, BM.

Robert Laine & Maria Blood, Sep. 13, 1834, by John Shane, J.P., Sep. 14, 1834.

Jacob B. Lasiter & Urithe Durin, Oct. 28, 1834. J. B. Lasiter Sr., BM.

Robert Laurence & Lydia Tatum, July 30, 1834, by Thos. Babb, J.P., Anderson Kirkpatrick, BM.

William B. Laurence & Sarah B. Laurence, Nov. 10, 1834. Alex S. Young, BM.

Jonathan Ligon & Lucinda Jolly, Oct. 7, 1834, by E. P. Horn, J.P., George W. Anderson, BM.

William Lillard & Polly Cook, May 24, 1834, by J. H. Davis, J.P., May 28, 1834. Reuben Tipton, BM.

Isham F. D. Maddox & Lucinda Sutton, Nov. 15, 1834. Jesse Sutton, BM.

Wilson L. Maddox & Mary Gouldstone, Aug. 4, 1834, by Thos. Babb, J.P., Elijah Maddox, BM.

Richard B. Marlow & Pamelia Hudson, Feb. 1, 1834, by Elisha Vaughan, Feb. 2, 1834. William Hudson, BM.

Wiley Meadle & Cynthia Woollard, Feb. 20, 1834, by C.
  Holman, J.P., Feb. 21, 1834. Allen W. Vick, BM.
William McCartney & Eveline Baird, Dec. __, ____. Henry
  M. Comer, BM.
Milton N. McGehee & Lydia Alexander, May 28, 1834.
  William C. Peller, BM.
William McGinnis & Anna Williams, April 15, 1834, by
  Williamson Williams, M.G., April 17, 1834. John Belt,
  BM.
Thomas McSpedin & Sarah Cropper, Dec. 31, 1834, by
  Robert H. Ellis, J.P., William McSpeddin, BM.
Neely Midget & Betsey Douglas, Sep. 10, 1834, by Solomon
  Caplinger, J.P., George Midget, BM.
Isaac R. Moore & Eliza D. Biles, Nov. 29, 1834, by M. T.
  Cartwright, J.P., Dec. 4, 1834. M. T. Cartwright, BM.
Zechariah P. Moore & Lydia Green, Dec. 3, 1834. Wilson
  Bloodworth, BM.
Elias A. Moser & Nancy M. Brinson, July 30, 1834, by
  Silas Tarver, J.P., A. S. Winford, BM.
John W. Moseley & Sarah Crittenden, Oct. 21, 1834, by
  Silas Tarver, J.P., Joseph L. Mosely, BM.
Payton Neel & Sally Blackburn, Jan. 29, 1834. Henry
  Blurton, BM.
William Neighbours & Susannah Haas, Jan. 28. 1834.
  Philip Haas, BM.
Garrett Nelson & Mary Ashby, Sep. 6, 1834, by Joshua
  Woollen, M.G., Sep. 7, 1834. Moses Woollen, BM.
Cordy Nickins & Manerva Murry, May 15, 1834. John
  Nickens, BM.
William Nunn & Elizabeth Wilson, Aug. 16, 1834, by J. B.
  Talor, J.P., Aug. 21, 1834. Henry Thornton, BM.
John O'Brien & Mary Edwards, May 9, 1834, by Jas.
  Williford, John Organ, BM.
Noah O'Neal & Eliza Henry, Dec. 8, 1834. James Bell BM.
John Organ & Patsy Johnson, Aug. 23, 1834, by John Borum,
  Aug. 28, 1834. John R. Edwards.
Rolly Organ & Rebecca Mabry, Nov. 19, 1834, by John Seay,
  Nov. 20, 1834. C. W. Jackson, BM.
Samuel Overton & Barbara Furgason, Dec. 24, 1834 by
  Thos. Holman, J.P., Thos. Bradley, BM.
Francis A. Owen & Elizabeth H. Hardin, Nov. 29, 1834, by
  A. L. P. Green, M.G., Robert L. Caruthers, BM.
Daniel Palmer & Lucinda Guess, Aug. 13, 1834. Green Bond,
  BM.
William B. Parham & Angaline Puckett, Oct. 13, 1834, by
  J. B. Lasater, J.P., Oct. 16, 1834. Sam'l T. Williams,
  BM.
Samuel F. Patterson & Eliza Compton, Dec. 29, 1834, by
  Solomon Caplinger, J.P., Pauldin Anderson, BM.
Isaac Peek & Malissa C. Duke, Aug. 20, 1834, by Wm. H.
  White, M.G., Aug. 21, 1834. James H. Cawthon, BM.
Rial Pennuel & Bidy Louisa Jennings, Nov. 17, 1834, by
  J. Lester, V.D.M., Nov. 19, 1834. Hosea Ward, BM.
John M. Porterfield & Annis Lea, Aug. 4, 1834, by Jno.
  F. Doak, J.P., Aug. 5, 1834. William H. Lea, BM.

John Pritchett & Edna Moore, Dec. 17, 1834, by W. B.
Taylor, J.P., William Corder, BM.
William M. Provine & Phardlias Bowers, July 7, 1834.
S. N. Provine, BM.
Edward Radford & Malinda Winters, Nov. 9, 1834. John C.
Drollinger, BM.
John Ramsey & Mary A. Yandell, Dec. 29, 1834. Thomas R.
Yandell, BM.
Thomas Reed & Sarah Springs, Aug. 30, 1834, by J. B.
Taylor, J.P., Aug. 31, 1834. Samuel Reed, BM.
James A. Richardson & Jane C. Edings, March 19, 1834, by
J. Lester, V.D.M.
Robert Rickets & Harriet Leath, Sep. 22, 1834. John
Barber.
Isaac J. Roach & Matilda Caroline Marshall, Dec. 13, 1834,
by John Beard, M.G., Dec. 16, 1834. Isaac J. Roach, BM.
Elijah Russell & Tempy Grisham, April 4, 1834, by
Obadiah Freeman, April 9, 1834.
William C. Rutland & Emily B. Miles, July 30, 1834.
Isaac J. Roach, BM.
Cullen Sanders & Sarah Baskin, June 4, 1834, by Joshua
Woollen, M.G., Robert Baskin, BM.
Samuel Sanders & Mary Sanders, April 8, 1834, by Thos.
Calhoun, M.G., James Lyon, BM.
William P. Sayle & Agnes F. Watkins, Jan. 7, 1834, by
John Beard, M.G., Jan. 9, 1834. Mc McCorkle, BM.
John A. Shannon & Winsey T. Coleman, Jan. 10, 1834.
Ezekiel Holloway, BM.
Samuel Shannon & Abigail Hobson, Oct. 28, 1834, by Wm.
M. Swain, J.P., David B. Moore, BM.
Robert Simpson & Susan Cooke, Dec. 10, 1834. John
Morehead, BM.
Prisley G. Smart & Selina Stewart, April 4, 1834. Calvin
Bennett, BM.
Thomas Smith & Nancy Belcher, July 16, 1834. Abner Reed,
BM.
William D. Smith & Caroline _____, Sep. 10, 1834, by
Geo. _____, V.D.M., Pleasant Smith, BM.
Henry D. Summers & Thankful Climer, Dec. 15, 1834, by
Wm. M. Swain, J.P., Feb. 18, 1834 (?). William Graves,
BM.
John Stacy & Emily Smith, Dec. 12, 1834, by James Somers,
Dec. 22, 1834. John Edwards, BM.
James Stewart & Sally Thornton, Jan. 1, 1835, by James
Somers, J.P.
Phillip Swan & Lucinda Starroll, Dec. 22, 1834. Solomon
Caplinger, BM.
Robert B. Sypert & Julett Jackson, April 18, 1834, by
Henry Hobson, J.P., William S. Walker, BM.
William Tate & Lucy York, Dec. 17, 1834. Henry L. Bush,
BM (?).
Iverson J. Thomas & Mary Ann Shelton, Jan. 18, 1834, by
Joshua McMinn, J.P., Jan. 23, 1834. James Grier, BM.
John B. Thompson & Elizabeth _____, Oct. 2, 1834, by
Walter Carruth, J.P., Oct. 4, 1834. Samuel Donnell, BM.

Thomas J. Thompson & Lucy Ann Peace, May 29, 1834. Wm. J. Martin, BM.

Josiah S. Tooly & Sarah N. Cloyd, March 19, 1834, by John Beard, M.G., Richard B. Tate, BM.

Washington Turner & Pheby Butcher, Oct. 18, 1834. Thomas Cox, BM.

David Vaughter & Elizabeth Lacifield, Jan. 15, 1834, by James Bond, V.D.M., Jan. 22, 1834.

Handley Vaughan & Elizabeth Wray, Feb. 17, 1834, by Joseph B. Wynne, Sumna Bloodworth, BM.

Henry Vivrett & Sarah Jolly, Oct. 29, 1834, by E. P. Hern, J.P., Joseph E. Holly, BM.

Dudley Wave & Sindi Langly, Oct. 27, 1834, by B. Pyland, John Banfield, BM.

Robert Wade & Sarah Ann Rogers, April 12, 1834, by Sion Bass, William Johns, Jr., BM.

Fielding Walden & Eliza Belcher, June 30, 1834, by Robert H. Ellis, M.G., William Chandler.

John Walden & Elizabeth Jane Lott, Dec. 26, 1834. Lodaway Dobbs, BM.

Joshua Walsh & Palma Wiley, April 12, 1834, by B. Pyland (Piland), April 17, 1834. Valentine Coker, BM.

James Warren & Mary Organ, March 24, 1834, by Robert H. Ellis, M.G., March 24, 1834. Jesse Jackson, BM.

Michael Warren & Polly Merritt, Aug. 30, 1834, by James Bond, V.D.M., John Cunningham, BM.

David Watkins & Mary Ramsey, Oct. 13, 1834, by B. T. Motley, J.P., Oct. 18, 1834. Robt. B. Martin, BM.

Rufus L. Watson & Nancy Morris, Oct. 4, 1834. Henry Hunt, BM.

Andrew Wetherly & Aseneth Sims, Feb. 8, 1834. Thomas L. Green, BM.

Claibourn Whitson & Mary Brown, Dec. 18, 1834. William T. F. Coles, BM.

Allen Williams & Mary Turpin, Oct. 22, 1834, by Wilson Pitner, J.P., M. McCorkle, BM.

Ephraim A. Williams & Jane Belt, April 8, 1834, by Williamson Williams, M.G., April 10, 1834. John Thompson, BM.

George W. Williamson & Elenor G. Steele, Jan. 22, 1834. Finis. E. Williamson, BM.

John A. Williams & Charity Davis, July 5, 1834, by B. Pyland, July 8, 1834. A. W. Boothe, BM.

Joseph Williams & Sarah Blankenship, July 26, 1834, by Williamson Williams, M.G., July 29, 1834. Isaac Williams, BM.

Samuel Williams & Martha Williams, Dec. 22, 1834. Lodaway Dobbs, BM.

George A. Wilford & Manerva Carlin, Jan. 17, 1834, by B. T. Mabry, Jan. 22, 1834. Jas. C. Wilford, BM.

John J. Winston & Mary Lackey, Oct. 27, 1834, by Abner W. Saison, V.D.M., April 28, 1835. William C. Winston.

Joseph Wright & Rachel Hamilton, Dec. 9, 1834. Solomon Wright, BM.

William Yandell & Jane D. Davis, Oct. 6, 1834. William Hamilton, BM.

Beverly Young & Sarah Little, Nov. 17, 1834, by Micajah Estes, M.G., E. S. Wright, BM.

Green B. Adams & Matilda R. Jennings, Oct. 17, 1835. John Reece, BM.

Hiram Alsup & Mourning Alsup, April 6, 1835. Nathan A. Alsup, BM.

Joseph M. Anderson & Mary D. Sypert, Sep. 24, 1835, by F. G. Gerguson, W. M. Hall, BM.

Purnal H. Andrews & Emiline Donnell, Dec. 4, 1835, by B. Pyland, M.G., Dec. 9, 1835. R. J. Andrews, BM.

Walkers G. Andrews & Margaret _____, Nov. 4, 1835, by M. T. Cartwright, J.P., Nov. 5, 1835. E. R. Stewart, BM.

Henry S. Arnold & Clarissa Underwood, Dec. 29, 1835, by Joshua Woolen, M.G., Dec. 29, 1835. John Drennon, BM.

Henry G. Arnold & Mary Whitlock, July 7, 1835, by B. W. Smith, J.P., Alfred H. Foster, BM.

Thomas Babb & Elizabeth Bridges, March 31, 1835, by E. P. Horn, J.P., William T. Powell, BM.

William Bachus & Martha Sims, July 30, 1835, by W. R. D. Phipps, J.P., John Sims, BM.

Merchant Baldwin & Martha C. Buckley, Dec. 29, 1835, by Williamson Williams, M.G., Dec. 31, 1835. Richard Barber, BM.

Joseph Barber & Martha M. Ligon, July 15, 1835. Henry Barber, BM.

Jacob Barber & Hester Barber, Oct. 22, 1835, by M. T. Cartwright, J.P., M. T. Cartwright, BM.

Joshua H. Hughlett & Hanny (Fanny) Harris, April 4, 1834. H. Johnson, BM (?).

William Barber & Margaret _____, April 19, 1835, by _____ Graves, J.P., James H. Baird, BM.

Jones Bass & Delila Ellis, June 15, 1835. John H. Dew, BM.

Henry Beadles & Mary Ann Alexander, Sep. 22, 1835. Joseph Beadles, BM.

Woodford Belcher & Lucy Chandler, Dec. 26, 1835. John Reece, BM.

Allen Bell & Eliza Marks, July 28, 1835, by Sion Bass, William Swan, BM.

John Bett & Aley Smith, Sep. 7, 1835. Benjamin Bett, BM.

James M. Billings & Sarah Organ, Sep. 5, 1835. James R. Ellis, BM.

M. H. Billings & Nancy Irby, Sep. 15, 1835. A. W. Leatherwood, BM.

Robert D. Black & Elizabeth Ann Baskins, March 2, 1835, by Joshua Woollen, M.G., Robt. M. Baskins, BM.

John Blankenship & Margaret McDaniel, Oct. 30, 1835, by Williamson Williams, M.G., Hosea Ward, BM.

Oscar F. Bledsoe & Martha A. Wynne, Jan. 28, 1835. J. Y. Blythe, BM.

John M. Bone & Lucy Webb, April 4, 1835, by Abner W. Tarver, V.D.M., Harrison Ward, BM.

John Bogle & John Bryson, Sep. 11, 1835. John Bryson, BM.
Joseph H. Bogle & Rachel Turney, Nov. 23, 1835, by John
  Sneed, J.P., Nov. 24, 1835.
Green C. Bowers & Susan Forbis, Feb. 6, 1835, by Stephen
  McDonald, Feb. 12, 1835. James M. Provine, BM.
Andrew J. Branch & Abigail Payne, Sep. 14, 1835. R. C.
  Branch, BM.
Robert C. Branch & Sarah Neal, Sep. 4, 1835, by Wm.
  Lawrence, J.P., Sep. 9, 1835. G. W. Clark, BM.
John Bridges & Nancy Amanda Calhoun, Aug. 8, 1835, by
  E. S. Allen, M.G., Aug. 12, 1835. John L. Layne, BM.
A. W. Brien & Sally P. Stewart, Oct. 26, 1835, by J.
  Lester, V.D.M., Nathaniel L. Orand, BM.
Amsted Brogan & Sarah Thomas, Dec. 5, 1835. A. H. Foster,
  BM.
Hugh Brown & Lucinda Booker, Feb. 6, 1835, by Thomas
  Smith, M.G., Samuel Booker, BM.
Hugh Brown & Lamizra McCarroll, Aug. 14, 1835, by John
  Beard, M.G., Aug. 20, 1835. John N. Roach, BM.
John H. Brown & Sarah Bass, Jan. 14, 1835. Robt. Lawrence,
  BM.
Ross Brown & Rosanah Brown, Sep. 1, 1835. Thomas
  Robinson, BM.
Lytle Bryant & Sarah Wilkerson, Aug. 1, 1835, by John
  Beard, M.G., Aug. 13, 1835. Nathl. Cartmell, BM.
John Bryson & Littoe Leech, Sep. 29, 1835, by James
  Thomas, M.G., Mark Alexand, BM.
Thomas Burton & Amanda Parham, Dec. 16, 1835. Isaac
  Rutland, BM.
James Camp & Hetty Bass, Dec. 29 (?), 1835. Soloman Bass,
  BM.
John W. Copeheart & Mary Reeves, Aug. 6, 1835. Newbern,
  BM.
George Carroll & Susan Blankenship, Jan. 27, 1835, by
  J. Lester, V.D.M., Saml. H. Porterfield, BM.
James L. Chapman & Mary Bettis (Bettie), Dec. 10, 1835.
  Saml. C. Anderson, BM.
Burrell Chick & Eleanor Sanders, Dec. 26, 1835. James
  Sanders, BM.
Mitchell Childen & Juliet B. Tarpley, Aug. 12, 1835, by
  John C. Parker, Nathan G. Jarratt, BM.
Jeptha Clemmons & Margarett Truett, ___. 28, 1835.
  William Clemmons, BM.
Eli Coggins & Nancy Ragsdale, Dec. 19, 1835, by G. H.
  Huddleston, J.P., Dec. 22, 1835. John L. Casilman, BM.
Joseph Cooksey & Lucinda Satterfield, March 2, 1835.
  Alfred Pride, BM.
James B. Comer & Martha Shanon, Jan. 21, 1835, by Levi
  Holloway, J.P., Jan. 22, 1835. James Johns, BM.
Samuel R. Comer & Jane Jackson, Aug. 20, 1835, by James
  Foster, J.P., A. H. Foster, BM.
Thomas W. Congers & Martha Walker, Dec. 16, 1835, by
  Henry Hobson, J.P., Dec. 17, 1835. Little Berry
  Wright, BM.

William H. Crenshaw & Delila Ann Hall, Dec. 9, 1835, by
Geo. Donnell, M.G., Edmund B. Drake, BM.
Robert Crudup & Caroline Harkreader, Sep. 28, 1835.
Samuel Walker, BM.
Isaac N. Curry & Jane Dobson, March 25, 1835, by J.
Hooker, M.G., Samuel B. Gibson, BM.
Samuel Davis & Margaret Steele, Oct. 7, 1835. Thos. E.
Everett, BM.
Alexander S. Dickson & Rebecca Patterson, Jan. 6 1835,
by John McMinn, J.P., Jan. 8, 1835. Mark C. Alexander,
BM.
Alfred E. Donnell & Adaline Donnell, Jan. 13, 1835, by
B. Pyland, M.G., Jan. 15, 1835. John Muirhead, BM.
Elusly A. Donnell & Mary McKee, Dec. 8, 1835, by B.
Pyland, Dec. 8, 1835. Charles F. McKee, BM.
Robert Donnell & Jane F. McMinn, Dec. 15, 1835, by B.
Pyland, Dec. 17, 1835. Howell Williams, BM.
Saml. H. Donnell & Mary Carter, Nov. 19, 1835, by Sion
Bass, M.G., Henry Major, BM.
George R. Dooley & Nancy Y. Jackson, Sep. 16, 1835, by
Jas. C. Willeford, J.P., Sep. 17, 1835. R. Barkley,
BM.
James Drennon & Deletha Shelton, Feb. 24, 1835, by Joshua
Woollen, M.G., Feb. 24, 1835. Danl. N. Alsup, BM.
Samuel Eagan & Nancy Johnson, July 1, 1835, by John W.
Bomer, M.G., Joseph E. Johnson, BM.
Sam'l. Eagan & Almyra Harris, July 30, 1835. William
Ames, BM.
John T. Echols & Luraney Clifton, Feb. 19, 1835. Mitchell
Perry, BM.
Henry Eddins & Milly Sparks, Oct. 12, 1835, by John Bone,
J.P., Oct. 14, 1835. (Little) Henry Eddins, BM.
Henry Edwards & Nancy Edwards, Nov. 13, 1835, by James
Bond, V.D.M., Nov. 16, 1835. Wiliam Fields, BM.
John Edwards & Jane Edwards, June 25, 1835, by James Bond,
V.D.M., Henry Edwards, BM.
James R. Ellis & Jane B. McSpedden, Oct. 6, 1835, by
Robt. H. Ellis, Oct. 7, 1835. Robert Harrison, BM.
Alfred Enoch & Malissa Hancock, Dec. 25, 1834, by Obadiah
Freeman, M.G., Wilson Bloodworth, BM.
William C. Fane & Mary C. Smith, Oct. 1, 1835, by John
Bone, J.P., B. W. Bond, BM.
William C. Fane & Mary Ann Jackson, May 9, 1835. Robert
D. S. McMinn, BM.
Jesse Fuller & Martha Caplinger, Sep. 9, 1835, by Solomon
Caplinger, J.P., Samuel Hooker, BM.
Benjamin M. Garrison & Nancy A. Cooper, Dec. 11, 1835, by
H. L. Mabry, J.P., N. G. Jarratt, BM.
Stephen Goodman & Malinda Clemons, Feb. 21, 1835, by
James Somers, J.P., Feb. 22, 1835. J. C. Bennett, BM.
Charles Green & _____ Edwards, April 5, 1835, by James
Bond, V.D.M., April 7, 1835. Robert B. Edwards, BM.
Jamez Grier & Emmz M. Thomas, Feb. 20, 1835, by John
McMinn, J.P., Feb. 25, 1835. John P. Patterson, BM.

William Griffin & Elizabeth Rye, Dec. 22, 1835. C. W. Cummings, BM.

Charles Hall & Polly Ann Pride, May 27, 1835, by John Beard, M.G., May 31, 1835. Daniel Searcy, BM.

James G. Hamilton & Margaret M. Barr, Aug. 22, 1835, by John Allison V.D.M., Aug. 27, 1835. William Hamilton, BM.

Josiah Harlin & Malissa Cason, Dec. 14, 1835. Reuben Saterfield, BM.

Nathan T. Harris & Elizabeth Woods, Nov. 13, 1835, by J. B. Lasater, J.P., Nov. 15, 1835. Amos Mount, BM.

Richard Harris & Myra Hamilton, April 7, 1835, by Stephen McDonald, J.P., April 9, 1835. Elijah Matsinger, BM.

Washington Harris & Helen Reeder, Aug. 26, 1835, by B. G. Barclay, J.P., Adam Reeder, BM.

Ainsworth Harrison & Rebecca Denton, May 7, 1835, by B. Mottley, J.P., May 9, 1835. Turner Vaughn, Jno. H. Dew, BM.

Edmund Hathaway & Francis Chumley, May 27, 1835. Leonard Hathaway, BM.

William J. Hawks & Sarah E. Chandler, Nov. 7, 1835. Finis E. Shannon, BM.

John A. Hearn & Sarah Caraway, Jan. 24, 1835, by B. G. Barclay, J.P., Eli M. Thompson, BM.

John Hearn & Eleanor Morris, March 5, 1835, by W. R. Phipps, Berry Wright, BM.

James W. Hearn & Polly Garrison, June 17, 1835. John Hearn, BM.

James G. Herron & Nancy Patterson, Aug. 4, 1835. Eli M. Thompson, BM.

Andrew H. Holbert & Martha Ann Moxly, Nov. 15, 1835, by B. Pyland, Nov. 19, 1835. D. C. Hibbett, BM.

Armstead Hocking & Mary Bell, Sep. 22. 1835, by Sion Bass, M.G., William Hastings, BM.

Henry Hooper & Mertha Little, Aug. 6, 1835. Payton Neal BM.

John Horsley & Elizabeth Dorch, May 9, 1835, by Thos. P. Holman, J.P., May 10, 1835. Radford Walker, BM.

Robards Howell & Puab B. Vance, Aug. 19, 1835, by Micjah Estes, M.G., Thomas Curd, BM.

Pleasant T. Hubbard & Lockey Owen, Nov. 16, 1835, by Wm. McKee, BM.

William Hunter & Margaret Scoby, Oct. 13, 1835, by Stephen McDonald, J.P., Alex H. Provine, BM.

Stephens T. Hutchings & Elizabeth G. Glass, Feb. 23, 1835. William Hutchings, BM.

Joseph C. Johnson & Mary Jane Moss, Sep. 7, 1835. Dabney Carr, BM.

Edmund A. Jackson & Lockey Cason, Jan. 19, 1835. W. C. Fane, BM.

Isaac Jackson & Sarah Ann Massey, Dec. 22 1835, by John Seay, M.G., Jno. White, BM.

Joel Jackson & Mary Bonner, Sep. 7, 1835, by Thomas Smith, J.P., David Evits, BM.

William P. Jackson & Adaline Martin, Oct. 20, 1835, by
J. Hooker, M.G., Oct. 22, 1835.

William Jarrell & Sarah Dill, Jan. 22, 1835. John Dill,
BM.

William B. Jenkins & Elizabeth Hobbs, Aug. 22, 1835, by
Sion Bass, James T. Phillips, BM.

Elihu B. Jewell & Malinda A. Thomas, July 31, 1835.
Joisons J. Thomas, BM.

Abram O. Johns & Elizabeth M. Hudson, Dec. 15, 1835, by
Thomas Smith, M.G., Alexander Lemons, BM.

Joseph C. Johnson & Mary Jane Moss, Sep. 7, 1835, by T.
Kirkpatrick, J.P., Sep. 10, 1835.

Alston B. Jolly & Rebecca Johnson, Jan. 3, 1835. J. C.
Bennett, BM.

Josiah Jones & Cynthia Copeland, Nov. 13, 1835, by J.
Lester, V.D.M., James H. Jones, BM.

William Jones & Susan Turner, March 23, 1835. Benjamin
Howell, BM.

William B. Kirby & Martha Hill, Jan. 28, 1835, by George
Donnell, V.D.M., Jan. 29, 1835. Jno. H. Dew, BM.

Isham Kitrell & Carry Ann Procter, Oct. __, 1835. B. D.
Hawkins, BM.

Jesse M. Knight & Elizabeth Kelly, Sep. 3, 1835. Hiram
Howell, BM.

Joseph Knox & Estha Evaline, Dec. 14, 1835, by Jesse
Alexander, V.D.M., Dec. 17, 1835. J. W. Smith, BM.

Christopher Lain & Lavinia Johnson, Nov. 18, 1835. W. B.
Baxter, BM.

Gibby Lane & Lewdy Jones, Oct. 8, 1835. William Nelson,
BM.

Robt. Lampkins & Mary Ragland, July 2, 1835, by B. T.
Mottley, J.P., J. T. Penny, BM.

Aquilla M. Leatherwood & Kiziah Robertson, July 15, 1835.
Pleasant Irby, BM.

William H. Lea & Sarah Brown, Sep. 10, 1835, by Jno. T.
Doak, J.P., Dec. 8, 1835. James H. Smith, BM.

Edward W. Lester & Elizabeth Jennings, Dec. 11, 1835, by
Joshua Lester, V.D.M., Dec. 15, 1835.

Manson B. Lester & Martha Word, Nov. 30, 1835, by J.
Lester, V.D.M.

William Lester & Mary Jane Duffy, Dec. 5, 1835, by J.
Lester, V.D.M., Thomas C. Word, BM.

Jefferson Link & Elizabeth Ann Price, Oct. 1, 1835, by
John Seay, M.G., John L. Hawkins, BM.

James Little & Burline Medline, Dec. 2, 1835. Henry
Hooper, BM.

David D. Mabry & Eliza Wilkinson, June 27, 1835, by Henry
Hobson, J.P., N. G. Jarratt, BM.

Francis E. Mabry & Malinda Hosley, July 28, 1835, by
Henry Hobson, J.P., Radford Walker, BM.

Timothy G. Mallory & Lavina Adamson, Sep. 28, 1835.
Isaac Smith, BM.

Isaac Mathis & Docia Kelly, Nov. 19, 1835. John Winston,
BM.

WILSON COUNTY MARRIAGES

James J. Mathis & Sarah Bell, April 28, 1835, by John
Sneed, J.P., May 4, 1835. Lewis Bond, BM.
Ezekiel W. Martin & Fredonia R. Winston, Feb. 12, 1835,
by Jeremiah Williams, Feb. 19, 1835. James T. Williams,
BM.
James Martin & Elizabeth Martin, Aug. 15, 1836. Amos
Martin, BM.
Robt. B. Martin & Cynthia Hegerty, March 26, 1835, by
B. T. Mattley, J.P., March 27, 1835. Robert J. Garison.
James B. McAdow & Mary Knight, Feb. 17, 1835, by John
McMinn, J.P., Feb. 19, 1835. Nathaniel Orand, BM.
Newbern S. McAdow & Julia F. Orrand, Feb. 6, 1836, by
J. Lester, V.D.M., Wm. B. Bryson, BM.
William McCulloch & Martha Jackson, Sep. 30, 1835. John
Lawrence, BM.
Andrew McMullin & Marinda D. Jennings, Sep. 28, 1835.
Thomas Belcher, BM.
William McNamor & Eliza Buckley, Jan. 13, 1835. Milton
A. McNamor, BM.
Nathaniel Merritt & Nancy Ragsdale, Dec. 28, 1835, by
Wm. M. Swain, J.P., Dec. 29, 1835. Green B. Merritt, BM.
Henry Miller & Mary Caplinger, Dec. 5, 1835, by J. B.
Taylor, J.P., Dec. 22, 1835. William Caplinger, BM.
Thomas E. Morriss & Eliza R. Burton, Feb. 25, 1835, by
John W. Bowan, James E. Sands, BM.
R. E. Moseley & Minserva Walker, Nov. 28, 1835. Wm.
Halbrook, BM.
David O. Moore & Cynthia Gatten, Sep. 10, 1835. Lemuel
Moore, BM.
Jabez Nooner & Jane Drollinger, May 29, 1835, by John
Beard, M.G., June 2, 1835. John C. Drollinger, BM.
Joseph Oneal & Elizabeth McBride, Sep. 16, 1835, by Sion
Bass.
Cameron Ozment & Susan Killis, June 8, 1835, by Levi
Holloway, J.P., June 9, 1835. John Davis, BM.
William W. Peace & Nancy Jenkins, Oct. 8, 1835. John
Campsey, BM.
Josiah Pemberton & Nancy Bull, May 28, 1835. Henry D.
Lester, BM.
Thomas Pentecost & Sarah Davis, Sep. 28, 1835, by B.
Pyland, Oct. 31, 1835. Calvin Donnell, BM.
Drury Perry & Nancy Vick, Dec. 30, 1835. Robert Creswell,
BM.
Jesse Phillips & Louisa Mallory, Dec. 29, 1835, by John
Sneed, J.P., Dec. 31, 1835. Timothy G. Mallory, BM.
Seth Phillips & Ann Harlin, Feb. 4, 1835. Henry Phillips,
BM.
Joseph K. Pierce & Mary Ann Latamore, Aug. 20, 1835,
by Robt. Andrews, M.G., Aug. 20, 1835. Jefferson _ink,
BM.
Jesse Pugh & Polly Adamson, April 28, 1835, by John Smith,
J.P., Timothy Mallory, BM.
Thomas Puckett & Ann Lasater, Sep. 5, 1835, by J. Lester,
V.D.M., Sep. 5, 1835. William Lester, BM.

WILSON COUNTY MARRIAGES

Thomas A. Puckett & Amanda G. Randle, Feb. 25, 1835,
by James Dew, J.P., Feb. 27, 1835. Thos. C. Telford,
BM.
James O. Roach & Elizabeth H. Barton, Feb. 6, 1835.
William Barton, BM.
Thomas R. Roach & Nancy W. Cloyd, July 15, 1835, by E.
Cloyd, M.G., June 16, 1835. Thomas C. Telford, BM.
George Romines & Cynthia Hearn, Dec. 22, 1835, by Henry
Hobson, J.P., Andrew Congers, BM.
Ezekiel Rouse & Betsy Jenkins, Jan. 14, 1835. John
Stewart, BM.
John Rouse (a free man of Color) & Jensey Jenkins (a free
woman of Color), March 14, 1835, by J. B. Lasater, J.P.,
Turner Jenkins, BM.
William A. Russell & Nancy M. Anderson, Feb. 5, 1835, by
John Kelley, M.G., John Webb, BM.
Richard Savage & Jane Telford, Aug. 10, 1835, by A. J.
McDonald, J.P., Aug. 12, 1835. Thomas J. Thompson, BM.
Andrew S. Sherrill & Sarah B. Hearn, Jan. 1, 1835, by
Robert L. Andrews, Joseph Peairs, BM.
Samuel W. Sherrill & Elizabeth Jane Moxley, June 1, 1835,
by B. Pyland, M.G., June 2, 1835. E. Sherrill, BM.
Jefferson Sneed & Lucy Rich, March 11, 1835. Alfred F.
Foster, BM.
John Sims & Susan Merritt, Sep. 9, 1835. John Smith, BM.
Matthius Sims & Sally Roberson, Sep. 15, 1835. W. S.
Sublett, BM.
Valentine Simpson & Lucretia Lane, March 12, 1835, by
Joshua Woollen, M.G.
Elisha Smith & Hannah Davidson, Aug. 27, 1835, by B. S.
Mottley, Aug. 28, 1835. James H. Lampkins, BM.
John P. Smith & Mary Dudly, March 11, 1835, by B. T.
Mottley, J.P., March 11, 1835. James T. Lampkins, BM.
John C. Smith & Pennue Nettles, July 20, 1835, by B.
Pyland, July 23, 1835. E. S. Cain, BM.
Saml. S. Smithwick & Martha Johnson, Nov. 28, 1835, by
John Bonner, J.P., Dec. 2, 1835. Valentine H. Brown.
Jefferson M. Sneed & Lucy Rich, March 11, 1835, by John
Sneed, J.P., March 19, 1835.
Calvin J. Spradley & Sarah Sweatt, June 4, 1835. Newbern
P. Stone, BM.
Micajah Stone & Elizabeth Woollard, Jan. 8, 1835. Calvin
W. Jackson, BM.
Elijah Strong & Elizabeth Cooper, Nov. 18, 1835. Thos.
J. Tezer, BM.
James Stewart & Sarah Thornton, Jan. 1, 1835. John
Stewart, BM.
Henry C. Summar & Lucinda Owen, Aug. 31, 1835, by B.
Smith, J.P., Fleming Owen, BM.
James Sommar & Rebecca Teppert, Jan. 12, 1835, by John
McMinn, J.P., Jan. 15, 1835. Frances Cooper, BM.
Jesse Sutton & Elizabeth Hite, Nov. 3, 1835. Felin
Maddox, BM.
Joel Swindle & Jane Lewis, Jan. 22, 1835, by B. T. Mottley,
J.P., Jan. 22, 1835. Elisha Smith, BM.

140

William B. Tarpley & Mary Harvey, June 23, 1835. Green
B. Adams, BM.
James Thomas & Polly Wilson, Jan. 31, 1835, by John
McMinn, J.P., Feb. 1, 1835. Elihu B. Jewell, BM.
John Tims & Susan Merritt, Sep. 9, 1835, by W. R. D.
Phipps, J.P.
Joseph Tippet & Tempy Harrison, Dec. 30, 1835, by M. T.
Cartwright, J.P., Dec. 31, 1835. Joseph Manning, BM.
Joshua H. Tipton & Rebecca Ann Rider, March 6, 1835, by
Elisha Vaughn, M.G., March 12, 1835. Wilson Bloodworth,
BM.
John W. Todd & Mahala Phillips, Dec. 11, 1835. P. Rison,
BM.
Joseph Trout & Lucretia Bell, Dec. 23, 1835, by A. J.
McDonald, J.P., Moses Watkins, BM.
Thomas Tuggle & Temperance Duke, Dec. 22, 1835. Harris
Fuller, BM.
Larry Vivrett & Harriet Cole, Jan. 30, 1835. Madison
Organ, BM.
Troylus N. Violet & Margaret C. Searcy, Aug. 11, 1835,
by M. T. Cartwright, J.P., Aug. 13, 1835. M. T.
Cartwright, BM.
Elisha Walker & Ann Eliza McDonald, Dec. 21, 1835. Davis
S. Dew, BM.
William T. Walker & Nancy McDaniel, April 4, 1835, by
_____, April 5, 1835. John Wiseman, BM, William
Moss, BM.
John Wallace & Fanny H. Sellas, Oct. 3, 1835, by Jesse
Alexander, V.D.M., Oct. 7, 1835. Saml. B. Killough, BM.
Robert B. Warren & Susan Gray, Nov. 9, 1835, by Robt. D.
Bell, Peter Rison, BM.
Thomas Webb & Martha Ann Guess, April 24, 1835, by James
Bond, V.D.M., April 30, 1835. William N. Davidson, BM.
David Weir & Ruth Reeves, April 12, 1835, by Robert M.
Ellis J.P., Robert Owen, BM.
Athur Williams & Louisa Blankenship, Aug. 6, 1835, by J.
Lester, V.D.M., Isaac Williams, BM.
Bennett Williams & Kiziah Webb, Feb. 21, 1835, by Micajah
Estes, M.G., Feb. 25, 1835. Calvin Williams, BM.
Elbert Williams & Mary Foutch, Nov. 20, 1835. Sam'l. T.
Williams, BM.
John P. Williams & Elizabeth Cox, Oct. 19, 1835, by Jas.
C. Willeford, J.P., Oct. 20, 1835. Patrick H. Hegerty,
BM.
William Gray Williams & Mary Smith, May 30, 1835, by
Micajah Estes, M.G., William R. Williams, BM.
William Williamson & Aggy Gothard, Dec. 8, 1835.
James W. White & Mary Palmer, Sep. 26, 1835. Robt. L.
Pulley, BM.
David F. Wood & Ann B. Brown, May 2, 1835, by John Beard,
M.G., May 7, 1835. Jno. N. Roach, BM.
John Woods & Joanna Johnson, May 9, 1835, by Obadiah
Freeman, May 10, 1835. Isaac Chatham, BM.
Losen B. Woollard & Amy Bandy, Jan. 24, 1835. John Johns,
Jr.

Whitehead Woodliff & Nancy W. Posey, Feb. 28, 1835, by
James Somers, J.P., March 7, 1835. S. J. Midwell, BM.
Thomas K. Wynne & Elizabeth Johnson, Oct. 13, 1835, by
John Seay, Adam Muirhead, BM.
John Young & Lockey Wasson, Dec. 15, 1835, by Joshua
Lester, V.D.M., Dec. 25, 1835. James Hamilton, BM.
Stacy Young & Jane Anderson, Sep. 14, 1835. Council L.
Crawford, BM.
Jeremiah H. Allen & Mary Holman, June 16, 1836, by John
Seay, M.G., June 18, 1836.
John W. Anderson & Mary Ann Bass, Sep. 21, 1836, by
Wilbon R. Winter, J.P.
Ichabod Archer & Ann Eliza White, May 3, 1836, by M.
Woollen, J.P., May 7, 1836.
Thomas Baird & Mary Martin, Sep. 5, 1836, by James Bond,
V.D.M., Sep. 8, 1836.
Richard Barker & Susanna Williams, March 15, 1836.
Robert Whittier, BM.

Thomas Bartholomew & Margaret Horton, Feb. 16, 1836, by
J. Kirkpatrick, J.P., Feb. 19, 1836.
John Bass & Susan Barbee, Sep. 14, 1836, by Sion Bass, M.G.
Sampson Bell & Polly M. Bradley, May 14, 1836, by John
Borum, May 16, 1836.
William Bickers & Mary Allen, July 18, 1836, by John Bell,
J.P., July 19, 1836.
Alexander F. Blair & Emily J. Tally, March 1, 1836, by
B. T. Mottley, J.P., March 2, 1836.
Wilson Bloodworth & Alsy Eagan, Feb. 14, 1836, by Elisha
Vaughn, M.G., Feb. 16, 1836.
Bassel C. Brown & Hannah Rutland, March 14, 1836, by
John Beard, M.G., March 16, 1836.
John B. Bryant & Katarine Waters, Oct. 17, 1836, by
Joshua Lester, V.D.M., Thomas McKee, BM.
Samuel B. Bryson & Elizabeth Davenport, Nov. 7, 1836, by
George Bogle, J.P., Dec. 23, 1836.
Christopher Butter & Mary McHaney, Nov. 19, 1836, by
Joshua Lester, V.D.M., James McHaney, BM.
Ruffin C. Caples & Sarah Eddins, Dec. 7, 1836, by L.
Fisher, M.G.
Elihu Caraway & Mary D. Richmond, Dec. 3, 1836, by Henry
Truett, J.P., Dec. 11, 1836.
Robert Chambliss & Susannah Johnson, Dec. 1, 1836.
Milton Climer & Polly Martin, May 2, 1836.
Benjamin Clifton & Nancy Johnson, Dec. 21, 1836, by B. S.
Mabry, M.G., Feb. 22, 1837.
Stephen E. Comer & Anna Marrs, Oct. 22, 1836, by R. Comer,
J.P., Oct. 28, 1836.
Edward Compton & Mason Booker, Feb. 20, 1836, by Sion
Bass, M.G.
William Compton & Martha Farrell, Dec. 21, 1836, by
Wm. _____.
Charles Coppage & Ann Kennedy, Jan. 27, 1836.
Nathan Corley & Sarah Terr, Oct. 29, 1836, by A. J.
McDonald, J.P.

Robert Craddock & Elizabeth King, June 20, 1836, by Anthony Owing.

James Cropper & Malinda Dellis, Feb. 29, 1836, by B. T. Mottley, J.P., March 1, 1836.

Thomas Curd & Melcenia E. Rutland, Oct. 12, 1836, by Wm. T. Luck.

Ezkiel S. Curry & Rebecca McDaniel, Sep. 22, 1836, by John Beard, M.G., Sep. 28, 1836.

John Davis & Elizabeth Hearn, July 27, 1836, by John Hearn, J.P.

Richard Dill & Elizabeth Douglass, Aug. 17, 1836.

Adnah Donnell & Elizabeth Donnell, Jan. 13, 1836, by John Bone, J.P., Jan. 14, 1836. Stephen Comer, BM.

John W. Donnell & Agnes Julia Ann Wommack, Sep. 1, 1836, by Geo. Donnell, V.D.M., Sep. 6, 1836.

Robert B. Donnell & Annie Lea, Oct. 20, 1836, by R. Comer, J.P.

William Dobson & Margaret Grayham, Aug. 19, 1836, by J. Hooker, M.G., Aug. 21, 1836.

William C. Douglas & Lucy Ann Sidwell, Jan. 12, 1836, by Arch B. Oneal.

John Drennan & Polly Bell, Feb. 6, 1836, by G. A. Huddleston, J.P., Feb. 25, 1836.

Williamson Dunnaway & Mary Burke, Oct. 11, 1836, by Joshua Lester, V.D.M.

James Eckols & Elizabeth Ferrel, Feb. 18, 1836, by Stephen McDonald, J.P.

Theophilus Edwards & Martha Edwards, Aug. 6, 1836, by Sion Bass, M.G., Joseph Maning, BM.

Mathew Ethridge & Nancy Frances Justice, April 5, 1836, by Joshua Lester, V.D.M.

Benjn. H. P. Estes & Sarah Mosier, April 4, 1836, by Levi Fisher, M.G., April 9, 1836. Jospehus Walker, BM.

Samuel Estes & Martha Estes, Oct. 29, 1836, by Levi Fisher, Nov. 3, 1836.

Ewing (James Ewing) & Malinda Beller, May 16, 1836, J. H. Fisher, BM.

Levi Fisher & Martha RES Guthrie, May 2, 1836, by Thomas Smith, M.G., May 3, 1836.

James Flanagin & Nancy Glanagin, Dec. 24, 1836, by B. T. Mabry, M.G., Dec. 25, 1836. Lewis Dies, BM.

Marcus Flanigan & Susan Flanigan, Dec. 24, 1836, by B. T. Mabry, Dec. 25, 1836.

John W. Foster & Nancy McMurry, July 13, 1835, by P. Y. Davis, M.G., Dec. 13, 1836.

Isham Fuller & Sarah Caplinger, June 8, 1836, by Solomon Caplinger, J.P.

Abraham George & Jemima Gibson, March 9, 1836. Robt. M. Baskins, BM.

Samuel B. Gibson & Lavina Climer, April 23, 1836, by J. Hooker, April 26, 1836.

Samuel Gibson & Elizabeth Ricketts, Nov. 30, 1836, by Thos. Miles, J.P., Dec. 1, 1836.

James D. Gill & Christine Caplinger, Oct. 19, 1836, by Solomon Caplinger, J.P., Oct. 20, 1836.

Felix R. Gleaves & Nancy M. Davis, June 28, 1836, by John
Beard, M.G., June 30, 1836.
Guy T. Gleaves & Harriet H. Hardy, Sep. 26, 1836.
Lewis Grantham & Eddy Trout, Dec. 3, 1836, by J. Thomas
M.G., Dec. 29, 1836.
William H. Grimmet & Elizabeth L. Briant, June 11, 1836,
by Joshua Lester, V.D.M., June 14, 1836.
Thomas C. Grissim & Sarah B. Crutchfield, Sep. 14, 1836,
by M. T. Cartwright, J.P., Sep. 15, 1836.
William Gwyn & Martha Woodrum, Nov. 14, 1836, by John
Beard, M.G., Nov. 24, 1836.
Samuel Hamilton & Jane Harris, Jan. 4, 1836. McGee
Harris, BM.
Thomas P. Hawkins & Eliza R. Scoby, Oct. 15, 1836.
Answorth H. Howell, BM.
Moses Harrison & Betsy Edwards, Aug. 20, 1836, by Solomon
Caplinger, J.P., Aug. 23, 1836.
James S. Harris & May S. Waters, Aug. 15, 1836, by
Solomon Caplinger, J.P., Aug. 16, 1836.
Samuel A. Hays & Jane Cloyd, July 27, 1836, by T. G.
Burney, M.G., Aug. 18, 1836.
Edward D. Hicks & Cornelis T. Hall, May 4, 1836, by Geo.
Donnell, V.D.M.
Nathaniel Hickman & Tabitha J. Kemp, April 1, 1836, by
B. Graves, J.P.
William Hobbs & Lucretia Wier, Oct. 5, 1836, by Cloyd
Ellis, J.P., Oct. 6, 1836. C. W. Jackson, BM.
Charles W. Huguly & Elizabeth Hooker, Aug. 26, 1836, A.
B. Rose, M.G., Sep. 1, 1836.
Washington H. Irwin & Sarah Smith, Nov. 2, 1836, by Sion
Bass, M.G., Dec. 1, 1836.
Warren Jackson & Martha Warren, Nov. 2, 1836, by J. W.
Locke, J.P., Nov. 2, 1836.
Elijah Johns & Delila York, Aug. 13, 1836, by Elisha
Vaughan, M.G., Aug. 18, 1836. Job T. Haysworth, BM.
Gregory D. Johnson & Susannah Hartsfield, Aug. 13, 1836,
by G. H. Glenn, J.P.
Isaac Johnson & Mary Telford, Nov. 26, 1836, by John
Beard, Dec. 1, 1836.
James H. Johnson & Susan Vinson, Feb. 25, 1836, by B.
Bridges, J.P.
William Johnson & Nicy Moon, May 4, 1836, by George
Bogle, J.P., May 6, 1836.
Levi Jones & Elizabeth K. Herald, Oct. 5, 1836. John E.
Dickinson, BM.
James T. Jones & May Stroud, Feb. 29, 1836, by Joshua
Lester, V.D.M.
Purses D. Jetton & Jane E. McGregor, Feb. 23, 1836, by
B. Graves, J.P.
William Kennedy & Maria Moore, Dec. 20, 1836, by George
Brown, J.P.
Joseph Kirkpatrick & Emeline Bently, June 13, 1836, by
H. B. Hill, M.G., June 15, 1836.
Hezekiah T. Lassater & Eliza Lang, Jan. 9, 1836. H. S.
Sypert, BM.

Thomas B. Leech & Alvira Alexander, Oct. 31, 1836, by George Bogle, J.P., Nov. 2, 1836.

Edward D. Lester & America Wasson, Jan. 21, 1836, by Joshua Lester, V.D.M., V. W. Cummings, BM.

David B. Smith & Nancy Lester, Aug. 18, 1836. J. L. Smith, BM.

Henry Major & Francina Donnell, Sep. 1 (or 24), 1836, by B. Pyland, Sep. 27, 1836.

Robert Marshall & Celia Lackey, Sep. 27, 1836, by Saml. Corley, Oct. 13, 1836.

John Martin & Dorcas Patterson, June 13, 1836, by B. Graves, J.P.

Thomas Marlin & Mary Wray, April 5, 1836, by Elisha Vaughan, M.G., April 6, 1836.

John McCray & Mary Horn, Dec. 31, 1836, by Isaac Hunter.

Joseph McDonald & Emily Furlong, July 16, 1836. Joel Algood, BM.

Thos. W. McDonald & Narcissa Allen, May 4, 1836, by John Hearn, J.P.

James McHaney & Nancy L. Sims, Nov. 19, 1836, by Joshua Lester, V.D.M.

Samuel McCinny & Martha Locke, Jan. 5, 1836, by Stephen McDonald, J.P., Jan. 7, 1836.

Russell S. Medling & Fary F. Patterson, Aug. 29, 1836, by J. B. Lasater, J.P., Sep. 6, 1836.

Little Berry Moore & Mary Ann Johnson, April 7, 1836, by John Sneed, April 15, 1836. William Bond, BM.

John Moran & Mary Williams, Oct. 10, 1836, by George Bogle, J.P., Oct. 11, 1836.

James Moore & Elizabeth Brooks, July 12, 1836, by John Bell, J.P., July 13, 1836.

Joseph L. Mosely & Elvira Drennan, May 2, 1836, by Silas Tarver, May 5, 1836.

Amos Mount & Eliza Patterson, Dec. 20, 1836, by J. B. Lasater, J.P., Dec. 21, 1836.

Almond Mullinax & Eliza Mellegan, Nov. 26, 1836, by George Bogle, J.P., Dec. 6, 1836.

Smith Oliver & Sarah Ann Sanders, Feb. 4, 1836, by Joshua Woollen, M.G., Robert Hester, BM.

Noah Oneal & Moranda Whitworth, July 7, 1836, by Thos. Davis, J.P., July 10, 1836.

Martin Owens & Zina Hollinsworth, Dec. 28, 1836, by Anthony Owen, J.P.

Robert L. Pulley & Susannah M. Cartwright, Oct. 25, 1836, by Solomon Caplinger, J.P., Oct. 26, 1836.

William R. Palmer & Louisa Green, Dec. 19, 1836, by Shelah Waters, J.P., Dec. 21, 1836.

William B. Parham & Rebecca McHenry, July 25, 1836, by G. H. Huddleston, J.P., July 28, 1836.

Wyatt Parkman & Margaret B. Douglas, Oct. 3, 1836, by John Hearn, J.P., Oct. 6, 1836.

Joshua Pemberton & Milly Dudley, June 13, 1836, by B. L. Mabry, M.G., June 14, 1836.

Baily Phillips & Amanda Harlin, Nov. 22, 1836, by John Borum, Nov. 24, 1836.

Josiah Phillips & Senny Cropper, Nov. 21, 1836, by Sion Bass, M.G.

Archibald Pugh & Lucinda Rickets, Nov. 17, 1836, by Wm. Lawrence, J.P., Dec. 20, 1836.

Joseph Putman & Lucinda Hearn, Dec. 3, 1836, by J. B. Lasater, J.P.

Peyton W. Randolph & Mary McCartney, Dec. 20, 1836, by Henry Truett, J.P.

Joel Rouse (a free man of Color) & Mary Jenkins (a free woman of Color), Aug. 10, 1836, by J. B. Lasiter, J.P., Aug. 12, 1836.

Robert Shannon & Mahulda McCartney, Sep. 14, 1836, by Henry Truett, J.P., Sep. 15, 1836.

Wood H. Sherron & Martha Walker, Sep. 1, 1836, by Wilbon R. Winter, J.P.

Samuel W. Sherrell & Eliza Ann Bomar, June 15, 1836, by Allen Clemmon.

Nicholas Smith & Penelope J. Summar, Feb. 13, 1836, George Harnet, BM.

McDaniel C. Smith & Mahulda Freeman, Dec. 5, 1836, by Allen Clemmons, Crawford Cragg, BM.

Thomas J. Smith & Elmira Jane Winter, Nov. 21, 1836, by John Seay, M.G.

Abram Sneed & Elizabeth Fuston, Sep. 5, 1836, by George Bogle, Sep. 6, 1836.

Alfred Soary & Catharine Francis, Jan. 6, 1836, by J. T. Cartwright, J.P., Jan. 7, 1836.

James Spears & Mary Tipet, Oct. 24, 1836, by A. Bass, M.G.

Moses Standly & Nancy An Miligan, June 7, 1836, by George Bogle, J.P.

John G. Stewart & Mary L. B. Williams, Aug. 30, 1836, by John Provine, Aug. 31, 1836.

Azur Sullivan & Delila Welch, May 24, 1836, by J. Hooker, M.G., May 25, 1836.

Cyrus C. Silliman & Abigail Edwards, Feb. 2, 1836, by A. F. Doak, J.P.

William W. Sullivan & Elizabeth P. Swan, Oct. 21, 1836, by B. Graves, J.P.

Samuel W. Sherrill & Polly Vicen (Vincen), Nov. 17, 1836, by Henry Truett, J.P.

William C. Sweatt & Sarah Ann Tuggle, April 8, 1836, by Allen Clemmons, April 27, 1836.

James M. Swain & Sarah E. Shannon, Dec. 5, 1836, by John Billenjoley, Dec. 8, 1836.

William Tate & Anna E. Guill, July 16, 1836, by Ezekiel Cloyd, M.G.

Archibald Tally & Rachel B. Williams, Dec. 20, 1836, by Jas. Baird, J.P., Dec. 29, 1836.

Samuel Telford & Katharine Cawthan, Oct. 5, 1836, by John Beard, M.G., Oct. 6, 1836.

Thomas C. Telford & Mary Ann Logan, Nov. 16, 1836, by Thos. Kirkpatrick, J.P., Nov. 18, 1836.

Jacob Thomason & Susan Marks, Nov. 26, 1836, by Sion Bass, M.G.

Dennis K. Thompson & Cynthia Ann Donnell, Aug. 13, 1836, by B. Pyland, Aug. 18, 1836.
James Calvin & Elizabeth D. Lester, Nov. 14, 1836, by Joshua Lester, V.D.M.
William Toombs & Martha Brown, March 29, 1836, by Thos. P. Holman, J.P.
Felin Vick & Caroline Rice, July 9, 1834, by Micajah Estes, M.G.
Joseph Vick & Mary Jackson, Feb. 5, 1836. Lemuel Rucker, BM.
Washington Vowell & Jane Whitworth, March 7, 1836, by B. Pyland, M.G., March 8, 1836.
John L. Vowell & Malvina Dukes, March 7, 1836, by B. Pyland.
Richard Wade & Mary Dougan, Sep. 6, 1836, by Moses Ellis, J.P.
Thomas Warren & Peggy Williams, July 8, 1836, by Anthony Anvey, Elijah Jennings, BM.
Ross Webb & Martha Smith, Nov. 21, 1836, by John Seay, M.G., Nov. 25, 1836.
Howell W. Williams & Sarah Bradly, March 29, 1836, by B. Pyland, M.G.
William C. Winston & Rebecca J. Cason, Feb. 20, 1836, by L. Fisher, M.G.
John W. Wright & Mary A. Harris, Oct. 29, 1836, by Elisha Vaughan, M.G., Oct. 30, 1836.
Edwin Adams & Lavina Ragsdale, Dec. 4, 1837, by Jacob Milton, M.G., Dec. 5, 1837.
Robert C. Allen & Susan F. Jarratt, Dec. 13, 1837, by G. H. Bransford, M.G., Claiborn Jarratt, BM.
Daniel N. Alsup & Susan Alsup, July 12, 1837. James D. Gollady, BM.
Wilbon Andrews & Martha Shanks, Oct. 17, 1837, by B. T. Mabry, L.E.C., Oct. 18, 1837. R. G. Andrews, BM.
William Axum & Mary H. Williams, Dec. 24, 1837. Newbern P. Stone, BM.
Bennett Babb & Rachael White, June 20, 1837, by Joseph B. Wynn, M.G., B. W. Ireland, BM.
James H. Bachus & Martha Echols, July 6, 1837, by John Hearn, J.P., Thos. Sypert, BM.
James H. Baird & Julia Jennings, Feb. 20, 1837, by J. T. Stevenson, J.P., March 1, 1837. Rutherford R. Barton, BM.
Leonard D. Baker & Sarah A. Johnson, July 15, 1837, by John Seay, M.G., July 18, 1837. Thomas R. Wynne, BM.
Joseph S. Barbee & Delpha Walker, Aug. 14, 1837, by Wilson Hearn, M.G., Aug. 15, 1837. Owen T. Barbee, BM.
Benjamin G. Barkley & Ann Eliza Wynn, Nov. 6, 1837. Berry Young, BM.
John Bates & Ann Brown, Dec. 1, 1837. William Bates, BM.
Joel A. Battle & Adaline Mosely, July 21, 1837, by F. E. Pitts, M.G., July 22, 1837. Geo. S. Golladay, BM.
Hezekiah Bell & Susan Fisher, Dec. 23, 1837, by Jonathan Bailey, J.P., Jan. 2, 1837 (1838). Wm. M. Caplinger, BM.

147

William O. Belcher & Frances C. Chandler, Nov. 28, 1837,
by Robert H. Ellis, J.P., Nov. 30, 1837. Benjamin
Gill, BM.
John C. Bennett & Martha A. Moore, Nov. 16, 1837, by
John Kelley, M.G., Thomas J. Stratton, BM.
Asap M. Bond & Levica Robertson, Oct. 23, 1837, by
William Alsup, J.P., Oct. 23, 1837. Henderson Esther,
BM.
Robert Bond & Elizabeth Climer, Nov. 9, 1836, by J. Hooker
M.G., Samuel B. Gibson, BM.
John Bowers & Jane Sypert, June 21, ____, by George
Donnell, V.D.M., June 22, 1837. Zechariah Wherry, BM.
David C. Bradley & Abigail Calhoun, Aug. 10, 1837. Thomas
G. Sanders, BM.
Hezekiah Bradley & Mary Dejernatt, May 10, 1837, by John
Borum, May 12, 1837. William Holland, BM.
William Brogan & Nancy Ann Montgomer, Oct. 6, 1837, by
Elihu _____, J.P., Oct. 12, 1837. William Hubbard, BM.
Andrew Brown & Catharine Worsham, Oct. 11, 1837. William
Bates, BM.
Thomas Bryant & Charlotte Jetton, June 5, 1837. J. C.
Spillars, BM.
Robert H. Bumpas & Eliza S. Craddock, Jan. 8, 1837, by
John Whitlock, V.D.M., Jan. 24, 1837. Geo. Smith, BM.
Fielding Burke & Anna Cluck, March 13, 1837, by Wm. Alsup,
J.P., March 15, 1837. James Cluck, BM.
Robert A. Burton & Elizabeth H. Donaldson, Nov. 16, 1837,
by George Donnell, V.D.M., George S. Golladay, BM.
Thomas Carney & Mary Jane Haley, Aug. 7, 1837, by Sion
Bass, M.G., William Vantrease.
Enos Carter & Celia Osburn, Nov. 27, 1837, by Moses
Woollen, J.P., Nov. 28, 1837. Solomon Carter, BM.
Littleton N. Carter & Charity D. Garrison, Feb. 23, 1837,
by John Hearn, J.P., John Hearn, BM.
Elijah Cason & Martha A. Clopton, May 9, 1837, by James
Bond, V.D.M., May 11, 1837. J. B. Rutland, BM.
_____ Casselman & Jane Jenkins, Aug. 12, 1837. Burrell
P. Casselman, BM.
Nicholas Chambers & Mary A. Jackson, Sep. 14, 1837. John
E. Bell, BM.
Beverly Chumley & Martha Bell, June 20, 1837, by Wm.
Lawrence, J.P., June 22, 1837. John Cumming, BM.
Pleasant Chumney & Betsey Panter, July 1, 1837, by W. G.
Bailey, J.P., July 2, 1837. James Panter, BM.
Samuel Clifton & Mary Pennebaker, July 15, 1837, by Jas.
Willeford, J.P., July 16, 1837.
Milton Climer & Adaline Cowthon, May 1, 1837. Wm. Graves,
BM.
James Coggins & Sarah Clifton, May 22, 1837, by John
Billingsley, May 23, 1837. A. G. Murhead, BM.
Stephen E. Comer & Anna Marrs, Oct. 22, 1836. Sam R.
Comer, BM.
William Compton & Rachel M. Nunn, Oct. 11, 1837, by Sion
Bass, M.G., Moses Atwood, BM.

WILSON COUNTY MARRIAGES

Charles Coppage & Harriet Brown, May 25, 1836. Thomas L.
Coppage, BM.
Minor Criswell & Catharine Gray, Jan. 1, 1837. Fletcher
Campbell, BM.
John Crudup & Elizabeth Graves, Oct. 23, 1837. C. B.
Lumpkins, BM.
James Crutchfield & Martha Spain, May 26, 1837, by Jas.
Baird, J.P., May 28, 1837. Thomas Brown, BM.
Price Curd & Elizabeth Hall, Nov. 25, 1837. William Curd,
BM.
Moses M. Currey & Margaret Dobson, Feb. 13, 1837, by J.
Hooker, M.G., Feb. 14, 1837. Isaac N. Currey, BM.
Charles N. Cutrell & Mary Ann Lewis, April 27, 1837, by
John Seay, M.G., May 4, 1837. John Rieff, BM.
John M. Davis & Eliza Turner, Oct. 21, 1837. William A.
Holbrook, BM.
Philander Y. Davis & Aleanor Dwyn, Dec. 20, 1837. C. W.
Jackson, BM.
Thomas Duffee & Nancy B. Glass, Nov. 15, 1837, by James
Bond, V.D.M., Nov. 16, 1837. Elijah Cason, BM.
John Earhart & Jane Hays, Dec. 9, 1837, by John Beard,
M.G., Dec. 10, 1837. H. Bernard, BM.
Samuel S. Eason & Elizabeth J. Warren, Sep. 20, 1837. R.
J. Evans, BM.
Thompson Eatherly & Harriet Eatherly, March 18, 1837.
Wm. Y. Eatherly, BM.
Peter P. Elliott & Susan J. Eddings, Nov. 29, 1837. John
A. Sneed, BM.
John A. Ellis & Martha Hearn, Sep. 18, 1837, by Markley
S. Fare, M.G., Jan. 1, 1838. William Ballender, BM.
James Eskew & Eliza Thornton, Jan. 24, 1837, by Thomas
Kirkpatrick, J.P., Jan. 25, 1837. William Guill, BM.
Duncan N. Estes & Frances Atwood, Sep. 18, 1837. A. J.
Pendleton, BM.
John Estes & Martha Griffin, Nov. 8, 1837. Robards
Howell, BM.
Mathew Estes & Fanny Lassater, Dec. 9, 1837, by J. B.
Lasater, J.P., Dec. 10, 1837. Henderson Estes, BM.
Tilman Ethridge & Polly McDaniel, Jan. 19, 1837. A. H.
Foster, BM.
William Axum & Mary H. Williams, Dec. 24, 1837, by J.
Irby, J.P., Dec. 25, 1837.
Robert Fakes & Susannah Alsup, July 3, 1837. S. J. Alsup,
BM.
Henry G. Flippen & Polly Lawrence, June 1, 1837, by M. J.
Cartwright, J.P., Joseph S. Barbee, BM.
Pascal Ford & Harriet Cawthon, Dec. 28, 1837. Thos. Ford,
BM.
Raneelear Foster & Matilda Robertson, Jan. 26, 1837, by
Geo. Donnell, V.D.M., R. D. Hankins, BM.
William Garmany & Agnes Smith, May 11, 1837, by Jas.
Baird, J.P., Jas. Johnson, BM.
William George & Kizziah Chumney, March 12, 1837, by Wm.
Lawrence, J.P., March 14, 1837. James George, BM.

Benjamin Gill & Martha Ann Belcher, Dec. 25, 1837. Samuel Allison, BM.

Joseph Graves & Elizabeth Prior, Feb. 22, 1837, by Thos. Davis, J.P., Burrell Reaves, BM.

William Graves & Winniford Lunceford, Jan. 29, 1834, by John Shane, J.P.

Hardy B. Gray & Sarah Sadler, Aug. 18, 1837, by Wm. H. Dott, J.P., Samuel Butt, BM.

Lewis Griffeth & Mizabel Briant, April 26, 1837. James Coldwell, BM.

William Griffin & Sarah Martin, Nov. 1, 1837, by Robert H. Ellis, J.P., James R. Ellis, BM.

Nicholas Grendstaff & Drucilla Tracy, July 11, 1837. David P. Tracy, BM.

William Guill & Jane A. Harelson, Jan. 28, 1837. James Eskew, BM.

William Halbrook & Harriett Oakley, May 21, 1837, by Wm. S. Walker, J.P., J. P. Summerhill, BM.

Samuel Hamilton & Sally Huguely, Aug. 30, 1837. William A. Hamilton, BM.

Eli Hancock & Mary H. Powell, Aug. 31, 1837, by John F. Hughs, M.G., C. W. Jackson, BM.

John Hancock & Martha Ann Hancock, March 21, 1837, by John Billingsly, March 23, 1837. Thomas Baird, BM.

Charles Harris & Margaret C. Duncan, Dec. 18, 1837, by Isaac Hunt, J.P., Dec. 25, 1837. John J. Swinney, BM.

John Harrington & Polly Ingram, Oct. 2, 1837, by Henry Truett, J.P., Samuel W. Sherrill, BM.

Landon Harrison & Mary Ann Hartsfield, June 1, 1837. William W. Johnson, BM.

John W. Harkreader & Sarah Babb, March 2, 1837, by John Beard, M.G., Sylvester Harkreader, BM.

John R. Hays & Peggy Amanda Fite, March 23, 1837. L. W. Davidson, BM.

Jacob Hearn & Martha Grindstaff, Jan. 11, 1837, by N. L. Norville, M.G., Jan. 12, 1837. H. M. Hancock, BM.

Jonathan Neil & Mary Baird, Jan. 17, 1837, by Sion Bass, M.G., James H. Branch, BM.

James Nichens & Esther Archer, Aug. 10, 1837. George Nichens, BM.

William Holland & Rhoda Bradley, May 10, 1837, by Moses Ellis, J.P., Oct. 15, 1837. James Borum, BM.

Levi Holloway & Elizabeth Marks, Jan. 24, 1837, by John Hearn, J.P., R. Holloway, BM.

Jesse W. Holt & Harriet C. Gregory, July 24, 1837. E. W. Gregory, BM.

Reuben D. Hubbard & Frances Pemberton, Oct. 31, 1837. John Cumming, BM.

John Hugeley & Martha M. Cawthon, Feb. 6, 1837. Isaac Rutland, BM.

Elijah Hunt & Julia Briant, Aug. 16, 1837. Josephus Walker, BM.

Thomas H. Hunt & Jane Holbrook, Feb. 17, 1837, by Wm. Watt, J.P., Feb. 17, 1837. John M. Davis, BM.

Elijah H. Jennings & Elizabeth Williams, June 5, 1837.
E. C. Jennings, BM.
Wiley T. Jennings & Sarah Roberson, Jan. 11, 1837, by
George Bogle, J.P., Eli Summers, BM.
John Johnson & Jane Aston, Sep. 19, 1837. A. L. Bell, BM.
William Johnson & Elizabeth McCaffry, Dec. 3, 1837, by
W. S. Bailey, J.P., John Johnson, BM.
David Jones & Elizabeth Lain, May 30, 1837, by Joshua
Woollen, M.G., June 14, 1837. Jesse Mullen, BM.
James H. Jones & Mary Wood, Sep. 28, 1836, by J. B.
Lasater, J.P., Sep. 29, 1836.
Mathew Jones (a free man of Color) & Priscilla Scott (a
free woman of Color), Oct. 30, 1837. Abraham Scott, BM.
Noah Jones & Eliza Ann Jones, Jan. 4, 1837. Thomas B.
Dunn, BM.
Tobins G. Jones & Elizabeth Gould, May 20, 1837, by
Barthel Figures, J.P., May 24, 1837. George W. Jones,
BM.
Mark Joplin & Delila Newby, Feb. 14, 1837, by Jas. Baird,
Feb. 18, 1837. Terrell Davis, BM.
Thomas H. Knight & Lucinda Thomas, Dec. 27, 1836, by
James Thomas, Jan. 24, 1837. Geo. Smith, BM.
Thomas B. Lain & Amelda Graves, Nov. 2, 183_, by John
Shane, J.P., Nov. 7, 1833.
Calvin Lasater & Martha Goldson, Dec. 18, 1837, by S.
Tarver, J.P., Dec. 20, 1837. Sam C. Anderson, BM.
David Lea & Arilla Lea, July 3, 1837, by Jas. Baird, J.P.,
Saml. Comer, BM.
Richard P. Lumpkins & Matilda C. Algood (A. Ford), Aug.
22, 1837. Archibald Carver, BM.
Meriot Ligon & Susan Debo, Feb. 27, 1837, by Robt. D.
Bell, M.G., Feb. 27, 1837. Samuel Sanders, BM.
Josiah Lockett & Almira Latimer, May 30, 1837, by Levi
Fisher, M.G., R. N. Latimer, BM.
Robert G. Logsden & Roda Ragsdale, July 17, 1837, by Henry
Truett, J.P., July 19, 1837.
Ebenezer K. Logsden & Evaline Hill, Dec. 12, 1837, by
Robert G. Loyd, J.P.
James H. Long & Elizabeth M. Wittey, April 13, 1837. B.
W. Ireland, BM.
William M. Lyon & Hannah B. Jones, Aug. 2, 18__, by
Barthel Figures, J.P., Sep. 6, 1836.
Seth W. Mabry & Martha A. Bell, Nov. 29, 1837, by P. Y.
Davis, M.G., C. W. Davis, BM.
Elijah L. Maddox & Piety Williams, Dec. 23, 1837, by Isaac
Hunter, J.P., Dec. 25, 1837. Benjamin Maddox, BM.
John Marks & Elizabeth Butler, June 5, 1837, by Jonathan
Bailey, J.P., Solomon Caplinger, BM.
Amos Martin & Sarah C. Truett, March 28, 1837. G. W. C.
Bond, BM.
Gideon C. Matlock & Anza C. Hardy, April 4, 1837, by
Thomas Kirkpatrick, Elijah B. Drake, BM.
Frederick Mays & Nancy A. Ford, Dec. 28, 1837. Thomas
Ford, BM.

Lewis McCartney & Martha Hawks, Jan. 2, 1837, by Henry Truett, J.P., Jan. 5, 1837. Wm. Johns, Jr.

Michael McDearman & Nancy Christopher, Jan. 5, 1837, by Thomas Miles, J.P., A. Simmons, BM.

Stephen McDonald & Lucy Warren, Nov. 1, 1837, by P. Y. Davis, M.G., A. H. Foster, BM.

Humphrey D. McElyea & Mary Rice, April 1, 1837, by J. Hooker, M.G., April 5, 1837. Thomas Richmond, BM.

Milton McGeehe & Mary Drollinder, May 10, 1837, by Ezekiel Cloy, M.G., May 11, 1837. R. H. Thompson, BM.

Henry McRoy & Martha Woodal, Sep. 5, 18__, by Isaac Hunter, J.P., Sep. 7, 1837. Reddin McRoy, BM.

James McWright & Malissa Peppers, Feb. 11, 1837, by Elisha Smith, J.P., James Glass, BM.

Cary Morris & Nancy Let, Feb. 8, 1837, by Jas. Baird, John S. Belt, BM.

Joseph Morrison & Elizabeth George, April 24, 1837. Miles M. Harvey, BM.

Azariah Moss & Adaline L. Alford, Dec. 12, 1837. M. Earheart, BM.

William D. Moss & Eliza J. Tarpley, Nov. 2, 1837, by George Donnell, V.D.M., B. D. Hankins, BM.

Isaac Mullinax & Hulda Turner, Nov. 13, 1837, by W. T. Bailey, J.P., Nov. 16, 1837. John Mullinax, BM.

Adam G. Murhead & Hannah Frazer, Dec. 26, 1837, by A. T. Scruggs, M.G., Geo. S. Golladay, Thos. J. Stratton, BM.

Nathaniel Murray & Jane Hearn, Dec. 18, 1837, by Markley S. Foard, M.G., Dec. 26, 1837. John Eskew, BM.

John B. Norris & Margaret B. Debow, Nov. 17, 1837. Robert P. Garrison, BM.

R. W. Odum & Lucy Rutland, Jan. 11, 1837, by Joshua Woollen, M.G., Jan. 24, 1837. E. W. Lester, BM.

Jennings Oliver & Rachel Jones, Oct. 11, 1837. Grandison Jones, BM.

John C. Organ & Elizabeth Stone, Jan. 18, 1837, by Thos. R. Jackson, J.P., Alfred H. Foster, BM.

George W. Overby & Sarah H. Ramsey, May 30, 1837, by George Donnell, M.G., May 31, 1837. W. H. Baxter, BM.

William H. Owen & Ann C. Penny, July 3, 1837, by John Billingsley, July 4, 1837. Robert R. Lampkin, BM.

James P. Patton & Mary Phillips, July 19, 1837. Anderson P. Payne, BM.

Micajah Peacock & Roses Smith, Jan. 3, 1837, by Moses Woollen, J.P., Jorden Robertson, BM.

Gassaway W. Peach & Eliza A. Drennon, Dec. 18, 1837. Samuel Edgar, BM.

Sherwood Pearcy & Polly Puckett, Dec. 19, 1837. F. W. Pearcy, BM.

William B. Pemberton & Phobe Brogan, Aug. 7, 1837. Alexr. Braden, BM.

Benjamin Phillips & Nancy Bass, Feb. 21, 1837, by Sion Bass, M.G., John Oakley, BM.

Charles A. Porterfield & Catharine Lemons, Dec. 19, 1837, by Saml. H. Porterfield, J.P., Alexander Lemons, BM.

William S. Prowell & Rachel Cartmelt, March 23, 1837, by
Jno. F. Hughs, M.G., Adam G. Murhead, BM.
Dudley W. Procter & Harriet A. Mabry, March 1, 183_, by
Wm. Watkins, J.P., March 6, 1837. Harry W. Robb, BM.
George R. Pugh & Jane Marks, Nov. 23, 1837, by Wm.
Lawrence, J.P., Joseph S. Pugh, BM.
Elzy Pugh & Martha Bradley, Dec. 14, 1837. Thos. Martin,
BM.
James M. Quarles & Mary Williams, Sep. 20, 1837, by
Williamson Williams, M.G., Sep. 21, 1837. David W.
Quarles, BM.
Hardin Ragland & Amelia A. Hanna, May 11, 1837, by F. E.
Pitts, M.G., May 12, 1837. Wm. Ragland, BM.
James Raines & Sarah Peppins, Oct. 2, 1837. Calvin
Williams, BM.
William Robb & Eliza McClain, Sep. 23, 1837, by John
Allison, V.D.M., John Allison, BM.
William Roberson & Manerva Spradley, June 8, 1837, by M.
T. Cartwright, J.P.
Robert G. Loesdon & Roda Ragsdale, July 17, 1837. E.
Holloway, BM.
George K. Robertson & Elizabeth Jane McClain, Feb. 25,
1837, by Silas Tarver, J.P., James H. McFarland, BM.
William A. Russell & Evaline Peak, Oct. 27, 1837, by
Wilson E. Winter, J.P., Oct. 29, 1837. Meeds P.
Anderson, BM.
Reuben M. Searcy & Frances B. Alloway, Feb. 11, 1837, by
Ezekiel Cloyd, M.G., Feb. 12, 1837. John B. Scoby, BM.
Robert Searcy & Norma Blurton, Feb. 1, 1837, by Wm. F.
Luck, William Sands, BM.
Andrew Sellers & Elizabeth Ann Donnell, Nov. 6, 1837.
Champ Smith, BM.
William C. Sellars & Eliza W. Smith, Sep. 16, 1837, by
Jas. Baird, J.P., Sep. 19, 1837. Robt. C. Grier, BM.
Green W. Shaw & Frances Loyd, April 10, 1837, by W. S.
Cartwright, James Bonner, BM.
James Shorter & Martha Wynn, June 1, 1837, by John
Billingsley, John Shorter, BM.
Elam Simmons & Lovisa Teague, Sep. 25, 1837, by Jas.
Baird, J.P., Sep. 29, 1837.
Sterling Simpson & Polly Johnson, Nov. 29, 1837, by W.
T. Bailey, J.P., Nov. 30, 1837. John Johnson, BM.
Henry F. Smith & Mary D. Morris, Sep. 14, 1837, by John
F. Hughes, M.G., J. W. White, BM.
Samuel C. Smith & Martha D. Foster, March 13, 1837, by
R. T. Comer, J.P., Steth Harrison, BM.
James A. Sneed & Elizabeth Bettis, Sep. 14, 1837, by
Isaac Hunter, J.P., Samuel J. Chapman, BM.
William H. Southworth & Henrietta Jackson, June 17, 1837,
by Barthel Figures, J.P., June 19, 1837.
William M. Spradley & Rachel Lash, Feb. 16, 1837, by
Solomon Caplinger, J.P., Wm. M. Spradley, BM.
Ebenezer Stewart & Bijah Sommars, May 10, 1837, by James
Somers, J.P., May 11, 1837. Green Stewart, BM.

Eli Somers & Lucy Lester, April 3, 1837. James Porterfield, BM. ‾

Edward Summerhill & Mary A. Thomason, Dec. 27, 1837, by
Wm. S. Watkins, J.P., Wm. Summerhill, BM.

LeRoy B. Suttle & Margery W. Grier, June 27, 1837 by F.
Witts, M.G., John G. Park, BM.

Robert Sweatt & Martha Sweatt, Dec. 19, 1837, by Solomon
Caplinger, J.P., Dec. 21, 1837. Thompson Anderson, BM.

William Sweatt & Elizabeth Sweatt, July 17, 1837, by
Solomon Caplinger, J.P., July 20, 1837. Robert Sweatt,
BM.

John J. Swiney & Celia Hamilton, Feb. 22, 1837, by Isaac
Hunter, J.P., John R. Belcher, BM.

James Tarpley & Eliza Geers, June 8, 1837, by Geo. Donnell,
M.G., William Moss, BM.

James Thompson & Harriet Coffrey, Dec. 27, 1837, by John
Sloan, M.G., Jan. 2, 1837 (?). John N. Thompson, BM.

Joseph Thompson & Mary A. M. Lester, Aug. 22, 1837.
Joseph Thompson, BM.

William G. Thorn & Elizabeth Scott, Sep. 14, 1837, by
Henry F. Bone, M.G., Sep. 14, 1837. A. H. Foster, BM.

Nicholas Loyd & Anna Turner, Jan. 6, 1837. A. W. Peacock,
BM.

William M. Turpin & Julia Thomas, Oct. 3, 1837. E. R.
Stewart, BM.

Larry Vivrett & Emely Gregory, Dec. 2, 1837, by H. B.
Hill, M.G., Dec. 7, 1837. Claiborn R. Jarratt, BM.

Andrew J. Wade & Louisa J. Geers, June 17, 1837, by Henry
Truett, J.P., June 20, 1837. Don D. Atwell, BM.

Adam Wall & Narcissa Hinson, July 27, 1837, by John Hearn,
J.P., Thos. D. Hearn, BM.

William H. Ward & Cynthia Hubbard, Dec. 26, 1837. Thomas
B. Florida, BM.

John M. Ware & Mary McDearman, Jan. 16, 1837. James E.
Foster, BM.

Moses Watkins & Sarah Wheeler, July 12, 1837. John E.
Bell, BM.

Thomas Weir & Mary C. Joplin, Feb. 6, 1837, by Jas. Baird,
J.P., Feb. 7, 1837. James Ware, BM.

Leonard Whitson & Elizabeth Tipton, March 15, 1837.
Summer Bloodworth, BM.

James F. Williamson & Louisa Walker, June 3, 1837, by E.
Cloyd, M.G., June 8, 1837. John N. Alexander.

James P. Williams & Prudence Beadles, Nov. 23, 1837, by
Williamson Williams, M.G., Seth P. Williams, BM.

Hiram Williams & Martha Jennings, May 1, 1837. E. C.
Jennings, BM.

Abner Wit & Isabella Stroud, March 24, 1837. Lewis
Grantham, BM.

Flemmings P. Wood & Lucy Williams, Jan. 29, 1837, by John
Bransford, M.G., Joseph Freeman, BM.

George Woollard & Anna Bundy (Bandy), Dec. 31, 1837.
James R. Johnson, BM.

James H. Yandle & Leanner C. Jones, May 18, 1837, by John
Beard, M.G., May 19, 1837. John Ramsey, BM.

WILSON COUNTY MARRIAGES

James Yergin & Jane Ballard, May 5, 1837. John W. Steele, BM.
Alexander S. Young & Frances Taylor, Nov. 29, 1837. A. H. Foster, BM.
Thomas Young & Mary Van Hoozer, Oct. 14, 1837. Wm. Young, BM.
Samuel Archer (a free man of Color) & Elizabeth Parker (a free woman of Color), Jan. 12, 1838. William Sypert, BM.
Don D. Atwell & Julia Gears, Jan. 9, 1838, by Geo. Donnell, V.D.M., Jan. 10, 1838. Tilmon J. Wilkerson, BM.
Alfred M. Ayers & Mary M. Knox, March 12, 1838, by John J. Sloan, M.G., March 13, 1838. J. H. Fisher, BM.
Alexander Baird & Margaret Smith, Oct. 10, 1838. C. L. Crawford, BM.
William Baird & Emeline C. Baird, Aug. 22, 1838, by Jas. Baird, J.P., Aug. 23, 1838. C. L. Crawford, BM.
James Barbee & Malinda Smart, April 20, 1838, by Sion Bass, M.G., April 30, 1838. C. W. Cummings, BM.
William Barnsfield & Mary Merchant, Dec. 22, 1838, by Jas. C. Willeford, Dec. 23, 1838. Allgood Woollard, BM.
Rutherford R. Barton & Avey Tilda McLarin, Aug. 21, 1838, by Wm. Barton, M.G., Zebulon Baird, BM.
William Bates & Margaret Wright, May 28, 1838, by Gideon H. Nransford, M.G., May 29, 1838. William Hester, BM.
James M. Bell & Elizabeth Oneal, Nov. 14, 1838, by Solomon Caplinger, J.P., Harris Fuller, BM.
William W. Bell & Sarah Ann Golladay, May 10, 1838, by George Donnell, V.D.M., Saml. Yerger, BM.
James Bernard & Martha Griffin, Sep. 14, 1838, by Wm. Barton, M.G., Sep. 16, 1838. Milton McGahe, BM.
William H. Blackford & Demaris Ann Parkell, Dec. 17, 1838. Henry Carter, BM.
Daniel A. Boaz & Cynthia Rice, April 3, 1838. William R. Dodson, BM.
Hiram Bright & Elizabeth Tims, Oct. 2, 1838, by Jas. Baird, J.P., Oct. 3, 1838. Asa Oneal, BM.
George C. Britt & Frances E. Mason, June 25, 1838, by Archb. B. Duval, G. W. C. Bond, BM.
James Buckner & Tempy Gibson, May 26, 1838. James T. Sims, BM.
George Campbell & Elizabeth Skean, Dec. 25, 1838, by John Billingsley, J.P., Dec. 26, 1838. Mathew Skean, BM.
James A. Campbell & Rebecca E. McNeill, Oct. 8, 1838, by Joseph B. Wynne, M.G., R. N. Campbell, BM.
Asa Carpenter & Eleanor Stephens, Dec. 20, 1838. John M. Payton, BM.
Addison Carroll & Lucetta R. Thomason, Nov. 26, 1838, by Moses Ellis, J.P., Nov. 28, 1838. E. B. Summerhill, BM.
James Cartwright & Martha Ann Coleman, June 18, 1838, by Elihu Jewel, June 19, 1838. Joseph Collier, BM.
Thomas Cartwright & Mary Fisher, Jan. 3, 1838, by Shelah Waters, J.P., Jan. 4, 1838. Thomas Hankins.
George W. Carver & Brunette P. Rice, Dec. 5, 1838. Thomas C. Osborn, BM.

Alexander Chambers & Jane Hunter, Jan. 25, 1838, by John
Borum, Jan. 28, 1838. Robert J. Garrison, BM.
Thomas Chapman & Verinda Snow, Aug. 16, 1838. William
Coggins, BM.
John A. Clark & Margaret Beard, Aug. 3, 1838, by J. A.
Young, J.P., James H. Branch, BM.
Edwin Clemmons & Patience Harris, March 21, 1838, by Jas.
Beard, March 22, 1838. Thos. Robertson, BM.
John Clemons & Elizabeth McHenry, Sep. 3, 1838, by G. A.
Huddleston, Sep. 5, 1838. Jesse Christopher, BM.
James J. Cluck & Rachel Robertson, Feb. 22, 1838, by John
Bond, V.D.M., Feb. 23, 1838. Jonathan Hall, BM.
Braxton Compton & Polly Underwood, Sep. 3, 1838, by J. W.
Locke, J.P., Sep. 4, 1838. William Acols, BM.
Benjamin Cooksey & Lydia Wier, Feb. 21, 1838, by Moses
Ellis, J.P., James Allen, BM.
Andrew J. Creswell & Frances Lane, Oct. 22, 1838. Hardy
B. Griffin, BM.
William T. Criswell & Matilda Lane, Dec. 1, 1838, by R.
S. Tate, Dec. 5, 1838. Henry T. Cropper, BM.
Thomas H. Cropper & Lerzah Telford, Aug. 29, 1838, by
John Beard, M.G., Henry S. Cropper, BM.
Charles C. Dale & Susan Harris, Oct. 27, 1838. Charles
Scott, BM.
Thomas Dallis & Nancy D. Chappell, July 10, 1838, by
Moses Ellis, J.P., Josiah Griffin, BM.
William N. Dawson & Martha Jane Hartsfield, Dec. 19, 1838.
John W. Wynne, BM.
Isiah B. David & Elizabeth Hays, Sep. 24, 1838, by H. W.
Puckett, M.G., Sep. 27, 1838. Gaben Dollarhede, BM.
Edmund Dillon & Hannah Tally, April 2, 1838, by John
Lester, V.D.M., April 2_, 1838. William A. Jennings,
BM.
Hiram Dickens & Charity Reese, April 10, 1838. J. W.
Barton, BM.
John E. Dickinson & Susannah N. Sims, April 23, 1838.
T. J. Sims, BM.
Jackson C. Dixon & Frances Welch, Feb. 28, 1838, by M.
Woollen, J.P., March 1, 1838.
Hardy M. Doak & Mary Charlotte, Oct. 15, 1838. James B.
Rutland, BM.
James H. Douglass & Margaret Rodgers, March 8, 1838, by
John Beard, M.G., Ramsey M. Mayson, BM.
George A. Duncan & Mary Poe, July 9, 1838. Henry Ward, BM
William Eason & Eliza N. Corley, June 23, 1838, by Jas.
Aston, J.P., June 26, 1838. David C. Wilson, BM.
Aaron Edwards & Elizabeth Hill, Oct. 1, 1838. G. B.
Edwards, BM.
Robert B. Edwards & Ann Ewing, July 3, 1838, by J. Hooker,
M.G., July 5, 1838. Robert Fakes, BM.
Miles Ellis & Martha Hancock, Dec. 27, 1838. Pollas
Lawrence, BM.
Sinclair England & Susan Kindred, Dec. 24, 1838. Edw.
Kindred, BM.

Robert C. Escue & Eleanor Myers, July 21, 1838, by
Micajah Estes, M.G., July 22, 1838. Thomas Williams,
BM.
Tilman Ethridge & Polly McDaniel, Jan. 19, 1838, by
Williamson Williams, M.G., Jan. 20, 1838.
Joseph H. Foster & Mary F. Davis, Dec. 14, 1838, by E.
James T. Tompkins, Dec. 18, 1838. J. B. Moss, BM.
James T. Gambell & Ann Wheeler, Nov. 27, 1838, by Silas
Tarver, J.P., Dec. 6, 1838. Silas Tarver, BM.
Isaac E. Gibson & Delila Browning, May 10, 1838. E. S.
Rhodes, BM.
William Gholston & Harriet Spickard, Dec. 10, 1838, by
Wm. Barton, Dec. 19, 1838. W. B. Jackson, BM.
Hardy B. Griffin & Sarah Ann Roberts, Dec. 1, 1838, by
R. S. Tate, M.G., Dec. 5, 1838. William T. Criswell,
BM.
Joseph Griffin & Elizabeth Anderson, Oct. 1, 1838.
William B. Vivrett, BM.
Josiah Griffin & Mahalia Martin, Sep. 18, 1838, by Moses
Ellis, J.P., Moses Ellis, BM.
William Hagan & Sarah Smart, Dec. 18, 1838, by Sion Bass,
M.G., Frances Smart, BM.
Zara Haralson & Margaret Ann Huguely, Oct. 5, 1838, by
A. B. Rogers, M.G., Oct. 9, 1838. Benjamin Walker, BM.
Samuel Harris & Rosey Cunningham, March 6, 1838, by
Joseph Aston, J.P., March 7, 1838. J. E. (?) Bell, BM.
West Harris & Angeline Brinkley, Jan. 2, 1838, by Jas.
Baird, J.P., J. W. Wynne, BM.
Elijah Hathway & Elizabeth Pedago, July 28, 1838, by Wm.
Lawrence, J.P., July 29, 1838. Wm. Adamson, BM.
Peter Harvel & Jane Chapple, Aug. 1, 1838, by Moses Ellis,
J.P., Gree Pugh, BM.
Martin Hawks & Sina Clifton, Sep. 25, 1838. C. Anderson,
BM.
Thomas Hawkins & Kiziah McBride, Jan. 29, 1838, by S.
Waters, J.P., Armsted Hawkins, BM.
William Hankins & Rebecca Allen, April 3, 1838, by
Solomon Caplinger, J.P., April 5, ____. Bailey Phillips,
BM.
Job T. Hayworth & Sewird Eskew, April 30, 1838, by Thos.
Burk, J.P., May 2, 1838. George F. Harris, BM.
James Hearn & Martha J. Ellie, Jan. 30, 1838, by Tho. R.
Jackson, J.P., Jan. 31, 1838. Joseph Griffin, BM.
Lewis W. Henry & Sophia Billingsley, Aug. 25, 1838, by
Gideon H. Braryford, Aug. 27, 1838. Samuel Major, BM.
Amzi C. Herron & Sarah Jane Potts, Sep. 1, 1838, by
Saml. H. Porterfield, J.P., John A. Herron, BM.
William H. Hill & Mary Rutland, Jan. 8, 1838. F. L.
Roulhoc, BM.
Archibald Huffman & Elizabeth Carter, Oct. 20, 1838, by
Jas. C. Williford, J.P., Oct. 21, 1838. William H.
Willeford, BM.
Joseph B. Hughes & Elizabeth M. Dabbs, Aug. 22, 1838, by
Levi Fisher, M.G., William J. Burress, BM.

Jesse Ingram & Nancy Sutton, Dec. 13, 1838, by Henry
Truett, J.P., Dec. 15, 1838. John Hancock, BM.
John Wesley Jarrell & Elizabeth Mitchell, Aug. 21, 1838,
by Gideon H. Bransford, M.G., Fountain Jarrell, BM.
Jacob A. Jennings & Nancy Robertson, July 20, 1838.
William H. Ward, BM.
James Jenkins & Martha Bradley, Nov. 22, 1838, by Shelah
Waters, J.P., Barnett Bradley, BM.
James T. Jewell & Malinda Thomas, Jan. 11, 1838, by Elihu
Juell, Feb. 1, 1838. John Baum, BM.
Gregory D. Johnson & Lucinda Vaughn, April 4, 1838, by
Jas. C. Webbfoset, J.P., Jeremiah Johnson, BM.
William Johns & Priscilla Russell, Jan. 24, 1838, by
Henry Truett, J.P., Finis E. Shannon, BM.
Nelson Jones & Nancy Williams, Dec. 3, 1838. Absolum
Earheart, BM.
Martin S. Keane & Maranda J. Hearne, June 23, 1838, by
Carlisle, M.G., June 27, 1838. Thos. D. Hearn, BM.
Joseph S. Lane & America Ann Puckett, Sep. 26, 1838,
by Henry Truett, Sep. 29, 1838. Allen Puckett, BM.
William Lane & Elizab Gholdstone, Sep. 4, 1838, by
Wm. Barton, M.G., Sep. 5, 1838. William A. Leach, BM.
Turner M. Lawrence & Sarah Taylor, Feb. 25, 1838, by Jas.
Young, J.P., Dec. 27, 1838. George Neal, BM.
John H. Lenoir & Malvira C. Bond, March 15, 1838, by G.
A. Huddleston, J.P., Joshua J. Bond, BM.
Marteell Mabry & Mary Tune, Dec. 19, 1838, by Wm. S.
Walker, J.P., Dec. 26, 1838. Wm. Holbrook, BM.
Azariah J. Maddox & Julia Ann Baxter, April 6, 1838,
Silas Tarver, J.P., April 8, 1838. James M. Baxter, BM.
John W. Martin & Martha Stone, Nov. 10, 1838, by Thos.
R. Jackson, J.P., Nov. 19, 1838. Thos. R. Martin.
J. W. Massey & Martha Morris, Dec. 7, 1838, by Levi
Fisher, M.G., Josephus Walker, BM.
James H. McFarland & Charlotte Walker, Nov. 1, 1838, by
Joseph B. Wynns, M.G., Nov. ___, 1838. Jesse B. White,
BM.
Edmund Melvin & Eleanor Myers, June 27, 1838, by Micajah
Estes, M.G., June 28, 1838. Zachariah T. Hays, BM.
William Melvin & Tabitha P. Gillespie, Jan. 30, 1838,
by John Beard, M.G., Jan. 31, 1838. Nathan C. Clampet,
BM.
William Moore & Elizabeth Carlin, Dec. 5, 1838, by Sion
Bass, M.G., James Robertson, BM.
Wm. L. Moxley & Elizabeth Coe, April 23, 1838, by M. T.
Cartwright, J.P., April 26, 1838. W. T. Cartwright, BM.
William B. Mumford & Amanda G. Johnson, Jan. 23, 1838,
by A. T. Scruggs, M.G., Jesse B. White, BM.
Raulston B. Murray & Susan Scott, March 27, 1838, by
George Brown, J.P., Joseph Nickins, BM.
Thomas G. Nevels & Ann Hagan, May 3, 1838. Thos B. Clarke
BM.
Ennis Organ & Diana Harrison, Nov. 12, 1838, by E. Smith,
J.P., Nov. 13, 1838. T. B. Brivard, BM.

WILSON COUNTY MARRIAGES

Cartwell Mabry & Mary Tune, Dec. 19, 1838, by Wm. S. Walker, J.P., Dec. 26, 1838. Wm. Holbrook, BM.

John Oneal & Martha Freeman, Dec. 19, 1838, by B. Tarver, J.P., Dec. 20, 1838. L. N. M. Cook, BM.

Francis Palmer, Sr. & Polly Bumpus, Sep. 3, 1838. Petters Ragland, BM.

William Parham & Ann Eliza Johnson, Oct. 1, 1838. L. B. Brinkley, BM.

Randle Partain & Lydia Bachus, Jan. 9, 1838, by R. Comer, J.P., Jan. 17, 1838.

Hartwell Patterson & Martha Chism, Jan. 23, 1838, by G. H. Bransford, Jan. 24, 1838. Hale J. Winsett, BM.

Jordan Patterson & Betsy Ann Johns, Aug. 6, 1838. Lewis Patterson, BM.

Kenchen Patterson & Martha Jennings, Feb. 13, 1838. Kindell Barlow, BM.

Wyand Pennybaker & Mourning Johnson, Nov. 12, 1838. Allen Jones, BM.

John Pemberton & Elizabeth Brogan, Sep. 6, 1838. Abner Jennings, BM.

Hiram Percell & Parthena Williams, Aug. 17, 1838. John M. Stroud, BM.

John C. Rainey & Evaline Organ, April 10, 1838, by E. Smith, J.P., April 19, 1838. Newbern Stone, BM.

William Reese & Nancy Woollard, July 13, 1838, by B. S. Mabry, July 16, 1838. Robert J. Goodwin, BM.

Robert Rhea & Lydia Williams, Dec. 22, 1838, by Sam H. Porterfield, J.P., Albert G. Lea, BM.

Anderson F. Roach & Margaret M. Alexander, Nov. 6, 1838, by John Beard, M.G., Thos. H. Roach, BM.

Moses Robertson & Manerva R. Oliver, Feb. 26, 1838, by H. W. Puckett, M.G., March 5, 1838. William H. Martin, BM.

George Romines & Elizabeth Underwood, Dec. 5, 1838, by Robert M. Ellis, J.P., Dec. 6, 1838. Andrew Conger, BM.

William Russell & Lucy Sinners, Jan. 30, 1838. J. R. Ashworth , BM.

John N. Sadler & Mary Jane Scott, Nov. 5, 1838. William T. Degernett, BM.

Bird Sands (of mixed blood) & Hettie McClendon (of mixed blood), April 25, 1828. William Sands, BM.

John Scott & Mary Aston, Feb. 5, 1838. Robert J. Garrison, BM.

Robert Scott & Elizabeth Vowell, May 29, 1838, by B. Pyland, M.G., James P. Scott, BM.

James A. Seat & Martha Griffin, Oct. 20, 1838, by Thomas David, J.P., Oct. 28, 1838. Alfred Ragsdale, BM.

Finis E. Shannon & Nancy M. Hearn, July 28, 1838, by Tho. R. Jackson, J.P., July 31, 1838. John M. Wynne, BM.

Jonathan Shores & Malinda McMullen, Sep. 24, 1838, by H. W. Puckett, M.G., Sep. 25, 1838. William Shores, BM.

James Singleton & Sarah Bagwell, Sep. 26, ____, by Henry Truett, J.P., Sep. 27, ____. John Fields, BM.

John L. Sloan & Rachel Thompson, Sep. 19, 1838, by Jesse Alexander, M.G., Sep. 20, 1838. James Thompson, BM.

Josiah Smith & Sarah A. F. Williamson, Dec. 10, 1838, by
John Beard, M.G., Dec. 11, 1838. Thomas J. Smith, BM.
Joseph Smith & Sarah Pemberton, Aug. 7, 1838. E. Smith,
BM.
Daniel Soaps & Sarah P. Askins, July 13, 1838, by Thomas
Kirkpatrick, J.P., July 15, 1838. David Bush, BM.
Joseph Stuart & Shilotte Ables, Sep. 11, 1838, by George
Donnell, M.G., David McGarr, BM.
Newbern P. Stone & Sarah Organ, April 10, 1838, by E.
Smith, J.P., April 11, 1838. John C. Raney, BM.
Thomas J. Stratton & Caroline Golladay, May 10, 1838, by
George Donnell, M.G., Sam Yergen, BM.
William A. Syblett & Rebecca Puckett, Jan. 1, 1838, by
Geo. Donnell, M.G., A. Harris, BM.
Barnet J. Sullivan & Elizabeth Sinclair, Dec. 22, 1838.
Eli Sinclair, BM.
Anthony Terrell & Eliza Bradshaw, July 25, 1838. Rich'd.
Terrell, BM.
Nathaniel Thurman & Claudia Need, Nov. 3, 1838. Josiah
Vick, BM.
Nathaniel Thurman & Mary Tuggle, April 23, 1838. Edmund
Jones, BM.
Albert Tomlinson & Nancy P. Afflack, Sep. 13, 1838. R.
J. Evans, BM.
Henry Tomlinson & Parilee Johnson, July 26, 1838, by
Joseph Astor, Aug. 8, 1838. Milus McCorkle, BM.
James Thompson & Lavina Ayres, Nov. 7, 1838, by Joshua
Lester, M.G., Nov. 8, 1838.
David R. Tracy & Susan Lawrence, Oct. 13, 1838, by Sion
Bass, M.G., John H. Vowell, BM.
Alexander Urie & Manerva Ferrell, Nov. 9, 1838, by M. T.
Cartwright, J.P., Nov. 15, 1838. John W. Foster, BM.
Valentine Van Hooser & Delila N. Zachary, July 9, 1838.
Thomas M. Young, BM.
Benjamin B. B. Walker & Louisa J. Crudup, Dec. 3, 1838,
by R. L. Tate, M.G., Dec. 11, 1838. John W. Hewgley,
BM.
William S. Walpole & Lydia Earnheart, Oct. 15, 1838, by
Cary James, M.G., Oct. 18, 1838. C. H. Walpole, BM.
William Watkins & Ann Eliza Ramsey, Dec. 26, 1838, by
P. Y. Davis, Moses Watkins, BM.
Ross Webb & Lucy Jane Bullard, June 26, 1838, by B. S.
Mabry, M.G., George M. McWhirter, BM.
William Webb & Frances Vaughn, March 16, 1838, by Jas. C.
Willeford, J.P., May 14, 1848. William N. Dawson, BM.
Thomas W. West & Martha Ann Allen, March 20, 1838.
Archibald Allan, BM.
John W. Whitlock & Nancy Brogan, Dec. 3, 1838. Thomas
K. Whitlock, BM.
William Whitson & Ann Criswell, March 17, 1838, by Thos.
Burke, J.P., March 18, 1838. William Lillard, BM.
Andrew J. R. Williams & Sarah Ann Ozment, Oct. 23, 1838,
by Saml. H. Porterfield, J.P., Isaac Williams, BM.
David Williams & Nancy Stambridge, Oct. 4, 1838, by John
Billingsby, J.P., Gregory J. Smith, BM.

WILSON COUNTY MARRIAGES

James P. Williams & Isabella C. Scoot, April 2, 1838, by
Thos. David, J.P., April 3, 1838. J. B. Booth, BM.
Seth R. Williams & Sally Sanders, May 3, 1838, by Moses
Woollen, J.P., Cullen Sanders, BM.
William T. Williams & Nancy W. Andrews, Nov. 6, 1838, by
B. Pyland, M.G., H. W. Williams, BM.
Tilman J. Wilkinson & Lucy M. Wade, Feb. 8, 1838, by Geo.
Donnell, M.G., Burton Underwood, BM.
James C. Williford & Alcey Carr, Jan. 24, 1838, by B. S.
Mabry, Geo. Smith, BM.
Charles Wilson & Elizabeth Leach, Jan. 30, 1838.
Richard Wommack & Matilda L. Moxley, May 12, 1838, by B.
Pyland, J.P., May 18, 1838. Jaes S. Wommack.
R. D. Wright & Lucinda Ozment, July 29, 1838. Wm. A.
Lea, BM.
James Wynns & Catharine Rieff, Feb. 5, 1838, by Joseph
B. Wynne, M.G., John Rieff, BM.
George B. Alexander & Eliza Merchant, Oct. 19, 1839, by
Thos. David, J.P., Oct. 20, 1839. Thos. Burke, BM.
James Allen & Nancy Neil, Nov. 15, 1839, by Sion Bass,
M.G., Robert Givan, BM.
Wilaon Baird & Eliza Baird, Aug. 19, 1839. Batt Baird, BM.
John Barber & Nancy Ware, Jan. 7, 1839, by J. Provine,
M.G., Jan. 8, 1839. E. Brantley, BM.
Kendell.C. Barton & Lockey Jarman, Jan. 7, 1839. J. C.
Word, BM.
Bailie H. Bell & Eleanor Carter, Nov. 7, 1839, by A. M.
Stone, M.G., John J. Carter, BM.
John Bell & Sarah Grogan, April 16, 1839, by Solomon
Caplinger, J.P., Baily Bell, BM.
Houston Bell & Sarah Bonds, April 25, 1839, by Thos.
David, J.P., Cary Morris, BM.
Thomas Belt & Mary Belt, Nov. 20, 1839, by Wm. Barton,
M.G., Nov. 29, 1839. Benj. Belt, BM.
Joseph Bennett & Nancy Merritt, Oct. 21, 1839, by Thos.
David, J.P., Oct. 22, 1839. Isham S. Green, BM.
James S. Bennett & Polly Edwards, Dec. 1, 1839, by James
Bond, M.G., Dec. 10, 1839. Jarratt W. Edwards, BM.
Perry P. Benson & Nancy M. Hill, Dec. 21, 1839. Wm. J.
Pride, BM.
Benjamine Berry & Mary Oakley, Nov. 4, 1839, by Archamab,
Bass, M.G., Nov. 6, 1839. Dake Young, BM.
William D. Bland & Viney Beadles, Dec. 26, 1839, by Saml.
H. Porterfield, J.P., John W. Bland, BM.
Robert R. Bogale & Elizabeth H. (?) Jennings, Oct. 8,
1839, by James Turner, J.P., Oct. 9, 1839. James
Turner, BM.
Samuel Booker & Mary Taylor, Aug. 13, 1839, by Silas
Tarver, J.P., Aug. 15, 1839. Elijah B. Drake, BM.
Daniel Bradley & Lydia Chasteen, Dec. 23, 1839, by Solomon
Caplinger, J.P., Dec. 24, 1839. Joseph Jenkins, BM.
James Bradley & Elizabeth White, Nov. 6, 1839, by Sion
Bass, M.G., D. G. Hankins, BM.
Alexander Brite & Malinda Jennings, March 28, 1839. W.
J. McClain, BM.

161

William C. Brown & Mary C. Johnson, Dec. 24, 1839, by
Melkijah L. Vaughn, M.G., Elijah M. Holt, BM.
Nathan Bundy & Martha G. Mullin, Sep. 23, 1839, by Jas.
C. Willeford, J.P., Sep. 24, 1839. Allgood Wollard, BM.
Robt. N. Campbell & Mary E. McNiel, Sep. 18, 1839, by
Joseph B. Wynns, Sep. 20, 1839. Fletcher Campbell, BM.
Wilson T. Cartwright & Elizabeth Tracy, Dec. 10, 1839.
R. H. Cartwright, BM.
Joseph T. Cason & Joanna Jarmon, Feb. 23, 1839. J. D.
Scott, BM.
Lazairus Casselman & Jane E. Summers, Aug. 7, 1839. Jacob
Casselman, BM.
John N. Chandler & Lucinda G. Rogers, Dec. 2, 1839, by
Wm. Barton, M.G., Dec. 5, 1839. J. B. Murray.
Payton Chadwell & Esther Jane Ricketts, July 25, 1839,
by G. A. Huddleston, J.P., July 29, 1839. John T.
Ricketss, BM.
James Clemmens & Nancy R. Casselman, Aug. 20, 1839, by
John Billingsley, J.P., Sep. 3, 1839. William Clemmons,
BM.
Uriah Cluck & Elizabeth Hall, Nov. 19, 1839, by John
Bond, M.G., Nov. 20, 1839. William Hall, BM.
Eli Coggins & Polly Penny, June 3, 1839, by John
Billingsley, J.P., June 25, 1839. John F. Hancock, BM.
William T. F. Coles & Lititia Shepherd, June 24, 1839,
by Melkijah S. Vaughn, M.G., June 25, 1839. Daniel
Barley, BM.
John H. Conyer & Mary Harrington, May 28, 1839, by G. H.
Bussard, J.P., Truman Harrington, BM.
Robert Compton & Elizabeth Warren, Jan. 4, 1839, by Wm.
S. Wallis, J.P., Jan. 5, 1839. Lofton Echols, BM.
William Corley & Eliza Jane Neelson, Jan. 9, 1839, by
P. Y. Davis, M.G., Montgomer J. Corley, BM.
Peter Cox & Thurza Phillips, Jan. 14, 1840, by Solomon
Caplinger, J.P., Dec. 14, 1849. Henry Phillips, BM.
Counsel L. Crawford & Aristem L. Hill, Jan. 2, 1839, by
Jas. T. Tompkins, Jeptha Clemmons, BM.
Martin Creswell & Harriet Eagan, Jan. 5, 1839, by Thos.
Burk, J.P., Jan. 6, 1839. Minor Creswell, BM.
Benjamin S. Dallis & Susan Allen, Dec. 11, 1839, by
Robert H. Allis, J.P., James E. Cropper, BM.
John McDaniel & Lucy Ozment, Oct. 16, 1839, by Joseph
Collins, J.P., Oct. 18, 1839.
John Davis & Catharine Hearn, Nov. 4, 1849. John W.
Wynne, BM.
James Dickerson & Sarah New, Nov. 29, 1839, by H. B. Hill,
M.G., Dec. 3, 1839. David W. Dickerson, BM.
John Durham & Mary M. Watkins, Aug. 12, 1839, by Wm.
Barton, M.G., Aug. 14, 1839. Robt. D. Reed, BM.
John Dwpe & Martha Hearn, April 13, 1839, by Isaac
Hunter, J.P., April 15, 1839. Wm. Holbrook, BM.
Henry Edwards & Jane Edwards, July 29, 1839, by Jas.
Baird, J.P., July 30, 1839. John A. Smart, BM.
John W. Ellis & Chelly Ann T. Sluder, April 30, 1839.
Wm. B. McLendon, BM.

Andrew Eskew & Matilda Caroline McFarlin, April 29, 1839.
Alfred Wskew, BM.
William Exum & Eliza Allen, July 23, 1839. L. Matherly,
BM.
Albert L. Fakes & Sarah B. Johnson, Dec. 3, 1839, by
Melkijah L. Vaughn, M.G., Dec. 5, 1839. Hugh Edwards,
BM.
Herrod Foutch & Susan Williams, Nov. 6, 1839. Benjamin
Cluck, BM.
John H. Foust & Louisa Violett, Aug. 20, 1839, by M. T.
Cartwright, J.P., Aug. 21, 1839. Peter A. Cartwright,
BM.
Richard J. Bone & Sarah Coutch, Sep. 29, 1839. Herod
Fourth, BM.
Robert J. Garrison & Elizabeth Horsley, Nov. 13, 1839, by
Wm. S. Watkins, J.P., Benjamin M. Garrison, BM.
Lucas George & Jane Forbis, Nov. 7, 1839, by James Warren,
M.G., Dec. 26, 1839. Ennis Organ, BM.
Joseph S. Gibson & Elizabeth Shaw, Oct. 10, 1839, by A.
J. Donnell, J.P., Lewis W. Herrell, BM.
Doctor Goodman & Rhoda Landrian, Sep. 2, 1839. Jacob
Thomas, BM.
William Graves & Elizabeth A. Russell, April 1, 1839. A.
J. Graves, BM.
James S. D. Green & Susan Bridges, Oct. 13, 1839. William
Sands, BM.
John A. Griffin & Margaret Anderson, Feb. 4, 1839, by
Micajah Estes, M.G., Feb. 6, 1839. Micajah Estes, BM.
Stephen Griffin & Elizabeth Jacobs, Oct. 5, 1839, by
Joseph Collins, J.P., Ephraim Williams, BM.
William Grissom & Mary D. Reed, Aug. 10, 1839, by John
Billingsley, J.P., Aug. 22, 1839. Wily Russel, BM.
Frances S. Grogan & Constant Ruffman, April 10, 1839, by
Solomon Caplinger, J.P., April 11, 1839. Bailee Bell,
BM.
Joseph Guill & Elizabeth M. Thaxton, Aug. 28, 1839. John
B. Fletcher, BM.
John J. Hagar & Harriet A. Duncan, Dec. 21, 1839. Beverly
W. Seay, BM.
John P. Hallyburton & Jane A. McDonald, Sep. 16, 1839,
by Robt. D. Bell, Sep. 27, 1839. David L. Crenshaw, BM.
William D. Hamblin & Mary Lane, March 20, 1839. Wm.
Barton, BM.
William Harris & Elizabeth Duffy, May 6, 1839. William
Jackson, BM.
Henry Hays & Susan B. Hughes, March 14, 1839, by Joseph
Astor, M.G., March 17, 1839. Wm. L. Sypert, BM.
Reuben G. L. Hays & Delila Litchfield, April 12, 1839, Thos.
R. Jackson, J.P., Robert M. Burton, BM.
Melbry P. Hearn & Elizabeth Jane Johnson, Jan. 23, 1839,
by J. John F. Hughes, M.G., Jan. 24, 1839. John F.
Hughes, BM.
William Henry & Mary Wroe, May 28, 1839. Florve McGregor.
William H. Hill & Sarah C. Jackson, Nov. 17, 1839, by J.
M. Peyton, J.P., Nov. 20, 1839. J. W. Jackson, BM.

WILSON COUNTY MARRIAGES

James Hobbs & Sarah Grissom, Jan. 21, 1839. Joseph Bell, BM.

Henry Hobson & Ann Maria Baker, May 1, 1839, by John Seay, M.G., May 2, 1839. William J. King, BM.

John Holland & Martha Piner, May 23, 1839, by Wm. Barton, M.G., Eli Sullivan, BM.

William Horn & Martha Carruth, March 2, 1839, by Jas. Astor, J.P., March 3, 1839. Daniel Nowlin, BM.

Elijah Hunt & Jane Graves, Nov. 5, 1839, by Thos. Davis, J.P., James M. Hunt, BM.

Washington B. Jackson & Mahalay Freeman, June 14, 1839, by A P. Richmond, J.P., June 18, 1839. T. H. Chandler, BM.

James Jennings & Rachel Shores, May 16, 1839, by Joshua Lester, M.G., Thomas Williams, BM.

William B. Harris & America S. Miles, Oct. 22, 1839, by W. H. Johnson, M.G., Oct. 24, 1839. C. T. Harris, BM.

William A. Jennings & Catharine James, April 2, 1839, by Joshua Lester, M.G., April 4, 1839. John Dillon, BM.

Jesse Johnson & Ebathan Tomlinson, June 22, 1839, by J. D. Ragland, J.P., L. B. Stevens, BM.

Mark Jopling & Ann McNicle, Jan. 29, 1839, by Isaac Hunter, J.P., Jan. 31, 1839. William Horn, BM.

Joseph H. Kennedy & Lucinda C. Ewing, Feb. 21 1839, by Joshua Lester, M.G., Feb. 28, 1839. Smith J. McAdow, BM.

John H. King & Sarah Ann Chandler, July 9, 1839, by Wm. Barton, M.G., July 10, 1839. A. G. Rogers, BM.

James Lanham & Nancy Snider, May 9, 1839, by Solomon Caplinger, J.P., Abraham McBride, BM.

Thomas Lannom & Nancy McBride, March 25, 1839, by Solomon Caplinger, J.P., March 26, 1839. Joseph Marrs, BM.

Harmon Lasater & Elizabeth Watkins, Oct. 2, 1839, by H. Truett, J.P., Oct. 3, 1839. Calvin Lasater, BM.

Jesse R. Laswell & Mary Baker, Aug. 27, 1839, by Joshua Woollen, M.G., Aug. 29, 1839. W. S. Bond, BM.

Robt. Liggon & Jane Wills, Sep. 13, 1839. Joshua Bartlett, BM.

William W. Lisles & Casendania Harris, July 30, 1839, by M. T. Cartwright, J.P., July 31, 1839. Thos. B. Hearn, BM.

John Malone & Elizabeth Hinson, July 29, 1839, by Henry Truett, J.P., July 30, 1839. Abraham Boyd, BM.

John W. Marshall & Annaliza McAdoo, Oct. 31, 1839. Oscar S. Ewing, BM.

James W. Martin & Mary E. Corley, Sep. 16, 1839, by Johnathan Wiseman, M.G., Sep. 18, 1839. F. G. Carney, BM.

Smith L. Matherly & Kitty T. Harrison, July 24, 1839. J. C. Word, BM.

John McDaniel & Lucy Ozment, Oct. 16, 1839. Geo. Donnell, BM.

Daniel A. Eachen & Mary Barber, Sep. 21, 1839, by Archamack, Bass, M.G., James Gill, BM.

WILSON COUNTY MARRIAGES

Robert McFarland & Martha Brown, Jan. 17, 1839. Ira McFarland, BM.
Moses McMillin & Lucinda Garrison, Jan. 1, 1839, by James Turner, J.P., Jan. 6, 1839. Moses Garrison, BM.
Robert D. McMinn & Mary Alford, June 11, 1839. Eli Donnell, BM.
James B. McNiele & Ann Ross, July 1, 1839, by Joseph B. Wynns, July 4, 1839. Allen Ross, BM.
Green Merrett & Lurany Graves, Sep. 18, 1839. L. J. Graves, BM.
Sylvanus Merrett & Eliza Bennett, Oct. 29, 1839, by John Bond, M.G., Oct. 31, 1839. Obadiah Ragsdale, BM.
William Miles & Emily Tomlinson, May 29, 1839, by Jas. Aston, J.P., May 30, 1839. Alexander Carruth, BM.
Garrett G. Mitchener & Frances H. Avery, Nov. 26, 1839, by R. R. Barden, M.G., Nov. 27, 1839. John P. Johnson, BM.
John Mobbs & Peggy Pugh, July 3, 1839. Elias Merrit, BM.
John Modglin & Nancy Webb, Jan. 19, 1839. Turner Thompkins, BM.
William D. Morrison & Jane L. Donnell, March 20, 1839, by B. Pyland, M.G., April 1, 1839. Jas. B. Rutland, BM.
Paul Motto & Mary Webster, Nov. 26, 1839, by G. H. Bussard, W. L. Wilburn, BM.
Mathias Mount & Bidy Emeline Jennings, Feb. 12 1839. Thomas B. Florida, BM.
James Mullinax & Nancy Oakley, March 31, 1839, by Jas. Turner, J.P., April 11, 1830 (?). John Mullinax, BM.
James Bradley & Jane Bradley, Oct. 2, 1839, by Jonathan Bailey, J.P., Nov. 11, 1839. Harrison Doughty, BM.
John M. Odum & Mary Lax, Oct. 18, 1839, by E. W. Haile, M.G. Oct. 21, 1839. Samuel C. Odum, BM.
James F. Organ & Lucy Bell, April 3, 1839. R. J. Evans, BM.
Joseph M. Payton & Elizabeth Jane Wier, Dec. 18, 1839, by Joseph B. Walker, M.G., Jesse Jackson, BM.
Willis Patterson & Jane Williams, April 10, 1839, by James Bond, M.G., Lewis Patterson, BM.
Nancy W. Phillips & Sarah Young, Feb. 4, 1839, by Archamack Bass, M.G., Feb. 10, 1839. Javill Grandstaff, BM.
John Pirtle & Martha M. Hubbard, May 1, 1839, by Levi Fisger, M.G., May 2, 1839. Geo. M. McWhirter BM.
William Porch & Sarah Waldens, May 7, 1839, by E. Smith, J.P., May 9, 1839. N. P. Stone, BM.
Edward Powell & Hicksey E. Babb, Nov. 6, 1839, by B. Tarver, J.P., D. G. Hankins, BM.
James N. Provine & Elizabeth J. Bradley, Nov. 30, 1839, by Robt. D. Bell, M.G., James C. Calhoun, BM.
Francis Puckett & Docy Sharp, Feb. 18, 1839. Geo. W. Hynds, BM.
Alfred Ragsdale & Nancy M. Seatt, Feb. 25, 1839 by Thos. Davis, Feb. 26, 1839. J. P. Ragsdale, BM.
John D. Ragland & Harriet Telford, Sep. 6, 1839 by Robt. D. Bell, M.G., J. A. Cartwright, BM.

William L. Reddete & Elizabeth Harrison, Jan. 15, 1839. Joseph Harrison, BM.

Ewing H. Roane & Martha K. Calhoun, Feb. 11, 1839. J. N. Embris, BM.

Thomas L. Robertson & Eleanor Oldham, Feb. 26, 1839, by John Seay, M.G., Feb. 27, 1839. Josephus Walker, BM.

Asa G. Rogers & Sarah Ann P. Chandler, Dec. 26, 1839, by Wm. Barton, M.G., Jan. 1, 1839 (?). E. W. Rogers, BM.

James B. Rogers & Mary Ann Prim, Oct. 3, 1839, by B. Tarver, J.P., G. W. Rogers, BM.

George W. Rose & Mary Corder, Jan. 22, 1839. George Ferrell, BM.

Samuel N. Ross & Susan G. Dolen, Jan. 2, 1839, by Joseph B. Wynns, Jan. 3, 1839. Josephus Walker, BM.

Thomas J. Russell & Mary Camel, Dec. 26, 1839. Thos. Tracy, BM.

William Russell & Sarah Chandler, Sep. 23, 1839, by Wm. Barton, M.G., Sep. 25, 1839. J. R. Ashworth, BM.

Thomas D. Scott & Eliza Jane Kelly, Nov. 5, 1839. G. L. Scott, BM.

William Searcy & Nancy Hill, Sep. 21, 1839. M. T. Cartwright, BM.

Wood H. Sherron & Martha R. Wood, Feb. 20, 1839, by John Seay, M.G., Feb. 21, 1839. T. L. Roberts, BM.

Richard Shores & Jane Emeline Jennings, Feb. 23, 1839, by C. Wroe, M.G., Jonathan Shores, BM.

Sam'l. C. Smith & Dicy Doak, Sep. 4, 1839. Saml. T. Williams, BM.

Thomas E. Spain & Nancy S. Foster, Dec. 16, 1839, by Saml. Corley, R. H. Foster, BM.

Samuel Springs & Jane McBride, June 15, 1839, by Solomon Caplinger, J.P., June 16, 1839. Joseph Snidger, BM.

James Stanley & Jane Wills, Dec. 18, 1839, by John Billingsley, J.P., Truman Harrington, BM.

Joseph J. Strawn & Roxilany Rison, Jan. 21, 1839, by G. H. Bussard, J.P., John C. Ash, BM.

Ahasahael Sullivan & Clarkey Patterson, June 15, 1839, by Wm. Barton, M.G., June 16, 1839.

Richardson Swann & Tabitha Hunt, Oct. 7, 1839, by B. Tarver, J.P., Oct. 8, 1839. C. C. Cummings, BM.

James J. Tate & Elizabeth R. Pike, June 24, 1839, by James T. Tompkins, Henry W. Ferrell, BM.

John Tatum & Jane Howdyshell, Feb. 6, 1838. Harry Brown, BM.

Solomon Taylor & Sarah May, Dec. 25, 1839, by John B. Vivrett, Wm. A. Jackson, BM.

Thomas B. Taylor & Mary Watten, Oct. 15, 1839, by J. D. Ragland, J.P., Oct. 27, 1839. G. W. Lewis, BM.

James Tilford & Sarah R. Eatherly, Nov. 4, 1849. Henry Eatherly, BM.

Samuel Thompkins & Margarett Whitson, Sep. 5, 1839, by Wm. H. White, M.G., Turner Tompkins, BM.

Thos. Thurman & Sarah Neal, Jan. 7, 1839. Alexander M. Cloyd, BM.

John Tumblin & Lydia Walden, June 20, 1839. Wm. Roach, BM.

Thomas Underwood & Fanny Petway, March 9, 1839. Braxton Compton, BM.

Edward Vance & Mary C. Brevard, Feb. 21, 1839, E. Smith, J.P., Daniel Vance, BM.

Henry B. Vaughn & Susan C. Vaughn, Aug. 27, 1839, by Melkijah L. Vaughn, M.G., Aug. 29, 1839. W. T. F. Coles, BM.

James W. Walton (Waltron) & Rachel Jane Tate, Feb. 25, 1839, by A. B. Rozett, M.G., Feb. 28, 1839.

James S. Wommack & Dorcas Hill, Aug. 5, 1839, by H. W. Puckett, M.G., Aug. 8, 1839. M. M. Maxwell, BM.

John Weaver & Sylvester Hardin, July 8, 1839, by J. S. Williams, J.P., Joseph Eaton, BM.

William Whitehead & Mary Boyd, Sep. 19, 1839, by John Billingsley, J.P., Abram Boyd, BM.

Reubin E. Whitsett & Dicy Ann McFarland, Nov. 6, 1839, by Peter Fuqua, M.G., J. H. White, BM.

Frank (?) Hinks (?) & Julia (?) Pritchett, Aug. 14, 1839, by James Little, J.P., Banja. Pritchett, BM.

Charles Wilson & Elizabeth Leach, Jan. 30, 1839. James B. Thomas, BM.

Wharles Wilson & Jane Shelton, March 30, 1839, by Elihu Jewel, J.P., July 25, 1839. Thomas Shelton, BM.

John B. Wisemen & Rebecca F. Jackson, Sep. 23, 1839, by Jonathan Wiseman, M.G., Sep. 26, 1839. Peter Townsend, BM.

Moses A. Wood & Delila Lawerence, April 9, 1839, by James Young, J.P., April 11, 1839. Ro. Donnell, BM.

Reuben M. Wood & Hester Ann _____, July 27, 1839, by Thomas Kirkpatrick, J.P., July 29, 1839. James H. Cawthron, BM.

Samuel M. Wright & Elizabeth Ann Hamilton, Oct. 2, 1838. Thos. H. Cawthon, BM.

Hiram T. Wroe & Mary Thompson, Nov. 20, 1839, by Joshua Lester, M.G., Nov. 28, 1839. John Tumblin, BM.

Benjamin Young & Louisa Phillips, Jan. 30, 1839, by Sion Bass, M.G., James H. Branch, BM.

Samuel Yandell & Harriet Wood, July 27, 1839, by Thos. Kirkpatrick, J.P., July 30, 1839. Hartwill S. Zachary, BM.

Simon Adamson & Avaona (Anna) Jane Measles, Nov. 5, 1840, by James Turner, Eli A. Puch, BM.

John H. Allen & Martha Neal, Oct. 16, 1840. George Neal, BM.

Leroy Allen & Polly S. Midget, July 10, 1840. Nathan Midget, BM.

Timothy M. Allison & Sarah M. Ewing, Jan. 21, 1840, by Joshua Lester, M.G., Jan. 23, 1840. Thos. Baird, BM.

Gideon M. Alsup & Sarah A. C. Ryan, Feb. 24, 1840, by Joshua Lester, M.G., Feb. 27, 1840. Thos. J. Baird, BM.

William T. Alsup & Frances Byrns, March 8, 1840, by H. W. Pickett, M.G., March 12, 1840.

William G. Astow & Elizabeth Walker, Nov. 9, 1840, by
John Borum, Nov. 10, 1840. William A. Bell, BM.
Harris Barkley & Martha Jones, Dec. 17, 1840, by Thos.
Davis, L. B. Green, BM.
Randle C. Barrett & Rhoda Reynolds, March 9, 1840, by
Joshua Lester, M.G., March 11, 1840.
Hugh F. Baskins & Sally Ann Lacefield, Dec. 16, 1840,
by Joshua Woollen, Dec. 22, 1840. Jacob M. Casilman,
BM.
Harmon T. Bass & Nancy W. Estes, Dec. 25, 1840, by E. J.
Allen, Dec. 27, 1840. William J. Pride, BM.
James M. Baxter & SArah R. Grant, Jan. 3, 1840, by S.
Tarver, J.P., Jan. 5, 1840. Jas. C. Word BM.
Joseph Beadle & Susan Lester, Sep. 9, 1840, by Archamack
Bass, Sep. 10, 1840. S. M. Alexander, BM.
Madison Belcher & Mary D. Young, June 20, 1840, by
H. W. Pickett, M.G., June 25, 1840. James S. Young, BM.
William Belcher & Louisa C. P. Aston, Nov. 5, 1840, by
R. D. Bell, M.G., Nov. 7, 1840. M. Golston, BM.
Joseph Bell & Mary Lain, Dec. 1, 1840, by James Bond,
Dec. 10, 1840. Henry Edward, BM.
Jeremiah Belt & Mary Reed, Sep. 17, 1840, by Williamson
Williams, M.G., Benjamin Belt, BM.
Ozburn Bettis & Martha Wilkinson, Aug. 19, 1840, by R. L.
Mayson, J.P., Thomas Goldston, BM.
Robert D. Bingham & Isbel Sims, Nov. 18, 1840, by B.
Pyland, M.G., Nov. 19, 1840. James G. Simms, BM.
Henry Blake & Joannah Ward, June 20, 1840, by A. B.
Richmond, J.P., July 2, 1840. N. F. Drake, BM.
Branch Flankenship & Prudence Cogwell, July 16, 1840.
Daniel Blankenship, BM.
Westin Bodine & Rebecca Moseley, Feb. 4, 1840, by Isaac
Hunter, J.P., Feb. 6, 1840. S. B. Murray, BM.
Geraldus Bottom & Emily M. Spinks, June 1, 1840, by Silas
Tarver, J.P., June 4, 1840. Mark Whitaker, BM.
Henry Borum & Martha Cartwright, Nov. 11, 1840, by
Jonathan Bailey, J.P., Nov. 12, 1830 (?). T. T.
Armstrong, BM.
Hiram Borum & Nancy Tucker, Feb. 3, 1840. George Jewell,
BM.
James H. Branch & Eleanor D. Neal, Feb. 21, 1830, by
James Young, J.P., Feb. 19, 1840. George Neal, BM.
John Brewer & Eliza Tims, June 11, 1840. Henry Adams,
BM.
Nelson B. Bryan & Manerva Jane Waters, Dec. 14, 1840, by
Joshua Lester, M.G., Dec. 16, 1840. Thos. Waters, BM.
John O. Briant & Elizabeth Walker, Dec. 20, 1840, by
R. S. Tate, Dec. 22, 1840. James Jackson, BM.
Alexander Brightwell & Adaline Pitlow, Aug. 15, 1840.
William W. McWhirter, BM.
John A. Brogan & Lucy Johnson, Jan. 14, 1840, by James
Thomas, J.P., Jan. 16, 1840. Jesse B. Pemberton, BM.
Edward Brown & Martha Swaner, May 25, 1840, by B. Tarver,
J.P., May 25, 1840. H. C. Brown, BM.

WILSON COUNTY MARRIAGES

Milton S. Bryne & Fredonia R. Martin, Jan. 2, 1840, by
J. B. Lasater, J.P., Wm. C. Winston, BM.
Edward Calas & Sarah Merchant, Oct. 24, 1840, by B. Pyland,
M.G., Oct. 29, 1840. John R. Billingsley, BM.
James C. Calhoun & Julia Ann Bradley, Feb. 3, 1840, by
J. Robt. D. Bell, M.G., Feb. 4, 1840. William Calhon,
BM.
Archibald Carver & Mary Ann Swingley, Feb. 3, 1840, by
John Kelly, M.G., Feb. 6, 1840. Andrew J. Spickard, BM.
Henry Carver & Alizabeth A. Hamblen, Dec. 23, 1840, by
John Kelly, M.G., Dec. 24, 1840. Wm. L. Martin, BM.
Joab P. Cawthon & Delanta A. E. J. Robbins, Nov. 15, 1840,
by Thomas Kirkpatrick, J.P., Nov. 23, 1840. James
Cawthon, BM.
Nicholas Chambers & Elizabeth Norris, Oct. 28, 1840, by
John Borum, Oct. 29, 1840. John Chambers, BM.
Tobias H. Chandler & Louisa H. Rogers, Jan. 1, 1840,
by Wm. Barton, M.G., Jan. 2, 1840. A. H. Russell, BM.
John S. Chastain & Amanda Bradley, Nov. 21, 1840, by
John Borum, M.G., Nov. 27, 1840. Isaac Bradley, BM.
Thomas H. Cheek & Julia A. Glenn, Jan. 13, 1840, by
Solomon Caplinger, J.P., Benjamine H. Glenn, BM.
Eliza Henderson & Eliza Henderson (error in recording),
Dec. 23, 1840. David C. Jackson.
Henry Cluck & Sally Upchurch, Sep. 14, 1840. Leven
Woollenn, J.P.
Fountain H. Cobb & Sarah Surlock, Jan. 1, 1840, by Wm.
Walker, J.P., Jan. 2, 1840. H. F. Johnson, BM.
James H. Cogwell & Sarah Ethridge, July 1, 1840. William
Turner, BM.
Nathaniel Cook & Elizabeth Sypert, Jan. 1, 1840. Joseph
J. Strong, BM.
Beverley A. Cromwell & Mary Young, Feb. 18, 1840, by
Robt. D. Bell, M.G., C. T. Harris, BM.
Simon Craddock & Maria Jane Vick, July 14, 1840, by James
Thomas, M.G., July 16, 1840. Leonard Walker, BM.
John A. Creswell & Nancy Mays, Sep. 7, 1840, by Melkijah
L. Vaughan, M.G., Sep. 8, 1840. Isaac G. Caler, BM.
Joseph W. Cummings & Dolly Ann Rideout, Aug. 3, 1840, by
Saml. H. Porterfield, J.P., Aug. 6, 1840. Nat. Bell,
BM.
Robert B. Curry & Ann Baker, July 4, 1840, by Wm. J.
Bonner, M.G., July 15, 1840. William W. Huddleston, BM.
John P. Dale & Elizabeth R. Harris, June 24, 1840.
Charles C. Dale, BM.
James M. Davis & Sarah Weir, Dec. 7, 1840, by Moses Ellis,
J.P., Dec. 8, 1840. Wm. B. Pursey, BM.
William Dudley & Jane Smith, Jan. 23, 1830, by J. Organ,
J.P., J. Organ, BM.
Thomas S. Dickson & Elizabeth Hollinsworth, Dec. 31, 1830.
Freeman R. Jackson, BM.
William Dill & Eliza Neely, Jan. 11, 1841. Eperson Bandy,
BM.
Elijah B. Drake & Sarah M. Rowlstone, Sep. 23, 1840, by
Geo. Donnell, M.G., James B. Rutland, BM.

169

E. M. Dunn & Nancy M. Somers, March 4, 1840, by Silas Tarver, J.P., March 5, 1840. J. A. Somers, BM.
Rufus Eatherly & Louisa Donaldson, Oct. 12, 1840. James Donaldson, BM.
John D. Irwin & Nancy Allen, Jan. 7, 1840. George Vaught, BM.
Wilie Eskew & Minerva Hooser, July 7, 1840, by Wm. Barton, M.G., July 8, 1840. James Smart, BM.
Sidney Forsher & Mary Ann Vaughan, Nov. 22, 1840, by M. T. Cartwright, J.P., Nov. 27, 1840. John Cummings, BM.
Charles Gaines (a free man of Color) & Missouri Collins (a free woman of Color), Sep. 4, 1840, by Thomas Kirkpatrick, J.P., Sep. 9, 1840. Henry Morris, BM.
John M. Garrison & Martha Smith, Oct. 8, 1840, by M. T. Cartwright, J.P., Samuel P. Smith, BM.
David George & Lucinda Kean, Oct. 21, 1840, by Thos. Kirkpatrick, Samuel Morriss, BM.
Lucus George & Nancy Forbus, Dec. 30, 1840, by Jas. Aston, J.P., Robert Lampkin, BM.
William H. Graves & Jane Johnson, Aug. 3, 1830. D. G. Hankins, BM.
John Hale & Julia Ann Bright, Aug. 17, 1840. Solomon Warren, BM.
William Hallum & Martha H. Calhoun, Aug. 11, 1840. Jesse B. White, BM.
Burr Harris & Mary Ann O. Harrison, ___. __, ___. J. W. Wynne, BM.
Simon T. Harris & Tabitha Jane Woodrum, Oct. 7, 1840, by Ezekiel Cloyd, M.G., Oct. 8, 1840. Lemuel Christian, BM.
Truman Harrington & Elizabeth Smith, Jan. 2, 1840, by John Billingsley, J.P., Caleb H. Smith, BM.
William Harrington & Polly Johnson, Feb. 24, 1840, by M. T. Cartwright, J.P., Truman Harris, BM.
James Hankins & Mary Elizabeth Nettles, March 31, 1840, by M. T. Cartwright, J.P.
Cyrus W. Haggard & Martha Harrison, Nov. 30, 1840, by Robert Hill, J.P., Robert Johnson, BM.
William F. Hearn & Eleanor Johnson, Dec. 23, 1840, by Achbd. B. Duval, Dec. 24, 1840. J. A. Cartwright, BM.
Stephen Henry & Delila Oneal, Jan. 13, 1840, by Archamack Bass, M.G., Jan. 14, 1840. Finis Edwards, BM.
James W. Herron & Jane McNamour, Sep. 17, 1840, by Saml. H. Porterfield, J.P., Jonathan Patton, BM.
James Hester & Susan Bates, Jan. 14, 1840, by Micajah Estes, M.G., William Hester, BM.
Samuel D. Higgason & Elizabeth Brown, July 21, 1840, by Melkijah L. Vaughn, July 22, 1840. Samuel Cole, BM.
Harmon L. Hollamon & Caroline C. Bullard, Jan. 21, 1840, by Joseph Walker, M.G., Wilson T. Cartwright, BM.
Henderson Horn & Sarah Ann Brooks, June 20, 1840, by Isaac Hunter, J.P., June 24, 1840. Edward Chambers, BM.
Green B. Howard & Lurany Comer, Nov. 18, 1840, by Wm. S. Walker, J.P., Nov. 19, 1840. Walter J. Rotranac, BM.

Lewis Hughley & Zuritha A. Anderson, Sep. 12, 1840, by
Jno. Baird, M.G., Sep. 17, 1840. Euclad M. Earnest, BM.
Benjamin B. Hunt & Evaline Moore, May 20, 1840, by
Melkijah L. Vaughn, M.G., May 21, 1840. A. C. Call, BM.
John D. Irwin & Nancy Allen, Jan. 7, 1840, by Archamack
Bass, M.G., Jan. 8, 1840.
Thomas J. Jacobs & Malvina Jane Swain, Sep. 20, 1830.
Etheldred Brantly, BM.
Calvin W. Jackson & Jane B. Green, Feb. 17, 1840, by J.
B. Walker, M.G., A. P. Blythe, BM.
Joseph Jenkins & Mary Swan, Dec. 26, 1840, by S. Waters,
J.P., Dec. 31, 1840. B. W. White, BM.
Labon Jenkins & Elizabeth Mays, May 16, 1840, by Melkijah
L. Vaughan, May 17, 1840.
Elijah H. Jennings & Priscilla Hackworth, July 10, 1840,
by E. C. Jennings, J.P., July 11, 1840. Richard Shores,
BM.
Clement Johnson & Martha Lain, Oct. 14, 1840, by J. Organ,
Oct. 15, 1840. H. A. Johnson, BM.
John W. Johnson & Martha A. Hickman, Oct. 24 1840, by
H. Truett, J.P., Claiborne R. Jarrett.
Robert Johnson & Mary Spencer, Jan. 23, 1840, by Williamson
Williams, M.G., Peter F. Johnson, BM.
William Johnson & Tempa Pilant, Sep. 29, 1840, by Claivory
H. Rhodes, J.P., James Johnson, BM.
George W. Jones & Nancy Ashby, Feb. 7, 1840, by Joshua
Woollen, M.G., Feb. 12, 1840. Jno. B. Drake BM.
Wiley E. Jones & Thursyan Graves, Aug. 15, 1840, by J. T.
Tompkins, Aug. 20, 1840. Wm. A. Mitchell, BM.
Alfred A. Kennedy & Sarah S. McFarland, Feb. 10, 1840.
Alanson A. Kennedy, BM.
Edward Kendred & Rachel Webb, May 27, 1840, by Wm. S.
Watkinson.
Henry S. Kennedy & Martha A. Hubbard, Feb. 11, 1840, by
Joshua Lester, M.G., Feb. 27, 1840. A. S. Ewing, BM.
Thos. B. Kenday & Patsy Jennings, May 20, 1840. William
S. Mount, BM.
Thomas S. Kindred & Mary Y. Duncan , Sep. 29, 1840, by
Robt. D. Bell, M.G., Oct. 6, 1840. James M. Horsley,
BM.
Abel Kellis & Elizabeth Ozment, Jan. 14, 1840, by John
Billingsley, J.P., John Ozment, BM.
Marion B. Kittrell & Tabitha Hicks, March 9, 1840. B.
Tarver, BM.
Johnson Lain & Clairnda R. Stevenson, Dec. 1 1840. Allen
Pucket, BM.
John Lanham & Susan Foust, Feb. 4, 1840, by Jonathan
Bailey, J.P., Feb. 10, 1840. Joseph Marks, BM.
Prisly Lannom & Mary Caroline Alsup, Sep. 23, 1840, by
Joseph Payton, T. W. Lannom, BM.
William Lea & Sarah Davis, Dec. 30, 1840, by William
Vantrease, Dec. 31, 1840.
Alexander Lemons & Vastile Chandler, May 27, 1840, by
Wm. Barton, M.G., James Somers, BM.

Harrison Lester & Nancy Adaline Jarmon, Nov. 9, 1840, by
Joshua Lester, M.G., Nov. 12, 1840. J. Lester, BM.
Elisha Lindsay & Susan Bass, Sep. 26, 1840, by Sion Bass,
M.G., Thos. Waters, BM.
Hardy Tom Linson & Nancy Ann Jones, Feb. 25, 1840, by
John Bell, J.P.
Hezekiah Turner & Alley Ellis, Feb. 5, 1840. Charles
Compton, BM.
William Mabry & Narcissa Brown, March 17, 1840, by Wm. J.
Walker, J.P.
Benjamin Maddox & Mary Baxter, Nov. 12, 1840, by Wood
H. Hearn, J.P., Isaac Golladay, BM.
James Martin & Elizabeth Martin, June 13, 1840. Wm. A.
Sherrill, BM.
John Marler & Lydia Cassida, March 3, 1840, by Sion Bass,
M.G., Benjamin Phelps, BM.
James W. McAdow & Elizabeth Hubbard, June 13, 1840, by
H. W. Pickett, M.G., O. S. Ewing, BM.
Baily McClennaham & Rachel Chumley, Sep. 28, 1840.
William George, BM.
Alex F. McDonnell & Elizabeth M. Atkinson, Nov. 3, 1840.
John B. Dickson, BM.
Benjamin F. McCullock & Eliza Gray, April 29, 1840, by
Jess Peyton, May 10, 1840.
Elisha McGinnis & Louisianea Pearcy, Dec. 28, 1840, by
_____ Lasater, J.P., Dec. 29, 1840. John H. Cook, BM.
George W. McPeak & Elizabeth Mariah Perry, N.D. Thomas
Drennon, BM.
James Measle & Nancy Turner, Aug. 26, 1840, by James
Turner, Aug. 27, 1840. Charles McKie, BM.
Jeremiah Meggiett & Susan Hearn, Jan. 6, 1840, by Wm. A.
Jarratt, John Slavett, BM.
James Mobbs & Mary Pugh, Feb. 17, 1840, by Thos.
Kirkpatrick, J.P., Feb. 18, 1840. Lewis Merritt, BM.
Pleasant H. C. Monday & Martha Ann Eliza Taylor, Feb. 5,
1840. Jacob G. Hall, BM.
William Moon & Susan Osborn, March 1, 1840, by Joshua
Lester, M.G., March 16, 1840.
Alston Morgan & Julia Ann Abernatha, April 15 1840, by
J. M. Payton, J.P.
William Morris & Priscilla Mathews, Feb. 22, 1840. Houston
Belt, BM.
Julius H. Mount & Louisa Patterson, May 14, 1840, by
Williamson Williams, M.G., May 17, 1840.
William C. H. Murphy & Amanda F. Rutland, Oct. 16, 1840,
by Thos. Kirkpatrick, M. S. Gardner, BM.
C. W. Neal & Margarett Woods, Nov. 2, 1840, by James
Young, J.P., Nov. 4, 1840. Js. H. Branch, BM.
George Neal & Mary Vantrease, July 24, 1840, by James
Turner, J.P., Nicholas Vantrease, BM.
Zachariah Nettles & Sarah Lawrence Aug. 24, 1840, by
James Young, J.P., John W. Shanks, BM.
William J. Owen & Tabitha Hicks, March 9, 1840, by Robert
H. Elly, J.P., March 10, 1840. H. W. Robbs, BM.

John S. Page & Martha Ann Duncan, Nov. 2, 1840, by N. L. Norvell, M.G., Nov. 10, 1840. G. A. Duncan, BM.

Jonathan Patton & Sarah E. McNamor, Aug. 13, 1840, by Saml. H. Porterfield, J.P., Aug. 20, 1840. Tho. Waters, BM.

Thos. G. Patterson & Martha Johns, Feb. 11, 1840. Samuel Rickett, BM.

Charles W. Pearson & Martha Jackson, Feb. 21, 1840, by J. D. Ragland, J.P., John Murhead, BM.

Eilliamson Pearcy & Elizabeth McGinnis, March 3, 1840, by J. B. Lasater, J.P., March 5, 1840. Francis W. Peary, BM.

Wm. J. Pride & Julia Ann Bass, Oct. 16, 1840. Henry P. Thomson, BM.

William A. Pruett & Armelia W. Smith, Nov. 14, 1840, by Archamack Bass, M.G., Nov. 25, 1840. James G. Sims, BM.

James F. Puckett & Rebecca Jane Smith, Feb. 20, 1840, by Joshua Lester, M.G., Feb. 26, 1840. Churchwell Anderson, BM.

Jas. H. Ragsdale & Laura Goodman, Oct. 3, 1840. William S. Wilburn, BM.

William H. Rideout & Polly Cummings, July 6, 1840, by Saml. H. Porterfield, J.P., July 14, 1840. Preston Henderson, BM.

John N. Roach & Elmira E. A. J. Robbins, Oct. 14, 1840. Thos. C. Telford, BM.

Alfred B. Rogers & Priscilla Clifton, Aug. 29, 1840, by Wilson Hearn, Sep. 6, 1840. William J. Rofgers (Rogers), BM.

Henry Rotramel & Nancy Lain, Dec. 26, 1840, by B. Tarver, J.P., Jan. 6, 1840 (?). A. _. S. Winford, BM.

Walter J. Rotramel & Lucinda Howard, Dec. 17, 1840, by Wm. S. Watkins, William Harris, BM.

Richard Rowden & Sarah Green, Feb. 3, 1840, by Thos. Davis, J.P., Feb. 5, 1840. Thos. Penecost, BM.

James Russell & Lory Carney, Jan. 3, 1840. Jno. W. Golliday, BM.

Richard Rutledge & Harriett Bush, Jan. 28, 1840, by Geo. Donnell, M.G., Jan. 29, 1840. John S. Evns, BM.

William Sands & Ann Pool, May 8, 1840, by B. L. Mayson, J.P., June 18, 1840.

Tobias M. Sawyer & Eleanor H. Smith, April 14, 1840. Wesley, M. Sellars, BM.

John B. Scoby & Sarah Branch, Dec. 9, 1840, by Shelah Waters, J.P., Dec. 10, 1840. A. R. Eatherly, BM.

Thomas Shepherd & Nancy Cox, Dec. 9, 1840, by Sion Bass, M.G., Allen Kizor, BM.

William M. Shores & Pamelia Green, Nov. 27, 1840, by M. T. Cartwright, J.P., Dec. 1, 1840. M. Bennett, J. P. Bone, BM.

John T. Simpson & Lucy G. Kelly, Dec. 7, 1840, by H. W. Pucket, M.G., Dec. 29, 1840. J. A. Sneed, BM.

Phillip B. Smith & Elizabeth Walker, Feb. 29, 1840, by Archanack Bass, March 6, 1840. Burr Feagure, BM.

Sam'l. P. Smith & Eliza B. Tanner, July 12, 1840, by M.
T. Cartwright, J.P., Thomas Johnson, BM.
Sydney Smith & Mahenry Bridges, Dec. 12, 1840, by B. Tarver
J.P., William T. King, BM.
Joseph Snider & Dorcas Springs, July 24, 1840, Jonathan
Barkley, J.P., July 27, 1840. Joseph Marks, BM.
Joses G. Starratt & Louraney Henry, Oct. 6, 1840, by
Archenack, M.G., James Edwards, BM.
Ely Sullivan & Elizabeth Spickard, March 9, 1840, by R.
R. Barton, M.G., March 10, 1840.
Sylvanus Sullivan & Malvina Clayton, Jan. 2, 1840, by
J. H. Britton, J.P., Jan. 5, 1840. H. F. Johnson, BM.
James Swan & Martha Gill, Nov. 4, 1840, by Jonathan
Barley, J.P., Nov. 5, 1840. James D. Gill, BM.
John Tarpley & Martha Chumley, Feb. 28, 1840, by T. C.
Wroe, J.P.
Darmon Taylor & Nancy Walker, June 20, 1840, by George
Brown, J.P., June 27, 1840. E. M. Holt, BM.
Alfred Tomlinson & Martha George Jones, Aug. 29, 1840,
by John Bell, J.P., Sep. 1, 1840. Simeon Tomlinson, BM.
Hardy Tomlinson & Nancy Ann Jones, Feb. 25, 1840. William
H. Tomlinson, BM.
Simeon Tomlinson & Nancy G. Goald, Dec. 31, 1840, by John
Bell, J.P., William H. Tomlinson, BM.
William H. Tomlinson & Orphy Carpenter Jones, Oct. 28,
1840. Simeon Tomlinson, BM.
Henry W. Traylor & Tabitha Jane McGinnis, Dec. 23, 1840,
by J. B. Lasater, J.P., Dec. 24, 1840. Isaac C. Hall,
BM.
Watt Tucker & Mary Craddock, Oct. 9, 1840. Hiram S.
Wroe, BM.
Hezekiah Turner & Alley Ellis, Feb. 5, 1840, by James
Young, J.P., Feb. 25, 1840.
John Underwood & Sarah Hendley, April 21, 1840, by Jas.
Aston, J.P.
Milner Walker & Caroline Tarpley, Dec. 20, 1840, by B.
Tarver, J.P., Dec. 23, 1840. Samuel Walker, BM.
Adam Weaver & Amelia Sellers, June 8, 1840, by J. M.
Peyton, J.P., June 9, 1840. A. W. Vick, BM.
John Weaver & Louisa Reese, Nov. 26, 1840, by W. D.
Sawrie, M.G., Wm. C. Hunt, BM.
James Whitehead & Elizabeth Jone, Feb. 14, 1840, by John
Bell, J.P., Feb. 17, 1840. Thomas Lyon, BM.
Ashkenay Williams & Susan Lester, Dec. 7, 1840, by Joshua
Lester, M.G., Dec. 15, 1840.
William B. Williams & Evaline Coles, Sep. 25, 1840.
Elihu L. Witherspoon & Sarah McKee, Nov. 14, 1840, by
Elihu Jewell, J.P., Nov. 15, 1840. N. Thomas, BM.
Benjamin F. Woodrum & Mary A. Rice, May 18, 1840, by
John Beard, M.G., May 21, 1840.
Elzi Wray & Louisa Pence, Feb. 3, 1840, by Melkiah L.
Vaughan, M.G., Feb. 6, 1840. John Baird, BM.
Isaac Wright & Marinda Jackson, July 31, 1840, by L.
Tarver, J.P., Feb. 24, 1841. S. W. Chandler, BM.

William A. Wyeen & Delila Ann Medlin, Dec. 23, 1840.
Jas. Griffin, BM.
Jonathan York & Mary Ann Nailor, March 22, 1840. J. R.
Jarrell, BM.

Section 2: 1841-1850

Asara Griffin & Patsy Swann, 15 Jan. 1841. B. Jonathan
J.P.
William H. Lyon & Martha F. McWherter, 6 Jan. 1841.
W. D. F. Lawrie, M.G.
Charles F. Mabus & Charlotte Tomlinson, 7 Jan. 1841.
William D. Smith, J.P.
William O'Neal & Maud Taylor, 8 Jan. 1841. William
(Starrell) J.P.
John S. Currey & Harriet M. Lannom, 12 Jan. 1841.
Thomas Bushe, J.P.
Robert Wicks & Candles Prichett, 11 Jan. 1841. James
Young, J.P.
William Dill & Eliza Neely, 12 Jan. 1841. M. S. Vaughn,
O.D.M.
Milijah Zachary & Margaret B. Robinson, 20 Jan. 1841.
Thomas Kirkpatrick, J.P.
Thomas Clay & Pamelia Andrews, 12 Jan. 1841. James
Tompkins, M.G.
John H. Johns & Mary F. Russell, 12 Jan. 1841. William
Barton, M.G.
James A. Moore & Elizabeth R. Ballard, 13 Jan. 1841.
John Beard, M.G.
John A. Link & Martha Johns, 12 Jan. 1841. Henry
Truett, J.P.
Hambleton Hester & Ann Eliza Baker, 19 Jan. 1841. Mica-
Jah Estes, M.G.
Jonathan Baily & Casandra H. Donnel, 21 Jan. 1841.
James Young, J.P.
Henry Hearne & Rebecca Ann Patton, 19 Jan. 1841. George
Donnell, O.D.M.
Moses Atwood & Permelee Allen, 26 Jan. 1841. Archibald
Bass, M.G.
David J. Smith & Martha Organ, 14 Jan. 1841. Thomas
Moore, M.G.
Anderson C. Breedlove & Lucinda Horn, 3 Feb. 1841.
William S. Walker, J.P.
Isham N. Morris & Anna Borum, 8 Jan. 1841. William
Flowers, Sr., M.G.
Thomas Bridges & Elizabeth Corder, 6 Feb. 1841.
John A. Sneed & Susan B. Hubbard, 8 Feb. 1841.
Bailey L. Woodall & Hardena F. Simmons, 10 Feb. 1841.
B____ Thomas, J.P.
Duncan Johnson & Elizabeth Nunley, 10 Jan. 1841. William
A. Stovell, J.P.
John C. Rice & Lavina Currey, 12 Feb. 1841. Thomas
Kirkpatrick, J.P.

John C. McCullock & Sarah Alexander, 12 Feb. 1841. Thomas Kirkpatrick, J.P.
William Clifton & Sarah Jane Conrod, 15 Feb. 1841. James Williams.
Elijah C. (Nelly) & Analiza Jennings, 15 Feb. 1841.
(   ) L. (   ) & Elizabeth Deco, 17 Feb. 1841. S. Tarver, J.P.
Elijah C. Jennings & Mary Ann Jewell, 25 Feb. 1841. Elihu Jewell, J.P.
Thomas Deloach & Lydia Ann Martin, 22 Feb. 1841.
John H. Lain & Martha J. Webb, 23 Feb. 1841. R. L. Tate, M.G.
James Hardy & Turga Harkreader, 23 Feb. 1841.
William Swan & Mary B. Gill, 25 Feb. 1841. Shelah Watson, J.P.
Levi Gilliam & Eliza J. Greathouse, 9 March 1841. W. W. Pickett, V.M.G.
Jacob R. Jennings & Nancy C. Jennings, 8 March 1841.
John D. Dismuke & Malvina Gleaves, 4 March 1841. George Donnell, O.D.M.
Etheldred Clemmons & Arrena Thornton, 18 March 1841. A. P. Richmond, J.P.
Williford Sandeford & Ann Woods, 10 March 1841. John Bell, J.P.
Hiram Putman & Harriet Nowlin, 9 March 1841. J. B. Laster, J.P.
Stephen Grissom & Ann Eliza Grissom, 9 March 1841. Henry Truett, J.P.
Absolum Con & Susan Bradly, 16 March 1841. William A. Stovell, J.P.
John A. Shannon & Lucy S. Clemmons, 13 March 1841.
John B. Clemmons & Sarah Ann Lain, 25 March 1841. William Clemmons, J.P.
Marchis H. Wright & Nancy Earhart, 22 March 1841.
Benjamin Tarver & Louisa Morris, 31 March 1841. W. D. F. (Lawrie), M.G.
William Merett & Eliza Jane Scott, 31 March 1841.
James Owen & Elizabeth Turner, 3 April 1841. John Borum.
Peterson Saller & Martha Mabry, 6 April 1841. William Walker, J.P.
Abner Lasater & Perlina Johnson, 15 April 1841. J. B. Laster, J.P.
Calvin Booker & Elizabeth Rhea, 29 April 1841. Joseph Collins, J.P.
Samuel Wommack & Elizabeth Nettles, 29 April 1841. B. Ryland, V.D.M.
William Jackson & Mary Bridges, 1 May 1841.
John B. Lea & Mary A. Putnan, 5 May 1842? J. B. Laster, J.P.
Jordan Robertson & Lucinda Baird, 11 May 1841. Joshua Woolen, M.G.
James Hamilton & Jane D. McFarland, 20 May 1841. John Kelly, E.M.C.C.
Daniel F. Payne & Sarah W. Dewke, 20 May 1841. John Kelly, E.M.C.C.

Richard Wamack & Elizabeth A. Baily, 3 June 1841. A. Bass, M.G.

Richard D. Johnson & Mary M. Todd, 27 May 1841. H. W. Pickett, V.M.G.

William R. Dobson & Margaret Brown, 26 May 1841. J. N. Roach, M.G.

Levin Woolen & Polly Gray, 27 May 1841. John Bond, V.D.M.

Alford W. Walker & Jane McMillen, 27 May 1841.

Joshua Patterson & Polly Ricketts, 30 May 1841. Samuel H. Porterfield, J.P.

William Perry & Eliza Baker, 1 June 1841.

Joseph Wier & Narcissa B. Dodd, 19 June 1841. Robert Ellis, J.P.

Eli C. Botts & Nancy Searcy, 15 June 1841. William Vantrease, M.G.

Samuel Jones & Sarah Wright, 17 June 1841. J. N. Roach, M.G.

James Wilson & Octava Jones, 15 June 1841. J. N. Roach, M.G.

Alexander A. Hill & Levicey D. Bone, 15 June 1841. Williamson Williams, M.G.

William Belcher & Elizabeth Joplin, 17 June 1841. Isaac Hunter, J.P.

Samuel M. Young & Nancy Grindstaff, 19 June 1841.

Alfred W. Cox & Eliza Jane Armstrong, 21 June 1841. E. C. Jennings, J.P.

Alderson Witt & Frances Wilie, 24 June 1841. M. T. Cartwright, J.P.

(Laban) Seatt & Martha Ann Webb, 24 June 1841. S. Organ, J.P.

William M. Swain & Rebecca Freeman, 24 June 1841. James Williams, J.P.

Howell J. Williams & Margaret Ann Reed, 14 July 1841. Joseph Collier, J.P.

Pleasant M. Markum & Nancy Telford, 1 July 1841. John Beard, M.G.

Abraham P. White & Celia Williams, 2 July 1841.

Robert C. Green & Lucy Lester, Feb. 1842. N. Carter, J.P.

Vincent L. Wadkins & Sarah Loyd, 15 July 1841. William Barton, M.G.

David Warford & Jane Putnam, 15 July 1841. J. B. Laster, J.P.

Wilson Taylor & Sarah A. Davidson, 20 July 1841. William Vantrease, M.G.

Sherwood G. Corley & Nancy David, 25 July 1841. George Brown, J.P.

Jesse Goodman & Sarah Johnson, 25 July 1841. Milkijah Vaughn, O.D.M.

John A. Carter & Anne M. Hughes, 29 June 1841. Isaac Hunter, J.P.

James B. Gibson & Arretter Steward, 14 Aug. 1841. A. P. Richmond, J.P.

WILSON COUNTY MARRIAGES

Hamilton Sneed & Nancy P. Martin, 3 Aug. 1841. Robert
Ellis, A.P.
M Mc N Ridley & Mary E. Baker, 3 Aug. 1841.
Jesse Alexander & Lucinda Jane Donnell, 5 Aug. 1841.
Thomas Davis, J.P.
James N. Patton & Ruth J. Godfred, 13 Aug. 1841. H. W.
Pickett, V.M.G.
Thomas Patton & Mary Jane Bland, 11 Aug. 1841. Joseph
Collier, J.P.
William G. Couch & Martha L. Thomas, 13 Aug. 1841.
McIntoish Averette & Rebecca Johnson, 19 Aug. 1841.
A. B. Dual, M.G.
Dennis Chumbly & Agnes Garrison, 18 Aug. 1841.
George A. Martin & Peggy N. G. Glenn, 19 Aug. 1841.
J. B. Stevens, J.P.
John E. Hager & Emeline Ramsey, 26 Aug. 1841. John
Beard, M.G.
Cameron Ozment & Catherine Ozment, 25 Aug. 1841. N.
Truett, J.P.
William P. F. Babb & Suntha D. Moser, 26 Aug. 1841.
Henry W. Ferrell & Moriah F. Johnson, 26 Aug. 1841.
William D. Smith, J.P.
William B. Wilson & Martha Jane Johnson, 30 Aug. 1841.
James Thomas, J.P.
John Peak & Sarah Dukes, 31 Aug. 1841. William H.
White, M.G.
Benjamin E. Partlow & Sarah Quarles, 3 Sep. 1841.
George W. Haynes & Sarah E. Andrews, 4 Sep. 1841.
E. W. Rye & Martha J. Eason, 8 Sep. 1841. Isaac Hunter,
J.P.
George W. Owen & Mary Rutledge, 16 Sep. 1841. M. L.
Cartwright, J.P.
(Lalberry) Ford & Abijah Lemmons, 18 Sep. 1841.
Ethelbert Sullivan & Elizabeth Ozment, 21 Sep. 1841.
Berry Moser & Mary Ann Pritchard, 28 Sep. 1841.
William Charlock & Nancy Nooner, 28 Sep. 1841. E. Cloyd,
M.G.
William D. Phepps & Mary F. A. Rodgers, 29 Sep. 1841.
Robert Sellars & Nancy Wallace, 30 Sep. 1841.
Euclud M. Earnest & Frency Hamilton, 4 Oct. 1841.
Thomas K. Yanette & Martha Weaver, 5 Oct. 1841.
John Bass & Mary Smith, 26 Oct. 1841. William Vantrease,
M.G.
Henry McFarland & Martha R. McCaffrey, 7 Oct. 1841.
Philip Earhart & Margaret A. Thompson, 14 Oct. 1841.
R. L. Tate, M.G.
William A. Ross & Elizabeth Webb, 9 Oct. 1841. Jubal
Grant, J.P.
Anthony Puryear & Ann Shingleton, 12 Oct. 1841. A. B.
Duvall, M.G.
Jonathan S. York & Martha Harris, 12 Oct. 1841. Jubal
Grant, J.P.
William F. Birch & Martha Dockins, 14 Oct. 1841.
William A. Starrett, J.P.

David W. Dickerson & Nancy Williams, 14 Oct. 1841. John Borum, M.G.

Dr. Andrew J. Winter & Margaret A. White, 15 Oct. 1841. Silas Tarver, J.P.

John Banks & Micky Webb, 16 Oct. 1841. J. Organ, J.P.

Samuel Cartwright & Manerva Ellis, 17 Oct. 1841. S. Waters, J.P.

John Tumblin & Mary Ann Stanley, 18 Oct. 1841. Henry Truett, J.P.

Thomas B. Oakley & Nancy Phillips, 20 Oct. 1841. A. Bass, M.G.

Alfred H. Russell & Ann Baird, 20 Oct. 1841. William Barton, M.G.

Robards York & Sally Eskew, 20 Oct. 1841. R. R. Barton, M.G.

Wilson A. Hearn & Sally Baird, 3 Nov. 1841. John Bond, V.D.M.

George H. Dill & Catherine Davis, 26 Oct. 1841. M. L. Cartwright, J.P.

Elias Merritt & Maryanne Askins, 29 Oct. 1841.

Davis L. Dew & Ruth Callis, 28 Oct. 1841. George Donnell M.G.

David C. Jackson & Parthena Sims, 2 Nov. 1841. B. Ryland, V.D.M.

Virgil Buckner & Sarah (   ), 30 Oct. 1841.

Calvin Williams & June Pippin, 1 Nov. 1841. Jubal Grant, J.P.

Robert A. Grant & Elizabeth Hutchison, 2 Nov. 1841. George Brown, J.P.

Braxton Compton & L____ Walker, 2 Nov. 1841. Samuel Walker, J.P.

O. B. (   ) & Lucy D. Lester, 6 Nov. 1841.

Alfred Beshears & Harriet Johnson, 6 Nov. 1841.

John W. Bridges & Permelia L. Alldridge, 9 Nov. 1841. William Barton, M.G.

Joel H. Swindle & Nancy Organ, 9 Nov. 1841, James Warren, M.G.

David Stockton & Clara A. Cook, 9 Nov. 1841. George Donnell, M.G.

Benjamin W. G. Winford & Harriet H. Harris, 10 Nov. 1841. George Donnell, M.G.

John W. ____esey & Martha Eatherly, 11 Nov. 1841. J. W. Wilson, J.P.

Thomas K. Roach & Elizabeth Martha Rhea, 15 Nov. 1841. Williamson Williams, M.G.

Edmond Wilson & Anna Marks, 17 Nov. 1841. Shelah Waters, J.P.

John B. Hays & Eliza H. Gippen, 17 Nov. 1841. E. C. Slater, M.M.E.C.

Etheldred Clemmons & Milly Edwards, 21 Nov. 1841. Henry Truett, J.P.

James C. Hamilton & Elizabeth Cunningham, 24 Nov. 184 William Vantrease, M.G.

Elias M. Hall & Sarah Tipton, 2 Dec. 1841. Milkijah S. Vaughn, U.D.M.

M. McKindred & Martha Gwynne, 23 Nov. 1841.
Micajah T. Bennett & Martha Palmer, 24 Nov. 1841. M.
Cartwright, J.P.
Russe J. Evans & Martha Jane Carter, 23 Nov. 1841.
Joseph Page & Mary McMinn, 2? Nov. 1841.
Warner P. M. Smith & Susan G. Dabbs, 27 Nov. 1841.
Otheel Johnson & Emeline E. Tarver, 28 Nov. 1841. B.
Tarver, J.P.
Robert Young & Nancy Neal, 1 Dec. 1841. B. A. Bass, M.G.
John A. Stewart & Elizabeth Donnell, 2 Dec. 1841. B.
Ryland, O.D.M.
Randle Grissom & Mary Ann Marrs, 4 Dec. 1841.
Edwin C. Wilburn & Eliza Ann Tatum, 2 Dec. 1841. John
Billingsley, J.P.
Gilbert B. Brittle & Sarah Marks, 8 Dec. 1841. William
Vantrease, M.G.
Winfield C. Jackson & Emily H. Steed, 9 Dec. 1841. John
Billingsley, J.P.
Elijah A. Pugh & Jane Dodd, 7 Dec. 1841.
Morgan Smith & Clarenda M. Johnson, 16 Dec. 1841. A. P.
Richmond, J.P.
Green Proctor & Nancy Ramsey, 9 Dec. 1841. B. Tarver, J.P.
Henry Vick & Elizabeth Perry, 11 Dec. 1841. J. N. Wilson,
J.P.
William Huflin & Lucinda Shepard, 11 Dec. 1841.
William Turner & Cinda Rilla Walker, 17 Dec. 1841. A.
Bass.
David Young & Elizabeth Pettway, 15 Dec. 1841. R. D.
Bell, M.G.
Thomas M. Edwards & Louisa F. Hearne, 15 Dec. 1841. A.
Matthews, M.G.
James W. Parsons & Charity J. S___awce, H. W., C.P.M.
Samuel T. Williams & Elizabeth Simpson, 19 Dec. 1841.
Isaac Neely & Elizabeth Cros___, 26 Dec. 1841. B. Tarver,
Johnny Johnson & Lockey Craddock, 19 Dec. 1841.
Joseph L. Manson & Martha Ann White, 1842. Edward C.
Slater, M.M.E.C.
Abner Dickson & Mary J. Wilkerson, 23 Dec. 1841. M. W.
Gray, M.G.
David W. Dickerson & Wincy Williams, 4 Dec. 1841.
William C. Ball & Abigail Braven, 23 Dec. 1841. John
Jarrott, M.G.
William M. Brien & Frances Young, 22 Dec. 1842. A. Bass.
John Malone & Elizabeth Boyd, 25 Dec. 1841. J. W.
Alexander, J.P.
Thomas W. Higgins & Martha Pemberton, 23 Dec. 1841. Thomas
R. Jackson, J.P.
William S. Rotmmel & Mrs. Eleanor D. Sanders, 23 Dec.
1841. Samuel Walker, J.P.
Robert Posey & Mary Chambless, 24 Dec. 1841.
Presley George & Dianna Porter, 24 Dec. 1841. Jubal
Grant, J.P.
Thomas Johnson & Sarah Cock, 25 Dec. 1841. J. Organ, J.P.
George W. Phepps & Elizabeth Palmer, 30 Dec. 1841. M.
Cartwright, J.P.

John J. Summers & Isabella Jackson, 27 Dec. 1841.
William W. Talley & Sarah Corley, 29 Dec. 1841. Thomas
Turner, J.P.
Orrand Walker & Evaline Hall, 30 Dec. 1841. J. T.
Tompkins.
Ebenezer D. Hearn & Esther Lea Hearn, 28 Dec. 1841. H.
Truett, J.P.
Edward Patterson & Elizabeth Green, 10 Feb. 1842. C.
W. Rhodes.
James M. Fisher & Elizabeth House, 29 Dec. 1841. J. B.
Taylor.
David H. Love & Tennessee A. W. Randell, 1 Jan. 1842.
J. B. Taylor.
William C. Rice & Catharine Gates, 4 Jan. 1842. A. P.
Richmond, J.P.
Abraham Boyd & Nancy Routon, 6 Jan. 1842. T. W. Alexander,
J.P.
Matthew Skeen & Fanny Young, 5 Jan. 1842. R. D. Bell, M.G.
William Congers & Parthena Walker, 5 Jan. 1842.
Joel N. Vanhook & Mary Hickman, 5 Jan. 1842.
James A. Link & Elizabeth Terrell, 6 Jan. 1842. John
Billingsley, J.P.
John R. Rutledge & Temperance Nowlin, 6 Jan. 1842. M. T.
Cartwright, J.P.
Jarrall Johnson & Sarah Clifton, 13 Jan. 1842. M. T.
Cartwright, J.P.
William Earnest & Martha Ann Williamson, 12 Jan. 1842.
R. S. Tate, M.G.
Richard H. Clark & Mary Neal, 13 Jan. 1842. James Young,
J.P.
Josiah C. Brenard & Sarah W. (Walkerd), 11 Jan. 1842.
John Beard, M.G.
Robert Harlin & J. Satterfield, 11 Jan. 1842.
Thomas Perry & Elizabeth Loyd, 11 Jan. 1842. M. T.
Cartwright, J.P.
Jordan Henry & Louisa Echols, 18 Jan. 1842.
Wesley Brown & Emerline Lannom, 19 Jan. 1842. Noah Cate,
M.G.
John L. Tribble & Mary Ayres, 23 Jan. 1842. E. C.
Jennings, J.P.
Wilie Russell & Hicksey Hearn, 27 Jan. 1842. John
Billingsley, J.P.
Lorenzo Graves & Polly (   ), 27 Jan. 1842. James Bond.
William P. Parker & Mary C. Brett, 26 Jan. 1842.
Mathias Crasnow & Louisa Bartlett, 26 Jan. 1842.
Samuel L. Ricketts & Miland Ann Paul, 1 Feb. 1842.
Archibald Campbell & Mary Ann Gather, 6 Feb. 1842. J. W.
Alexander, J.P.
John Wilson & Mary Ann Underwood, 2 Feb. 1842.
Smith Hudson & Ruth Jane Porterfield, 5 Feb. 1842. A. C.
King, J.P.
Lewis Lantem & Lourany Archer, 5 Feb. 1842.
William Collins & L. Nickens, 6 Feb. 1842. Joshua Woolen,
M.G.

WILSON COUNTY MARRIAGES

William Hancock & Sophia Hines, 10 Feb. 1842. John
  Billingsley, J.P.
Samuel McDonald & Adelia B. Warren, 9 Feb. 1842.
Jeremiah Harrison & Sarah Owens, 9 Feb. 1842.
Isham Davis & Sarah Hoozer, 9 Feb. 1842.
Lewis G. Hobson & Betsy Ann King, 12 Feb. 1842. William
  Barton, M.G.
Alexander Sanders & Ann Chick, 14 Feb. 1842.
John Boyd & Martha Marks, 17 Feb. 1842. William Vantrease,
  M.G.
John W. Shanks & Jane Burke, 23 Feb. 1842. James Young,
  J.P.
John Padgett & Jane Gray, 8 March 1842. Millejah Vaughn.
Jacob Archy & Roxelany Jane Nickens, 24 Feb. 1842.
Joseph Thompson & Eliza J. Knox, 3 March 1842. H. W.
  Pickett, V.M.G.
Thomas E. Everett & Evaline Lasater, 2 March 1842. Barton
  B. Brown, M.G.
Arthur Tarver & Nancy Irby, 3 March 1842.
Adam Wall & Rebecca Mahaffee, (Returned by Adam Wall; no
  ceremony performed).
Ewing M. Earnest & Moriah H. Hornsberry, 7 March 1842.
Mansfield Furgurson & Malvina McCulley, 17 March 1842.
  John Beard, V.D.M.
H. H. Summons & Letitia S. Bond, 4 March 1842.
James Stewart & Sally Manly, 12 March 1842. Joshua
  Woolen, M.G.
Freeman R. Jackson & Sarah E. Winter, 10 March 1842.
E. R. Satterfield & Nancy Sweatt, 10 March 1842. J. Organ,
  J.P.
Hugh Wiley & Hicksey A. (Sims), 13 March 1842. A. M.
  Pickens, M.G.
William H. Bates & Mary Ann Sellars, 15 March 1842.
  N. Cates, M.G.
Jackson Walden & Martha Thrower, 15 March 1842. Henry
  Truett, J.P.
Merrett Caraway & Sophia Henry, 22 March 1842. A. P.
  Richmond, J.P.
William H. Wells & J. D. Calhoun, 22 March 1842.
Zachariah Blake & Ann Jane Pemberton, 31 March 1842.
  A. C. King, J.P.
William H. Wynne & Rebecca E. Babb, 1 April 1842. J. A.
  Walker, M.G.
A. Armstrong & Malinda M. Knox, ? April 1842. H. W.
  Pickett, V.M.G.
Abner Ferguson & Nancy Smith, 31 March 1842.
William Parks & Rhoda Ann Sullivan, 2 April 1842.
B. L. Green & Martha Coe, 6 April 1842. Shelah Waters,
  J.P.
John Berry & Nancy Bass, 4 April 1842.
John Smith & Elizabeth Bass, 8 April 1842.
John Bonds & Sarah Shaw, 12 April 1842. A. C. King, J.P.
George W. C. Bond & Martha Ann Craddock, 13 April 1842.
Richard J. Ragsdale & Jincy Ragsdale, 13 April 1842.
  Samuel Bond, J.P.

Isham P. Pool & Eliza Parton, 24 April 1842. H. H. Hancock, J.P.

Elisworth P. Scales & Mary R. H. Campbell, 20 April 1842. R. L. Green, M.G.

Robert R. Taylor & Allyfare Partain, 21 April 1842. J. Grant, J.P.

Joseph Price & Cinthia Thompson, 25 April 1842. Ezekiel Cloyd, M.G.

Benjamin F. Marshall & Mary E. Thomas, 24 April 1842. E. C. Jennings, J.P.

J. W. Tunnar & Charlotte B. Hearn, 29 April 1842. John Seay, M.G.

Zachariah ___ bbitts & Nancy Underwood, 3 May 1842. W. C. Towson, J.P.

William L. Heraldson & Mary Brooks, 7 May 1843? William C. Clemmons.

Rodney Earhart & Mary Brooks, 9 May 1842.

Abner Christian & Martha E. Preston, 10 May 1842.

Christopher Coble & Charity David, 10 May 1842.

Isaac G. Barr & Caroline Huddleston, 12 May 1842. John Beard, M.G.

Robert Johns & Mary Jane Casselman, 13 May 1842. Henry Truett, J.P.

William Williams & Mary Donnell, 12 May 1842.

James Tarpley & Iby Ann Donnell, 15 May 1842. J. P. Scott, J.P.

John Haley & Mary Vantrase, 17 May 1842.

Jeremiah J. (   ) & Eden D. Pool, 19 May 1842. John Beard, M.G.

Samuel Vick & Martha Wynne, 20 May 1842.

Preston Hawks & Casander Pennybaker, 22 May 1842. J. P. Scott, J.P.

William J. Ashby & Aletha Griffin, 24 May 1842.

John Mount & Ann Eliza Thomas, 30 May 1842.

Jeremiah Collins & Priscilla Archer, 2 June 1842. Joshua Woolen, M.G.

James Harris & Matilda Jane Waters, 8 June 1842. William Swann, J.P.

Amos Campbell & Nancy Belt, 11 June 1842.

Alfred Underwood & Mary Ann Miles, 19 June 1842. William C. Touson, J.P.

Crawford M. Craig & Eliza E. Jackson, 18 June 1842.

Isaac E. Gibson & Jincy Clemmons, 24 June 1842. William L. Clemmons, J.P.

John A. Donnell & Mary Ann Donnell, 23 June 1842. J. P. Scott, J.P.

William Mayson & Louisa Jane Tomlinson, 29 June 1842. William C. Touson, J.P.

William H. Jones & Louisa Bloodworth, 27 June 1842. J. Grant, J.P.

William E. Denton & Patience C. Hall, 30 June 1842.

Westly Prichard & Maryanne Bostick, 7 June 1842. A. C. King, J.P.

Thomas C. Marlin & Almedia Prim?, 4 July 1842.

William A. Overstreeght? & Catherine Mitchel, 4 July 1842.

Barret Moss & Malinda Ozment, 7 July 1842.
Stephen N. May & Mary Kingsberry?, 9 July 1842. J. Grant, J.P.
John B. Woodrum & Manerva C. Bradberry, 13 July 1842. J. H. Payton, J.P.
Russell White & Susan Owen, 20 Oct. 1842. C. H. Rhodes, J.P.
Ebenezar Harris & Elizabeth Tally, 17 July 1842. J. P. Scott, J.P.
Herman M. Robbins & Mary Jane Ray, 21 July 1842. John Beard, M.G.
Absolum Parrish & Jane Crocket, 19 July 1842. Samuel Walker, J.P.
James K. Harris & Nancy Ashworth, 20 July 1842.
Hiram Patton & Lucinda Taylor, 20 July 1842. James H. Britton, J.P.
Samuel Tucker & Martha White, 21 July 1842. S. Water, J.P.
Wilson Cage & Mary Jane Creswell, 21 July 1842.
Britton Collins & Mary George, 20 Oct. 1842. C. H. Rhodes, J.P.
John Smith & Elizabeth Leach, 25 July 1842.
Augustus Cole & Martha Corley, 27 July 1842. James H. Britton, J.P.
John Smith & Elizabeth Bass (daughter of Cader Bass), 26 July 1842.
George Sweatt & Sarah Harlin, 28 July 1842. Thomas P. Moore, M.G.
John Weaver & Louisa Reece, 31 July 1842. L. Sypert, J.P.
Shelton Robertson & Sarah R. Alsup, 2 Aug. 1842. Samuel Bond, J.P.
Harvy Brown & Marinda Lawrence, 4 Aug. 1842. James H. Britton, J.P.
Francis Anderson & Mary Jane Thomas, 11 Aug. 1842. H. L. Sypert, J.P.
Jonathan Williams & Mary Ann Ryan, 10 Aug. 1842.
William Carr & Rebecca McMinn, 13 Aug. 1842.
Thomas Blake & Nancy Jane Pemberton, 25 Aug. 1842. Edmund Gilliam, J.P.
George W. Lewis & Sophia Allen, 16 Aug. 1842. C. W. Jackson, J.P.
John Brooks & Polly Goodner, 18 Aug. 1842. Isaac Hunter, J.P.
Matthew Alexander & Manerva C. Pickett, 28 Aug. 1842. H. L. Sypert, J.P.
Thomas McMullin & Elizabeth Stroud, 28 Aug. 1842. H. L. Sypert, J.P.
James N. Cartwright & Adaline M. Turner, 26 Aug. 1842.
Sterling B. Hardy & Susan B. Jarman, 29 Aug. 1842.
John H. Davis & Elizabeth Marks, 1 Sep. 1842. William Vantrease.
Demascus H. (Scrugg) & Elizabeth C. W. Sands, 30 Aug. 1842. J. B. Wynns, M.M.E.C.
James Brian & Nancy Horn, 31 Aug. 1842. Isaac Hunter, J.P.
Stephen Owen & Mary Jane Harris, 31 Aug. 1842.

Edmund Clanton & Francis Wright, 1 Sep. 1842. John Jarratt, M.G.

William Ames & Alice Wade, 6 Sep. 1842. L. Sypert, J.P.

James Porter & Elizabeth Ann Hobson, 6 Sep. 1842.

Levi L. Sanders & Elizabeth E. Gibson, 15 Sep. 1842. William L. Clemmons, J.P.

Summer Hamilton & Eleanor Hays, 16 Sep. 1842. H. Sypert, J.P.

Andrew Thompson & Martha Ward, 15 Sep. 1842. James L. H. Henderson, M.G.

William Shepard & Martha Carlin, 15 Sep. 1842. Thomas P. Moore, M.G.

William E. Davis & Malissa Tribble, 16 Sep. 1842.

Melchezedick Francis & Elizabeth Bogle, 19 Sep. 1842. Anthony Owen, J.P.

Samuel S. (Luckey) & Sarah E. Jackson, 20 Sep. 1842.

Wiley Mitchell & Martha Wilkerson, 21 Sep. 1842. T. J. Wilkerson, J.P.

Thomas Bennett & Maria Dillard, 22 Sep. 1842. Joel Algood, J.P.

William B. Williams & Evaline Coles, 23 Sep. 1842.

Neely Brown & Francis Ann Young, 24 Sep. 1842.

Joseph Burge & Mary Jackson, 5 Oct. 1842. William Swann, J.P.

David Jones & Matilda Briant, 20 Oct. 1842. C. H. Rhodes, J.P.

James C. Foster & Ann W. Bell, 28 Sep. 1842. William L. Clemmons, J.P.

John W. L. Bettes & Martha E. Summerhill, 28 Sep. 1842. L. Sypert, J.P.

Edward Adams & Adaline Abernatha, 30 Sep. 1842. Samuel Bond, J.P.

Adam Wall & Rebecca Mahaffey, 1 Oct. 1842. L. Sypert, J.P.

Ezekiel Bass & Mary Smith, 1 Oct. 1842.

James Edwards & Lucinda J. Holland, 2 Oct. 1842. John B. Spain, M.G.

Lewis W. Sherrell & Eliza B_____, 5 Oct. 1842. B. B. Hunt, M.G.

Benjamin D. Clifton & Louisa H. Forbes, 3 Oct. 1842.

Tapley W. Edwards & Prudence J. Alsup, 4 Oct. 1842.

Joshua L. Bond & Martha M. Kelly, 8 Oct. 1842.

Thomas Gates & Amanda M. Sullivan, 21 Oct. 1842. William L. Clemmons, J.P.

Jordan Stokes & Martha Jane Frazer, 11 Oct. 1842. F. E. Pitt, M.M.E.C.

William D. Jennings & Mary Ann (Byrn), 18 Oct. 1842. H. W. Pickett, V.M.G.

Thomas R. Hankins & Martha Ann Davidson, 13 Oct. 1842. L. Waters, J.P.

Leonidas Cook & Eliza J. Thompson, 19 Oct. 1842. J. B. Wynns, M.M.E.C.

Isaac Sparks & Jane L. Morrison, 18 Oct. 1842. D. Buowe.

James B. Rutland & Asenath A. Abbe, 19 Oct. 1842. George Donnell, V.D.M.

Comodore Kelly & Elizabeth C. Forbes, 20 Oct. 1842.
James Scott, J.P.
Francis R. Overstreet & Elizabeth W. Mitchell, 20 Oct.
1842. R. R. Barton, M.G.
Jeremiah Malone & Margaret Halpain, 20 Oct. 1842. George
Brown, J.P.
William McIntire & Nancy Hearn, 25 Oct. 1842. H. W.
Pickett, V.M.G.
Lasater Matthews & D. Morris, 24 Oct. 1842. C. H. Rhodes,
J.P.
William Finney & Eliza J. Cloyd, 25 Oct. 1842.
W. B. Cawthorne & Mary Osborne, 25 Oct. 1842.
Wadkins Hamblin & Sarah F. Cloyd, 3 Nov. 1842. John
Beard, M.G.
John N. Chandler & Ardenia Gibson, 3 Nov. 1842. William
L. Clemmons, J.P.
Edward Attesey & Elizabeth Killingsworth, 1 Nov. 1842.
L. Sypert, J.P.
James Pickett & Jane Farmer, 2 Nov. 1842. H. L. Sypert,
J.P.
Asa H. Sanders & C. H. Clemmons, 10 Nov. 1842. William
L. Clemmons, J.P.
John (   ) & Sarah Pennybaker, 5 Nov. 1842.
Thomas Bond & Jane Mount, 7 Nov. 1842.
John Bond & Elva Patterson, 22 Nov. 1842. C. H. Rhodes,
J.P.
Algernon Jones & Julia A. Cook, 8 Nov. 1842. H. L. Porter,
M.G.
Horace H. Patterson & Ellen Jarman, 10 Nov. 1842.
James M. Jelton & Elizabeth Hearn, 10 Nov. 1842.
William J. Taylor & Martha Ann Davis, 16 Nov. 1842.
Samuel Walker, J.P.
Alfred Coble & Jane Smith, 17 Nov. 1842. A. Bass, M.G.
Tyre Robinson & Elizabeth Carr, 14 Nov. 1842. T. J.
Wilkerson, J.P.
N. R. Jones & Mary Ann Huddleston, 17 Nov. 1842. James
Drennan, J.P.
William Neely & Jane Cartwright, 21 Nov. 1842.
Richard Briant & Susan G. Robberts, 22 Nov. 1842.
Thomas G. Richmond & Nancy Poiner, 23 Nov. 1842. William
L. Clemmons, J.P.
Jasper R. Ashworth, Jr. & Eliza Adalaid Seawell, 22 Nov.
1842. F. E. Pitt, M.M.E.C.
Thomas B. Stroud & Catharine E. Swingley, 23 Nov. 1842.
John Kelly, M.M.E.C.
George J. Wood & Elizabeth A. Bandy, 23 Nov. 1842.
Hope Skean & Winny Jones Vanhook, 23 Nov. 1842. J. H.
Payton, J.P.
H. G. Moser & Lucinday Taylor, 24 Nov. 1842. J. A. Walker,
M.G.
George W. Myres & Elizabeth Telford, 3 Dec. 1842.
John Montgomery & Lucy Andrews, 8 Dec. 1842. William Paul,
J.P.
Ethel___ Sullivan & Rebecca Patterson, 6 Dec. 1842,
William Barton, M.G.

John Hancock & Jemima Sweatt, 7 Dec. 1842. James P.
Scott, J.P.
Sleth T. New? & Minerva J. Gore, 5 Dec. 1842. Samuel
Walker, J.P.
Joseph G. Stewart & Martha A. Brien, 7 Dec. 1842. H. L.
Sypert, J.P.
Willis A. Simmons & Indiana Huddleston, 12 Dec. 1842.
James Bond.
Stephen Spain & Nancy Bennett, 11 Dec. 1842. Phillip
Smart, M.G.
James H. Graham & Martha M. Willis, 10 Dec. 1842.
John M. Jackson & Martha J. Jackson, 12 Dec. 1842.
James Guill & Rachel Eskew, 13 Dec. 1842.
Benjamin A. Latimer & Nancy Puckett, 15 Dec. 1842. John
Kelly, M.M.E.C.
Mayson Jenkins & Sarah Ann Stewart, 20 Dec. 1842. Samuel
Walker, J.P.
Benjamin Harper & Martha Ann Shoemaker, 29 Dec. 1842.
Benjamin F. Butler, Pastor of Bethel & Dry Fork Churches.
Andrew J. Bradford & Rebecca E. Duncan?, 21 Dec. 1842.
A. Bass, M.G.
William L. Smith & Jane Tippitt, 20 Dec. 1842.
Alexander Rutledge & Margaret A. Cox, 21 Dec. 1842. T.
J. Wilkerson, J.P.
James S. Lay & Pembrose Jones, 22 Dec. 1842. James L.
Scott, J.P.
John Ross & Margaret McNichol, 22 Dec. 1842.
David Dodd & Elizabeth Burton, 22 Dec. 1842.
Phocian Morgan & Elizabeth Pryor, 22 Dec. 1842.
George W. Modglin & Juritha Walls, 22 Dec. 1842. L.
Sypert, J.P.
Evan Wall & Elizabeth Ames, 24 Dec. 1842. J. H. Payton,
J.P.
Joseph N. Wood & Anna Sanford, 26 Dec. 1842. W. W.
Ferrell, J.P.
Mark Collier & Martha Leaman, 9 Jan. 1843. A. C. King,
J.P.
Moses H. Fite & Louisa Haas, 3 Jan. 1843. Henry Fite.
Hiram M. Fite & Mary Anne Wilson, 3 Jan. 1843. Henry
Fite.
Herman Williams & Nancy Brown, 4 Jan. 1843.
Pallace Lawrence & Nancy Taylor, 10 Jan. 1843. James
Young, J.P.
Thomas Rogers & Jane Rogers, 12 Jan. 1843. J. M. Wilson,
J.P.
Benjamin E. Partlow & Mary L. Paynor, 18 Jan. 1843.
William C. Lowson, J.P.
Owen Melvin & Hulda Earhart, 16 Feb. 1843. John Beard,
M.G.
Ezekiel Bass & Sally Murphy, 31 Jan. 1843. William
Vantrease.
John A. Webb & Sarah Modglin, 18 Jan. 1843.
George Chick & Mary Williams, 20 Jan. 1843.
James W. McCartney & Petro Hamson, 22 Jan. 1843. T. J.
Wilkerson, J.P.

WILSON COUNTY MARRIAGES

Joseph B. Murray & Cuelda T. Chandler, 26 Jan. 1843. William L. Clemmons, J.P.

Richard H. Harris & Nancy C. Thompson, 23 Jan. 1843. Micajah Estes, M.G.

William N. McPherson & Mary Johnson, 26 Jan. 1843. Harry Fite.

John McHaney & Sarah Sims, 31 Jan. 1843. A. C. King, J.P.

A. Jackson & Martha Averitt, 27 Jan. 1843. P. Y. Davis, M.G.

John Pugh & Elizabeth Brewer, 28 Jan. 1843.

William A. Easte & Sarah C. Carter, 30 Jan. 1843.

G. G. Craddock & Martha Ann Jennings, 5 Feb. 1843. H. W. Pickett, V.M.G.

Hardy C. Neal & Eliza Brown, 7 Feb. 1843. W. M. Barton, M.G.

James F. Jackson & Elizabeth Davis, 8 Feb. 1843. L. Sypert, J.P.

Andrew Chandler & Elizabeth Ann Edge, 12 Feb. 1843. H. L. Sypert, J.P.

Edmund D. Jennings & Susan F. Jennings, 14 Feb. 1843. H. W. Pickett, V.M.G.

Wiley Sanders & Virginia Tennessee Rucker, 14 Feb. 1843.

Joseph F. Tucker & Mary E. Hancock, 15 Feb. 1843. James Young, J.P.

Thomas Marks & Louisa Jane Butler, 7 Feb. 1843. William Vantrease

Thomas P. Richmond & Rachel C. Caraway, 7 Feb. 1843.

Simpson Bennett & Charity Bowdine, 16 Feb. 1843. W. C. Lowson, J.P.

John Harrison & Nelly Foosher, 17 Feb. 1843. L. Waters, J.P.

John Baird & Martha A. Bennett, 16 Feb. 1843. J. A. Walkup, M.G.

Griffin W. Rutherford & Mary Irena Lambeth, 22 Feb. 1843. R. J. Edwards, J.P.

John L. Patterson & Emily J. Johnson, 23 Feb. 1843. R. L. Sypert, J.P.

James Young & Mary M. Donnell, 20 Feb. 1843.

David Nowlin & Clarissa Corley, 23 Feb. 1843. W. C. Lowson, J.P.

David Chandler & Elizabeth C. Hays, 1 March 1843. John Beard, M.G.

Thomas L. Martin & Emaline Bomar, 5 March 1843. Samuel Bond, J.P.

Jordan Rea & Elizabeth Jane Massey, 8 March 1843.

Calvin H. Quenly & Veleria R. Rice, 12 March 1843. James Drennan, J.P.

Francis A. Youree & Josaphine McSpedin, 16 March 1843.

Alexander H. Manier & Francis P. Harrison, 18 March 1843.

Henry Clay & Loretha Markham, 23 March 1843. James Drennan, J.P.

Charles Carnes & Elizabeth Cluck, 24 March 1843. Joshua Woolen, M.G.

Isaac Bartlett & Jane Cox, 23 March 1843. James P. Scott, J.P.

William West & Mary F. Powell, 23 March 1843. J. W. Alexander, J.P.

Dickson D. Hickman & Francis Rotramel, 25 March 1843. J. N. Wilson, J.P.

Jeremiah M. Hedgepeth & Margaret Dobson, 30 March 1843. James Drennan, J.P.

L. A. Pope & Eliza Bowen, 4 April 1843. L. B. Haynie, M.G.

William Ellis & Mary Ann Hudson, 30 March 1843. William Vantrease.

Jacob Allen & Martha Ann Rhodes, 4 April 1843.

John Campbell & Emily ____ain, 13 April 1843. A. Matthews, M.G.

John R. Davis & Caroline Hunter, 13 April 1843. George Donnell, V.D.M.

James B. Alloway & Ann Hays, 11 April 1843. J. N. Wilson, J.P.

Alexander Stewart & Rhoda K. Mitchell, 21 April 1843. T. J. Wilkerson, J.P.

Martha Thornton & Asccey Mahaley Clemmons, 12 April 1843. Henry Truett, J.P.

Joseph Harper & Sarah La____s, 17 April 1843.

Daniel A. Boaz & Nancy A. Rice, 19 April 1843.

John P. Lawrence & Mary J. A. F. Alvis, 27 April 1843. J. A. Walkup, M.M.E.C.

James S. Cartmell & Mary E. L. Guthrie, 26 April 1843. John Kelly Elder, M.E.C.

Washington Bass & Margaret Wood, 28 April 1843. W. Swann, J.P.

Joseph Roland & Martha Davis, 5 May 1843.

Abram Beadle & Melison Helen Reed, 6 May 1843.

William L. Heraldson & Mary A. Gibson, 6 May 1843.

Granville Corley & Sarah Beasley, 9 May 1843. William C. Lowson, J.P.

Edmund Burton & Martha Eagan, 16 May 1843. R. R. Barton, M.G.

Dolphin Bass & Ruth Bennett, 30 May 1843. A. C. King

J. Wesley Horn & Mary Robertson, 31 May 1843. W. C. Lowson, J.P.

Nathaniel G. Davis & Francis Chambers, 22 June 1843. J. A. Walkup, M.G.

Phillip C. Lanius & Docia Davis, N.D.

John H. Ligan & Emmaline Artrecy Jolly, 7 June 1843. William Barton, M.G.

Paschal K. Williamson & Maria E. Davis, 6 June 1843.

Ira W. King & Deborah Brown, 7 June 1843.

Andrew J. McCartney & Sarah R. Hill, 15 June 1843. William White, M.G.

William N. Mitchell & Polly D. Hunt, 8 June 1843. W. Swann, J.P.

Edward Richards & Elizabeth Mooney, 22 June 1843. Hugh B. (Lansden), M.G.

Thomas J. Holmes & Frances Bradley, 24 June 1843.

Isaac J. Dobson & Lavina Edwards, 29 June 1843. Wilson Hearn, M.G.

WILSON COUNTY MARRIAGES

Joseph Burke & Harriet Piles, 4 July 1843. C. W. Jackson, J.P.
Edmund Newbill & Louisa Dority, 20 July 1843. J. L. Dillard, M.G.
James P. Richmond & Rachel C. Caraway, 8 Feb. 1843. William L. Clemmons, J.P.
Henry R. Thompson & Almedia Pride, 19 July 1843. John Beard, M.G.
Jonathan Prichard & Elizabeth Bostick, 20 July 1843. A. C. King, J.P.
Hiram Gatlin & Mary M. Brashaw, 27 July 1843. William Vantrease, M.G.
Seth Howard & P. Compton, 24 July 1843.
Elijah Jennings & Nancy Baily, 26 July 1843.
Hugh R. Gwynn & Jane Wright, 28 July 1843. James Drennan, J.P.
James A. Hatcher & Lucy Ann Ellis, 27 July 1843. R. J. Evans.
James A Summerhil & Sarah Ann Sypert, 27 July 1843.
Holden Smith & Pamelia MacKee, 30 July 1843. Samuel Walker, J.P.
William L. Dickinson & Mary Ann Coleman, 6 Aug. 1843. A. C. Hill, J.P.
David James & Malinda Jennings, 10 Aug. 1843. H. W. Pickett, V.M.G.
William C. Hunt & Doza A. Moore, 9 Aug. 1843. George Brown, J.P.
John W. Martin & Peggy E. Fite, 11 Aug. 1843.
James Johnson & Serina Tomlinson, 15 Aug. 1843. W. C. Lowson, J.P.
Thomas Vivrette & Julia Ann Hornsberry, 22 Aug. 1843. J. N. Wilson, J.P.
Robert Edwards & Pamelia Belcher, 24 Aug. 1843. R. J. Evans, J.P.
Nathan E. Lyon & Harriet Dellivan, 24 Aug. 1843. W. C. Lowson, J.P.
William J. Stanford & May C. McDonald, 7 Sep. 1843. E. B. Haynie, M.G.
William M. Cawthorn & Esther Telford, 26 Aug. 1843.
Charles E. Woodruff & Elizabeth D. Patton, 28 Aug. 1843.
John M. Alexander & Hardinia L. Drennan, 29 Aug. 1843. A. C. King, J.P.
William H. James & Catharine W. Alexander, 5 Sep. 1843. John Beard, M.G.
John Knox & Naomi Hill, 31 Aug. 1843. H. L. Sypert J.P.
James H. Fisher & Ann C. Cossett, 29 Aug. 1843. C. G. MacPherson, M.G.
Robert E. Thompson & Mary E. Tolliver, 1 Sep. 1843. C. W. Jackson, J.P.
Harvey L. Lain & Belzey C. Hagar, 4 Sep. 1843.
John Sims & Frances Watkins, 15 Sep. 1843. Henry Truett, J.P.
Samuel Arnold & Manerva Stevenson, 13 Sep. 1843.
J. W. Elliott & Lucy Barclay, 16 Sep. 1843.

James R. Horn & Sarah Ann Hunter, 17 Sep. 1843. William
Smith, J.P.
Enoch James & Ellen S. Thomas, 21 Sep. 1843. J. Turner,
J.P.
Robert Allen & Elizabeth Jane Lasater, 24 Jan. 1844.
C. H. Rhodes, J.P.
Doctor Franklin Harris & Elizabeth Clopton, 21 Sep. 1843.
Edmund Gilliam, J.P.
Washington Hatcher & Elizabeth Bradshaw, 20 Sep. 1843.
R. J. Evans, J.P.
Thomas Daniel & Leanna Smith, 27 Sep. 1843. H. L. Sypert,
J.P.
Thomas Puckett & Elizabeth Hood, 24 Jan. 1844. C. H.
Rhodes, J.P.
Albert Hankins & Mariah Johnson, 27 Sep. 1843. R. J.
Evans, J.P.
George Hawks & Martha Ozment, 1 Oct. 1843. Henry Truett,
J.P.
Phillip Comer & Emerline Cluck, 28 Sep. 1843. N. M.
Green, M.G.
William A. Smith & Seneath R. Thomas, 26 Sep. 1843.
Anthony (   ), J.P.
Thomas E. Williamson & Mary Haas, 11 Oct. 1843. Jeremiah
Turner, J.P.
Lucillus D. Lindsey & Sarah H. Crutchfield, 2 Nov. 1843.
A. C. King, J.P.
George W. Lester & Sarah Word, 3 Oct. 1843.
James Taylor & Sophia Babb, 5 Oct. 1843. John Kelly,
Elder M.E.C.
James M. Hunt & Missouri F. Tunstill, 5 Oct. 1843. George
Brown, J.P.
Edward Edge & Delany Ricketts, 17 Oct. 1843. Jeremiah
Turner, J.P.
Young Herondon & Lucy Hardwick, 8 Oct. 1843. Jeremiah
Turner, J.P.
John Shorter & Martha Burchett, 12 Oct. 1843. Not present.
Jonathan Shores, Jr. & Mary Ann Bailey, 13 Oct. 1843.
(Returned unexecuted 23 Feb. 1844).
Lewis Jones & Polly Hale, 14 Oct. 1843.
Jeremiah Hodges & Sarah Mooney, 17 Oct. 1843. H. L.
Sypert, J.P.
Louis Hawk & Elise Schertzer, 17 Oct. 1843. C. W. Jackson,
J.P.
James Sanders & Polly Baskins, 17 Dec. 1843. Joshua
Woolen, M.G.
Lewis B. Green & Nancy Bennett, 19 Oct. 1843. James
P. Scott, J.P.
William Neal & Catharine Vantrees, 19 Oct. 1843. James
Young, J.P.
Thomas P. Jones & Elizabeth Payne, 21 Oct. 1843. H. L.
Sypert, J.P.
C. Bennett & Matilday Gray, 19 Oct. 1843.
John Lannom & Mary Howard, 25 Oct. 1843. N. M. Green,
M.G.

WILSON COUNTY MARRIAGES

Samuel J. Newbitt & Sarah Walker, 25 Oct. 1843. James
    H. Britton, J.P.
James Organ & Amanda Cartwright, 26 Oct. 1843. R. J.
    Evans, J.P.
David Bass & Nancy Vowell, 26 Oct. 1843.
Thomas Blackwell & Martha Jenkins, 24 Oct. 1843. N. M.
    Green, M.G.
William P. Favoir & Mourning Alsup, 27 Oct. 1843. N. M.
    Green, M.G.
George W. Lain & Mary Rogers, 29 Oct. 1843. Henry Truett,
    J.P.
Samuel Shoemaker & Nancy Arnold, 29 Oct. 1843. Henry
    Truett, J.P.
Clem Jennings & Elizabeth Brett, 1 Nov. 1843.
William P. Hickerson & Mary Marks, 1 Nov. 1843.
William Anderson Sherrell & Martha C. Martin, 9 Nov. 1843.
    A. P. Richmond, J.P.
Jesse B. Pemberton & Mary Ann Womack, 9 Nov. 1843. A. C.
    King, J.P.
Robert Dillard & Harriet Larten, 10 Nov. 1843. Not present.
James Gray & Cindis Bates, 16 Nov. 1843. R. R. Barton,
    M.G.
James G. Sim____ & Martha Smith, 14 Nov. 1843. James P.
    Scott, J.P.
Martin Edwards & Cynthia Hynes, 13 Nov. 1843. H. H.
    Hancock, J.P.
William C. Gill & Elizabeth Hearn, 17 Nov. 1843. W.
    Swann, J.P.
James H. Mosely & Merneva Underwood, 15 Nov. 1843.
William B. Guthrie & Mary E. Jackson, 16 Nov. 1843. John
    Kelly, M.G.
Thomas Weir & Martha Blake, 23 Nov. 1843. A. P. Richmond,
    J.P.
Albert H. Powell & Martha Ann Page, 28 Nov. 1843. A. C.
    King, J.P.
James Spinks & Elizabeth Ozment, 22 Nov. 1843. Henry
    Truett, J.P.
Thomas N. Cox & Sarah Spears, 21 Nov. 1843. James P.
    Scott, J.P.
William J. Ashby & Manerva Johnston, 21 Nov. 1843. James
    P. Scott, J.P.
Lemuel Wright & Sarah Hickman, 22 Nov. 1843. John R.
    Wilson, J.P.
Jacob Bennett & Adaline Gray, 24 Nov. 1843. J. P. Lewis,
    J.P.
Thomas Berry & Martha Ann Phillips, 28 Nov. 1843. James
    Young, J.P.
Joseph Chastin & Martha Vowell, 27 Nov. 1843. Benjamin
    G. Barclay, J.P.
William Littleberry Belcher & Rebecca Wilson, 28 Nov. 1843.
    Jeremiah Turner.
John Spinks & Rebecca Denton, 28 Nov. 1843.
Benjamin Standley & Nancy Johnson, 3 Dec. 1843. Thomas
    Turner, J.P.

James M. Lucky & Omi E. Echols, 5 Dec. 1843. Jonathan
Bailey, J.P.
James Ferrell & Mary A. McSpadden, 5 Dec. 1843. R. J.
Williams, J.P.
Robert P. Sweatt & Jane Sherrell, 7 Dec. 1843. L. Waters,
J.P.
George Williamson & Jane E. Kirkpatrick, 28 Nov. 1843.
B. B. Hunt, M.G.
William R. Williams & Almira Puckett, 12 Dec. 1843.
John R. Belcher & Tennessee ( ), 12 Dec. 1843. P. Y.
Davis, M.G.
Nathaniel Puckett & Elmyra Ryan, 24 Jan. 1844. C. H.
Rhodes, J.P.
John Robert Parrish & Martha N. Mabry, 11 Dec. 1843.
Samson Harpole, J.P.
Edward Williams & Frances White, 18 Dec. 1843.
Bartlett E. Sawyer & Mary E. Sublett, 24 Dec. 1843. N.
M. Green, M.G.
John Eatherly & Margaret J. Williams, 18 Dec. 1843.
John B. White & Eleanor Barton, 4 Jan. 1844. L. Waters.
Miles Henry & Jane Marrs, 3 Jan. 1844. Benjamin G.
Barclay, J.P.
C. Kelly & Martha Andrews, 11 Jan. 1844. Thomas Turner.
Franklin Dockins & Sally Hobbs, 5 Jan. 1844. Jonathan
Bailey, J.P.
Alexander Sinclair & Elizabeth Bush, 7 Jan. 1844. A. P.
Richmond, J.P.
Henry Tomblin & Eliza Kidwell, 7 Jan. 1844. Henry Truett,
J.P.
Edwin B. Powell & Nancy Alford, 16 Jan. 1844. N. M.
Green, M.G.
Jonathan McMean & Sarah Beasley, 8 Jan. 1844. Samson
Harpole, J.P.
John Cawthon & Mary Ann Eddings, 9 Jan. 1844.
Thomas Wommack & Nancy Douglas, 11 Jan. 1844.
James M. Smith & Margaret A. Sands, 10 Jan. 1844. P. Y.
Davis, M.G.
Enoch Warner & Nancy King, 13 Jan. 1844.
Demascus McPeak & Sally Howard, 16 Jan. 1844. N. M. Green,
M.G.
Francis Earl & Susan Brown, 15 Jan. 1844. W. C. Lowson,
J.P.
Edward Denton & Elizabeth Foster, 15 Jan. 1844. Wood N.
Shearm, J.P.
John H. Sanders & Martha Jane Dillard, 18 Feb. 1844. P.
Y. Davis, M.G.
Churchwell Anderson & Elizabeth Lawrence, 17 Jan. 1844.
George Donnell, V.D.M.
Benjamin Clifton & Harriet B. Grant, 17 Jan. 1844. John
Seay, M.G.
David Phillips & Elizabeth Thompson, 19 Jan. 1844. A.
Bass, M.V.D.
William Bryant & Francis Collier, 21 Jan. 1844. Edmund
Gilliam, J.P.

WILSON COUNTY MARRIAGES

James N. Davis & Frances Wood, 21 Dec. 1843. N. B. Hill,
C.P.M.
Francis Redditt & Elizabeth Harrison, 20 Dec. 1843. J.
P. Scott, J.P.
James Coe & Martha Irby, 27 Dec. 1843. James P. Scott,
J.P.
Elias Hubbard & Susan L. Donelson, 26 Dec. 1843. James
J. Trott, M.G.
John Robertson & Clarissa Horn, 24 Oct. 1843. Samson
Harpole, J.P.
Richard Mount & Lively Patterson, 27 Jan. 1844.
Silas Lain & Elizabeth Nowlin, 26 Jan. 1844. William
Barton, M.G.
Andrew R. Eatherly & Elizabeth W. Tate, 27 Jan. 1844.
Lancelot Vivrett & Mary Links, 30 Jan. 1844. Henry
Truett, J.P.
James H. Scoles & Elizabeth W. Payton, 30 Jan. 1844.
T. E. Pitts, M.M.E.C.
D. G. Hankins & Elizabeth R. Grissom, 30 Jan. 1844.
E. D. Johnson & Elizabeth Harris, 22 Feb. 1844. L. Waters.
Albert Moser & Martha Ann Dawson, 30 Jan. 1844. J. P.
Scott, J.P.
Andrew C. Jackson & Mary Ann Ozment, 31 Jan. 1844.
James Williamson & Jane Adams, 1 Feb. 1844. Jeremiah
Turner, J.P.
William W. Swain & Nancy Webb, 3 Feb. 1844. T. J.
Wilkerson, J.P.
William Harris & Mary Eatherly, 8 Feb. 1844. L. Waters,
J.P.
Henry D. Kemp & Mary Bass, 7 Feb. 1844.
John E. Spillam? & Elizabeth Vick, 9 Feb. 1844. J. R.
Watson, J.P.
Carnes Logue & Margaret Braden, 13 Feb. 1844. William L.
Clemmons, J.P.
M. J. Green & M. M. Willis, 15 Feb. 1844.
Thomas Ellis & Nancy Griffin, 20 Feb. 1844. James B.
Scott.
Jackson Fox & Eliza Tribble, 21 Feb. 1844. H. L. Sypert,
J.P.
Henry Jackson & Nancy Spears, 21 Feb. 1844. W. C. Lowson,
J.P.
Michael E. Jones & Emily B. Provine, 21 Feb. 1844.
Richard H. Puckett & Cornelia Puckett, 23 Feb. 1844. D.
Bass, J.P.
John L. Bell & Martha J. Weir, 28 Feb. 1844. John Seay.
Josiah Guill & Mary Catharine Lyon, 26 Feb. 1844.
John Owen & Polly Harrison, 26 Feb. 1844.
George H. Lineum & Mary E. Woodrum, 27 Feb. 1844.
Leon W. Davis & Jane W. Mitchell, 28 Feb. 1844. Wood
H. Shearin, J.P.
William Babb & Sarah Newby, 29 Feb. 1844. John Kelly,
M.M.E.C.
John C. Ash & Mary Gould, 5 March 1844. T. J. Wilkerson,
J.P.

Johnson Kelly & Louisa Morand, 7 March 1844. Jeremiah Turner, J.P.

Joel King & Martha Ann Johnson, 7 March 1844. Wood H. Shearin, J.P.

Alfred Payne & Rebecca P. Horn, 13 March 1844. John Kelly, M.M.E.C.

Eli J. Summars & Elizabeth M. Long, 14 March 1844. H. W. Pickett, V.M.G.

Wilson B. Baird & Martha A. Baird, 21 March 1844. William L. Clemmons, J.P.

Henry J. Drew & Jenny Morris, 16 March 1844. J. N. Wilson, J.P.

William (   ) & Lavinia Moxley, 21 March 1844. James P. Scott, J.P.

William Davis & Elizabeth Ann Sullivan, 23 March 1844.

Elijah H. Jennings & Margaret Malissa Tucker, 24 March 1844.

William Lannom & Sarah Cluck, 28 March 1844. N. M. Green.

James Flaniken & Aletha Griffin, 29 March 1844. Samuel Bond, J.P.

William H. Carver & Rebecca A. Russell, 4 April 1844. William L. Clemmons, J.P.

Thomas H. Durham & Edy? Clark, 31 March 1844. Joshua Woolen, M.G.

Rufus P. Rice & Diadema Rice, 3 April 1844. James Drennan, J.P.

John Cowger & Elizabeth Halbrook, 3 April 1844. T. J. Wilkerson, J.P.

Peter Melvin & Mary Jackson, 7 April 1844. Ezekiel Cloyd, M.G.

John McRoy & Elizabeth Horn, 11 April 1844.

Andrew Horn & Julia Ann Corley, 17 April 1844. Sarah Harpole, J.P.

Albert Fagan & Martha Shores, 18 April 1844. H. L. Sypert, J.P.

Jesse Fowler & Louisa Hatcher, 16 April 1844.

Micajah Estes & Elizabeth Griffin, 17 April 1844.

James Chambers & Susannah Chan____, 18 April 1844.

George Burchett & Susannah Lawson, 20 April 1844.

James Wright & Margaret Posey, 21 April 1844. George Brown, J.P.

James Calhoun & Elanor Anderson, 1 May 1844.

Charles Williams & Elizabeth Green, 5 May 1844. James Drennan, J.P.

Michael Archer & Martha Jane Shoecroft, 16 May 1844. Samuel Bond, J.P.

Henry J. Watson & Sarah Adamson, 2 June 1844. Sebastian Williams.

Benjamin Good & Delila Watkins, 15 May 1844. George Donnell, V.D.M.

Thomas Height & P. Gregory, 15 May 1844. J. N. Wilson, J.P.

Milus Ayres & Susan B. Godfrey, 23 May 1844. H. L. Sypert, J.P.

John G. Ligon & Elizabeth Todd, 18 May 1844. J. N. Wilson, J.P.
James Warren & Julia Owen, 22 May 1844.
Samuel Flankkin & Jane Allen, 30 May 1844. J. B. Taylor, J.P.
Joseph Camper & Elizabeth A. Brewer, Evening of 30 May 1844. B. B. Hunt.
John Proctor & Julia Ann Lankford, 22 June 1844. Jonathan Bailey, J.P.
William Donaldson & Martha A. Graves, 24 June 1844. J. N. Waters, J.P.
John B. Fletcher & Sarah Pool, 24 June 1844. J. N. Wilson.
Robert L. Bumpass & Mary Ann Tipton, 27 June 1844. M. L. Vaughn, V.D.M.
Henry Williams & Eliza Sinclair, 29 June 1844. James Drennan, J.P.
Green B. Lannom & Margaret McCullock, 1 July 1844.
William Bennett & Jane Shores, 2 July 1844. James Young, J.P.
Tarpley G. Logue & Nancy Ann Bass, 4 July 1844.
S. A. White & Mary E. Bradberry, 4 July 1844. William Barton, M.G.
James C. Pickett & Parthenia Ann Hamilton, 16 July 1844. A. P. Richmond, J.P.
Caswell C. Craddock & Louisa Jane Rhodes, 16 July 1844.
John Hancock & Susannah Chambless, 16 July 1844. L. Yarborough, M.G.
Calvin Tally & Abigail Williams, 18 July 1844. H. W. Pickett, V.M.G.
Joel D. Foutch & Eliza McHenry, 18 July 1844. A. P. Richmond, J.P.
Wiley Hutchcroft & Elizabeth L____ax, 23 July 1844. J. Jarratt, M.G.
Thomas Tarpley & James Hardwich, 7 Aug. 1844. Isaac Mullinax, J.P.
Robert C. Dalton & Mary Carson, 30 July 1844. George Donnell, V.D.M.
George A. Estes & Elizabeth M. Gill, 31 July 1844. John Seay, M.G.
Larkin Allen & Sarah Harris, 1 Aug. 1844. H. B. Hill.
Harvy Spickard & Martha Ann Blackburn, 19 Aug. 1844. William Barton, M.G.
John Marshall & Sarah A. Hubbard, 13 Aug. 1844. H. W. Pickett, V.M.G.
William A. Grocer? & Sally Johnston, 20 Aug. 1844. Joshua Woolen, M.G.
Isham H. Partin & Sarah Emeline Pickett, 2 Aug. 1844. Samuel Bond, J.P.
James A. Kirkpatrick & Oliva Wray, 28 Aug. 1844. James Drennan, J.P.
Richard H. Mack & Susan Brien, 21 Aug. 1844. Green Proctor, J.P.
William R. Betty & Mary E. Martin, 27 Aug. 1844.
Samuel Ricketts & Francina Elizabeth Nancy Alexander, 28 Aug. 1844. J. W. Alexander, J.P.

William A. Smith & Louisa Jackson, 30 Aug. 1844.
Logun Belcher & Martha Ann Elizabeth Bailey, 2 Sep. 1844.
H. W. Pickett, V.M.G.
Caroll Johnson & Evaline Carlin, 1 Sep. 1844. B. G.
Barclay, J.P.
William Jennings & Rebecca Ann Gibson, 5 Sep. 1844.
Sebastian Williams, J.P.
( ) Harris & Manerva Green, 3 Sep. 1844. Edmund
Gilliam, J.P.
Abel W. Williams & Julia F. Stovall, 4 Sep. 1844. J. P.
Scott, J.P.
Thomas Earheart & Manerva A. Pride, 11 Sep. 1844. John
Beard, M.G.
William Sherman & Chaney Lain, 10 Sep. 1844. W. L.
Clemmons, J.P.
Nathan Oakley & Ann Webb, 10 Sep. 1844. Isaac Mullinax,
J.P.
Plesant G. Gears & Amanda E. Ash, 14 Sep. 1844.
John Holme & Nelly Modglin, 16 Sep. 1844. J. Grant, J.P.
Samuel Caplinger & Rebecca Bodine, 18 Sep. 1844.
Richard M. Hunt & Susan E. Mathews, 24 Sep. 1844. Hugh
B. Lansden, M.G.
Ila Douglas & Sarah W. Martin, 23 Sep. 1844.
Ansel Jackson Moran & Mahala Moran, 24 Sep. 1844. Isaac
Mullinax, J.P.
Christopher C. Blankenship & Mary H. Porterfield, 24 Sep.
1844.
Samuel J. Kitrell & Catharine F. Warren, 25 Sep. 1844.
B. B. Hunt.
John Carnes & Priscilla Hagan, 26 Sep. 1844. Elder John
P. Spain.
Edmund B. Drake & Sarah Jane Sypert, 29 Sep. 1844. George
Donnell, V.D.M.
Jeptha Clemmons & Francis D. Carver, 2 Oct. 1844. John
Beard, M.G.
William Foust & Elizabeth Lester, 2 Oct. 1844. J. A.
Bullard, M.G.
Robert W. Rutherford & Harriet Jane Pursley, 2 Oct. 1844.
Richard W. May & Evaline Bloodwoth, 2 Oct. 1844. John
Seay, M.G.
Isaiah Tribble & Mary M. Ward, 9 Oct. 1844. James
Thomas, J.P.
John W. Bland & Malinda J. Porterfield, 9 Oct. 1844.
H. W. Pickett, V.M.G.
William E. Bridges & Mary Clemmons, 7 Oct. 1844.
Fountain Daniel & Evelina Williams, 10 Oct. 1844. Milkijah
Vaughn, V.D.M.
John W. Wilcut & Jane Frances Sweatt, 15 Oct. 1844.
James L. Steed & Mary Ann Baird, 17 Oct. 1844. A. P.
Richmond, J.P.
William B. Worsham & Maria Caroline Green, 17 Oct. 1844.
Rutherford R. Barton, M.G.
Robert M. Elliott & Sally H. Currey, 17 Oct. 1844.
David Horn & Mary Jane Freeman, 18 Oct. 1844.
James A. Blankenship & Mary Ann Henderson, 19 Oct. 1844.

John Blackburn & Anna Sutton, 19 Oct. 1844. T. J. Wilkerson, J.P.

Lewis Marks & Sarah Neal, 24 Oct. 1844. William Vantrease, M.G.

Othiel Johnson & Ann Eliza Walker, 28 Oct. 1844.

John Bailey & Charlotte Neal, 29 Oct. 1844.

Samuel Hamilton & Fredonia Rice, 31 Oct. 1844. James Drennan, J.P.

William S. Duncan & Eliza Chamber, 7 Nov. 1844. J. L. Dillard, M.G.

Edmund McWhirter & Jane Vivrett, 31 Oct. 1844.

William Griffin & Mary Wood, 4 Nov. 1844.

Richard Jones & Sarah George, 8 Nov. 1844. Isaac Mullinax, J.P.

James Scott & Catharine Lomas, 11 Nov. 1844. Samuel Walker, J.P. ("Executed & set for trial whenever the parties are present. This was all done in the dark & I think it a dark case anyway. It turned out to be a free Negro & a white woman I understand."--Note by Clerk.)

Richard Barnsfield & Ann Eliza Williams, 8 Nov. 1844. James P. Scott, J.P.

William B. Smith & Letta B. Eatherly, 11 Nov. 1844. J. N. Wilson, J.P.

Ephraim H. Williams & Catharine Belcher, 14 Nov. 1844. Isaac Mullinax, J.P.

Felix Taylor & Louisa Ann Motheral, 15 Nov. 1844. M. S. Vaughn, V.D.M.

James Fisher & Eliza Medford, 18 Nov. 1844. William Swann, J.P.

George W. Martin & Martha Ann Robertson, 1 Nov. 1844.

Barnabas Eagan & Sarah Ann Holt, 21 Nov. 1844. R. R. Barton.

Thomas Kitrell & Mary Tarver, 21 Nov. 1844. B. B. Hunt, M.G.

Leonard Henley & Jenetta Underwood, 22 Nov. 1844. Robert Corley, J.P.

Woodson Cawthon & Cordelia Hewgley, 26 Nov. 1844.

Young Gresham & Elizabeth Luck, 28 Nov. 1844. James Young, J.P.

Frances Chandler & Elizabeth M. Reed, 3 Dec. 1844. Henry Truett, J.P.

William Beagles & Jane Alexander, 5 Dec. 1844. H. W. Pickett, V.M.G.

Richard Mitchell & Prudence Jackson, 4 Dec. 1844. W. C. Lowson, J.P.

Isham F. D. Maddox & Mary (Horseley), 5 Dec. 1844.

Benjamin A. Goosetree & Sarah C. Gibson, 5 Dec. 1844. George Donnell, V.D.M.

Joseph Dossier & Martha Bell, 5 Dec. 1844. George Donnell, V.D.M.

Jasper Rice & Kiziah Swindell, 10 Dec. 1844. J. N. Waters, J.P.

John D. Bass & Elizabeth Satterfield, 11 Dec. 1844. Thomas P. Moore, M.G.

Benjamin D. Clifton & Sarah Ann Calas, 11 Dec. 1844. Jos. Camper, M.G.

James M. Carter & Eleanor D. Walker, 17 Dec. 1844. John Beard, M.G.

George Henry Wheeler & Louisa Fisher, 12 Dec. 1844. William Swann, J.P.

Richard R. Ramsey & Lucy B. D. Dickerson, 12 Dec. 1844. D. Smith, J.P.

James Dement & Lauretta Jane Bond, 19 Dec. 1844. N. M. Green, M.G.

Jonathan Eatherly & Nancy Ann Thompson, 17 Dec. 1844. J. N. Wilson, J.P.

Wilson Waters & Christiany G. Bryan, 14 Dec. 1844. H. W. Pickett, B.M.G.

Edwin C. Sally & Sarah Ann Johnson, 18 Dec. 1844. Thomas Petroon, M.G.

Samuel L. Seagraves & Sarah Robertson, 18 Dec. 1844. J. A. Bullard, M.G.

Green L. Medlin & Eliza Young, 19 Dec. 1844.

John Paul & Rebecca Cate, 21 Dec. 1844.

John A. Haynes & Elizabeth Harrington, 21 Dec. 1844. J. A. Bullard, M.G.

Meedes P. Anderson & Milberry Bass, 23 Dec. 1844. J. N. Wilson, J.P.

Thomas Moore & Elizabeth Whitson, 25 Dec. 1844.

Green B. Hudson & Eliza Jane Sellars, 31 Dec. 1844.

Nicholas Green & Elizabeth Bloodworth, 20 Dec. 1844. R. R. Barton, M.G.

William McDaniels & Mary Ann Partain, 29 Dec. 1844. Dolphin Bass, J.P.

Matthew B. Andrews & Lucy Thomas, 1 Jan. 1845. R. R. Barton, M.G.

William J. Rogers & Ann Eliza Baird, 2 Jan. 1845. Henry Truett, J.P.

John Johnson & Martha Baker, 2 Jan. 1845.

James P. Putman & Marinda Putman, 8 Jan. 1845. Martin Clark, Elder M.E.C.

William R. Randolph & Eliza McRoy, 7 Jan. 1845. Reverend H. Telford.

John W. Orrand & Eliza Jane Tally, 14 Jan. 1845. H. W. Pickett, V.M.G.

Moses Pool & Nancy G. Willis, 9 Jan. 1845. D. B. Moore, M.G.

Thomas Borum & Susan A. Oakley, 7 Jan. 1845. James Young, J.P.

James Lambeth & Susan Wall, 8 Jan. 1845. Green Proctor J.P.

John G. B. Graves & Nancy Brown, 8 Jan. 1845.

George W. Sanders & Harriet Singleton, 11 Jan. 1845. Samuel Bond, J.P.

Thomas Lasater & Eliza Murphy, 20 Jan. 1845. C. H. Rhodes, J.P.

John Flowers & Martha Cook, 11 Jan. 1845. Micajah Estes, M.G.

Welles S. Stroud & Rhoda A. Patterson, 15 Jan. 1845.

WILSON COUNTY MARRIAGES

Frederick Terry & Eliza Jane Bell?, 15 Jan. 1845.
Nathaniel Edwards & Malvina Bennett, 17 Jan. 1845.
Dolphin Bass, J.P.
Samuel Caraway & Catharine Smart, 21 Jan. 1845. William
L. Clemmons, J.P.
John Alexander & Rebecca Vire?, 23 Jan. 1845. Isaac
Mullinax, J.P.
John Lehue & Jane McCullock, 24 Jan. 1845. James Drennan,
J.P.
George Williamson & Mary B. Prim, 20 Jan. 1845.
Eldridge P. Bell? & Eleanor Grissom, 30 Jan. 1845. D.
Bass, J.P.
Lewis W. Mabry & Sarah Mann, 22 Jan. 1845. Martin Clark,
Elder, M.E.C.
Hardy Morris & Lucy Ann Jones, 22 Jan. 1845.
William Word & Mary Phipps, 23 Jan. 1845.
William Jenkins & Ann Shane?, 23 Jan. 1845.
Hiram Cate & Lucy Ann P. Summerhill, 26 Jan. 1845. C. W.
Jackson, J.P.
Leander Hager? & Amanda Ann Kirkpatrick, 6 Feb. 1845.
Milkijah Vaughn, V.D.M.
Henderson Irby & Aletha Jane Gibson, 27 Jan. 1845. J. A.
Bullard, M.G.
Edmund Tompkins & Lenae Satterfield, 24 Jan. 1845. Thomas
Pehoone, M.G.
Kinchen Odum & Faithy Beard, 20 Jan. 1845. William
Vantrease.
James Rankin & S. Eagan, 6 Feb. 1845. R. R. Barton, M.G.
William W. Patterson & Elizabeth Burgess, 2 Feb. 1845.
William H. Grimmett, M.G.
A. N. Davis & Frances Brown, 4 Feb. 1845. L. G. Yarborough,
M.M.E.C.
Benjamin D. Powell & Mary G. Davis, 5 Feb. 1845. E. H.
Hatcher, M.M.E.C.
James L. Young & Mary M. Donnell, 23 Feb. 1845. Jesse
Alexander, V.D.M.
Samuel Major & Frances Davis, 12 Feb. 1845.
Henderson Taylor & Mary Ann Johnson, 15 Feb. 1845. J. N.
Wilson, J.P.
William W. Goodwin & Harriet F. Williamson, 18 Feb. 1845.
John Beard, M.G.
Sterling B. Payton & Abigail Babb, 18 Feb. 1845. L. G.
Yarborough, M.M.E.C.
William Bryant & Dolly Lain, 25 Feb. 1845. C. H. Rhodes,
J.P.
John H. Hawkins & Sarah D. Pugh, 24 March 1845. John
Davis, J.P.
Arthur Thompson & Mary Amanda Bett, 26 Feb. 1845.
William Pard, J.P.
Jonathan Sholes? & Lucy Wilkerson, 2 March 1845. John
Wiseman, M.G.
Robert P. Hardwick & Susan Kelly, 7 March 1845. Isaac
Mullinax, J.P.
James Bradberry & Margaret H. Johnson, 7 March 1845.

John L. W. Phillips & Mary Lavina Warren, 12 March 1845.
Thomas P. Moore, M.G.
Robert Wade & Serilda C. Carter, 16 March 1845. J. A.
Bullard.
John H. Davis & Lucy Ann Frazer, 20 March 1845. James
Arrington, J.P.
F. P. Hankins & Eliza Pugh, 5 April 1845.
Herman Stewart & Mary Ann Price, 6 April 1845. Samson
Harpole, J.P.
Cader Bass & Elizabeth Tompkins, 7 April 1845. J. Grant,
J.P.
George W. Grant & Catharine Hutchinson, 6 Feb. 1845.
John Davis, J.P.
James Woods & Martha Williams, 10 April 1845. Dolphin
Bass, J.P.
William Bayne & Elizabeth E. Wilson, 9 April 1845.
Elijah M. Massey & Laura Bradley, 15 April 1845.
Lemuel Cook & Elvira Lasater, 16 April 1845. John Kelly,
Elder, M.E.C.
George W. Buie & Catharine W. G. Donaldson, 17 April 1845.
William Polk & Susan Omohundro, 21 April 1845.
Eli Cherry & Martha Davis, 22 April 1845.
Franklin P. Swann & Elizabeth Bass, 23 April 1845.
Charles Bradley & J. Shepher, 23 April 1845.
Thomas W. Bond & Elizabeth Alsup, 29 April 1845. James
Bond.
Shadrack Jarman & Sophia Alford, 30 April 1845.
Robert M. Crittenden & Matilda Ann Hays, 30 April 1845.
John Seay, M.G.
George Warren & Mary Jackson, 3 May 1845.
William Clark & Nancy Stewart, 5 May 1845.
William Rice & Jane Swindell, 6 May 1845.
James M. Bucks & Martha J. Woods, 11 May 1845. Samson
Harpole, J.P.
Thomas H. Dale & Marilda Ford, 20 May 1845. C. H. Rhodes,
J.P.
John J. Loyd & Ann Booker, 21 May 1845.
Benjamin F. Briggs & Nancy McFarland, 25 May 1845.
John Seay, M.G.
Mashack Green & Sarah McMinn, 23 May 1845. Robert Corley,
J.P.
Samuel J. Moore & Julia Ann Hale, 27 May 1845.
Daniel Dean & L. Graves, 27 May 1845.
Alexander Brett & Louisa Carter, 27 May 1845.
William Hastings & Elizabeth Lanham, 29 May 1845.
Jonathan Bailey, J.P.
John Moore Smith & Mary Elizabeth Conyer, 3 May 1845.
Samson Harpole, J.P.
George Washington Tompkins & Sarah Ann Frances Wall, 29
May 1845. F. Johnson, M.C.P.C.
William R. Rogers & Martha Jane Emeline Horn, 5 June
1845. John Kelly, Elder M.E.C.S.
Samuel Ford & Susan Owen, 6 June 1845. Robert Corley, J.P.
James Smith & Sally L. Roberson, 12 June 1845. James
Drennan, J.P.

WILSON COUNTY MARRIAGES

Wlliam Mitchell & Martha J. M. Taylor, 10 June 1845.
(Returned by Mitchell).
Alfred Turner & Elizabeth A. J. Tompkins, 11 June 1845.
James M. Graves & Betsy Ann Conyer, 12 June 1845. R. R.
Barton, M.G.
Sterling B. Prichard & Matilda Robertson, 3 July 1845.
Isaac Mullinax, J.P.
McCollester Edwards & Nancy O'Neal, 11 July 1845.
William Swann, J.P.
John G. Bell & Martha S. Duncan, 10 July 1845.
William Patterson & Elizabeth Patterson, 22 July 1845.
Williamson Williams, M.G.
Thomas Swann & Martha Hawkins, 14 July 1845. Jonathan
Bailey, J.P.
Nathan Mullinax & Martha Jane Williamson, 16 July 1845.
Isaac Mullinax, J.P.
Alonzo Graves & Mary A. Graves, 19 July 1845.
William M____ & Rebecca Frances Wiseman, 21 July 1845.
John W. Briant & Susan Lax, 24 July 1845. Anthony Owen.
Nathaniel F. Davis & Martha C. Burton, 22 July 1845. J.
M. McMurry, M.G.
Andrew W. Thompson & Rachel M. Seaborn, 22 July 1845.
David James Wallace & Elizabeth Scott, 22 July 1845.
Williamson Williams, M.G.
Wilie Powell & Mary Smith, 22 July 1845.
L. C. Rembert & Mary Jane Jackson, 23 July 1845. John
Seay, M.G.
Brantlye Merritt & Eleanor M. Grissom, 25 July 1845.
D. B. Moore, M.G.
John F. Hall & Justin Donaldson, 23 July 1845.
John M. Allen & Felicia Ann Lasater, 1 Oct. 1845. C. H.
Rhodes, J.P.
Thomas J. Brasher & T. A. Jennings, 1 Aug. 1845. Isaac
Mullinax, J.P.
Gazaway Peach & Eleanor Logue, 7 Aug. 1845. James Drennan,
J.P.
Philander Owen & Manerva G. Hill, 26 July 1845.
Benjamin L. Martin? & Margaret E. Drenon, 26 July 1845.
A. C. Towsen & Elizabeth B. Martin, 31 July 1845. R. B.
Hill, M.C.P.CH.
John Prewitt & Elizabeth Barber, 29 July 1845. Jonathan
Bailey, J.P.
Francis M. Medlin & Elizabeth Richmond, 31 July 1845.
William L. Clemmons, J.P.
William W. Lindsey & Elizabeth Pope, 30 July 1845.
John J. Afflack & Susannah Joplin, 31 July 1845. William
D. Smith, J.P.
Benjamin Trusty & Emely Wray, 3 July 1845. Wood H.
Shearin, J.P.
John F. Hill & Marion W. Williams, 7 Aug. 1845. Williamson
Williams, M.G.
John Robertson & Lucinda Prichard, 7 Aug. 1845. Edmund
Gilliam, J.P.
Josiah Hunt & Nancy Campbell, 7 Aug. 1845.

William H. Pursell & Mary Mooney, 9 Aug. 1845. H. L.
Sypert, J.P.
Washington Patterson & Elizabeth McDaniel, 7 Sep. 1845.
Williamson Williams, M.G.
William P. West & Elizabeth Bass, 12 Aug. 1845.
Charles P. Stewart & Mary B. McNichols, 14 Aug. 1845.
Samson Harpole, J.P.
Dillard P. (Abby) & Milly C. Johnston, 23 Aug. 1845. J.
Organ, J.P.
Bob Major & Nancy Whurley, 23 Aug. 1845. D. B. Moore, M.G.
Andrew Melvin & Nancy Melvin, 25 Aug. 1845. John Beard
M.G.
John (Weener) & Sarah Smith, 24 Aug. 1845. C. W. Jackson,
Isaac N. Reed & Jane H. Thrift, 25 Aug. 1845.
William Bell & Abigail Ellis, 26 Aug. 1845.
Jonathan Eatherly & Agnes Harrison, 4 Sep. 1845. James
Warren, Elder Christian Church.
John H. L___ & Margaret H. Dowell?, 1 Sep. 1845.
McFanning Coulter & Sarah Jane Singleton, 5 Sep. 1845.
Thomas Holmes & Nancy W. Jackson, 11 Sep. 1845.
Ralph Martin & Elizabeth C. Burton, 10 Sep. 1845. D.
Lowry, M.C.
Thomas P. Walker & Feriby F. W. Smith, 10 Sep. 1845. John
Beard, M.G.
Richard Price & L. Jacobs, 9 Sep. 1845. T. J. Wilkerson,
J.P.
John Huddleston & Elvira W. Stratton, 9 Sep. 1845.
Benjamin Corder & Polly Tally, 10 Sep. 1845. Duncan
Johnson, J.P.
Edward Sweatt & Sarah Coe, 10 Sep. 1845. J. A. Bullard,
Henry (Con) & Nancy Loyd, 27 Aug. 1845. B. B. Hunt, M.G.
David F. C. Rankins & Susan Young, 25 Sep. 1845. J. N.
Philips.
R. P. Lain & Martha Lumpkin, 11 Dec. 1845. William
Barton, M.G.
Archibald H. Stroud & Elizabeth Bailey, 19 Sep. 1845.
C. H. Jackson, J.P.
Alexander P. Wiley & J. F. Allen, 19 Sep. 1845.
Bluford Hodges & Elizabeth Duncan, 21 Sep. 1845. J. J.
Trott, M.G.
William Brown & Mary E. Johnson, 21 Sep. 1845. T. J.
Wilkerson, J.P.
Joseph (Thornton) & Amanda Lain, 24 Sep. 1845. William
L. Clemmons, J.P.
James R. Green & Priscilla Sparks, 24 Sep. 1845. D. B.
Moore, M.G.
Thomas D. Lemon & Pamelia W. Cox, 27 Sep. 1845.
George W. Lea & Martha Jane Patterson, 27 Sep. 1845.
Jeremiah Newby & Elizabeth Jane Hancock, 8 Oct. 1845.
J. W. Phillips.
Andrew J. Hager & Martha Ann Porterfield, 9 Oct. 1845.
Thomas P. Moore, M.G.
Henderson Carter & Nancy Bailey, 12 Oct. 1845. T. J.
Wilkerson, J.P.

Pinkney H. Russell & Elizabeth F. Jones, 16 Oct. 1845.
B. D. Moore, M.G.
William Ricketts & Martha Bonds, 15 Oct. 1845.
Andrew J. Dillard & Rebecca Swain, 15 Oct. 1845. T. J.
Wilkerson, J.P.
James A. Stevens & Martha Ann Reed, 16 Oct. 1845.
Henry L. Cropper & Elizabeth M. Ellis, 16 Oct. 1845.
Thomas P. Moore, M.G.
Benjamin Holland & Cintha Johnson, 16 Oct. 1845. T. J.
Wilkerson, J.P.
Joseph Lane & Julia Dobbs, 17 Oct. 1845. William Nelson,
J.P.
James Allen & Anna Phillips, 19 Oct 1845. James Young,
J.P.
Robert A. Davis & Mary P. Sweatt, 20 Oct. 1845. S. Jones,
Church of Christ Minister.
William Carpenter & Christiana Williams, 21 Oct. 1845.
Williamson Williams, M.G.
Isaac C. Williams & Harriet Jane Ozburn, 20 Oct. 1845.
David Hudson & Martha Jane Partin, 21 Oct. 1845. Henry
Truett, J.P.
William Smith & Nancy S. Spinks, 21 Oct. 1845.
John Scott & Martha Ann Barclay, 23 Oct. 1845. J. Organ,
J.P.
Richard H. Mack & Mildred A. McDaniel, 22 Oct. 1845.
Thomas Lomax & Jane Carney, 2 Oct. 1845. James Arrington,
J.P.
Hardy Wherry & Mary Ann Jolly, 6 Nov. 1845. R. R. Barton,
M.G.
Charles H. Mullen & Elizabeth Estes, 29 Oct. 1845. J.
Organ, J.P.
Allen Dillard & Scelitta Ann Goostree, 30 Oct. 1845. D.
Lowry, C.P.C.
Vinson Compton & Elizabeth A. Garrison, 6 Nov. 1845.
John Wiseman, M.G.
Elisha Williams & Sarah Ann Finley, 4 Nov. 1845. D. Lowry.
Joseph Conyers & Elizabeth Eskew, 5 Nov. 1845. R. R.
Barton, M.G.
William Vantrease & Mary J. Wommack, 6 Nov. 1845. William
Vantrease, M.G.
Thoms J. Campbell & Agness Hunt, 7 Nov. 1845.
Jeremiah Owen & Peggy Owen, 9 Nov. 1845.
John Wright & Sophia Hunt, 9 Nov. 1845.
Isaac Stewart & Amanda C. Green, 12 Nov. 1845.
George W. Thompson & Martha Baird, 9 Nov. 1845.
Absolum G. Harkreader & Mary A. H. Smith, 11 Nov. 1845.
John Seay, M.G.
Richard Patrick & (Mime) Watkins, 11 Nov. 1845. William
Nelson, J.P.
John W. Austin & Martha Bell, 13 Nov. 1845. Duncan
Johnson J.P.
Edwin Berry & Margaret Scott, 13 Nov. 1845. B. G. Barclay,
J.P.
James Hicks & D. Hancock, 16 Nov. 1845. D. Lowry, M.C.P.C.
A. B. Ewing & Emily J. Nelson, 17 Nov. 1845.

A. Allen & Eliza Vantrease, 22 Nov. 1845.
Robert Craddock & Mary Ann Bailey, 25 Nov. 1845. T. J. Wilkerson, J.P.
John W. N. Stone & Margaret E. Tate, 25 Nov. 1845. James Arrington, J.P.
Hiliary F. Smith & Mary Perry, 28 Nov. 1845. Micajah Estes, M.G.
Thomas J. Orrand & Cynthia Young, 29 Nov. 1845.
James Ingram & Catharine Loyd, 29 Nov. 1845. J. Organ, J.P.
John Bailey & Elizabeth Ward, 30 Nov. 1845. J. C. Craddock
Elijah Whitson & Anna Wray, 3 Dec. 1845. George Brown, J.P.
M. J. Corley & M. Hains, 9 Dec. 1845. B. J. Algood, J.P.
Nathan Kelly & Charity Pugh, 2 Dec. 1845. Isaac Mullinax, J.P.
Obadiah Spradlin & Martha Jane Avery, 2 Dec. 1845. Green Proctor, J.P.
James W. Travis & May Ann Clark, 2 Dec. 1845.
J. Crudup & Louisa Wright, 2 Dec. 1845.
John Phillips & Rebecca J. Williams, 5 Dec. 1845. Williamson Williams, M.G.
Paschal E. Callis & Mary Jane Patton, 5 Dec. 1845. Williamson Williams, M.G.
William Link & Amanda Randolph, 4 Dec. 1845. Henry Truett, J.P.
William Patterson & Mary H. Williams, 7 Dec. 1845. William Paul J.P.
Alvin Smith & Hannah Hamilton, 11 Dec. 1845. John Beard M.G.
William A. McCaffree & Rebecca Ozment, 13 Dec. 1845 J. C. Craddock, J.P.
William McDearman & Cynthia E. Williams, 18 Dec. 1845. J. Grant, J.P.
William W. (   ) & Frances Grandstaff, 16 Dec. 1845.
John Lucas & Pamelia Partin, 18 Dec. 1845. N. Ledbetter, M.G.
Herman Dill & Martha Blalock, 21 Dec. 1845. George Brown, J.P.
Robert Redden & Nancy Flaniken, 21 Dec. 1845. Samuel Bond, J.P.
Isham Green & Frances Hancock, 22 Dec. 1845. C. W. Jackson.
Benjamin F. Ward & Eliza Jane Wood, 23 Dec. 1845.
Burtes Griffin & Lucy A. Hester, 25 Dec. 1845. Micajah Estes, M.G.
Burr Harris & Nancy Bartlett, 23 Dec. 1845. Wilson Hearn, M.G.
James Figures & Nancy Jane Dew, 24 Dec. 1845.
James McNeal & Mary Jacobs, 25 Dec. 1845. J. A. Bullard, M.G.
Andrew Lyon & Anna Araminta Owen, 29 Dec. 1845. P. Y. Davis.
William Brown & Elizabeth Robertson, 30 Dec. 1845.

WILSON COUNTY MARRIAGES

H. B. Grissom & Mary Phillips, 31 Dec. 1845.
Asa Brashere & Mary Martin, 2 Jan. 1846.
William B. Denton & Jane Calhoun, 3 Jan. 1846. P. Y.
Davis, M.G.
George D. Young & Miranda Thompson, 3 Jan. 1846.
Elijah G. Bass & Martha Bennet, 15 March 1846. William
Nelson, J.P.
James M. Sheppard & Mary G. Roberts, 5 Jan. 1846.
Elam Hill & Cynthia McDearman, 7 Jan. 1846. R. R. Barton,
M.G.
Temple O. Harris & Martha M. McGregory, 13 Jan. 1846.
D. Lowry, M.C.P.C.
Presley Clemmons & Martha E. Davis, 8 Jan. 1846.
Williamson Williams, M.G.
Jesse Adamson & Mary Painter, 8 Jan. 1846. Isaac Mullinax,
J.P.
A. F. Thompson & Lydia Ann Young, 8 Jan. 1846. James
Young, J.P.
William Bennett & Lucinda Foster, 8 Jan. 1846. J. D.
Moore, M.G.
Phillip McDaniel & Catharine Collier, 9 Jan. 1846. A. B.
Fisher, J.P.
Phillip McDaniel & Catharine Collier, 11 Jan. 1846. R.
R. Barton, M.G.
Sanford Sadler & Mary Ann Harrington, 11 Jan. 1846. Henry
Truett, J.P.
Rolly W. Craddock & Nancy M. Jennings, 11 Jan. 1846.
Sebastian Williams, J.P.
Browning Barker & Elivira Gibson, 14 Jan. 1846.
John Henson & Esther Harrington, 11 Jan. 1846. Henry
Truett, J.P.
John Swingley & Sarah McFarland, 15 Jan. 1846. John
Kelly, E.M.E.C.
John Logue & Catharine Harkreader, 17 Jan. 1846. John
Seay, M.G.
James H. Casselman & Nancy White, 17 Jan. 1846. John
Kelly, Elder M.E.C.
William Hewgley & Hannah Jones, 21 Jan. 1846.
Lewis Hewgley & Martha C. Rutland, 21 Jan. 1846.
Presley Boley & Elizabeth Hodge, 25 Jan. 1846. Duncan,
J.P.
Daniel G. Tally & Mary B. Kelly, 26 Jan. 1846.
J. P. Williams & Martha Williams, 31 Jan. 1846.
George Melvin & Hessey O'Briant, 5 Feb. 1846. John
Beard, M.G.
James Pride & Peggy Starks, 6 Feb. 1846.
J. P. Phelps & Martha Williamson, 25 May 1846. Sebastian
Williams, J.P.
John W. Moore & Cloey Martin, 9 Feb. 1846.
Berryman White & Docea Clay, 12 Feb. 1846. John Seay,
M.G.
Israel R. Mitchell & Rebecca J. Summers, 12 Feb. 1846.
Green Proctor, J.P.
William P. Harris & Susan Allen, 19 Feb. 1846. W. H.
Johnson, M.G.

Houston Jackson & Nancy Caroline Gregory, 20 Feb. 1846.
Samuel Bond, J.P.
Thomas Waters & Susan F. Taylor, 24 Feb. 1846. James
Young, J.P.
John B. Baird & Rebecca Gwyn, 24 Feb. 1846. C. W. Jackson,
J.P.
Elihu C. Compton & Sarah Carr, 26 Feb. 1846. Samson
Harpole J.P.
James White & Calpeony Dillard, 27 Feb. 1846. Joel
Algood J.P.
William Hendrix & Martha Eliza Lott?, 3 March 1846.
George Brown, J.P.
Isaac Johns & Lucy Patterson, 10 March 1846. Williamson
Williams, M.G.
Matthew Stewart & Baderick Hammons, 10 March 1846.
Jeremiah Arnold & Nancy Donnell, 19 March 1846. N. M.
Green, M.G.
William L. Duke & Nancy Jennings, 24 March 1846. R. R.
Barton, M.G.
William Tatum & Sarah Ann Goldstone, 24 March 1846.
William L. Clemmons, J.P.
Thomas Mitchell & Jane Cocke, 25 March 1846. R. R.
Barton, M.G.
Albert Ellis & Martha Escue, 25 March 1846. R. R. Barton,
M.G.
James A. Liggan & Elizabeth Ann Benson, 25 March 1846.
Robert D. Reed & (   ) Horn, 29 March 1846. T. J.
Wilkerson, J.P.
Elisha Collins & Lucretia Warner, 28 March 1846.
Cal___ M. Wrather & Sarah E. Alvis, 2 April 1846. W.
H. Johnson, M.M.E.C.
Calvin (   ) & Mary A. Thomas, 2 April 1846. Anthony
Owens, J.P.
Anderson Sadler & Patsy Vinson, 4 April 1846. T. J.
Wilkerson, J.P.
Isaac W. McElroy & Mary Gibbs, 8 April 1846. William
Swann, J.P.
Charles Wade & (   ) Henson, 6 April 1846.
Samuel Ellis & Elizabeth Parton, 7 April 1846. C. P.
Turrentine, M.G.
William Neely & Jane Green, 9 April 1846. R. R. Barton,
M.G.
Isaiah J. Pughe & Rachel J. Underwood, 18 April 1846.
Isaac Mullinax, J.P.
Hiram Hester & Mildred Graves, 15 April 1846. R. R.
Barton, M.G.
Radford B. Ozment & Martha Carpenter, 15 April 1846.
Andrew J. Vinson & Francis Sadler, 16 April 1846. T. J.
Wilkerson, J.P.
William Green & Missouri Brown, 21 April 1846. R. R.
Barton, M.G.
John A. Hodge & Eliza Haley, 24 April 1846.
Theodore Criswell & Mary Jane Parrish, 27 April 1846.
John Barbee & Mary Grandstaff, 29 April 1846. James
Young, J.P.

Berryman H. Bilbro & Frances F. Martin, 4 May 1846.
James F. Roberts & Sarah E. Jenkins, 9 May 1846.
Andrew Stroud & Nancy Mooney, 11 May 1846. N. L. Arnold, J.P.
Richard Evans & Johanna Johnson, 11 May 1846.
Benjamin Williams & Martha D. Jackson, 11 May 1846.
Ebenezer Hearn & Eliza Crutchfield, 14 May 1846. Henry Truett, J.P.
James Prichard & Jane R. Arnold, 4 June 1846. D. B. Moore, M.G.
Wiley Rowland & Elizabeth Sullivan, 5 June 1846. William Barton, M.G.
Charles W. Simpson & Fanny Jennings, 1 June 1846. N. L. Orrand, J.P.
John Williams & Rhoda Beuells, 4 June 1846.
George W. Hudson & Eliza Vantrease, 6 June 1846. James Young, J.P.
John (   ) & Nancy Johnson, 10 June 1846. R. R. Barton, M.G.
Nicholas F. M. Drake & Martha F. Wier, 10 June 1846. F. P. Scruggs, M.G., in presence of M. Payton, Anderson Davis, etc.
Cornelius Graves & Nancy C. Martin, 11 Jan. 1846.
Nicholas Estes & Emeline Carter, 11 June 1846. Jonathan Bailey, J.P.
Alvin C. Lesley & Elizabeth Jewell, 12 June 1846.
Calvin Jones & Susannah Lindsey, 18 June 1846. James Young, J.P.
Hartwell Rideout & Lucind Fouch, 24 June 1846. Williamson Williams, M.G.
Archibald Allen & Nancy Oakley, 24 June 1846. James Young, J.P.
Thomas C. Gray & Sarah Jane Smith, 2 July 1846. M. S. Vaughn, V.D.M.
Joseph S. Jones & Nancy Williams. 4 July 1846.
Alexander Orrand & Joannah Craddock, 8 July 1846. N. L. Orrand, J.P.
James Jordan & Zaney Johns, 1 Jan. 1847. C. H. Rhodes, J.P.
Henry Ramsey & Harriet Numbley, 7 July 1846. W. C. Lowson, J.P.
Ashley B. Rozell & Martha Ann Chambers, 15 July 1846. Martin Clark, Elder M.E.C.
John Hearn & Mary E. Hicks, 8 July 1846. F. P. Scruggs, M.G., in presence of M. Welch, Davis Turner, etc.
William Owen & Mary Hunt, 1 Jan. 1847. C. H. Rhodes, J.P.
John Patton & Lucy Davis, 13 July 1846.
B. D. Hankins & Tabbitha A. Owen, 14 July 1846. F. P. Scruggs, M.G., in presence of M. Jackson, Pearce Smith, etc.
Daniel Taylor & Mary Jennings, 15 July 1846.
John Moore & Vina Bales, 22 July 1846. N. L. Orrand, J.P.
G. B. Knight & Narcissa Howard, 28 July 1846. Dolphin Bass, J.P.

Thomas B. Oakley & Mary Phillips, 29 July 1846. James Young, J.P.

Joseph Harrison & Rebecca Whitehed, 27 July 1846.

M. W. Shryer & Mary Atkinson, 30 July 1846. W. W. McConnell.

James Armstrong & Sarah Armstrong, 1 Aug. 1846.

James M. Lester & Jennette Katharine Clemmons, 1 Aug. 1846.

Henry A. Baird & Almeda Lain, 19 Aug. 1846. William L. Clemmons, J.P.

E. All Wright & Peggy Ann Morris, 1 Jan. 1846. C. H. Jones, J.P.

James M. George & Elizabeth Williams, 9 Aug. 1846. Sebastian Williams, J.P.

Albert B. Hornsberry & Amanda E. Fields, 12 Aug. 1846.

John M. Williams & Elizabeth E. Rice, 20 Aug. 1846.

Joseph K. Pierce & Sarah Jane Compton, 30 Aug. 1846. C. W. Jackson, J.P.

William H. Evans & Margaret C. T. Williamson, 31 Aug. 1846.

John Jolly & Lucinda Mackey, 3 Sep. 1846. R. R. Barton, M.G.

Clement J. Baird & Matilda Johnson, 3 Sep. 1846. R. H. Hancock, J.P.

Joseph Thompson & Elizabeth Godfrey, 7 Sep. 1846.

Thomas Walker & Elizabeth D. Holt, 10 Sep. 1846. R. R. Barton, M.G.

Jacob L. Horn & Margaret J. Payne, 8 Sep. 1846. F. P. Scruggs, M.G.

William Telford & Mary Ann Johnson, 10 Sep. 1846.

James P. Johnson & Martha Carr, 13 Sep. 1846. J. Organ, J.P.

Reuben Tipton & Mary Green, 15 Sep. 1846. R. R. Barton, M.G.

Robert D. Reed & Mary Ann Horn, 15 Sep. 1846. James Arrington, J.P.

Charles Wade & Sally Hinson, 16 Sep. 1846.

Jonathan Jones & Manerva Cook, 17 Sep. 1846. Dolphin Bass.

Calvin D. Mitchell & Susan Petway, 21 Sep. 1846. W. C. Lowson, J.P.

Mathew Hill & Lucy A. Grimmett, 21 Sep. 1846.

James P. McSpedin & Elizabeth L. Ellis, 26 Sep. 1846. James C. Willeford, J.P.

William Rogers & Martha Patton, 8 Oct. 1846. Joseph Pitt, M.G.

Daniel B. Bonds & Pamelia E. (Cloddy), 28 Sep. 1846.

John H. Baird & Fanny Cason, 1 Oct. 1846. W. M. Green, M.G.

Alligood Woolard & Tabbitha Hankins, 4 Oct. 1846. J. Organ, J.P.

George A. Allen & Sarah Bond, 1 Oct. 1846. Henry Truett, J.P.

James G. Patton & Mary Patton, 5 Oct. 1846.

William Smith & Elizabeth Frances Glen, 7 Oct. 1846.
Jesse Johnson, M.G.
James Tomlinson & Lucy Jones, 7 Oct. 1846. Robert Corley,
J.P.
Thomas Keaton & Elizabeth Houston, 14 Oct. 1846. Sebastian
Williams, J.P.
John Anderson & Pamelia McClain, 12 Oct. 1846.
James O. (   ) & Mary Blankenship, 15 Oct. 1846.
Williamson Williams, M.G.
John J. Alsup & Rachel Davidson, 15 Oct. 1846. John C.
Craddock, J.P.
Milton Lain & Izelea W. Graves, 19 Oct. 1846.
John Shreves & Louisa Lain, 19 Oct. 1846.
W. R. Rutland & Elizabeth Eatherly, 20 Oct. 1846.
James M. Allen & Elizabeth M. Tally, 22 Oct. 1846.
Joseph Johnson & Sarah E. McNeely, 22 Oct. 1846. John
Organ, J.P.
Thomas Castleman & Caroline Steele, 25 Oct. 1846. Henry
Truett, J.P.
Jesse B. Delay & Frances Ann Word, 26 Oct. 1846.
John Floyd & Rachel Bagwell, 29 Oct. 1846. Henry Truett,
J.P.
George W. Patterson & Delila Barker, 4 Nov. 1846. James
Young, J.P.
Robert (   ) & Sally Ann Sneed, 12 Nov. 1846. Samuel
Stone, J.P.
Francis H. Posey & Nelly L. Bridges, 10 Nov. 1846.
Jackson Vantrees & Francis Jane Neal, 12 Nov. 1846.
William Vantrease.
Jeremiah McIntire & Caoline Wall, 13 Nov. 1846. James
Arrington, J.P.
Robert Brown & Susannah Norris?, 11 Nov. 1846.
James Con? & Elizabeth L. Williams, 18 Nov. 1846.
Thomas C. Peace & Louisa A. Cook, 18 Nov. 1846. J. H.
Payton, J.P.
Joseph Graves & Lucy Katherine Martin, 15 Nov. 1846. H.
H. Hancock, J.P.
Alford D. Crawford & Margaret Baird, 23 Nov. 1846.
Henry Tally & Eleanor Maddox, 26 Nov. 1846.
Zacheriah Newby & Elizabeth H. Edwards, 29 Dec. 1846.
H. H. Hancock, J.P.
Martin Hancock & Martha Ann Eliza Hancock, 29 Nov. 1846.
A. B. Fisher, J.P.
Joseph A. Patterson & Martha J. Alsup, 30 Nov. 1846.
John A. Shannon & Eliza J. Hearn, 2 Dec. 1846. James
Camper, M.G.
William Taylor & Eleanor Bumpass, 2 Dec. 1846. A. B.
Fisher, J.P.
John Hankins & Nancy Shepard, 30 Nov. 1846. William
Swann, J.P.
Robert Telford & Ann Drennan, 2 Dec. 1846.
P. Cole & Louisa M. Hays, 3 Dec. 1846.
Benjamin Burks & Frances Williamson, 4 Dec. 1846. Isaac
Mullinax, J.P.

Alexander Simmons & Eliza Hudson, 4 Nov. 1846. William Nelson, J.P.

Lemuel Robbins & Patsy Joiner, 7 Dec. 1846. Henry Truett, J.P.

Theophilus (West) & Martha Sadler, 7 Dec. 1846. Sebastian Williams, J.P.

John Thompson & Abigail Branch, 7 Dec. 1846.

William A. Mahan & Evaline Jackson, 7 Dec. 1846.

R. Franklin & Emily B. Calhoun, 17 Dec. 1846. James F. Johnson, M.C.P.C.

Sion M. Bass & Mary M. Chick, 16 Dec. 1846. R. R. Barton, M.G.

John F. Posey & Margaret Shannon, 15 Dec. 1846.

J. C. Williams & Priscilla Mount, 17 Dec. 1846. Williamson Williams, M.G.

William W. Donnell & Eady Harris, 17 Dec. 1846. D. B. Moore, M.G.

Ed. B. Drake & Mary Manerva Davis, 15 Dec. 1846.

William Caraway & Polly Clemmons, 18 Dec. 1846. Henry Truett, J.P.

Samuel W. Cook & Mary Wright, 24 Dec. 1846. John Davis.

William May & (   ) (   ), 21 Dec. 1846.

Robert W. Rosell & Mary O. Foulks?, 22 Dec. 1846.

Henry Peace & Martha J. M. Taylor, 23 Dec. 1846. C. W. Jackson, J.P.

Alexander Blythe & Nancy George, 24 Dec. 1846. Sebastian Williams, J.P.

Samuel Neal & Mary Jane C____der, 30 Dec. 1846. William Barton, M.G.

Green Proctor & Mary C. Caruth, 24 Dec. 1846.

Thomas Walton & Sarah Johnson, 27 Dec. 1846. W. C. Lowson, J.P.

Matthew Corley & Sarah Whitsett, 27 Dec. 1846.

William Alexander & Martha E. Poe, 28 Dec. 1846.

Benjamin Jones & Elizabeth A. Sellars, 28 Dec. 1846.

J. D. Donnell & Mary E. Jones, 28 Dec. 1846.

Henry Jones & M. A. M. Puckett, 28 Dec. 1846.

Stephen Pearson & Mary Ann Glenn, 29 Dec. 1846. W. C. Lowson, J.P.

Joseph Knox & Jane Bradford, 30 Dec. 1846.

Joseph Burks & Amelia Williamson, 31 Dec. 1846. James Thomas, J.P.

William Durell & Malvina Ozment, 2 Jan. 1847. John Bond, V.D.M.

Hugh H. Harris & Amanda A. Bell, 3 Jan. 1847. Henry Truett, J.P.

James M. Underwood & Elizabeth Haass, 6 Jan. 1847. Sebastian Williams, J.P.

Robert Campbell & Nancy J. Craddock, 6 Jan. 1847. N. L. Ozment.

Green B. Hatcher & Mary P. Ellis, 6 Jan. 1847. Loyd Richardson, M.G.

James H. Lain & Martha J. Martin, 6 Jan. 1847.

Patterson Taylor & Mary G. Partin, 8 Jan. 1847. Micajah Estes, M.G.

Cader Bass & Lucinda Young, 12 Jan. 1847. R. R. Barton, M.G.
H. A. Goodall & F. M. (Suggs), 7 Jan. 1847.
James R. Moran & Mary Hatcher, 14 Jan. 1847. Isaac Mullinax, J.P.
William Parrish & Mary Jane Goostre, 17 Jan. 1847. Robert Donnell, M.G.
William Tipton & Matilda Ann Collier, 21 Jan. 1847. R. R. Barton, M.G.
John Patton & Rhoda C. Casity, 18 Jan. 1847.
Thomas Bloodworth & Mary Ann Jones, 24 Jan. 1847. R. R. Barton, J.P.
Robert Hankins & Mary W. Gold, 21 Jan. 1847. E. Lewis Dies.
Robert D. Bell & Sarah J. Duncan, 19 Jan. 1847. P. Y. Davis, M.G.
William G. Goldstone & Elizabeth Jackson, 21 Jan. 1847. William Barton, M.G.
Joseph Lindsey & Nicy Ann Cates, 24 Jan. 1847. J. Organ, J.P.
James Bundy & Nancy Donnell, 27 Jan. 1847. R. Donnell, M.G.
Robert E. Forrester & Mary J. Orrand, 15 Jan. 1847.
James D. Bettes & Margaret Perkins, 26 Jan. 1847. Green Proctor, J.P.
George E. Ward & Mary Ann Word, 26 Jan. 1847.
James Le____ & Frances L. Koonse, 26 Jan. 1847.
Benjamin Dobson & Manerva Jane Woolen, 31 Jan. 1847. Thomas Spane Elder.
James Allen & Lucy Ann Williams, 26 Jan. 1847. James Young, J.P.
William Garrett & Ruth Jane Stone, 26 Jan. 1847. T. J. Wilkerson, J.P.
John Conyers & Martha J. Frazer, 2 Feb. 1847. James Arrington, J.P.
(Spearmon) Robenson & Lucinda Kitrell, 3 Feb. 1847.
Pleasant M. McBride & Nancy J. Midget, 4 Feb. 1847. Duncan Johnson, J.P.
David A. Grier & Armandy C. Browning, 19 Feb. 1847. H. B. Lansden, M.G.
Robert Flanekin & Mary Edwards, 8 April 1847. Edmund Gilliam, J.P.
Samuel Averett & Mary C. Moore, 11 Feb. 1847. William C. Lowson, J.P.
John G. Carter & Eliza B. Browning, 11 Feb. 1847. J. P. Campbell, M.G.
W. Thompson & Mary Campbell, 10 Feb. 1847. T. J. Wilkerson, J.P.
Andrew J. Warren & Lucinda Ragland, 9 Feb. 1847. T. J. Wilkerson, J.P.
Warfield Thompson & Mary Campbell, 10 Feb. 1847.
Kindred G. Bobo & Julia Ann Waters, 16 Feb. 1847. E. Curlee, Elder Ch. Church.
M. W. McConnell & Martha J. Kirkpatrick, 18 Feb. 1847. M. G. Vaughn, V.D.M.

Thomas Gholson & Martha Smith, 17 Feb. 1847. James
Thomas, J.P.
Winfield C. Jackson & Nancy Jackson, 18 Feb. 1847. P. Y.
Davis, M.G.
William H. Lanair & Mary Brazzel, "Believed married March
1847". J. S. McClain, Clerk.
Berry Bryant & Nancy Ann Tolbert, 22 Feb. 1847. N. L.
Orrand, J.P.
George W. Payton & Temperance P. Hall, 24 Feb. 1847. R.
Donnell, M.G.
Madison Rains & Frances Moseley, 25 Feb. 1847. James
Arrington, J.P.
Allen H. Goodwin & Sarah H. Stewart, 25 Feb. 1847. A. B.
Fisher, J.P.
William Edwards & Martha Elvira Woolen, 28 Feb. 1847.
D. B. Moore, M.G.
Samuel Williams & Mary M. Fite, 2 March 1847. B. F.
Ferrell.
William Wagoner & Christiana Compton, 2 March 1847. T.
J. Wilkerson, J.P.
Richard Strothers & Mourning Walker, 4 March 1847. James
Arrington, J.P.
Charles J. Hancock & Achasy C. Warren, 8 March 1847.
Joseph F. M. Martin & Martha J. Dr____man, 9 March 1847.
Sherley J. Russell & Mary J. Neal, 11 March 1847.
William Barton, M.G.
Richard Felts & Susannah Lanair, 11 March 1847. William
Vantrease, M.G.
Henry M. Lawson & Mourning C. Moss, 18 March 1847. James
Arrington, J.P.
George W. Goodwin & Frances Stewart, 17 March 1847. T.
J. Wilkerson, J.P.
Alexander Jones & Fany Stone, 26 March 1847. Samuel
Harpole, J.P.
John Bond & Nancy Hall, 31 March 1847. N. M. Green,
Pastor at Fellowship in Rutherford County.
William Waters & Saraphonia E. Sherrell, 31 March 1847.
J. C. Goodall, J.P.
Henry Horn & Martha Ann Bandy, 31 March 1847. T. J.
Wilkerson, J.P.
E. A. Kennedy & Elizabeth E. Smith, 31 March 1847.
Anthony Owen, J.P.
James Williams & Mary C. Finley, 6 April 1847. Thomas
Randle, M.G.
Samuel M. Young & Amanda Cooksey, 5 April 1847.
William M. Mathews & Nancy Owen, 15 April 1847.
William W. Carpenter & Ellen Ozment, 19 April 1847.
William F. Rich & Eliza Ann H. Purnel, 28 April 1847.
Nathaniel Hay, M.G.
Thomas A. Partlow & Margaret Williamson, 18 April 1847.
A. G. Kelly, M.G
Jesse J. Pearson & Judy R. Jackson, 27 April 1847. W. C.
Lowson, J.P.
James M. Allen & Nancy Booker, 9 May 1847. A. G. Kelly,
M.G.

Patrick B___er & Alesey Cobb, 4 May 1847. Tilman J.
Wilkerson, J.P.
Henry Steel & Malinda Ann Barefoot, 15 May 1847.
Commodore P. Patton & Martha S. Wroe, 20 May 1847. A. L.
Ivy.
Charles J. Johns & Elizabeth Davis, 17 May 1847.
Joseph Abbenatha & Elizabeth Reynolds, 19 May 1847.
Samuel Bond Esquire.
William Henry Campbell & Ruth C. Gilliam, 20 May 1847.
Miles W. McConnell, M.G. (Regular).
Joseph Marks & Margaret Swann, 20 May 1847. Jonathan
Bailey, J.P.
Thomas Tilghman & Mary Ann McGregor, 22 May 1847.
Armstead W. Jolly & Jane Bettes, 27 May 1847. Green
Proctor, J.P.
Anson Ball & Maroney Pridey, 3 June 1847. William
Vantrease, M.G.
John Guy & Harriet Horn, 27 May 1847. Loyd Richardson,
M.G.
James C. Handy & Nelly Johnson, 28 May 1847.
James B. McHenry & Diretha Freeman, 30 May 1847. Joshua
Woolen, M.G.
Edward B. Williams & Rachel A. Telford, 29 May 1847.
Alexander J. Porter & Martha Watson, 1 June 1847. Robert
Donnell, M.G.
Benjamin L. Posey & Elizabeth Blalock, 3 June 1847.
George Brown, J.P.
A. Stamps & Matilda Rice, 1 June 1847.
El___dam Barrett & Laritha Bennett, 3 June 1847. Thomas
Spain, Elder.
Howard Joplin & Mary Ann Gibson, 15 June 1847. Samson
Harpole, J.P.
James W. Wilkerson & Sarah Walpole, 23 June 1847. William
Barton, M.G.
David A. Wilkins & Indiana Cooper, 9 June 1847.
Benjamin Wright & Clarissa Hambleton, 9 June 1847. William
Woodrum, J.P.
Alexander Brett & Mary P. Birthright, 16 June 1847.
James C. (   ) & Ann G. Wood, 16 June 1847.
Lafayette Ware & Martha M. Spinks, 23 June 1847. B. B.
Hunt, M.G.
Isaac Sanders & Mary J. Richmond, 29 June 1847. N. M.
Green, Pastor at Baptist Church at Fellowship in
Rutherford County.
Rossan Keith & Mary Chumley, 2 July 1847. Isaac Mullinax,
J.P.
William M. Knight & Nancy M. Edwards, 6 July 1847.
William Nelson, J.P.
John P. Dale & Adaline H. Craddock, 5 July 1847.
John A. Brogan & Eliza Ann Gates, 11 July 1847. James
Thomas, J.P.
Newton Underwood & Manerva Jackson, 8 July 1847. D. B.
Moore, M.G.
Benjamin M. McFarland & Martha Young, 11 July 1847.
John Seay, M.G.

Watson Ozment & Caroline Ozment, 10 July 1847.
James D. Reve & Elizabeth A. Mabry, 5 Aug. 1847. James
Arrington, J.P.
Hezekiah Seatt & Charlotte M. Seatt, 12 July 1847. T.
J. Wilkerson, J.P.
J. H. Barkley & Sarah Berr, 13 July 1847.
Samuel Ricketts & Litty Alexander, 20 July 1847. John
C. Craddock, J.P.
Joshua G. Bennett & Nancy Merritt, 23 July 1847. Samuel
Bond, J.P.
John Jolly & Nancy J. Guill, 27 July 1847. Joseph
Turrentine, M.G.
Daniel Malone & Sally Wright, 29 July 1847. B. G.
Barclay, J.P.
James Coleman & Elizabeth Campbell, 26 July 1847.
William Williams, M.G.
Elisha B. Simmons & Amanda Tomlinson, 30 July 1847.
William D. Smith, J.P.
R. P. Seatt & Eliza Cate, 3 Aug. 1847. T. J. Wilkerson,
J.P.
N. Alford & Dicey Bilbro, 6 Aug. 1847.
Daniel Vaughn & Lucy Ann Mahan, 10 Aug. 1847. P. Y.
Davis, M.G.
Alfred Bass & Sally B. Binkley, 12 Aug. 1847. John
Beard, M.G.
Jonathan Hall & Roxanna Bond, 12 Aug. 1847. N. M. Green,
M.G.
Jackson Rowland & Araminta Blackburn, 12 Aug. 1847.
William Barton, M.G.
Andrew Williams & Malissa Seatt, 12 Aug. 1847. T. J.
Wilkerson, J.P.
Ransom G. Thornton & Mary Ann Lain, 15 Aug. 1847. S. E.
Jones, C.C.M.
C. A. Steed & Sephronna H. (Penny), 22 Aug. 1847. Henry
Truett, J.P.
Coleman Tally & Julia Ann Orrand, 22 Aug. 1847. N. L.
Orrand, J.P.
Samuel A. Hunt & Sarah D. Moore, 24 Aug. 1847. James
Tompkins, M.G.
James R. Str___d & Sarah E. Lester, 24 Aug. 1847.
Green Ball & Abigail Ball, 26 Aug. 1847. Duncan Johnson,
J.P.
William McRoy & Susan E. Brien, 26 Aug. 1847. Samson
Harpole, J.P.
Ransom Tucker & Martha Jane YOung, 30 Aug. 1847. D. B.
Moore, M.G.
Charles Compton & Sarah Tucker, 31 Aug. 1847. Duncan
Johnson, J.P.
Franklin Castleman & Nancy Jenkins, 31 Aug. 1847.
Thomas Cook & Eliza Cartmell, 1 Sep. 1847. Wood H.
Sherin, J.P.
William Lanier & Ruth Malissa Ann Herron, 1 Sep. 1847.
John Donaldson & Elizabeth A. Graves, 4 Sep. 1847.
Marshall W. Huddleston & Julia A. Sellars, 7 Sep. 1847.
Reverend John Booker.

Isham H. Puckett & Malinda Guill, 8 Sep. 1847.
John C. Foster & Mary Donnell, 16 Sep. 1847. John Beard,
M.G.
Jacob G. Hancock & Virginia Ann Lanier, 13 Sep. 1847.
(Returned 22 Sep. 1847).
Houston Hunt & Nancy J. Baird, 14 Aug. 1847. D. B.
Moore, M.G.
John W. Foster & Mary F. Orrand, 14 Sep. 1847.
Robert Doak & Clementine R. Hancock, 14 Sep. 1847. A.
G. Kelly, M.G.
John Williams & Elizabeth Thompson, 14 Sep. 1847.
William F. Jones & L. Nettles, 15 Sep. 1847. James
Young, J.P.
Andrew J. Singleton & Margaret A. Putman, 15 Sep. 1847.
John W. Booker.
William Morgan & Jane Thompson, 15 Sep. 1847.
James M. Johnson & Elizabeth Susan Bettes, 15 Sep. 1847.
T. J. Wilkerson, J.P.
Alfred Bass & Elizabeth Andrews, 21 Sep. 1847.
Bennett M. Ewing & Amanda Bruswell?, 23 Sep. 1847.
Isaiah P. Sublett & Susan Cawthon, 25 Sep. 1847. N. M.
Green, M.G.
William P. Hearn & N. P. Hearn, 29 Sep. 1847. L. Fisher,
M.G.
Stephen Owen & Judith Robinson, 25 Sep. 1847.
John B. Burdin & Flotell Blacknall, 29 Sep. 1847.
James W. Ewing & Elizabeth M. Alman, 30 Sep. 1847. John
Booker.
John C. Calhoun & Martha Hall, 29 Sep. 1847.
John Moran & Zilpha Sanders, 30 Sep. 1847. (Returned).
William G. F. Underwood & Mary J. Lester, 30 Sep. 1847.
J. Covey, M.G.
Lucy W. Johnson & Sally Wadkins, 4 Oct. 1847. Joshua
Woolen.
W. C. Hudson & Mary Pritchett, 5 Oct. 1847. James Young
J.P.
Richard Jones & Mary Sadler, 6 Oct. 1847. Sebastian
Williams.
Albert G. Hearn & L___ory Hearn, 12 Oct. 1847.
John Baxter & Mary A. Campbell, 5 Oct. 1847.
James H. Biter & Elizabeth Drennan, 12 Oct. 1847.
Albert Hendrix & Nancy By____, 12 Oct. 1847.
Frances Baker & Jane Johnson, 13 Oct. 1847. William
Lanius, J.P.
William Cobb & Martha A. Bartlett, 14 Oct. 1847. T. J.
Wilkerson, J.P.
Richard Hodges & Nancy C. Powell, 19 Oct. 1847. John
Kelly, Elder M.E.C.
Gad Smith & Mary L. W. Bullard, 16 Oct. 1847.
Samuel W. Crosnow & Adaline A. Clayton, 7 Oct. 1847.
James Arrington, J.P.
George W. Williams & Susan Blankenship, 14 Oct. 1847.
James Bond.
Henry Jackson Rogers & Elizabeth Frances Sullivan, 21
Oct. 1847. Henry Truett, J.P.

Harvy Lawrence & Elizabeth Hunt, 20 Oct. 1847.

Thomas E. Williamson & Frances McFarland, 20 Oct. 1847.

John Kelly, Elder M.E.C.

John B. McConnell & Mary Cassandra B____e, 20 Oct. 1847.
J. E. (   ), M.G.

Caleb H. Smith & Martha M. Vaughn, 21 Oct. 1847. T. J.
Wilkerson, J.P.

Asbury D. Overall & Lucy Crutchfield, 26 Oct. 1847.
Loyd Richardson, M.G.

Charles Stone & Thersey C. Wollard, 4 Oct. 1847. Samson
Harpole, J.P.

William Shanks & Louisa W. Edwards, 27 Oct. 1847.

B. Belcher & Perlina Williamson, 28 Oct. 1847. Isaac
Mullinax, J.P.

George A. Tunstell & M. P. O'Neal, 29 Oct. 1847. James
Tompkins, M.G.

John Blount & Leah Sanders, 31 Oct. 1847. Duncan Johnson,
J.P.

James Stubblefield & Bethena Melton, 31 Oct. 1847. Samuel
Bond, J.P.

Robert W. Hudson & Rachel Caselman, 2 Nov. 1847. Henry
Truett, J.P.

Plesant Tarpley & Sarah McKee, 4 Oct. 1847. Isaac
Mullinax, J.P.

Andrew B. Phillips & Salena Taylor Glenn, 10 Nov. 1847.
Thomas P. Moore, M.F.

James Thomas Horn & Arminty Reed, 8 Nov. 1847. Samson
Harpole, J.P.

William Eatherly & Sarah Jane Lain, 9 Nov. 1847.

Sterling B. Suggs & Nancy Patterson, 10 Nov. 1847.

William F. Alsup & Louisa Owen, 11 Nov. 1847. N. M.
Green, M.F.

John Sims (free man of Color) & Martha Gibson (free
woman of Color), 11 Nov. 1847. Samuel Bond, J.P.

Robert A. Baskins & Mary Frances Green, 11 Nov. 1847.
Joshua Woolen, M.G.

John Oakley & Martha Phillips, 11 Nov. 1847. James
Young, J.P.

Joel Preston & Susan Davis, 14 Nov. 1847. Duncan
Johnson, J.P.

William Tally & Nancy Whitehead, 13 Nov. 1847.

Thomas E. Stephens & Louisa Organ, Thomas P. Moore, M.G.

Thomas B. Davis & Elizabeth (Haster), 18 Nov. 1847.
Duncan Johnson, J.P.

William Whitsett & Patsy Keton, 23 Nov. 1847. Sebastian
Williams, J.P.

Lucian A. Puckett & Sarah Hawk, 21 Nov. 1847. Henry
Truett, J.P.

Joshua Guin & C. A. Chick, 25 Nov. 1847.

John Clemmons & Martha J. Sherrell, 1 Dec. 1847. D. B.
Moore, M.G.

William Gates & Elizabeth Rice, 2 Dec. 1847. William
Woodrum, J.P.

John N. Porterfield & Nancy C. Craddock, 1 Dec. 1847.
William Paul, J.P.

Alfred Vowell & Mary Brazzell, 5 Dec. 1847. William
    Paul, J.P.
Joel Wommack & Sarah Ann Lea, 2 Dec. 1847. Henry Truett,
    J.P.
William Waters & Lucinda Holmes, 3 Dec. 1847.
William J. Kincaid & Mary Stubblefield, 5 Dec. 1847.
    Henry Truett, J.P.
James Ferguson & Nancy Carr, 19 Dec. 1847. D. Barr, M.G.
Edward Rouse & Sally Ann Collier, 11 Dec. 1847.
Alanson G. Wynne & Dicy McFarland, 14 Dec. 1847. James
    Arrington, J.P.
Charles R. Puckett & Sarah C. Sellars, 15 Dec. 1847.
    John W. Booker, M.G.
Henry B. Vaughn & Martha Campbell, 15 Dec. 1847. James
    Plummer, M.F.
Ennis Douglas & Maria Bennett, 16 Dec. 1847. Joel Algood,
    J.P.
Thomas H. Thomas & Lavina (   ), 16 Dec. 1847.
Thomas N. Clymer & Martha Ames, 16 Dec. 1847. William
    Barton, M.G.
John Moran & Martha Armstrong, 19 Dec. 1847. Isaac
    Mullinax, J.P.
Samuel Martin & Rebecca McMillon, 20 Dec. 1847.
James Debow & Evaline Harris, 21 Dec. 1847.
John Bell & Mahala Allen, 21 Dec. 1847. Duncan Johnson,
    J.P.
John Britton & Manerva Coles, 22 Dec. 1847. Robert
    Donnell.
Charles Conyers & Harriet Arrington, 23 Dec. 1847.
    Samson Harpole, J.P.
Abraham Eddins & Martha Whitson, 29 Dec. 1847. R. R.
    Barton, M.G.
John P. Boothe & Amanda Young, 28 Dec. 1847. John Kelly,
    Elder M.E.C.
Jordan Hackney & Manerva Young, 28 Dec. 1847. John Kelly,
    Elder M.E.C.
William J. Styles? & Anna Turner, 30 Dec. 1847. Isaac
    Mullinax, J.P.
William E. Walker & Edney D. Bell, 30 Dec. 1847. John
    Seay.
Edwin A. Mabry & Louisa A. Mabry, 30 Dec. 1847. James
    Arrington, J.P.
James R. Bomar & louisa Davis, 6 Jan. 1848. Duncan
    Johnson, J.P.
Glennis Blankenship & Prudence Blankenship, 30 Dec. 1847.
Charles Cox & Charlotte Stone, 1 Jan. 1848. Samson
    Harpole, J.P.
Hardy W. B. Mitchell & Lucinday E. Chappell, 2 Jan. 1848.
    H. H. Hancock, J.P.
Edward P. Bass & Mary Ann Cloyd, 4 Jan. 1848. Jesse
    Alexander, V.D.M.
John L. Gleaves & Tabitha P. Moore, 7 Jan. 1848. John
    Kelly, Elder M.E.C.
Thomas A. Reeves & Elizabeth Turner, 6 Jan. 1848. Isaac
    Mullinax, J.P.

Francis Harris & Mary Carr, 6 Jan. 1848. J. Organ, J.P.
James W. Gray & Jane Edwards, 6 Jan. 1848. William
Wilson, J.P.
William Thomason & Margaret Ann Pugh, 6 Jan. 1848. Isaac
Mullinax, J.P.
John Stubblefield & Betthew Bell, 17 Jan. 1848. D. B.
Moore, M.G.
Allen H. Grissom & Malinda Stubblefield, 13 Jan. 1848.
D. B. Moore, M.G.
John H. Droun & Dolly Jackson, 11 Jan. 1848. P. Y. Davis,
M.G.
Thomas Vaught & Mary Neal, 20 Jan. 1848. James Young,
J.P.
William J. Moore & Sarah H. Hughes, 12 Jan. 1848. James
Tompkins.
John Clemmons & Elizabeth Bagwell, 13 Jan. 1848. Henry
Truett, J.P.
Samuel P. Patton & Nancy C. Godphrey, 11 Jan. 1848.
Abraham Jolley & Rachel F. Eskew, 12 Jan. 1848. Phillip
Smart, M.G.
Gideon M. Rutherford & Mary C. Duke, 12 Jan. 1848.
Thomas Jones & Harriet Ellison, 13 Jan. 1848. John
Booker, M.G.
Alva James & Lavice L. Thomas, 13 Jan. 1848. N. L. Orrand,
J.P.
John Bloodworth & Rebecca Griffin, 13 Jan. 1848.
Elijah J. Jones & Frances Gould, 14 Jan. 1848. Richard
Lyon, M.G.
William Winters & Mary Jane Rye, 17 Jan. 1848. J. V. E.
C___vey, J.P.
Samuel C. Criswell & Sarah M. Gray, 20 Jan. 1848. R. R.
Barton, M.G.
John C. Carpenter & Amanda M. Vivrett, 19 Jan. 1848.
Henry Truett, J.P.
Allen Dockins & Sarah Sweatt, 27 Jan. 1848. William
Swann, J.P.
William B. Sweatt & Elizabeth Ragland, N.D. James Warren,
E.C.C.
William Eaks & Frances Rakes, 23 Jan. 1848.
John W. Wynne & Margaret L. Donnell, 25 Jan. 1848. D. B.
Moore, M.G.
Thomas Smithwick & Judy Whitehead, 27 Jan. 1848. Thomas
P. Moore, M.G.
Thomas Allen & Harriet Wilkerson, 30 Jan. 1848. T. J.
Wilkerson, J.P.
Albert C. Thomas & Martha Jewell, 1 Feb. 1848.
James M. Huddleston & Isabella C. Donnell, 2 Feb. 1848.
John W. Booker, M.G.
David Gilliam & Martha Brewer, 3 Feb. 1848. William
Woodward, J.P.
Robert Reaves & Nancy D. Davis, 7 Feb. 1848.
William P. Alexander & Charity Williams, 8 Feb. 1848.
Isaac Mullinax, J.P.
William Tally & Lucy Webb, 9 Feb. 1848.
Hiram W. Tucker & Elizabeth Williams, 9 Feb. 1848.

Richard H. Lain & Harriet Jones, 10 Feb. 1848. Isaac
  H. Dennis, J.P.
Thomas Cassity & Julia Ann Patton, 11 Feb. 1848.
William L. White & Mary Ann Bradly, 12 Feb. 1848.
James C. (   ) & H. Trout, 15 April 1848. Thomas P.
  Moore, M.G.
James B. Martin & Caroline (Chambless), 21 Feb. 1848.
  T. J. Williams, J.P.
James R. Ross & Martha McIntire, 22 Feb. 1848.
Robert Davis & Lucy Simmons, 23 Feb. 1848. George Brown,
  J.P.
William (Sims) & Elizabeth O'Neal, 1 March 1848. Edward
  Gilliam, J.P.
Richard C. Lock & Mary L. Beasly, 4 March 1848. W. D.
  Smith, J.P.
P. S. Sherrill & Martha Adkinson, 8 March 1848. John
  Kelly, M.G.
Joshua B. Williams & Mary McKee, 3 March 1848. N. L.
  Orrand, J.P.
Joseph Bogle & Erisma Thomas, 9 March 1848. N. L. Orrand,
  J.P.
Thomas Chambless & Mary Cox, 9 March 1848. Samson
  Harpole, J.P.
William Bradly & Julia Ann Sweatt, 9 March 1848.
Josiah N. Burke & Josephine Huddleston, 14 March 1848.
  N. M. Green, M.G.
H. C. Finney & Elizabeth S. Alexander, 14 March 1848.
Andrew J. F___y & Margaret R. Cloyd, 14 March 1848.
Joseph Telford & Nancy Ramsey, 16 March 1848. Richard
  Lyon, M.G.
Ezekiel Huddleston & Lavinia Cawthon, 18 March 1848.
Elijah Collins & Nancy Hall, 16 March 1848. Joshua
  Woolen, M.G.
James B. Binkley & Susan David, 25 March 1848.
William D. Smart & Dicy Harlin, 26 March 1848.
Isaac Swann & Lucy Wilson, 30 March 1848. Duncan Johnson,
  J.P.
Crawford Walker & Eliza Cowger, 30 March 1848. James
  Arrington, J.P.
William H. Heughley & Rachel A. Bridges, 7 April 1848.
  William L. Clemmons, J.P.
William H. Vantrease & Isabella Duncan, 12 April 1848.
  William C. Bransford, M.G.
Marcus Lafayette Reeves & Malissa Nettles, 9 April 1848.
  A. A. Massey, J.P.
Moses A. Byers & Lucretia Prichard, 10 April 1848.
Samuel Thompson & Martha Fisher, 13 April 1848. William
  Swann, J.P.
James C. Lanier & Mary Jane Watkins, 17 April 1848.
Henry Akers & Mary Scott, 20 April 1848. Fletcher
  Campbell, J.P.
Hiram Williams & Eliza Ann Duke, 20 April 1848.
John McRoy & Caroline Ferguson, 21 April 1848.
Richard J. Bond & Emily Jones, 24 April 1848 ("at hour
  by sun P.M."). A. A. Massey, J.P.

Lewis W. Eason & A. Woolard, 24 April 1848. William D. Smith, J.P.

Joel Algood & Nancy W. Moore, Wednesday 26 April 1848. J. L. Dillard, M.G.

William Organ & Sophia Irby, 3 May 1848. Isaac H. Dennis, J.P.

James L. Adams & Elizabeth Drennan, 12 May 1848. Jesse Ballintine, J.P.

Caleb J. Barr & Martha Scoby, 8 May 1848.

Michael J. ___cher (Colored) & Catharine J. (   ), 11 May 1848.

William D. Barker & Cynthia A. Barker, 13 May 1848. Jesse Ballintine, J.P.

Moses J. Evits & Mary D. Burdine, 15 May 1848. (Returned but not certified).

Samuel Bett & Elizabeth Bett, 24 March 1848. William Thomas, J.P.

B. J. Cox & Anna Randell, 30 May 1848. Thomas Kirkpatrick, J.P.

Edmund Grigg & Martha Thompson, 30 May 1848.

Reuben M. Ray & Mary Ann Gerguson, 31 May 1848.

William Echbaum & Amelia Chumbley, 11 June 1848. T. J. Wilkerson, J.P.

Joseph Fowlkes & Rebecca Ann Cawthon, 12 June 1848.

Robert A. (Hailey) & Sopha Ann Jennings, 21 June 1848.

James King & Betsy Ann Alford, 4 July 1848. Thomas P. Jones, J.P.

John A. Andrews & Louisa Jennings, 12 July 1848. R. R. Barton, J.P.

William B. West & Araminta Jane Seatt, 4 July 1848. T. J. Wilkerson, J.P.

Albert W. Brooks & Sarah Eatherly, N.D.

Charles Compton & Elizabeth Stroud, 27 July 1848. William Vantrease, M.G.

William H. Mac___kin & Ann E. L. Bullard, 6 July 1848. J. N. E. Covey.

John Hackney & Sally Abernathy, 9 July 1848. Samuel Bond, J.P.

L. W. Fitts & Harriet L. Bell, 4 July 1848. John Seay, M.G.

John G. Drennan & Elvira Graves, 12 July 1848.

Edward Williams & Martha Jones, 17 July 1848. Abram A. Massey, J.P.

William Swindall & Margaret Halsey, 18 July 1848.

Jacob Thomas & Mary Ann Daniel, 22 July 1848.

Isaac J. Vanhoozer & Nancy E. Thompson, 24 July 1848.

Answorth Harrison & Parmelia A. Carver, 26 July 1848.

Rufus A. Rozell & Elizabeth W. Harkreader, 26 July 1848. John Seay, M.G.

E. B. Scott & Sarah Ann Cox, 21 July 1848. R. P. Donnell, J.P.

Anderson Ferggerson & Jane Turner, 27 July 1848.

L. McAdny & Elizabeth Bates, 3 Aug. 1848. H. L. Wroe, J.P.

WILSON COUNTY MARRIAGES

Lewis McRoy & Susan McRoy, 31 Jan. 1848.
Thomas Baird & Martha Clemmons, 1 Aug. 1848. (   ) Baird,
    J.P.
George W. Keaton & Mary Elizabeth Davis, 3 Aug. 1848.
    Nathaniel Hays, M.G.
Thomas Nowlin & Martha Sadler, 6 Aug. 1848. Isaac
    Mullinax, J.P.
Daniel McBride & Nancy Lanum, 4 July 1848. William Swann,
    J.P.
Green Strong & Jane Bryan, 6 Aug. 1848. J. T. Goodall,
    J.P.
Robert C. Lain & Johanna Rutland, 8 Aug. 1848. P. D.
    Jetton, J.P.
William P. O'Neal & Nancy Louisa Johnson, 9 Aug. 1848.
    William Nelson, J.P.
Alfred Jackson Taylor & Ruth Jane Williams, 10 Aug. 1848.
    C. S. Sims, J.P.
Henry C. Jackson & Nancy Sharp, 10 Aug. 1848.
Lemuel M. Shaw & Levina C. Woolen, 16 Aug. 1848. Elder
    Thomas Spain
William C. Sparks & Sarah R. Justiss, 16 May 1848. J. B.
    Moore, M.G.
Matthew Summers & Sally Gunn, 27 Aug. 1848. John H.
    Johnson, J.P.
Ezekiel Vantries & Catharine Alexander, 23 Aug. 1848.
    Abram A. Massey, J.P.
John Pippins & Angeline Creswell, 24 Aug. 1848. R. R.
    Barton, M.G.
Robert Bass & Malissa Philips, 23 Aug. 1848.
John Justiss & Rachel Debow, 24 Aug. 1848. W. C. Sparks,
    M.G.
Elijah Hickey & Sarah Pritchett, 27 Aug. 1848. E. B.
    Haynie, M.G.
John K. Cartwright & Sarah Ann Jones, 29 Aug. 1848. N.
    G. Alexander, J.P.
Alvis Spain & Sinai Jones, 5 Sep. 1848. William Nelson,
    J.P.
James Birchett & Mary Alloway, Sep. 1848. Duncan Johnson,
    J.P.
James T. Word & Luicy Jane Jennings, 2 Sep. 1848.
M. Sanderson & Jane Sanderson, 3 Sep. 1848.
Alexander Wade & Sarah F. Word, 4 Sep. 1848.
John Haley & Margaret George, Sep. 1848. Duncan Johnson,
    J.P.
Martin Fisher & Elizabeth Griffin, 6 Sep. 1848. William
    Swain, J.P.
William Putman & Cintha Weir, 6 Sep. 1848.
Ptolemy McMullin & Jane Marler, 12 Sep. 1848.
James E. D___m & Emily C. Tate, 15 Sep. 1848.
John McAdny & Penelope Kelly, 16 Sep. 1848.
Charles G. Carter & Frances E. Stevenson, 19 Sep. 1848.
    M. L. Vaughn, V.D.M.
Peter Owens & (Lucy) D. Matthews, 18 Sep. 1848.
Granderson P. Huddleston & Elizabeth Smith, 17 Jan. 1849.
    Joshua Woolen, M.G.

George W. Fisher & Amy Caroline Fisher, 21 Sep. 1848. William Swann, J.P.

Edward Hunter & Rachel Harvil, 21 Sep. 1848. Thomas P. Moore, M.G.

Albert Scott & Sally Ann Collins, 28 Sep. 1848. P. D. Jetton, J.P.

John A. Underwood & Elvira Alexander, 21 Sep. 1848. Isaac Mullinax, J.P.

Daniel Fakes & Clementine M. B. Baird, 21 Sep. 1848. R. Donnell, M.G.

Thomas H. Dunn & Rachel Chumley, 24 Sep. 1848. Z. McMillon, J.P.

Wesley N. Tate & Mary Jane Reeves, 26 Sep. 1848.

Green Ledbetter & Elizabeth Hays, 26 Sep. 1848.

George R. Bogle & Louissiania Gibson, 26 Sep. 1848.

James C. Taylor & Susannah Wray, 5 Oct. 1848. William L. Clemmons, J.P.

John P. Patterson & Mariah H. Robertson, 2 Oct. 1848.

Gasaway Peach & Mary F. Partlow, 26 Oct. 1848. Thomas Kirkpatrick, J.P.

Jordan Goodwin & Margaret Hunt, 3 Oct. 1848. J. R. Plummer, M.G.

James L. Sims & Sarilda Ann Puckett, 15 Oct. 1848.

William Blankenship & Mary Elizabeth Taylor Moore, 5 Oct. 1848. John Kelly, M.M.E.C.S.

Thomas J. Bonds & Lavina Sullivan, 11 Oct. 1848. William Woodrum, J.P.

George W. B. Shannon & Mary C. Baird, 11 Oct. 1848. D. B. Moore, M.G.

Benton P. Williams & Mary Holland, 10 Oct. 1848. N. G. Alexander, J.P.

John Partin & Polly Sherrell, 12 Oct. 1848. D. B. Moore, M.G.

John L. Baker & Harriet Brown, 18 Oct. 1848. A. D. Jetton, J.P.

Green M. Garrett & Dianna Mackey, 22 Oct. 1848. R. R. Barton, M.G.

Joshua F. Ashby & Rebecca Patterson, 18 Oct. 1848. William Nelson, J.P.

Edmund Jackson & Martha Ann Cherry, 26 Oct. 1848. John Kelly, M.G.M.E.C.S.

John Olliver Bennett & Ledection Philips, 25 Oct. 1848. P. A. Alexander, J.P.

William (Swainey) & Elizabeth Moser, 25 Oct 1848. William D. Smith, J.P.

Edward Bodiley & Alemed Hewgley, 8 March 1849. L. E. Gardner, M.G.

Harvey G. Moser & Eliza Ann Smith, 7 Nov. 1848. Edmund Gilliam, J.P.

Peyton Cowgill & Mahala Melvin, 31 Oct. 1848.

John W. Clifton & Mary Louisa Carlin, 1 Nov. 1848. Isham Green, J.P.

James Barrett & Mary Ann Andrews, 2 Nov. 1848. T. J. Wilkerson, J.P.

Jeremiah Ward & Mary E. Sullivan, 6 Nov. 1848.

C. W. Hazard & Betty Glenn, 16 Nov. 1848. M. L. Vaughn, V.D.M.

William Partin & Lucy Ann Burke, 7 Nov. 1848. William Woodrum, J.P.

John William Chandler & Elizabeth Ann Sullivan, 8 Nov. 1848. W. H. Johnson, M.G.

Robert Dellis & Katharine Lyon, 8 Nov. 1848. B. L. Bell, J.P.

Lasater Matthews & Patsy Ann Cook, 9 Nov. 1848. John H. Johnson, J.P.

Algernal Bryan & Elizabeth C. Philips, 9 Nov. 1848. N. G. Alexander, J.P.

Berryman G. L. Warren & Tabitha Ann McDonald, 14 Nov. 1848.

Joseph Gray & Mary Jane Eagan, 16 Nov. 1848. R. R. Barton, M.G.

Thomas Philips & Henrietta Henderson, 16 Nov. 1848. James Bond.

Jacob M. Castleman & Martha Vanhook, 14 Nov. 1848. R. Donnell, M.G.

George W. McCullock & Rachel W. Tate, 18 Nov. 1848.

William H. Robb & Caroline E. Davis, 21 Nov. 1848. J. W. Hume, M.G.

Fauer Cason & Mary H. Sharp, 23 Nov. 1848. J. L. Martin, M.G.

Alvah Sperry & Nancy Ann Wright, 13 Dec. 1848. William L. Young, J.P.

David Young & Nancy Caroline Neal, 21 Nov. 1848. N. G. Alexander, J.P.

Pallais Neal & Mary Young, 22 Nov. 1848. N. G. Alexander, J.P.

William J. Wilson & Narcissa Catharine Earhart, 22 Nov. 1848.

Joseph Parrish & Mary Frances Griffin, 22 Nov. 1848.

William Nickens & Elizabeth Nickens, 23 Nov. 1848. Thomas J. Thompson, J.P.

Gray Whitehead & Sarah Ann Elizabeth Hawkins, 27 Nov. 1848. B. L. Bell, J.P.

Robert Winter & Nancy Terrell, 4 Dec. 1848.

James A. Hankins & Samanthy Jane Cox, 3 Dec. 1848. Jacob Thomason, J.P.

George A. Armstrong & Mary Ann Forbes, 9 Dec. 1848.

John W. Sherrell & Mary Caroline Hudson, 14 Dec. 1848. D. B. Moore, M.G.

John Rutland & Almananda Eatherly, 14 Dec. 1848.

Lewis W. Hewgley & Margaret Ann Wray, 14 Dec. 1848. William L. Young, J.P.

Oma F. Tatum & Sarah E. Lawson, 17 Dec. 1848. James Arrington, J.P.

Henry L. Tally & Martha Swann, 18 Dec. 1848. Wilson Hearn, M.G.

James Evans & Martha Morris, 21 Dec. 1848. A. M. Green, M.G.

George Oakley & Elizabeth Foust, 21 Dec. 1848. Duncan Johnson, J.P.

Archibald Cawthon & Sarah C. Wilson, 23 Dec. 1848.
Carlos M. Buckley & Mildred Norris, 6 Jan. 1850. P. Y.
Davis, M.G.
Andrew Petty & Elizabeth D. Owen, 26 Dec. 1848.
Lemuel Wright & Mary Elizabeth Wright, 4 Jan. 1849.
William L. Young, J.P.
Enoch J. Floyd & Sarah E. Parton, 29 Dec 1848. William
Woodrum, J.P.
John L. Johnson & Elizabeth F. Dudley, 31 Dec. 1848.
Richard Lyon, M.G.
Granville Medlin & Martha K. Jarman, 4 Jan. 1849. J. J.
Martin, M.G.
William A. Groom & Samuel E. Rich, 3 Jan. 1849. Nathaniel
Haass, M.G.
Thomas D. Baker & Candes England, 3 Jan. 1849. Wood H.
Shearin, J.P.
William B. Ramsey & Frances Ann Baker, Jan. 1849. P. Y.
Davis, M.G.
Purnel Lain & Polly Lasater, 9 Jan. 1849. William Nelson,
J.P.
James Hearn & Mary Jane McBride, 9 Jan. 1849.
Benjamin J. Eskew & Susan E. Zackery, 10 Jan. 1849.
William L. Clemmons, J.P.
John H. Ashby & Dolly Anne Mason, 10 Jan. 1849. William
Nelson, J.P.
Elijah L. Brinkley & Sarah Billingsley, 9 Jan. 1849.
William Baird, J.P.
Buchanan James & Rachel Jane Ayres, 18 Jan. 1849. A. S.
Ivy, V.D.M.
Christopher Baker & Sarah F. Webber, 17 Jan. 1849. P. D.
Jetton, J.P.
Thompson Weatherly & Harriet Amanda Lasater, 17 Jan. 1849.
John H. Johnson, J.P.
L. Kennedy & Martha Jane Ewing, 18 Jan. 1849. Nathaniel
Hay.
Joel L. Horn & Frances Alkinson, 19 Jan. 1849. John
Kelly, M.G.
Samuel B. Smith & Elizabeth Raines, 24 Jan. 1849. R. R.
Barton, M.G.
David H. Wheeler & Louisa McDonald, Jan. 1849. P. Y.
Davis, M.G.
Matthias Johnson & Sarah Elizabeth Hickman, 24 Jan. 1849.
T. J. Wilkerson, J.P.
Samuel C. Ellis & Nancy Duke, 30 Jan. 1849.
Elijah E. Travilian & Nancy Carr, 11 Jan. 1849. James
Arrington, J.P.
Alexander McRoy & Sarah Adcock, 4 Feb. 1849. Hugh
Telford, M.G.
William Murry & Frances Ann Woodrum, 8 Feb. 1849. D. B.
Moore, M.G.
Robert Ozment & Caroline Weatherly, 9 Feb. 1849. William
Baird, J.P.
John J. Martin & Elizabeth (   ), 10 Feb. 1849.
John Dukes & Mary Smith, 13 Feb. 1849. R. R. Barton, M.G.

Abner (   ) & Susan Briant, 13 Feb. 1849. John H.
Johnson, J.P.
Robert P. Monroe & Louisa C. Medlin?, 19? Feb. 1849.
William Nelson, J.P.
Wilshere Washburn & Sally Jane Phillips, 15 Feb. 1849.
N. G. Alexander, J.P.
James L. Haralson & Eliza Ann Young, 22 Feb. 1849. L. E.
Gardner, M.G.
James Monroe Skelton & Nancy L. McKnight, 16 Feb. 1849.
Eli Archer & Sarah Hutchison, 19 Feb. 1849. Thomas J.
Thompson, J.P.
Thomas Patterson & Nancy Patterson, 22 Feb. 1849. William
Nelson, J.P.
Asa B. Douglas & Sarah Palmer, Feb. 1849. P. Y. Davis,
M.G.
Thomas E. Spradlin & Emily A. Ellington, 22 Feb. 1849.
Wood H. Shearin, J.P.
Anthony Marler & Casander Williams, 14 March 1849.
Zadock McMullin, J.P.
Jesse Rowland & Elizabeth Bradberry, 27 Feb. 1849. L. W.
Robertson, J.P.
Thomas Wright & Mary Ann Vaughn, 2 March 1849. J. W.
Fields, J.P.
Munroe Sanderson & Jane Sanderson, 6 March 1849.
William Robertson & Sarah A. Capell, 9 March 1849. John
M. Millers, J.P.
James G. Ross & Mary Ellis, 15 March 1849. Joseph (   ),
M.G.
Nathaniel L. Overall & Dicy Cartwright, 12 March 1849.
William C. Baskin & Ch____ Howard, 22 March 1849. Jesse
Ballintine, J.P.
Thomas E. Spradlin & Emily A. Ellington, 26 Feb. 1849.
William Robertson & Malissa Jane Campbell, 22 March 1849.
Edmund Gilliam, J.P.
Richard M. Gibson & Mahala M. Lannom, 21 March 1849.
Thomas Kirkpatrick, J.P.
Ransom R. Gwyn & Susan E. C. Kirkpatrick, 22 March 1849.
D. B. Moore, M.G.
Richard Adkins & Jane Puckett, 22 March 1849. Elder
Thomas Spain.
Joseph D. McKnight & Sarah M. Armstrong, 29 March 1849.
Jesse Alexander, V.D.M.
John Paul & Lavina Belt, 28 March 1849. Abram A. Massey,
J.P.
Silas Higginbottom & Nancy Ann Elliott, 28 March 1849.
Jesse Ballintine, J.P.
John W. Perdue & Ann E. Browning, 29 March 1849. J. R.
(   ), M.G.
Henry Moser & Martha Bradley, 3 April 1849. John M.
Miller, J.P.
William A. Patterson & Darcus Cox, 3 April 1849. Thomas
P. Jones, J.P.
Eli Grissom & Matilda Griffin, 5 April 1849.
Zechariah W. Frazer & Frances W. Harris, 5 April 1849.
John F. Hughs, M.G.

William L. Hobson & Sarah Ann Martin?, 8 April 1849.
James Arrington, J.P.
Robert A. Burford & Mary E. Low, 7 April 1849.
Benjamin Organ & Elizabeth C. Powell, 15 April 1849. L.
N. Lankfort, M.G.
John M. Bland & Elizabeth Dobson, 10 April 1850. John
H. Hessey.
George Morris & Eliza Ray, 29 April 1849. T. J.
Wilkerson, J.P.
William Herenden & Nancy George, 25 April 1849.
Joel H. Smith & Mary A. E. S. Rey, 10 May 1849. D. B.
Moore, M.G.
John C. Craddock & Martha Jane Ryan, 10 May 1849. Thomas
P. Moore, J.P.
James E. Sands & Martha Jane Williams, 6 May 1849. Wood
H. Shearin, J.P.
Zechariah P. Hankins & Mary Ann Hester, 21 May 1849.
John Gold, M.G.
Dennis Sullivan & Martha Emeline McNamer, 24 May 1849.
Samuel Hobson & Nancy Ann Hewgley, 31 May 1849. William
Lanier, J.P.
Thomas Alloway & Esther C. Graves, 1 June 1849.
James M. Shuder & Elizabeth W. Rice, 6 June 1849. D. B.
Moore, M.G.
Levi M. Williams & Sarah Ann Patterson, 2 June 1849.
Joseph O'Neal & Mary Horn, 4 June 1849. John M. Miller.
Abraham Eddins & Frances Ann Smith 6 June 1849. R. R.
Barton, M.G.
James Skelton & H. Jane Gold, 7 June 1849. John Gold,
M.G.
Thomas Pugh & Martha Ann Reynolds, 9 June 1849. J. H.
Henry, M.G.
Cicero Murphy & Sarah A. Palmer, 9 June 1849.
Tyrie Daulton & Susan E. Shavers, 16 June 1849. I. H.
Dennis, J.P.
Cadenalleder W. Jones & Martha Jones, 21 June 1849.
James W. Bashaw & Elizabeth B. Crutchfield, 27 June 1849.
John W. Jarrell & Eleanor Jane Riddle, 28 June 1849.
Joseph Johnson, J.P.
Joshua G. Bennett & Sarah Bass, 1 July 1849. William
Thompson, J.P.
Thomas L. Guy & Eliza Bettes, 6 July 1849. (License
returned, but no certificate).
Zechariah L. Wright & Malinda Ballard, 23 July 1849.
William Woodrum, J.P.
Joshua A. Jackson & Mary Averett, 15 July 1849.
Eli Purdue & Matilda M. Loyd, 9 Aug. 1849. William L.
Clemmons, J.P.
Bedford B. Rice & Parthena A. Sullivan, 29 July 1849.
William Woodrum, J.P.
William Powell & Margaret Jane Donnell, Jesse J. Vowell,
J.P.
Isaac Chatham & Susan Johnson, 8 Aug. 1849. T. J.
Wilkerson, J.P.

WILSON COUNTY MARRIAGES

Samuel Jones & Martha Ann Gilliam, 9 Aug. 1849.
Micajah Bennett & Nancy Tarver, 14 Aug. 1849. P. A.
Cartwright, J.P.
Ausborn C. Bettes & Harriet Woolard, 9 Aug. 1849. Wood
H. Shearin, J.P.
Anderson P. Seatt & Mary Ann Chatham, 14 Aug. 1849. T.
J. Wilkerson, J.P.
John Carter & Susan Curry, Aug. 1849. A. W. O'Neal, M.G.
John M. Bland & Elizabeth Dobson, 19 April 1849. D. B.
Moore, M.G.
Eli Purdue & Matilda M. Loyd, 9 Aug. 1849. William L.
Clemmons, J.P.
Bedford B. Rice & Parthena A. Sullivan, 29 July 1849.
William Woodrum, J.P.
William Powell & Margaret Jane Donnell, Jesse J. Vowell,
J.P.
Isaac Chatham & Susan Johnson, 8 Aug. 1849. T. J.
Wilkerson, J.P.
Samuel Jones & Martha Ann Gilliam, 9 Aug. 1849.
Micajah Bennett & Nancy Tarver, 14 Aug. 1849. P. A.
Cartwright, J.P.
Ausborn C. Bettes & Harriet Woolard, 9 Aug. 1849. Wood
H. Shearin, J.P.
Anderson P. Seatt & Mary Ann Chatham, 14 Aug. 1849. T.
J. Wilkerson, J.P.
John Carter & Susan Curry, Aug. 1849. A. W. O'Neal, M.G.
William A. Witty & Harriet E. Page, 15 Aug. 1849.
John H. Eakin & Elizabeth Mitchell, 17 J___ (   ).
Isaac H. Dennis, J.P.
John Robertson & Rebecca Alsup, 23 Aug. 1849. N. M.
Green, M.G.
George Thompson & Eliza Ann Jennings, 21 Aug. 1849.
William Bradley & Sally J. England, 21 Aug. 1849. Sion
Bass, M.G.
Calvin Cowger & Abigail (Sooter), 22 Aug. 1849. James
Arrington, J.P.
Bob Mitchell & Martha Murry, 16 Aug. 1849. W. W. Bell,
M.G.
William Wright & Mary Lawrence, 28 Aug. 1849. William
Vantrease, M.G.
David Hamilton & Margaret McRoy, 29 Aug. 1849. William
Woodrum, J.P.
Francis Harris & Sarah Sweatt, 1 Sep. 1849.
A. J. Davis & Mary Patton, 1 Sep. 1849.
Joseph Tally & Nancy Webb, Sep. 1849. Zado McMullon, J.P.
John B. Weir & Polly Wyley, 2 Sep. 1849. James C.
Williford, J.P.
Wilie McFarlin & Martha E. Page, 3 Sep. 1849.
Smith King & Catharine N. Leeman, 4 Sep. 1849. Abram A.
Massey, J.P.
James McKnight & J___sey Bennett, 6 Sep. 1849.
Uriah Jennings & Huld Turner, 10 Sep. 1849.
John F. Brishnton & Nancy E. Fuqua, 7 Aug. 1849. N. M.
Green, M.G.

Henry Da____von & Elizabeth Wall, 13 Sep. 1849. W. P.
Wilburn, M.G.
Joseph P. Coleman & Julia Ann Brogan, 17 Sep. 1849. H.
L. Wroe, J.P.
Josiah M. Morris & Nancy Tarrett, 17 Sep. 1849.
E. S. Smith & Martha F. Huddleston, 17 Sep. 1849.
William C. D. M. Davis & La____iza P. Prim, 17 Sep. 1849.
Briant Green & Lodusky Winters, 20 Sep. 1849. William
Lanius, J.P.
James F. Coggin & Margaret Barkley, 19 Sep. 1849. T. J.
Wilkerson, J.P.
Winfield S. Duger & S. White, 19 Sep. 1849.
James P. Hearn & C. Tatum, 20 Sep. 1849. M. S. Vaughn,
V.D.M.
Andrew Joyce & Angeline Marable, 20 Sep. 1849. John M.
Miller, J.P.
William Freeze & Eliza Jane Christopher, 22 Sep. 1849.
William G. Avery & Lenore E. Ellington, 23 Sep. 1849.
Wood H. Shearin, J.P.
John B. Hays & Elizabeth A. Horn, 21 Sep. 1849. A. W.
Meacham.
Bethel Phillips & Hicksey Bass, 26 Sep. 1849.
John A. Haynes & Martha Ann Smith, 26 Sep. 1849.
Allen Tomlinson & Polly Hobbs, 25 Sep. 1849.
James Johnson & Susan Hudson, 30 Sep. 1849. Isham Green,
J.P.
T. M. ____awyer & Ellen Quarles, 29 Sep. 1849.
Alansen Kennedy & Eliza Daniel, 7 Oct. 1849.
Robertson Johnson & Lelitha Foley, 1 Oct. 1849.
Nathan Harsh & Mary Jane Rutherford, 4 Oct 1849. P. Y.
Davis, M.G.
Wammack P. Wilburn & Lucinda Justiss, 4 Oct. 1849.
William C. Sparks, M.G.
Dr. Richmond Baker & Rachel Melvin, 5 Oct. 1849. J. H.
Hessey.
William C. (Lax) & Saluda Bell, 10 Oct. 1849. H. L.
Wroe, J.P.
Josiah Bridges & Lelitha Hayworth, 9 Oct. 1849. Fletcher
Campbell, J.P.
Hezekiah Jennings & Lockey Odum, 9 Oct. 1849.
F. L. Dillard & Lucinda Tomlinson, 5 April (   ). John
Gold, M.G.
Henry Walker & Sarah A. V. Bell, 11 Oct. 1849. John
Kelly, M.G.
Joseph Jenkins & Elizabeth Bell, 11 Oct. 1849. William
Swann, J.P.
William A. Warren & Mary Elizabeth Callis, 11 Oct. 1849.
Littleberry Driver & Sarah M. Burk, 18 Oct. 1849. J. W.
Paty, Local Preacher.
William Thomas Kirkpatrick & Susan Malissa (Barr), 18 Oct.
1849. D. B. Moore, M.G.
John Pearson & Mary Ellen Cossett, 15 Oct. 1849.
John C. White & Harriet J. Wortham, 16 Oct. 1849.

WILSON COUNTY MARRIAGES

Alfred Bone & Amanda Edwards, 25 Sep. 1849. J. C.
Provine, M.G.
Yancy F. Clardy & Martha E. ___s___, 14 Nov. 1849.
Reverend Richard Lyon.
Joshua Woolen & Mary Baird, 30 Oct. 1849.
Matthew L. Breedlove & Mary Carr, 11 Nov. 1849. James
Arrington, J.P.
William A. Bettes & Mary Corum, 11 Nov. 1849. James
Arrington, J.P.
George H. Callis & America Ann Warren, 11 Nov. 1849.
William Nelson, J.P.
Andrew D. Bell & Rebecca Lanier, 6 Nov. 1849. William
Vantrease, M.G.
James Weir & Elizabeth M. Lyon, 7 Nov. 1849. Thomas P.
Moore, M.G.
Green Proctor & Eliza Latimer, 6 Nov. 1849. John F.
Hughes, M.G.
William J. Wood & Jane C. Neal, 8 Nov. 1849.
John Echols & Nancy Henry, 8 Nov. 1849. C. Curlee, E.C.C.
William J. Brown & Nancy Henderson, 11 Nov. 1849.
John M. Vaught & Elizabeth J. Thompson, 23 Nov. 1849.
William Thompson, J.P.
Robert A. Gregg & Sarah Jane Elizabeth Holloway, 15 Nov.
1849. William L. Clemmons, J.P.
Purnel N. Hearn & Nancy L. Gill, 15 Nov. 1849. A. N.
Reaves, M.G.
James N. Gwyn & Nancy L. Zackery, 23 Jan. 1850.
Louis J. Duprie & Amelia M. Jones, 19 Nov. 1849.
Silas Chapman & Louisa Hill, 19 Nov. 1849. T. J. Wilkerson,
J.P.
John Sullivan & Avina Jarrell, 19 Nov. 1849. H. B. Hill,
C.P.M.
Jesse W. Rowlett & Lucy Hickman, 21 Nov. 1849. W. P.
Wilborn, M.G.
Jarratt Ross & Mary Ann Thrift, 22 Nov. 1849.
William Smith & Susan McElroy, 23 Nov. 1849. John M.
Miller, J.P.
Frederick O. Sims & Nancy Ann Hearn, 28 Nov. 1849. P. A.
Cartwright, J.P.
Jarrott Sanders & Sidney C. Murry, 27 Nov. 1849.
John Williamson & Nancy Kirkpatrick, 27 Nov. 1849.
Carlos G. Clay & Salina C. Taylor, 2 Oct. (   ). P. Y.
Davis, M.G.
William D. Chadick & Mary Jane Cook, 5 Dec. 1849. L. C.
Anderson, M.G.
John J. Pitman & Levina Ross, 6 Dec. 1849. Robert M.
(   ), M.G.
John M. Fakes & Elizabeth Ann Hibbitts, 10 Dec. 1849.
L. C. Anderson, M.G.
John Dies & Elizabeth Ramsey, 11 Dec. 1849. William D.
Smith, J.P.
John Miles & Penny Tomlinson, 12 Dec. 1849. William D.
Smith, J.P.
Alexander Young & Parmelia Beard, 12 Dec. 1849.
John W. Anderson & Jane Bass, 12 Dec. 1849.

Thomas Hudson & Nancy Prichett, 13 Dec. 1849.
Albert Griffin & Martha Jane Sullivan, 17 Dec. 1849.
Sand J. Creswell & Mary Ann Coles, 11 Dec. 1849. James
Johnson, J.P.
John C. Goldstone & Parallee Catharine Young, 19 Dec. 1849.
D. M. Moore, M.G.
Joseph Young & Nancy Marks, 20 Dec. 1849. L. Davis, J.P.
Benjamin B. Hunt & Eliza Reiff, 18 Dec. 1849.
John J. Hartsfield & Martha Hurland, 19 Dec. 1849. A. W.
M___, M.G.
Newman Tolliver & Amelia Britton, 20 Dec. 1849.
James R. Gwyn & Nancy Zackery, 26 Jan. 1850. William L.
Clemmons, J.P.
George J. Morris & Maria Estes, 20 Dec. 1849. T. J.
Wilkerson, J.P.
James Leach & Lucy Jane M___, 27 Dec. 1849. N. M. Green,
M.G.
James H. Hunt & Sarah Jane Wright, 24 Dec. 1849. John M.
Miller, J.P.
William Winford Walker & Brunetta G. Cowger, 25 Dec. 1849.
James Arrington J.P.
James M. Hall & Elizabeth Johnson, 27 Dec 1849. T. J.
Wilkerson, J.P.
John Gavin & Mary J. Mosley, 27 Dec. 1849. T. J.
Wilkerson, J.P.
David Rogers & Mourning Keaton, 29 Dec. 1849. Isaac
Mullinax, J.P.
William Swinny & Elizabeth M___, 25 Oct. 1850. William
D. Smith, J,P.
John H. Bell & Louisa Walker, 5 Jan. 1850. P. Y. Davis,
M.G.
Stephen Forbes & Mary Nowlin, 3 Jan. 1850. C. J. Barr,
M.G.
Robert P. Hatcher & Nancy R. Ferrell, 30 Jan. 1850 (at
night). James C. Williford, J.P.
Thomas Baker & Elisha Baker, 8 Jan. 1850. John W. Booker,
M.G.
John B. Putman & Matilda J. Bone, 4 Jan. 1850.
William Williams & Caroline Drennan, 6 Jan. 1850. Hugh
Telford, M.G.
David J. Drennan & Evaline Jane Hewgley, 8 Jan. 1850.
William (   ) & Lutilia Brown, 8 Jan. 1850. A. W.
Meacham, M.G.
Stephen M. Woodrun & Susan B. L. Curry, 14 Jan. 1850.
William Woodrum, J.P.
Mark Miller & Susan Shelton, 8 Jan. 1850.
Sampson Hughs & Missouri E. Foster, 8 Jan. 1850. C. J.
Barr, M.G.
Thomas R. Baird & Sally C. Steele, 8 Jan. 1850. William
Baird, J.P.
David W. Quarles & Eliza A. Quarles, 8 Jan. 1850. John
W. Booker, M.G.
Martin Steed & Missouri J. Holloway, 8 Jan. 1850. William
Baird, J.P.
John Dockins & Nancy Weir, 14 Jan. 1850.

WILSON COUNTY MARRIAGES

John L. Williamson & Martha Jane Hass, 17 Jan. 1850.
Isaac Mullinax, J.P.

William Harlin & Margaret E. Bradshaw, 16 Jan. 1850 (at
night). James C. Williford, J.P.

Samuel H. Carpenter & Mary Ann Vivrett, 16 Jan. 1850.
William Baird, J.P.

James H. Young & Mary Anderson, 17 Jan. 1850.

James P. Wright & Sarah Gatton, 24 Jan. 1850. William
Vantrease, M.G.

Abram McRoy & Mary Bush, 25 Jan. 1850. William Woodrum,
J.P.

Pleasant Corley & Elizabeth Robertson, 22 Jan. 1850.
C. J. Barr, M.G.

Tilman L. Tarver & Martha E. Carter, 23 Jan. 1850. P. A.
Cartwright, J.P.

Houston W. Patterson & Angeline C. Matthews, 25 Jan. 1850.
John H. Johnson, J.P.

Henry (Tapley) & Lavinia Paul, 27 Jan. 1850. A. A. Massey,
J.P.

William L. Alexander & Mary Ann Cunningham, 30 Jan. 1850.
William Thompson, J.P.

Miles W. Wilburn & Mary Jane Petty, 29 Jan. 1850. W. P.
Wilburn, M.G.

Hardin Goodall & Elizabeth Compton, 6 Feb. 1850. T. J.
Wilkerson, J.P.

Finis Ewing Kirkpatrick & Margaret Isabella Rea, 7 Feb.
1850. D. M. Moore, M.G.

Moses Riley & Margaret Jane Harris, 23 Feb. 1850. W.
Burr, M.G.

Matthew L. Ramsey & Nancy Tomlinson, 19 Feb. 1850. Thomas
P. Moore, M.G.

Harvey W. Robb & Margaret A. Palmer, 20 Feb. 1850. P. Y.
Davis, M.G.

John Beard & Martha Phillips, 20 Feb. 1850.

Levi R. Jennings & Rebecca Byrn, 25 Feb. 1850.

Allen Tomlinson & Mary Owen, 27 Feb. 1850. Thomas P.
Moore, M.G.

John M. Leeman & Elizabeth Emeline Ashworth, 26 Feb. 1850.

William H. Lanier & Elizabeth Frances King, 26 Feb. 1850.

Henry L. Joplin & Sarah O'Neal, 26 Feb. 1850.

William G. Gears & Emily Woolard, 27 Feb. 1850: Joseph
Willey, M.G.

William G. Bishop & Mary Ann Heralson, 28 Feb. 1850.

John Henry Williams & Cynthia Williams, 3 March 1850.
William Thompson, J.P.

William H. Pridey & Anthony H. Ball, 7 April 1850. Thomas
P. Jones, J.P.

Amos Campbell & Esther Williams, 9 March 1850.

N. G. Hart & Malinda Rucker, 12 March 1850. John W.
Booker, M.G.

William H. Crittenden & Fanny Nailer, 13 March 1850.
William Jolly, J.P.

John Miles & Sarah Bodine, 14 March 1850.

Robert Reed & Elizabeth Sherrell, 20 March 1850. D. B.
Moore, M.G.

Absolum Shain & Zem____budy White, 17 March 1850. P. Y.
Davis, M.G.
Joseph W. Cawthon & Mary P. Cartwright, 23 March 1850.
Archibald Allen & Martha L. Ellis, 24 June 1850. N. G.
Alexander, J.P.
William H. Quarles & Nancy Adlman, 27 March 1850. John
W. Booker, M.G.
Thomas Bruce & Martha King, 30 March 1850. William
Nelson, J.P.
Frances Lahew & Frances Ann Barlow, 21 April 1850. John
H. Johnson, J.P.
Andrew J. Chandler & Mary Donnell, 10 April 1850. William
Chadick, M.G.
Lafayette Becks & Sarah A. Dillard, 6 April 1850. P. D.
Jetton, J.P.
Robertson Bryant & Pamelia Ann Johnson, 9 April 1850.
Joshua Alexander Cunningham & Mary Cox, 10 April 1850.
William Thompson, J.P.
Franklin Johnson & Lucretia Hickman, 15 April 1850. W.
W. Bell, M.G.
Joseph S. Rutland & Sarah E. Buckner, N.D. ("The couple
were never married").
Isaac McBride & Mary Jane Holderfield, 18 April 1850.
C. J. Barr, M.G.
Roland G. Andrews & Susan C. Green, 23 April 1850.
James Collins & Mary Matilda Watkins, 25 April 1850.
Joshua Woolen, M.G.
P. Y. Davis & Louisiana Young, 26 April 1850. J. C.
Provine, V.D.M.
William R. Boyd & Martha Ann Jones, 25 April 1850.
James Wade & Nancy Lain, 25 April 1850. W. P. Wilburn,
M.G.
Jacob G. Hancock & Virginia Lanier, 30 April 1850.
William Vantrease, M.G.
Ben Dechard & Mary McClain, 14 May 1850. L C. Anderson,
M.G.
Milberry H. Andrews & Mary F. Maholland, 15 May 1850.
P. A. Cartwright, J.P.
Jasper J. White & Martha J. White, 17 May 1850.
Andrew J. McDonald & Lucinda Margaret Nelson, 21 May 1850.
J. L. Dillard, M.G.
William James Moss & Susan Dill, 22 May 1850. R. E.
Mosley, J.P.
Bird W. Mays & Martha E. Wilson, 23 May 1850. Joseph
Johnson, J.P.
Blake Baker & Elizabeth Organ, 22 May 1850. P. D. Jetton,
J.P.
Robert W. Whitlock & Nancy C. Wood, 27 May 1850.
William C. Dobson & Ramy Griffin, 30 May 1850. Hugh
Telford, M.G.
George W. Burke & Frances Jetton, 14 June 1850. Jesse
Ballentine, J.P.
Robert Bonds & Frances Cawthon, ?16 June 1850. Joshua
Woolen, M.G.

WILSON COUNTY MARRIAGES

Robert F. Powers & Sarah Eagan, 6 June 1850. James
Arrington, J.P.
Charles H. Cook & Rachel Carver, 11 June 1850.
William P. O'Neal & Elizabeth Jane Johnson, 16 June 1850.
William Nelson.
Jackson L. Owens & Milberry P. Petty, 21 June 1850.
Thomas Strain & Mary Frances Rogers, 21 June 1850. W.
Burr, M.G.
Samuel N. Thomas & Drucella Sneed, 22 June 1850.
William H. Tribble & Margaret A. Patterson, 26 June 1850.
H. L. Wroe, J.P.
Lemuel Scott & Catharine Collins, 27 June 1850. Joshua
Woolen, M.G.
Elisha Collins & Esther Nickens, 28 June 1850. Joshua
Woolen, M.G.
Allen P. Robertson & Kiziah Leatherwood, 30 June 1850.
Wood H. Shearin, J.P.
John Kincaid & Ann Eliza (Lin), 3 July 1850. Isham Green,
J.P.
George W. Oglesby & Emeline Briant, 4 July 1850. L.
Davis, J.P.
Joshua Davis & Mary Elizabeth Eatherly, 11 July 1850.
P. D. Jetton, J.P.
John Drake & Calantha Mottley, 11 July 1850. John F.
Hughes, J.P.
James Adams & Sarah Bennett, 14 July 1850. Jesse
Ballentine, J.P.
Richard Ashworth & Jane M. Ricketts, 16 July 1850. William
Thompson, J.P.
Commodore Perry Jennings & Nancy Johnson, 17 July 1850.
H. S. Wroe, J.P.
Henry B. Stevens & Ann Elizabeth Ferrell, 16 July 1850.
William D. Smith, J.P.
James Bryant & Unity Bryant, 16 July 1850.
C. L. Bond & Sarah Jane Baird, 20 July 1850. William
Nelson, J.P.
Paul J. Nailer & Catharine Francis Wright, 20 July 1850,
William Randle, M.G.
Isaac Stanly & Mary Stokes, 22 July 1850. Thomas J.
Thompson, J.P.
Wesley B. Wright & Mary L. Yerger, 22 July 1850.
Daniel W. Nye & Virginia G. Hooper, 8 Aug. 1850. William
Randle, M.G.
Omer L. Partain & Mary B. Tuggle, 23 July 1850.
Hudson Tomlinson & Elizabeth Hunter, 24 July 1850. William
D. Smith, J.P.
James Hays & Juliana Orrand, 27 July 1850.
John C. Garrison & Elizabeth Harrison, 2 Aug. 1850.
Griffin Jones & Happy Ann Lane, 5 Aug. 1850. N. M. Green,
M.G.
Jonathan Ward & Martha McAffrey, 9 Aug. 1850. P. Jones.
Joseph Berry & Rebecca Paul, 11 Aug. 1850. A. A. Massey,
J.P.
Richard Mount & Eliza Jane Height, 10 Aug. 1850.

James A. Lemmons & Mary Jane Clemmons, 12 Aug. 1850.
H. Harris & Nancy Vanatty, 12 Aug. 1850.
David England & Mary Jane Bradley, 12 Aug. 1850. J.
Thompson, J.P.
Samuel Powers & Martha J. Ragland, 16 Aug. 1850. A. W.
Meacham, M.G.
James Clemmons & Elizabeth Merritt, 22 Aug. 1850. Isham
Green, J.P.
William A. D. Jones & Emeline Holloway, 22 Aug. 1850.
J. A. Hobbs, J.P.
Benjamin F. Kennedy & Lucy Sneed, 20 Aug. 1850.
Elias Bass & Jane Bailey, 21 Aug. 1850.
Thomas R. Ashworth & Hette L. Ricketts, 27 Aug. 1850.
William Thompson, J.P.
James H. Ward & Lavina Williams, 21 Aug. 1850.
Melchesdick Francis & Louisiana Puckett, 21 Aug. 1850.
Rankin R. Lannom & Mary L. Smith, 25 Aug. 1850. A. A.
Massey, J.P.
Isaac Preston Grindstaff & Tabitha J. Compton, 25 Aug.
1850. Z. McMullon, J.P.
Payton S____rls & Martha Calton, 28 Aug. 1850. J. B.
Fletcher, M.G.
Thomas N. Lankford & Mary W. Alford, 17 Aug. 1850. W.
Burr, M.G.
James H. Curry & Eleanor P. Long, 30 Aug. 1850.
William J. W. Kidder & Elizabeth C. Lasater, 3 Aug. 1850.
Isaac N. Carver & Mary Ann Jenkins, 2 Sep. 1850. L. E.
Gardner, M.G.
Reuben Tomlinson & Martha R. Carver, 3 Sep. 1850. Thomas
P. Moore, M.G.
James Tally & Louisa Cooksey, 8 Sep. 1850. Z. McMullon,
J.P.
William E. Davis & Nancy E. Ewing, 3 Sep. 1850. W. Hays,
M.G.
Charles Oldham & Mary Horn, 10 Sep. 1850. J. Kelly, M.G.
Levi D. Philips & Nancy P. Bonds, 10 Sep. 1850. John
Philips, V.D.M.
Zadock McMullon & Elizabeth Meazles, 11 Sep. 1850. Isaac
Mullinax, J.P.
Wilie H. Grissom & Isabella Mahaffa, 21 Sep. 1850. James
Hobbs, J.P.
Harrison A. Goodall & Martha J. Tuggle, 12 Sep. 1850.
S. E. Jones, C.C.M.
George Vantreas & Susan Taylor, 11 Sep. 1850. William
Vantrease, M.G.
William A. H. Hackney & Lucinda Carnes, 15 Sep. 1850.
William Nelson, J.P.
Etheldred Bass & Nancy Vanatty, 15 Sep. 1850. William
Vantrease, M.G.
Minor (Creswell) & Mary Eleanor Wilson, 16 Sep. 1850.
R. E. Mosely, J.P.
John F. Waters & Marinda Waters, 18 Sep. 1850. S. E.
Jones, M.G.
Richard Green & Mary Frances Woods, 19 Sep. 1850. James
Arrington, J.P.

WILSON COUNTY MARRIAGES

Harvy Bond & Susan B. Mount, 19 Sep. 1850. John Phillips, V.D.M.
John Bond & Mary Ann Brotherton, 18 Sep. 1850.
William Ausborn & Piney Koonse, 1 Oct. 1850. John H. Johnson, J.P.
James Floyd & Nancy Odum, 22 Sep. 1850. J. Thomason, J.P.
Enoch C. (Seawood) & Cassa Emeline Ward, 23 Sep. 1850. H. D. Reed & Nancy E. Horn, 24 Sep. 1850. C. J. Barr, M.G.
John M. Bennett & Mary Parker, 25 Sep. 1850. William Swann, J.P.
Patrick Kelly & Mary Jane Blankenship, 26 Sep. 1850.
Zachariah H. Warren & Marion W. Hill, 30 Sep. 1850.
William L. Ozment & Sarah Owens, 30 Sep. 1850.
John L. Bass & Pamelia Eleanor Andrews, 2 Oct. 1850.
Henry Cartmell & Adaline E. Hunt, 1 Oct. 1850.
Thomas George & Penelop Hammons, 4 Oct. 1850. William Barton, M.G.
William J. Walden & Sarah Ann Belcher, 2 Oct. 1850.
John Thomas Jolly & Semantha A. Carr, 3 Oct. 1850. William Randle, M.G.
George W. Reed & Martha Ann Wright, 5 Oct. 1850.
Stephen Grissom & Martha J. Partin, 8 Sep. 1850. R. R. Barton, M.G.
Jesse Poyner & Eliza Wright, 10 Oct. 1850. William L Clemmons, J.P.
William J. Allison & Ann Warren, 18 Oct. 1850. T. J. Wilkerson, J.P.
William Hays & Martha E. Gibb, 10 Oct. 1850. J. T. Goodall, J.P.
Robert H. Davis & Martha E. Kelly, 12 Oct. 1850.
John W. Sullivan & Susan F. Hawks, 12 Oct. 1850.
George W. Jennings & Mary Thomas Lester, 14 Oct. 1850.
Isham P. Pool & Mary Qusenberry, 17 Oct. 1850. D. B. Moore, M.G.
Nathan Green, Jr. & Betty McClain, 15 Oct. 1850. D. Lowry, M.G.
Pleasant Chumley & Mary Williams, 16 Oct. 1850. Isaac Mullinax, J.P.
Jesse Powell & Louisa P. Wilson, 16 Oct. 1850.
Elijah B. Hudson & Nancy Reeder, 18 Oct. 1850. N. G. Alexander, J.P.
Robert Hankins & Sephronia M. Sims, 20 Oct. 1850. P. A. Cartwright, J.P.
Isaac Horton & Jane Coppage, 16 Oct 1850. James C. Johnson, J.P.
Houston Terrell & Harriet Jane Lea, 19 Oct. 1850. E. Holloway, J.P.
Archibald A. Carter & Mary A. Hodges, 29 Oct. 1850. T. J. Wilkerson, J.P.
Abraham Britton & Jane M. Barbee, 23 Oct. 1850. J. C. Provine, V.D.M.
James G. Thompson & Orpah L. Thompson, 27 Oct. 1850. William Thompson, J.P.

Spencer W. Tally & Aceneth H. Williams, 2 Nov. 1850.
N. M. Green, M.G.
Hughy Midgett & Sina Oakley, 31 Oct. 1850. Jacob
Thomason, J.P.
Charles H. Spears & Frances Snow, 31 Oct. 1850. Jacob
Thomason, J.P.
John W. Wright & Elizabeth H. Howell, 2 Nov. 1850.
William J. Baird & Martha Williams, 5 Nov. 1850. John
Phillips, V.D.M.
Silas M. Donnell & Martha E. Donnell, 4 Nov. 1850.
E. S. Sims, J.P.
John A. Herron & Virginia Ann (   ), 4 Nov. 1850. William
Vantrease, M.G.
William J. Coleman & Elizabeth (   ), 5 Nov. 1850.
Albert Bettes & Lucinda Moseley, 7 Nov. 1850. R. Lyon,
M.G.
John Walton & Elizabeth Richardson, 7 Nov. 1850. J. B.
Fletcher, M.G.
Wilson Branch & Malissa Jane B___les, 8 Nov. 1850.
Aaron V. Ragan & Harriet G. Estes, 11 Nov. 1850.
John L. Vantrease & Rachel Bass, 13 Nov. 1850.
John L. Jackson & Sarah J. Bangham, 15 Nov. 1850. John
Kelly, M.G.
William W. Lasater & Susan Kingbrook, 16 Nov. 1850.
William Nelson, J.P.
James Edwards & Polly Ann Bass, 19 Nov. 1850. C. S. Sims,
J.P.
James M. Bone & Mary E. Hight, 19 Nov. 1850. John Phillips
D.M.
Henry Kenton & Martha Ayers, 21 Nov. 1850. Isaac Mullinax,
J.P.
Taylor Lindsay & Elizabeth Stanton, 24 Nov. 1850. P. D.
Jetton, J.P.
John Organ & Elizabeth Lash?, 23 Nov. 1850.
Seth Philips & Sarah Glidden, 24 Nov. 1850.
William H. Walden & Elizabeth F. Patton, 27 Nov. 1850.
D. B. Moore, M.G.
William Thompson & Martha Chastain, 27 Nov. 1850. William
Thompson, J.P.
William Kimbro & Mary Ann Carloss, 26 Nov. 1850.
John Summers & Elizabeth Bett, 28 Nov. 1850. A. A. Massey,
J.P.
Evan Garner & Cassey McDougen, 28 Nov. 1850. William
Vantrease.
James H. Hudson & Ruth Ann Jane Burton, 28 Nov. 1850.
Thomas Hundsley & Martha E. Hudson, 5 Dec. 1850. William
Vantrease, J.P.
James H. Smith & Mary Jane Radford, 3 Nov. 1850. J. B.
Fletcher, M.G.
Thompson Wall & Ann McDearman, 2 Dec. 1850.
Josiah L. Trice & Elizabeth Davis, 5 Dec. 1850. E.
Holloway, J.P.
Francis M. Shearin & Martha A. Babb, 5 Dec. 1850. W.
Burr, M.G.

WILSON COUNTY MARRIAGES

William Oakley & Susan Turner, 8 Dec. 1850. Zadock
McMullon, J.P.
Dr. G. Dismukes & Margaret Britton, 10 Dec 1850. D.
Lowry, M.G.
William C. Blackburn & Matilda F. Hamblin, 11 Dec. 1850.
Thomas P. Moore, M.G.
Theophilus J. Johnson & Caroline Ramsey, 11 Dec. 1850.
John M. Cason & Evaline Baird, 12 Dec. 1850. N. M.
Green, M.G.
Richard Adkins & Elizabeth Bailey, 12 Dec. 1850. John
H. Johnson, J.P.
Frances Buchanan & Anna E. Wharton, 17 Dec. 1850. D.
Lowry, M.C.P.
William C. Hodge & Missouri Martha Tate, 17 Dec. 1850.
Richard Henry Bennett & Rebecca M. Gwyn, 27 Dec. 1850.
Chapman Kinton & Elizabeth Thompson, 19 Dec. 1850.
William Dudley & Nancy J. Smith, 19 Dec. 1850.
George R. Ward & Catharine K. Stroud, 22 Dec. 1850.
Thomas P. Jones, J.P.
Thomas Waters & Mary C. Jones, 22 Dec. 1850. Hugh Telford,
M.G.
George Harsh & Mary S. A. Guthrie, 23 Dec. 1850. W. Burr,
M.G.
Henry R. Rose & Sarah Allison, 23 Dec. 1850. T. J.
Wilkerson, J.P.
Presley Lester & Elizabeth C. Crutchfield, 24 Dec. 1850.
William R. Jennings & Sarah Jane Sullivan, 24 Dec. 1850.
Thomas C. Calhoun & Elizabeth Lowry, 25 Dec. 1850.
Samuel Burk & Mary Vantrease, 26 Dec. 1850. William
Vantrease, M.G.
Isaiah R. Lanum & Mary C. Lanum, 26 Dec. 1850. Joshua
Woolen, M.G.
James Scroggins & Margaret Ann Dias, 1 Jan. 1851. Thomas
P. Moore, M.G.
Joshua Felts & Harriet Criswell, 29 Dec. 1850. R. R.
Barton, M.G.
John Hancock & Martha Wilson, 29 Dec. 1850. Isham Green,
J.P.
William Nickens & Mariah Jane Merry, 30 Dec. 1850.
Washington Cox & Franky Bradley, 15 Jan. 1851. J. Thompson,
J.P.

CORRECTIONS

PAGE NO.	NOW READS	SHOULD READ
14	Pleasan- Tally	Pleasant Tally
19	Polly Donslon	Polly Donelson
19	Duplicate Entry of "Isaac Griffen and Ibby Wiley"	
25	Ryland Chamdler	Ryland Chandler
29	Lieu Ellen Th ompson	Lieu Ellen Thompson
43	Henry Hichols	Henry Nichols
58	Jesse Alexznder	Jesse Alexander
62	Jacob Sullibam	Jacob Sullivan
62	Pstaey Adams	Patsey Adams
64	JOhn H. Stoneman	John H. Stoneman
67	Rhoda HOlland	Rhoda Holland
69	Elizabeth	Elizabeth Moss
72	Hugh Campbell, GM	Hugh Campbell, BM
73	John DAvis	John Davis
73	Sally WArren	Sally Warren
74	Chrostopher Cooper	Christopher Cooper
108	Wm. Neigh Jiowrs	Wm. Neighbours
114	ALfred Bloodworth	Alfred Bloodworth
114	Martha C. SMith	Martha C. Smith
116	Julia Gerguson	Julia Ferguson
117	Silas M. Rgasdale	Silas M. Ragsdale
122	Caoline Herd	Caroline Herd
124	Eeddin D. B. Price	Reddin D. B. Price
128	Micholas Chambers	Nicholas Chambers
134	F. G. Gerguson	F. G. Ferguson
136	Wiliam Fields	William Fields
141	Athur Williams	Arthur Williams
143	Ewing (James Ewing)	James Ewing
148	Nancy Ann Montgomer	Nancy Ann Montgomery
162	Montgomer J. Corley	Montgomery J. Corley
168	SArah R. Grant	Sarah R. Grant
174	Joses G. Starratt	Moses G. Starratt
184	Heraldson & Mary Brooks	Heraldson & Mary Gibson
198	Evaline Bloodwoth	Evaline Bloodworth
202	J. Shepher	J. Shepherd
203	Wiliam Mitchell	William Mitchell
211	Caoline Wall	Caroline Wall
216	Martha Jane YOung	Martha Jane Young
219	louisa Davis	Louisa Davis
222	Mary Ann Geruson	Mary Ann Ferguson

Armstrong (cont.)
Elijah 14
Eliza Jane 178
George A. 225
James 112, 210
James M. 30, 54, 70, 99
Knox 60, 89
Martha 219
Minervey 93
Samuel 60
Sarah 210
Sarah M. 227
Syrus 83
T. T. 168
Arnet, Mossy 29
Arnold, Ann 77
Butler 25, 87
Coaley 116
David (2) 25
Davis 96
Green 113
Frances 45
Henry G. 134
Henry S. 134
James 47, 53, 65
Jane R. 209
Jeremiah 208
John 25, 68, 96
John B. 89
Lucretia 67
Mary 59
Nancy 56, 80, 193
Pleasnt 56
Polly 35, 49
Richard 113
Samuel 191
Susan 90
Thomas 56
Thos. 56
William 113
Arnton, Charles W. 2
Prissola 2
Arrington, Aggey 120
H. 117
Harriet 219
Thomas 30
Ash, Amanda E. 198
John C. 166, 195
Ashby, John H. 226
Joshua F. 224
Mary 131
Nancy 171
William J. 184, 193
Asher, Walter W. 56
Ashew, Andrew 113
Ashford, Hannah 15
John 4
Moses 16
Polly 24
Sarah 107
Ashworth, Elizabeth Emeline 233
Jasper E. 35
Jasper R., Jr. 187
J. R. 81, 159, 166
Nancy 185
Richard 235
Thomas R. 236
Askew, Alford 113
Andrew 113 (See ASHEW)
Elizabeth 65
Askin, Ethalinda 107
Askins, Adison 125
Maryanne 180
Sarah P. 160
William 71
Aspey, George 30
Aspy, Lucretia 48

Astan, Daniel 30
Aster, Nancy 86
Astoce, James 78
Aston, Jane 151
Louisa C. P. 168
Mary 159
Astor, Joseph 128
Astow, William G. 168
Atherly, Elizabeth 82
James 39, 101
Jane 71, 101
John 39
Jonathan 119
Atkinson, Elizabeth M. 172
Frances 226 (See ALKINSON)
Joseph S. 83
Mary 210
Royal 51
Attesey, Edward 187
Atwell, Don D. 154, 155
Atwood, Frances 149
Moses 148, 178
Nancy 115
Ausborn, William 237
Aust, Elizabeth 30, 120
Frederick 71
Sally 61
Austin, John W. 205
Avains (Evins), Catharine 63
Averett, Mary 228
Samuel 213
Averette, McIntoish 179
Averitt, Martha 189
Avery, Allen 30
Ann 32
Elizabeth 31
Frances H. 165
George S. 56
John W. 65 (See AVORY)
John W. 77
Martha Jane 206
Nancy 107
Polly 65
Sally 24
William (2) 30, 31
William G. 230
Avory, John W. 65
Axum, William 147, 149
Ayers, Alfred M. 155
Martha 238
Ayres, Lavina 160
Mary 182
Rachel Jane 226
Aytes, John 39
Sally 47
Azachary, Allen 126
B (?), Eliza 186
B (?) e, Mary Cassandra 218
B (?) er, Patrick 215
B (?) les, Malissa Jane 238
Babb, Abigail 201
Bennet 30
Bennett 147
Cleary 23
Cloe 26
Elizabeth 3
Henry B. 51
Hicksey E. 165
Martha A. 238
Martha T. 32
Rebecca E. 183
Sarah 150
Sophia 192
Thomas 39, 51, 134
William 32, 33, 39, 41, 95, 195
William P. F. 179
William W. 72

Bachelor, Jno. 18
Bachus, James H. 147
Lydia 159
William 134
Badgett, Jesse 96
John 96
Baget, Thomas 77
Bagwell, Elizabeth 220
Lumford 51
Rachel 211
Sarah 159
Bailey, (?) iam 35
Cornelius W. 83
Elizabeth 204, 239
James S. 77
Jane 236
John 199, 206
Joseph 98
Martha Ann Elizabeth 198
Mary Ann 192, 206
Nancy 204
Baily, Claibourne 83
Cornelius 83
Elizabeth A. 178
George B. 126
James S. 108
Jonathan 176
Nancy 128, 191
William 39, 108
Bains, Joshua 4
Baird, Alexander 155
Andrew 7, 19
Ann 53, 180
Ann Eliza 200
Bartholomew 71
Batt 65, 161
Clement J. 210
Clementine M. B. 224
Clinton 56
David 19, 59, (2) 65
D. H. 77
Eliza 161
Elizabeth 37
Ellennor 4
Evaline 239
Eveline 131
Hardy H. 71
Henry A. 210
James 39, 65, 91
James H. 134, 147
John 65, 115, 174, 189
John B. 111, 208
John H. 210
Levi 119
Liddy 88
Lindley 83
Lucinda 71, 177
Margaret 211
Martha 87, 205
Martha A. 196
Mary 150, 231
Mary Ann 198
Mary C. 224
Nancy 71
Nancy J. 217
Patriser 100
Sally 180
Sarah 92
Sarah Jane 235
Seldon 71
Thomas 142, 150, 223
Thomas R. 232
Thos. 167
Thos. J. 167
Unice 115
Wilaon (?) 161
William 71
William J. 238

244

252

253

Craddock (cont.)
Francis 6
G. G. 189
Joannah 209
John 61, 67
John C. 228
Lockey 181
Martha Ann 183
Mary 174
Nancy 27, 33
Nancy C. 218
Nancy J. 212
Richard 104
Robert 143, 206
Rolly W. 207
Simon 169
Sopha 48
William 25
Wm. 89
Cragg, Crawford 146
Craig, Crawford M. 184
David 1
Elizabeth 124
Nancy 1
Crasnow, Mathias 182
Craton, Elizabeth 4
James 6
Crawford, A. J. 42
Alford D. 211
C. L. 155
Council L. 142
Counsel L. 162
Edmant 97
Elizabeth 110
James 13
John 4
Peggy 13
Polly 25
William 13
Craver, Isaac 55
Craze, Abner G. 90
Creighton, Jane 34
Crenshaw, David L. 163
W. H. 127
William H. 128, 136
Creswell, Andrew 10
Andrew J. 156
Angeline 223
Eli 29
Halem 52
John A. 46, 169
Mary Jane 185
Martin 162
Minor 162, 236 (?)
Robert 118, 139
Samuel 84, 85
Sand J. (?) 232
Cribbs, Gilbert 9
Crisp, Mahala 126
Criswell, Ann 160
Harriet 239
Mathew 115, 121
Minor 149
Robert 109
Samuel C. 220
Theodore 208
William T. 156, 157
Crittenden, Robert M. 202
Sarah 131
William H. 233
Crocker, Elizabeth 87
Jesse 84
Martha 124
Polly 127
Crocket, Archibald 8
Jane 8, 185
Cromwell, Beverley A. 169
Crook, Caty 23

Crook (cont.)
James 23
Robertson 46
William M. 67
Crooker, Nancy 43
Crooms, James 26
Crooper, Rachel 71
Cropper, Elizabeth 52
Henry L. 205
Henry T. (2) 156
James 6, 67, 143
James E. 162
James P. 115
Levi 54
Nancy 73
Polly 26
Sally 31
Sarah 131
Senny 146
Tho. H. 115
Thomas H. 156
Cros, Elijah 32, 43
Cros (?), Elizabeth 181
Crosland, Sally 57
Crosnow, Samuel W. 217
Cross, Elijah 20, 28, 33, 34,
   38, 123
James 5
John 21
Nancy 35
Polly 20
Rachel 55
William 27
Crowder, David 84
Crowley, Elizabeth G. 108
Crudup, Elisha 63 (See CRUPUP)
J. 206
John 149
Louisa J. 160
Robert 136
Crudupe, Elisha B. 84
Robert 52
Crupup, Elisha 63
Crutcher, Carter 27
Edmund 12 (See CRUTHER), 28,
   29, 123
Elizabeth 55
F. G. 67, 77, 85, 93
Foster 57
Foster G. 46
Mary Ann 25
Thomas 65
Crutchfield, Dicy H. 120
Eliza 209
Elizabeth B. 228
Elizabeth C. 239
George 84
Hannah 24
James 149
James M. 128
Lucy 218
Nancy 89
Samuel 19
Sarah B. 144
Sarah H. 192
Cruther, Edmund 12
Cumming, John 148, 150
Cummings, Arthur 115
Caleb C. 108
C. C. 166
Charles M. 94
Charles W. 90
C. W. 114, 137, 155
Elizabeth 54
Geo. D. 129
George 34, 73
Harriet 68
Jane 34

Cummings (cont.)
John 94, 170
Joseph W. 169
Mary 73
Polly 173
Sally 124
Sarah 6, 29, 32
V. W. 145
William 44, 48, 68
Cunningham, Elizabeth 180
James 73
Jesse 2
John 73, 233
Joshua Alexander 234
Mary Ann 233
Moses 26, 73
Polly Ann 85
Rody 85
Rosey 157
Sarah 96
Curd, Aaron B. 21, 121
Elizabeth 91
James 97
John 115
Martha 55
Nancy 69
Polly Ann 44
Price 149
Sally 52
Thomas 137, 143
William 97, 115, 149
Currey, Isaac N. 149
John S. 176
Lavina 176
Moses M. 149
Sally H. 198
Curry, Elijah 18, 35
Elizabeth 98
Ezkiel S. 143
Isaac N. 118, 136
James H. 236
Mary 108
Robert B. 169
Susan (2) 229
Susan B. L. 232
Susannah B. 22, 123
Cutchen, Lemuel 84
Cuthrel, Joseph 61
Cutrall, Midget 104
Cutrell, Charles N. 149
Joseph 53
M. 99
Cutrull, Nancy 10
D (?) m, James E. 223
Da (?) von, Henry 230
Dab, Edward 22
Dabbs, Elizabeth M. 157
Samuel 128
Susan G. 181
Dakes, Alfred 90
Dale, A. 24
Charles C. 156, 169
John P. 169, 215
Thomas H. 202
Dallas, Hannah 63
Robert 54
Sally 70
Dallis, Benjamin s. 162
Thomas 156
Dalton, Robert 57
Robert C. 197
Dance, Christina G. 33, 80
Drury 70, 83
Daniel, Eliza 230
Elly 13
Fountain 198
James 78
Mary Ann 222

258

261

Garrison (cont.)
John M. 8, 170
Lucinda 165
Moses 165
Pearson 58
Robert J. 139 (See GARISON),
156, 159, 163
Robert P. 152
Sally 21
Sam'l 124
Gate, Jas. 100 (See CATO)
Gates, Catharine 182
Eliza Ann 215
James 47
John 129
Thomas 186
Valentine 129
William 218
Gather, Mary Ann 182
Gatlin, Hiram 191
Gatten, Cynthia 139
Gatton, Sarah 233
Gavin, John 232
Gay, John 65, 79
Miles 10
Gears, Julia 155
Plesant G. 198
William G. 233
Gee, John 91
Geers, Eliza 154
Louisa J. 154
Gentry, William 90
George, Abraham 143
Charles 91
David 170
Dudema 124
Elizabeth 152
Hugh 73, 106
James 10, 149
James M. 210
Jenney 10
Katherine 113
Lucas 163, 170
Lurana 118
Margaret 223
Mary 117, 185
Nancy 212, 228
Presley 181
Sarah 199
Solomon 6
Thomas 237
William 18, 149, 172
Gholdstone, Elizab 158
Gholson, Thomas 214
Gholston, William 157
Gibb, Martha E. 237
Gibbs, Henry M. 121
Jesse 50
Joshua 51
Mary 208
Giddins, Pleasant 129
Gideon, Pleasant 129
Gibson, Aaron 30, 62
Aletha Jane 201
Amos 26
Archibald 62
Ardenia 187
Biddy 24
Cinthea 22
David 10
Elivira 207
Elizabeth 15, 18
Elizabeth E. 186
Epsly 59
Isaac E. 157, 184
Ivey 32
Ivy 47
James 104, 121

Gibson (cont.)
James B. 178
Jemima 143
Jesse 73, 92, 99
John C. 62, 82
Joseph S. 163
Joshua 2
Louissiania 224
Martha 52 (?), 218
Mary 184
Mary A. 190
Mary Ann 215
Narcissa 103, 109
Rachael 2
Rebecca 4
Rebecca Ann 198
Richard M. 227
Sally 113
Sam'l 2
Samuel 2, 143
Samuel B. 136, 143, 148
Sarah C. 199
Solomon 26
Tealy 124
Tempy 155
Thomas 110
William 4, 93, 103, 104
Gilbert, Evenezer, 10, 26, 109
Elizabeth 98
John F. 129
Mary 73
Patsey 53
Gill, Benjamin 148, 150
Elizabeth 14
Elizabeth M. 197
James 164
James D. 143, 174
Martha 174
Mary B. 177
Nancy 14
Nancy L. 231
William 14
William C. 193
Gillespie, Amanda Ann 128
Chinea 34
Tabith P. 158
Gilliam, David 220
Henry 85
Levi 177
Levi S. 104
Margarett 103
Martha Ann (2) 229
Ruth C. 215
Sarah M. 111
Gillispie, David 73
Gillum, Edmund 62
Gilmore, Samuel 121
Gippen, Eliza H. 180
Givan, Robert 161
Givin, Betsey 21
Mary 24
Samuel 13
Givins, Jno. 2
John 7
Polly 79
Gladstone, Eli 90
Glanagin, Nancy 143 (?)
Glanton, Delia 44
Nancy 68
Glas, Elizabeth 60
Glasgow, Patsey 54
Glass, Elizabeth 95
Elizabeth G. 137
James 152
Nancy B. 149
Gleaves, Caroline 116
Felix R. 144
Guy T. 144

Gleaves (cont.)
John G. 91
John L. 219
Malvina 177
Mary S. 82
Missouri 88
Sarah 108
William 19 (See GLEEVES)
William B. 79
Gleeves (Gleaves), William 19
Glegly (?), George 25
Glen, Benjamin 48
Elizabeth Frances 211
Giles H. 41
Hannah 48
Thompson 41
Glenn, Benjamine H. 169
Betty 225
David 29
Don'l 104
Elizabeth 44
Jemimah 84
Julia A. 169
Mary Ann 212
Peggy N. G. 179
Salena Taylor 218
Thompson 79
Glidden, Sarah 238
Goald, Nancy G. 174
Goalston, Sarah 102
Goard, Lucy 70
Peter 67
Godd, Asa 18
Goddy (Gaddy), James 52
(Gaddy?), Mary 29
Godfred, Ruth J. 179
Godfree, James 11
Mary 11
Godfrey, Abegale 60
Elizabeth 210
James 32, 62
Rachel 5
Ruth 76
Susan B. 196
Godphrey, Nancy C. 220
Godwin, Joseph 14
Gold, Jane 228
Margaret S. 119
Martha S. 79
Mary W. 213
Nancy G. 174 (See GOALD)
Pleasant 119
Goldman, Jesse 41
Goldson, Martha 151
Goldston, Eli 26
Sally 24
Thomas 168 (Also GHOLSON?)
Goldstone, John C. 232
Sarah Ann 208 (GOALSTON?)
William G. 213 (GHOLSTON?)
Golgly, Stephen 77
Golladay, Caroline 160
Geo. S. 147
George S. 148
Isaac 172
John W. 122
Sam 104
Sarah Ann 155
Gollady, James D. 147
Golliday, Jno. W. 173
Golston, Barsheba 30
Charles 15
Elizabeth 25 (GHOLDSTONE?)
M. 168
Martha 74
Nancy 77
Good, Benjamin 196
Goodall, Cahrlotte 40 (?)

263

Griffet, Elizabeth 78
Griffeth, Lewis 150
Griffin, Albert 232
Aletha 184, 196
Asara 176
Burtes 206
Celia 15
Elizabeth 41, 196, 223
Handy B. 130 (?)
Hardy B. 156, 157
James 19, 115
Jas. 175
Joab 106
John 31
John A. 163
Joseph (2) 157
Josiah 156 /
Martha 149, 155, 159
Mary Frances 225
Matilda 227
Nancy 195
Patsey 31
Quinney 130
Ramy 234
Rebecca 220
Sally 129
Stephen 163
Thomas 62
William 137, 150, 199
Griffis, Lucinda B. 90
Griffith, Zachariah 37
Grigg, Edmund 222
Grimes, Elizabeth 2
Francis M. 122
Jesse 85
Nancy 5
Grimmet, William H. 144
Grimmett, Lucy A. 210
Grindstaff, Catharine 82
David 79
Elizabeth 95
Martha 150
Nancy 178
Polly 125
Grisham, Tempy 132
Thomas 109
William 122
Grisim, James 57
Philip 47
Rowland W. 47
Grisom, Thos. 22
Grissam, Rutland W. 8
Grissim, Martha P. 98
Nancy H. 127
R. W. 42
T. C. 127
Thomas C. 144
Grissom, Allen H. 220
Ann Eliza 177
Eleanor 201
Eleanor M. 203
Eli 227
Elizabeth R. 195
H. B. 207
James 26
Joseph 98
Milton W. 61
Randle 181
Sarah 164
Stephen 177, 237
Wilie H. 236
William 163
Grissum, Sarah 83
Grocer (?), William A. 197
Grogan, Frances S. 163
Sarah 161
Groom, William A. 226
Grubbs, Dolly 21

Grubbs (cont.)
Elizabeth 67
James G. 67
Sealy 38
William 124
Guess, Lucinda 131
Martha Ann 141
Thomas 122
Guill, Anna E. 146
Barnett 105
James 188
James A. 129
John H. 105
Joseph 163
Josiah 195
Malinda 217
Nancy J. 216
Susan 60
Thomas 67
William 149, 150
Guille, Byrd 36
Guin, Joshua 218
Gun, John 79
Polly S. 40
Sally 71
Gunn, Peggy 83
Sally 223
Thomas 110
Thomas L. 112
Gunter, John 101
Gunthrie, Abegal 30
Robert 47
Guston, James 47
Guthrie, Daniel J. 73
James 41
James B. 40, 85
Jas. 80
John 26
Martha RES (?) 143
Mary 83
Mary E. L. 190
Mary S. A. 239
Thomas 39, 41, 72, 73
William B. 193
Guy, John 215
Thomas L. 228
Guyn, Polly 94
Gwil, Bird 71
Gwin, Sally 35
Gwyll, Polly 52
Gwyn, Aleanor 149 (See DWYN)
Andrew 53
Elijah
Hugh 53, 65
James N. 231
James R. 232
John 109 (See DWYN)
Margaret 85
Martha 48
Ramson 50
Ransom 7, 227
Rebecca 208
Rebecca M. 239
Robert 102
Sally 53
William 144
Gwyne, Joanna 127 (See DWYNE)
Gwynn, Hugh R. 191
Robt. 105
Gwynne, Martha 181
Haas, Louisa 188
Mary 192
Philip 22, 131
Susannah 131
Haass, Elizabeth 212
Hackney, John 222
Jordan 219
Seth 22

Hackney (cont.)
William A. H. 236
Hackworth, Priscilla 171
Hagan, Ann 158
Priscilla 198
William 157
Hagar, Belzey C. 191
Elizabeth 116
John J. 163
Hager, Andrew J. 204
Hollis 122
John E. 129, 179
(?) Leander 201
Vilet 120
Hagerty, Harriett 123
Haggard, Cyrus W. 170
Hagor, Stealey 41
Hail, Caty 17
John T. 82
Suckey 5
Hailey (?), Robert A. 222
Haily, Patsey 28
Polly 57
Stephen 73
Hains, M. 206
Moody P. 41
Halbrook, Elizabeth 196
Noah W. 109
William 150
Wm. 105, 139
Hale, James Thomas 109
John 170
Jonas 55
Joseph 129
Julia Ann 202
Polly 192
Thomas 110
Haleman, Susannah 57
Haley, Eliza 208
John 184, 223
Mary Jane 148
Hall, Bennerr W. 41 (?)
Charles 137
Charlotte 94
Cornelis T. 144 (?)
Delila Ann 136
Drury 26
Elias M. 180
Elizabeth 104, 149, 162
Evaline 182
Isaac C. 174
Jacob G. 172
James 8
James M. 232
Jane Hughes 48
John F. 203
John N. 48, 53
John W. 63
Jonathan 156, 216
Joseph 32
Joshua 118
Martha 217
Nancy 214, 221
Patience C. 184
Polly 18, 26 (See HULL)
Sally 16
Temperance P. 214
William 18, 20, 162
W. M. 134
Hallum, Elizabeth 34, 43
George 3
Gilpin 73
James 91
John 3, 34
John, Jr. 5
Nancy 52
Polly 21
Robert 67, 70
Robt. 129

264

Harris (cont.)
Ebenezar 185
Eli 22
Elijah 93
Elizabeth 17, 36, 67, 195
Elizabeth R. 169
Elvira 18
Ephram G. 32
Evaline 219
Fanny (?) 134 (See Hanny)
Forgust S. 79
Frances W. 227
Francis 220, 229
Franklin (Doctor) 192
Furges G. 18
George 105
George F. 129, 157
H. 236
Hannah R. 110
Hanny (Fanny) 134
Harriet 83
Harriet H. 180
Harrison 22
Henry H. 74
Henry R. 105
Hugh 26
Hugh H. 212
James 26, 184
James K. 185
James S. 144
James W. 67
Jane 144
Jesse 98
John (2) 10, 116
John B. 62, 70
John D. 108
John R. 110
Joshua 11
Lucinda 57
Lucy 89
Margaret Jane 233
Martha 98, 102, 179
Mary A. 147
Mary E. 108
Mary Jane 185
McGee 79, 144
Michael 101
Michial 37
Moses 37
Nancy 23, (2) 32, 39, 57
Nathan S. 110
Nathan T. 137
N. T. 110
Patsey 2, 56
Priscilla 69
Richard 137
Richard H. 189
Robert 6
Rutha 126
Sally 18, 53, 54
Sam'l 10, 18
Samuel 7, 22, 157
Sarah 113, 197
Sarah C. 126
Sela 89
Simon T. 170
Sneed 91
Susan 108, 156
Temple O. 207
Thomas 26, 122
Thomas J. 116
Truman 170
Washington 137
West 157
William 105, 163, 173, 195
William B. 164
William F. 19, 116
William P. 207

Harris (cont.)
William S. 110
Wm. 15
Harrison, Agnes 204
Ainsworth 137
Ann 59
Answorth 126, 222
Ashworth 129
Caroline 104
Casendania 164
Coloe 84
Diana 158
Edmund R. 91
Elenor 80
Elizabeth 119, 166, 195, 235
Frances 70
Francis P. 189
Isaac 110
Jeremiah 183
John 189
Joseph 166, 210
Joshua 73, 110
Kitty 69
Kitty T. 164
Landon 150
Martha 170
Mary Ann O. 170
Moses 91, 101, 144
Nancy P. 73
Polly 195
Richard 45, 122
Robert 136
Sally 42
Sam'l C. 116
Samuel C. 108
Sterling 32
Steth 153
Stith 91, 96
Tempy 141
Zara 74, 75
Harsfield, William 39
Wm. 35
Harsh, George 239
Nathan 230
Hart, N. G. 233
Winston 105
Hartgrove, William 6
Hartsfield, Abagail 88
John J. 232
Martha Jane 156
Mary Ann 150
Susannah 144
William 40, (2) 47, 84, 100
Harvel, Peter 157
Harvey, Betsey 68
Mary 141
Miles M. 152
Nancy 68
Susannah 88
Thomas W. 85
Harvil, Rachel 224
Harville, Peter 37
Hass, Martha Jane 233
Haster (?), Elizabeth 218
Hastings, William 98, 137, 202
Hasty, Elizabeth 38
Hatcher, Green B. 212
James A. 191
Louisa 196
Mary 213
Robert P. 232
Washington 192
Hathaway, Edmund 137
Leonard 41, 137
Rhody 69
Rody 76
Susanah 56
Hatheway, Sarah 126

Hathway, Elijah 157
Haus, Hugh 101
Haw, James 26
Hawk, Louis 192
Sarah 218
Hawks, George 192
Martha 152
Martin 157
Preston 184
Susan F. 237
William J. 137
Hawkins, Armsted 157
B. D. 138
Frances 98
Grief B. 122
Harvey 85
James L. 85
John H. 201
John L. 138
J. W. 111
Martha 203
Mary 125
Mathew 98
Rebecca 91
Sally 127
Sam 107
Sarah Ann Elizabeth 225
Thomas 157
Thomas P. 144
Hay, James 68
Hayes, Rachel M. 125
Haynes, George W. 179
John A. 200, 230
Hays, Andrew 2
Ann 1, 190
Campbell 2
Charlotte 118
Eleanor 186
Elizabeth 74, 102 (See BAYS).
156, 224
Elizabeth C. 189
Harman 1
Henry 163
Hugh 68, 85, 105
James 68, 74, 85, 235
James P. 127, 129
Jane 149
John (2) 15
John B. 180, 230
John R. 150
Joseph 15
Louisa M. 211
Matilda Ann 202
Preston 85
Rachel S. 8
Reuben G. L. 163
Sam'l 15
Samuel A. 144
Thomas 27, 85
William 237
William J. 105
Zachariah T. 158
Haysworth, Job T. 144
Hayworth, Job T. 157
John 74
Lelitha 230
Micajah 74
Hazard, C. W. 225
Hazelwood, Elizabeth 23
John 32
Thos. 23
Hearn, Albert G. 217
Alliphair 79
Catharine 162
Caty (?) 98 (See City)
Charlotte B. 184
City (Caty) 98
Cleopatry 104

266

Hearn (cont.)
Cynthia 140
Easter 80
Ebenezer 27, 126, 209
Ebenezer D. 182
Edmund 105
Edward 109
Eliza J. 211
Elizabeth 143, 187, 193
Esther Lea 182
Hicksey 182
Jacob 150
James 27, 42, 157, 226
James P. 230
James W. 137
Jane 152
Jas. 81
John 32, 73, 85, (2) 92,
  95, 137, 148, 209
John A. 137
Joseph M. 129
Kasandany 118
L (?) ory 217
Lucinda 146
Martha 149, 162
Martha W. 109
Mathew 75
Melbry P. 163
Melby 6
Mitchell 79
Nancy 25, 42, 69, 187
Nancy Ann 231
Nancy M. 159
N. P. 217
Purnel 129
Purnel N. 231
Rebecca 109
Putha 88
Sarah 78, 126
Sarah B. 140
Sarah R. 96, 103
Stephen 79
Stephenson L. 96
Susan 172
Tabitha 86
Thomas 68, 85
Thos. B. 164
Thos. D. 154, 158
Wikson (?) 55
Wilson 92
Wilson A. 180
William F. 170
William H. 79
William P. 217
Hearne, Henry 176
Louisa F. 181
Maranda J. 158
Hedgepath, Silas 74
Hedgepeth, Jeremiah M. 190
Hedgpath, Silas 108, 129
Hefley, Elizabeth 91
Heflin, David 9
Eliza 55
Joab 85
Joseph 53
Nancy 4
Heflon, Mabry 74
Hegarty, Allis 40
Hegerty, Cynthia 139
Patrick H. 141
Heiflim, Charlotte 47
Height, Eliza Jane 235
John S. 122
Thomas 196
Henderson, Edness 15
Eliza (2) 169 (?)
Henrietta 225
Mary Ann 198
Michael D. 92

Henderson (cont.)
Malone 71 (See HINDERSON)
Nancy 231
Parthena 71
Peggy 23
Permilia 12
Preston 23, 27, 173
Rollins 92
Sam 114
Tobias 40, 51, 58
William H. 92
Hendley, Sarah 174
Hendrick, Jeremiah 10
Hendricks, Hannah 6
Hendrix, Albert 217
Drucilla 3
William 208
Henley, Leonard 199
Henrison, Jonathan 105
Henry, Alexander 74
Charles 10, 13, 14
Eliza 131
Enoch 53
Hugh 13
James 42
James P. 70, 78
Jordan 182
Levy 115
Lewis W. 157
Louraney 174
Mary 82
Miles 194
Nancy 231
Sophia 183
Stephen 170
William 163
Henson, (?) 208
John 207
Herald, Elizabeth K. 144
Heraldson, William L. 184, 190
Heralson, Mary Ann 233
Herd, Armstrong 22
Caroline 122
Herenden, William 228
Hern, Ebenezer 26
John 33
Lucy 78
Mary 26
Priscilla 33
Prudence 8 (Horn?)
Sally 25 (See HORN)
William 42 (See HORN)
William H. 62
Herndon, John R. 110
Young L. 68
Herondon, Young 192
Herrel, Eli 16
Herrell, Lewis W. 163
Samuel 117
Herring, Birdsong 98
Herrod, Lear 2
Mary Ann 69
Samuel 2
Herron, Amzi C. 157
Frederick 122
James G. 137
James W. 11, 170
John A. 157, 238
Ruth Malissa Ann 216
Hessey, Amy 75
Mary Ann 95
Hessy, James 105
John 130
John Huguley 130
Margaret 74
Rhewry 81
Hester, Elizabeth 118
Hambleton 176
Hiram 208

Hester (cont)
James 170
Lucy A. 206
Mary Ann 228
Robert 145
Samuel 129
William 155, 170
Heughley, William H. 221
Hewgley, Alemed 224
Cordelia 199
Evaline Jane 232
John W. 160
Lewis 207
Lewis W. 225
Nancy Ann 228
William 207
Hibbett, D. C. 137
Hibbitts, Elizabeth Ann 231
Hichan, Nancy 55
Hickerson, William P. 193
Hickey, Elijah 223
Hickman, Betsey 24
Dickson D. 190
Elizabeth 38
John 27, 50, 60, 70, 122
Julian 55 (?)
Juliann 50
Lemuel 105
Lemuel, Jr. 53
Lemuel, Senr. 53
Lucretia 234
Lucy 231
Martha A. 171
Mary 182
Nancy 45, 112
Nathaniel 144
Polly 70
Samuel 38
Sarah 193
Sarah Elizabeth 226
Snoden 53, 98, 104
Snodon 90 (See HICMMAN)
William 27, 43, 53, 64
William, Jr. 53
William, Senr. 53
Wright 32, 98
Wyatt 64 (See PICKMAN,
  RICKMAN)
Hicks, A. W. 103
Charles 79
Edward D. 144
Hannah 2
James 5, 205
Mary E. 209
Richard 2
Ruth E. 61
Tabitha 171, 172
Thomas 58
Hicmman (?), Snodon 90
Higarty, Thussey 37
Higdon, Ceyley 61
Gabriel 11, 28
James 3, 11
Higerty, Patrick 75
Higgans, Evilina 123
Higgason, Samuel D. 170
Higgin, Westley 18
Higginbottom, Silas 227
Higgins, Nancy 39
Peggy 14
Thomas W. 181
Hight, John S. (2) 105
Joseph W. 105
Lively 34
Mary E. 238
R. H. 54
Richard 32, 72
Robert 20

Hightower, Mary 88
Nancy 47
Hill, Abner 98
Alexander A. 178
Alfred M. 74
Allen 54, 74
Aristem L. 162
Bracton 85
Dorcas 167
Elam 207
Eliza 118
Elizabeth 21, 156
Evaline 151
G. W. (3) 129
Hugh B. 126
Isaac 86, 92, 130
Isaac W. 92
Israel M. 122
J. L. 111
John F. 203
Judith 29
Judy 58
Lewis 130
Lewis C. 98
Louisa 231
Luke 130
Manerva G. 203
Marion W. 237
Martha 138
Mathew 210
May 123
Meecy 52
Morning 77
Nancy 166
Nancy M. 161
Naomi 191
Peggy (? late P. Bradley) 28
Polly 92, 105, 113
Rebecca 53
Sally 57, 77
Samuel 122
Sarah N. 103
Sarah R. 190
Sousannah 7
Thomas (2) 47
Thomas L. 32
William 53, 92
William H. 157, 163
William S. 113
Hillsman, Nancy 115
Hinderson, Malone 71
Hines, Parthena 70
Sophia 183
Hings, Josiah W. 47
Hinks (?), Frank (?) 167
Hinson, Elizabeth 164
Narcissa 154
Sally 210
Hintson, Philip 2
Hite, Elizabeth 140
Hobbs, Elizabeth 138
James 164
James B. 105
Joseph C. 98
Micajah 6
Polly 50, 230
Sally 194
Thomas 13
William 144
Hobson, Abigail 132
Benjamin 10, 16, 42
Drusella 123
Elizabeth Ann 186
Henry 38, 62, 164
Joseph 99
Lewis G. 182
Louisa 110
Samuel 228

Hobson (cont.)
William L. 228
Hocking, Armstead 137
Hodge, Elenor 33
Elizabeth 207
George 33
John A. 208
Sarah 102
William C. 239
Hodges, Bluford 204
David 79
Elisha 20
Eliza 104
Elizabeth 56
Fanny 6
James 11
James W. 47
Jeremiah (2) 6, 192
Jesse 12
Josiah 20
Mary A. 237
Mary D. 95
Richard 217
Tabitha 12
Thomas 47
Wm. 79
Hogan, Anthony 110
Manerva 109
Hogg, Sam'l 1, 8
Sophia M. 46, 66
Holbert, Andrew H. 137
Joel B. 74
Holbrook, Jane 150
Martha 75
William A. 149
Wm. 10, 158, 159, 162
Holderfield, Jacob 92
Mary Jane 234
Holebrook, William 2
Holme, John 198
Holmes, Thomas 204
Thomas J. 190
Hollamon, Harmon L. 170
Holland, Alexander Z. 102
Ambros 58
Benjamin 205
Emily B. 101
James 11
John 99, 164
Levi 2
Lucinda J. 186
Mary 224
Mary E. 86
Reed A. 67
Richard 2
Rhoda 67
Sarah 27
Susan 73
William 2, 148, 150
Hollandworth, James 11
William 11
Hollaway, John 122
Hollerman, Mark 48
Hollingsworth, Isaac 74, 85
Jacob 32
James 16, 32, 52
Jas. 16
Jeney 80
John 85
Peter 53
Ranny 85
William 74
Hollinsworth, Elizabeth 169
Zina 145
Hollis, James E. 130
Holloman, Elliott 42
Holloway, E. 153
Emeline 236

Holloway (cont.)
Ezekiel 73, 132
Levi 150
Martha 76
Missouri J. 232
Pickward 98
R. 150
Richard 122
Sally 82
Sarah Jane Elizabeth 231
Holly, Joseph E. 133 (Jolly?)
Sarah 133 (See JOLLY)
Holman, John B. 92
Mary 142
Robert M. 99
Holmes, James 110
Lucinda 219
Holt, Elijah M. 162
Elizabeth D. 210
E. M. 174
Jesse 6, 129
Jesse W. 150
Sarah Ann 199
Holton, Martha 49
Holtzclaw, Hurnard 110
Honner, Lucy D. 69
Hood, Elizabeth 192
Hooker, Benjamin 68
Cloe 43
Elizabeth 23, 144
Johnie 30
Jonathan 85
Joshua 85
Mathew H. 99, 105
Matt. H. 110
Polly 19, 103
Rebecca Ann 120
Samuel 136
Sarah 91
Hooks, David 2
Hooper, George S. 62
Henry 137, 138
Virginia G. 235
Hooser, Valentine 17
Minerva 170
Hoover, Betsey 17
Hoozer, Mary Van 155
Sarah 183
Hopkins, Mary 87
Rebecca 53, 58
Sally 70
Stephen 2, 7
Susanah 7
Hopson, Agness 2
Nancy 24
Sally 86
Horn, (?) 208
Andrew 196
Charles 2
Clarissa 195
David 198
Elizabeth 4, 92, 196
Elizabeth A. 230
George W. 71
Harriet 215
Henderson 170
Henry 32, 214
Howel 42
Jacob L. 210
James R. 192
James Thomas 218
Joel L. 226
J. Wesley 190
Lucinda 176
Lucy 46
Martha Jane Emeline 202
Mary 145, 228, 236
Mary Ann 210

268

M_(?)_ (cont.)
Lucy Jane 232
William 203
Mabry, Cartwell 159
David D. 138
Edwin A. 219
Elizabeth A. 216
Evans 71
Francis E. 138
Harriet A. 153
Lewis W. 201
Louisa A. 219
Marteell 158
Martha 177
Martha N. 194
Rebecca 131
Seth W. 151
William 172
Mabus, Charles F. 176
Mac_(?)_kin, William H. 222
Mack, Richard H. 197, 205
MacKee, Pamelia 191
Mackentire, William 61
Mackey, Charles 123
Dianna 224
Levin 19
Lucinda 210
Macnatt, Levin 1
Polly 58
Maddock, Celia 70 (See MAD-
DOXK)
Lucy 23
Maddox, Azariah J. 158
Benjamin 151, 172
Celia 70 (See MADDOXK)
Eleanor 211
Elijah 130
Elijah L. 151
Eliza 111
Felin 140
Frances 118
Isham F. D. 130, 199
John 42
John P. 27, 33
Richard 80
Thankful 10
William 75
Wilson L. 130
Wm. W. 99
Maddoxk, Celia 70 (?)
Madlock, Littleberry 22
Magness, Sally 12
Susanah 3
Mahaffa, Isabella 236
Mahaffee, Rebecca 183
Mahaffey, Rebecca 186
Mahafy, Isaac 86
Marge 61
Mahan, Lucy Ann 216
William A. 212
Maholland, Elizabeth 6
Mary F. 234
William 70, 86
Mainier, James 58
Major, Bob 204
Henry 109, 136, 145
John 70, 106
Lucinda 91
Mary 68
Patsey 20
Samuel 157, 201
William 68
Makwell, William 12
Malone, Booth 33
Daniel 216
Jeremiah 187
John 164, 181
Mallory, Louisa 139

Mallory (cont.)
Timothy 139
Timothy G. 138, 139
Malsinger, Elizabeth 82
Manfield, Granwell 76
Manier, Alexander H. 189
Maning, Joseph 143
Patsy 91
Manly, Levi 99
Sally 183
Mann, Mary 86
Nancy 10
Polly 16
Sarah 201
William 11
Manneere, John 117
Manner, Clark D. 123
Mannin, Clark D. 106
Manning, Hardy 86
James 75, 86
John 47
Joseph 141
Polly 5
Robert 75
Mansfield, Garret 48
Granville 75 (See also
MANFIELD)
Grasty 63
Nancy 58
Manson, Joseph L. 181
Marable, Angeline 230
March, Henry B. 22
Rebecca 84
Mark, James 99
Margret 23
Markham, Loretha 189
Pleasant 53
Marks, Anna 180
Eliza 134
Elizabeth 150, 185
Jane 153
John 151
Joseph 171, 174, 215
Lewis 199
Martha 183
Mary 193
Nancy 232
Sarah 181
Susan 146
Thomas 189
Markham, Pleasant M. 178
Marler, Anthony 99, 227
Jane 223
John 172
Marlin, Thomas 145
Thomas C. 184
Marlow, Abram 75
B _(?)_ 17
Betsey 17
George 22
Hezekiah 27
James 27
McKensey 16
Meredith 89
Patsey 89
Payton 38, 48
Rich 1
Richard (2) 16, 48
Richard B. 130
Sarah 1
Thomas 38
Maro, Lucy 62
Marrich, George 27
Marrs, Alexander 8, 75
Anna 142, 148
Jane 194
Joseph 164
Julia 125

Marrs (cont.)
Mahala 103
Martin 75
Mary Ann 181
Rachel 94
Marshall, Ann 80
Benjamin F. 184
Catharine 16
Eliza 39
Elizabeth 20
John 8, 123, 197
John W. 164
Martyha (Martha) 32
Matilda Caroline 132
Polley 13
Rebecca 25
Robert 20, 17, 47, 145
Sally 26
William (2) 8, 13, 16
Martain, James 123
Martin, Adaline 130, 138
Alitha 88
Alley 16, 17
Amos 139, 151
Benjamin L. 203
Cloey 207
David 54
Elizabeth 27, 37, 128, 139,
172
Elizabeth B. 203
Ezekiel W. 139
Frances F. 209
Fredonia R. 169
Geo. 35
George 8
George A. 179
George N. 104
George W. 199
Hugh 42
James 56, 75, 139, 172
James B. 221
James M. 86
James W. 164
Jane 101
John 8, (2) 11, 95, 145
John J. 226
John P. 111
John W. 158, 191
Joseph F. M. 214
Lucy 53
Lucy Katherine 211
Lydia Ann 177
Lynsey 1
Mahalia 157
Maria 95
Martha C. 183
Martha J. 212
Mary 42, 66, 72, 142, 207
Mary E. 197
Matt 109
Nancy C. 209
Nancy P. 179
Pleasant 107
Polly 9, 142
Ralph 204
Robert 54
Robert Y. 86
Robt. B. 133, 139
Sally 42
Samuel 219
Sarah 150
Sarah Ann 228
Sarah W. 198
Seills 127
Theodelia 13 (See MARTON)
Thomas 66, 75
Thomas L. 189
Thos. 101, 153

Martin (cont.)
Thos. R. 158
William 86, 116
William H. 159
Wm. 108, 113
Wm. J. 133
Wm. L. 169
Marton, Theodelia 13
Masey, Garrett 54
Jane 53
Martha 51 (See MOSEY)
Nancy 46
Rebecca 45
Samuel 76 (See MOSEY)
Yancey 65
Masheras (?), John 28
Mason, Dolly Anne 226
Frances E. 155
Henry 69
James 58
John 79, 82
Requear H. 80 (?)
Reynear H. 72
Reynor H. 78
Susannah 79
Teynear H. 69 (?)
Thomas 69
Massey, Abram 86
Benjamin L. 108
Eli 69
Elijah M. 202
Elizabeth 125
Elizabeth Jane 189
Emaline 93
J. W. 158
Mansfield 71
Peggy 24
Sarah Ann 137
Yoncy 86 (See also MASEY)
Mathas, Alfred 99
Matherly, L. 163
Smith L. 164
Mathew, Alfred 80
Henry 80, 123
Mathews, Charlotte 113
Nathan C. 80
Priscilla 172
Samuel 59
Susan E. 198
William 123
William M. 214
Mathis, Alfred 99 (See MATHAS)
Isaac 138
James J. 139
Pollt 99 (Polly?)
Matlock, Alethea 124
Alethia S. 106
Gideon C. 151
Matsinger, Elijah 137
Matthews, Angeline C. 233
Lasater 187, 225
Lucy (?) D. 223
Sophia 103
William 113
Mattox, Elizabeth 64
Inde 76
Maxey, Elihu 42
Maxwell, Jane 83
John 86
Malonie 37
M. M. 167
Naomi 119
Seanath 84
William 12 (See MAKWELL), 34
May, Polly 27
Richard W. 198
Sally 34
Sarah 166

May (cont.)
Stephen N. 185
William 212
Mayho, Martha 88
Mayo, Jacob 106
Sally 42
Sarah 102
William 42
William I. 69
Mayor, Patsy 124
Mays, Bird W. 234
Drury 80
Elizabeth 171
Frederick 151
James 13, 78
Martha 46
Nancy 169
Sarah 84
Warren M. 115
Mayson, Ramsey M. 156
William 184
McAdams, Sam'l 17, 42
McAdny, John 223
L. 222
McAdoo, Annaliza 164
Sinthy 76
McAdow, Anne B. 61
Elizabeth 61
James 4, 16, 18
James B. 139
James W. 172
John 29, (2) 33, 60
Martha 17
Newbern S. 139
Polly 4
Smith J. 164
William 4
McAffrey, John 33
Martha 235
McAffy, Alesy 130
McAlpen, Polly 6
McBride, Abraham 27, 164
Daniel 223
Elizabeth 139
Isaac 234
Jane 116, 166
Kiziah 157
Mary Jane 226
Nancy 164
Pleasant M. 213
McCaffree, William A. 206
McCaffrey, John 60, 92
Martha R. 179
McCaffry, Elizabeth 151
McCarroll, Lamizra 135
McCartney, Andrew J. 190
James 11
James W. 188
John B. 123
Lewis 8, 152
Mahulda 146
Mary 146
Nancy 110
William 131
McCathon, D. A. 111
Mccerary, Robert 21 (?)
McCinny, Samuel 145
McClain, Alex F. 59
Alfred 48
Betty 237
Eliza 153
Elizabeth Jane 153
John A. 78
Josiah L. 84
Josiah S. 99
J. S. 108
Martha D. 118
Mary 234

McClain (cont.)
Pamelia 211
Rufus H. 111
William 108
William P. 117
W. J. 161
Wm. 10
W. P. 108, 113
McClendon, Hettie 159
McClennaham, Baily 172
McCombs, Nancy 127 (See McDOMBS)
McConnell, James L. 33
John B. 218
M. W. 213
McCorkle, Edwin A. 80
M. 133
Mc 132 (?)
Miles 123
Milus 48, 160
Richard B. 13
Samuel 38
Samuel M. 59
McCown, Elizabeth 6
James 63
Jane 107, 112
McCoy, Caty 44
Daniel 9
Hugh 2
James 2
Maryon 81
McCrairy, Thomas H. 69
McCrary, Aaron 75
Ann 29
Moses 75
McCray, John 145
McCreary, Robert 21 (See MCCERARY)
McCrory, Ann 26
McCulla, William 28
McCulley, Malvina 183
McCulloch, William 139
McCullock, Benjamin F. 172
George W. 225
Jane 201
John C. 177
Margaret 197
McCullough, Nathan 92
McCully, David D. 80
McDaniel, Alex. 54
Andrew 23, 38
Elias 99
Elizabeth 39, 204
James (2) 16, 23, 85, 96
Jas. 101
John 4, 92, 162, 164
John F. (2) 28
Margaret 134
Mildred A. 205
Nancy 141
Norman 16
Phillip (2) 207
Polly 87, 149, 157
Randolph 92
Rebecca 143
Samuel 23
Sarah 51
Stephen 38, 54
Synthia 58
McDaniels, William 200
McDeamon, Briant 93
Elizabeth 93
McDearman, Ann 238
Cynthia 207
James 118
Joseph 117
Mary 154
Michael 152

279

Moser (cont.)
Daniel 75
Elias A. 131
Elizabeth 129, 224
Harvey G. 224
Henry 28, 227
H. G. 187
Malinda 124
Suntha D. 179
Susan 81
Moses, David 15
James W. 103
Mosey (Masey), Martha 51
(Masey), Samuel 76
Mosier, Mary 89
Sarah 143
Mosley, Asa 93, 106
John 82
John C. 81
Mary J. 232
Priscilla 75
Samuel 38
Sarah 82
Moss, Agnes 44
Azariah 152
Barret 185
Dandridge 43, 54, 63
Elizabeth 69, 80
J. B. 157
John 59
Lethi 72
Mary Jane 137, 138
Moore L. 100
Moore S. 81
Mourning C. 214
Nancy 31
Parthenea 78
Stephen 76
Susanah 14
Thomas B. 93
William 26, 31, 100, 141,
154
William D. 152
William James 234
Wilzabeth R. 102
Wm. 12
Mosse, Elizabeth 26
Motheral, Aseneth 47
Elizabeth 38
John 23
Louisa Ann 199
Mary 47
Robert 33
Samuel 33
William 89
Motley, Benj. T. 90
Benjamin 28, 87
Bryant T. 45
B. T. 116
Motsinger, Christina 45
Jefferson 102, 124
Lucy 93
Mottley, Calantha 235
Motto, Paul 165
Mount, Alfred 54
Amos 137, 145
Elizabeth 66
Jane 187
John 184
Julius H. 172
Mary 95
Mathias 100, 165
Priscilla 212
Richard 9, 124, 195, 235
Sarah 105
Susan B. 237
Tellitha 110
Theos. 100

Mount (cont.)
William 8, 16, 100
William S. 171
Moxley, Caty 79
Elizabeth Jane 140
Joseph 28
Lavinia 196
Matilda L. 161
Wm. L. 158
Moxly, Martha Ann 137
Moyers, Grissam 6
Muckle, Hiskey 6
Muirhead, Adam 142
John 136
Mulinax, Zadock 43
Mullen, Charles H. 205
Jesse 151
Mulligan, Allen 28
Mullin, Martha G. 162
Zedie 113
Mullinall, Zeddock 83
Mullinax, Almond 145
Isaac 152
James 165
John 152, 165
Nathan 203
Mullings, Tabitha 28
Mumford, William B. 158
Munday, Aldey 3
Munnett (Monnett?), James 13
Murfrey, Gibson 93
Nancy 110
Murhead, Adam G. 152, 153
A. G. 148
John 173
Murphy, Cicero 228
Eliza 200
Lewereasy 53
Sally 188
William C. H. 172
Murray, Abram 48
James 49
J. B. 162
John 48, 63, 74, 75
John M. 92 (See MURRAYM)
Joseph B. 189
Mary Elizabeth 130
Nathaniel 152
Raulston B. 158
S. B. 168
Susan 59
William 124
Wm. 65
Murraym, John M. 92
Murry, Aseneth 126
Elizabeth 42
James 43
James B. 65
Jeremiah 81, 87
Louiza 92
Manerva 131
Mark 121
Martha 94, 229
Mary 130
Sally 121
Sidney C. 231
Tempsey 85
William 87, 106, 226
William 130 (Rev.)
Myers, Eleanor 157, 158
Nicholas 19
Peter 63, 73 (See MIRES)
Myres, Catherine 73
George W. 187
Myrick, Nancy 6
Walter 6
Nailer, Fanny 233
Paul J. 235

Nailor, Mary Ann 175
Naird, William 71
Nasworthy, Joseph 121
Nattles, Burwell 100
Nawlen, Thomas 75
Naylor, James 83
Neal, Amy 94
Ashley 63
C. 103
Charlotte 199
Clayburn 187
C. W. 172
Eleanor D. 168
Francis Jane 211
George 84, 158, 167, 168,
172
Hardy C. 189
Isaac 87, 90
James 69
Jane C. 231
Joseph 43, 130
Martha 167
Mary 182, 220
Mary J. 214
Nancy 181
Nancy Caroline 225
Pallais 225
Payton 137
Polley 44
Samuel 212
Sarah 90, 118, 135, 166,
199
William 192
William O. 78
Neel, Charles 27
Dorcas 122
Elizabeth 15, 22
Paton 127
Payton 131
Polly 27
Neelson, Eliza Jane 162
Neely, Eliza 169, 176
Isaac 181
John 49
William 187, 208
Neighbours, Polly 119
Rebecca 96
William 131
Neil, Drucilla 9
George 69
John 53
Jonathan 150
Margaret E. 46
Nancy 161
Neily, John 117
Nellum, James 43
Nelly (?), Elijah C. 177
Nelms, Norfleet 75
Norfleet B. 97
Nelson, Allen 93
Emily J. 205
Garrett 131
Harriet 114
Levicy 104
Lucinda Margaret 234
Nancy 64
Nathan 124
William 104, 111, 138
Nesbitt, Sam'l J. 100
Nettle, Benjamin 106
Nettles, Benjamin 68, 75
Darkus K. 93
Elizabeth 68, 177
James 40, 43
John 69
L. 217
Malissa 221
Mary Elizabeth 170

284

Ramsey (cont.)
Matthew L. 233
Nancy 5, 47, 181, 221
Richard 5, 30, 34, 38
Richard R. 200
Sarah H. 152
William B. 226
Wyatt 87
Randell, Anna 222
Tennessee A. W. 182
Randle, Amanda G. 140
Randolph, Amanda 206
Lavina 92
Peyton W. 64, 146
Sarah 34
William R. 200
Raney, John C. 160
Rankin, James 201
Rankins, David F. C. 204
Rather, James 12
Nancy 18
Patsey 12
Rathers, Betsey 8
James 8
Ratterce, Sally 62
Rattern, James 125
Rawlings, James L. 10
Rawls, John 79
Mary 79 (See ROLLS)
Ray, Archibald 29
Eliza 228
Hollon 42
Lucinda 106
Luke 13
Margaret 76
Mary Jane 185
Reuben M. 222
Salley 77
Sally 34, 71 (WRAY?)
Samuel (2) 100
Simpson 98
William 59
Willis 35
Raymay, Robert 83
Rea, Jordan 189
Margaret 83
Margaret Isabella 233
William 113
Reader, Alfred A. 107
Reading, Lewis (Leevis) 12
Polley 12
Reaves, Burrell 150
Jeremiah 38
Robert 220
Reay, Margaret 85
Rece, Nancy 46
Redden, Robert 206
William 54
Reddete, William L. 166
Redding, Anna 123
Elizabeth 46
Lavina 68
Nathan 46
Redditt, Francis 195
Reding, Nathan 49
Reece, John (2) 134
Louisa 185
Nancy 46 (See RECE)
Reed, Abner 132
Araminta 30, 35
Ardminta 128
Arminty 218
Easter 72
Eli 125
Elizabeth M. 199
Elum 76
George W. 237
H. D. 237

Reed (cont.)
Henry (2) 76
Isaac N. 204
James 46, 55, 59
Levy 72
Margaret Ann 178
Margaret B. 123
Martha 120
Martha Ann 205
Mary 168
Mary D. 163
Melison Helen 190
Polly 83
Robert 76, 111, 233
Robert D. 70, 208, 210
Robt. D. 162
Sally 14, 70
Samuel 132
Thomas 132
William 43
Reeder, Adam 125, 137
Alfred A. 107 (See READER)
Caty 50
Cynthea 75 (See PEEDER)
Harris 100
Helen 137
Lydia 40
Nancy 237
Rachel 100
Sarah 95
Reedy, Samuel 16
Rees, Thomas B. 79
Reese, Addison 107, 117
Alsey 93
Betsey 19
Charity 156
Eliza 54
Evalina 36
John 117
Louisa 174
Margaret 76
Murfree 20
Murphy 43
Nancy 59
Thomas B. 79 (See REES), 125
William 20, 70, 159
Reeves, Burwell 58
Drury 12
Hooker 39, 124
Jenney 28
Marcus Lafayette 221
Mary 135
Mary Jane 224
Ruth 141
Thomas A. 219
Reggs, John 49
Reif, Taurus 94
Reiff, Eliza 232
Rembert, L. C. 203
Renshaw, Nancy 51
Reve, James D. 216
Rey, Mary A. E. S. 228
Reyland, Hughy 55
Reynold, John 87
Reynolds, Ambrose 92
Betsey (Rynols) 18
Charlotte 58
Elizabeth 215
Harriet W. 125
Harruet (?) 76
John H. 93
Martha Ann 228
Rhoda 168
Shelby 107
Rhea, Archibald 125
Elizabeth 177
Elizabeth Martha 180
Jane 116

Rhea (cont.)
Milly 97
Polly 127
Robert 159
Rhode, Hezekiah 22
Rhodes, Claiborne H. 40
Elisha L. 81
E. S. 157
Frederick L. 118
Louisa Jane 197
Martha Ann 190
Thomas 24
Rhody, Hezekiah 29
Rice, Anderson C. 118
Ann 21
Bedford B. 228, 229
Benjamin 43
Brunette P. 155
Caroline 147
Cynthia 155
Diadema 196
Elijah 34
Elizabeth 64, 218
Elizabeth E. 210
Elizabeth W. 228
Esther 53
Fredonia 199
Henry 23
James 38, 59, 100
James P. 118
Jasper 199
John 5, 20, 106
John C. 176
Lytia 7
Mary 86, 152
Mary A. 174
Matilda 215
Nancy 43, 117, 129
Nancy A. 190
Nathaniel 29, 43
O. M. 121
Peggy 87
Polly 67
Rebecca 74
Rebecca W. 59
Rufus P. 196
Sarah 108
Susan 82
Susannah 63
Verleria R. 189
William 121, 202
William C. 182
Rich, Elizabeth 60
George 108
Lucy (2) 140
Mary 108
Obadiah 119
Obediah 70
Samuel E. 226 (?)
William F. 214
Richamond, Mary J. 215
Richard, Anna 5
Kinchen 94
Lewis 55
William 81
William M. 19
Richards, David C. 87
Edward 190
Richardson, Dorothy 35
Elizabeth 238
James A. 132
Martha 47
Milly 53
Susan 46
Thursey 75
Richmond, Andrew 107
Daniel 94, 107
Elizabeth 39, 107, 203

Rogers (cont.)
  Thomas 188
  William 210
  William J. 173 (See ROFGERS),
    200
  William R. 202
Rogersdale (Ragsdale), Richard
  20
Roives, Burnell 64
Roland, Joseph 190
Rollman, Margaret Ann 76
Rolls, Elizabeth 96
  Mary 79 (Rawls?)
Romine, Aaron 16, 34
Romines, George 140, 159
  Mary 107
Roper, Levin 34
Rose, George W. 166
  Henry R. 239
  Hermon 54
Rosell, Robert W. 212
Ross, Allen 3, 23, 165
  Ann 4, 165
  Elizabeth 72
  George 3, 18, 25
  Hanah 9
  James G. 227
  James R. 221
  Jarratt 231
  John 20, 188
  Jordan 10
  Levina 231
  Nancy 14, 39
  Polly 59
  Robert 8
  Samuel 4
  Samuel N. 109, 117, 166
  Samuel W. 130
  Theodore 17
  William A. 179
  William C. 128
Rosse, Minerva 111
Rotmmel, William S. 181
Rotrambee (?), Frederick 70
Rotramel, Francis 190
  Frederick 76
  Henry 173
  Walter J. 173
Rotranac, Walter J. 170
Rotranate, Frederick F. 99
Rotranel, David 125
  Henry 111
Roulhoc, F. L. 157
Rouse, Edward 219
  Ezekiel 140
  Joel 146
  John 140
Routon, Nancy 182
  Sarah 96
Roveling (?), Elizabeth 18
Rowden, Richard 173
Rowland, Kissiah 12
  Jackson 216
  Jesse 227
  Rebecca 20
  Richard 44
  Richardson 93
  Sally 30
  Tericy 125
  Wiley 209
Rowlett, Jesse W. 231
Rowlstone, Sarah M. 169
Rowton, Rebecca 66
Rozell, Ashley B. 209
  Rufus A. 222
Rucker, Edmund 81
  John W. 81
  Lemuel 147

Rucker (cont.)
  Malinda 233
  Virginia Tennessee 189
Rucks, Howell 112
Ruff, John 9
  Mary 127
Ruffman, Constant 163
Ruiff, Nancy 4
Ruleman, Justes 11
Russel, John 100
  William 88
  Wily 163
Russell, A. H. 169
  Alfred H. 180
  Elijah 132
  Elizabeth A. 163
  Hiram 38
  James 173
  Mary F. 176
  Pinkney H. 205
  Priscilla 158
  Rebecca A. 196
  Sherley J. 214
  Susan 116
  Thomas J. 166
  Vicy 111
  Wilie 182
  William 61, 159, 166
  William A. 140, 153
  Wm. 111
Russle, Jeremiah 23
Rutchledge, Nancy 45
Rutherford, Elizabeth 61, 128
  Gideon M. 220
  Griffin W. 189
  John R. 51, 88
  Mary Jane 230
  Robert W. 198
  Sophia 124
Rutland, Amanda F. 172
  Elizabeth 38
  Emily 55
  Hannah 142
  Henry 86, 107
  Isaac 135, 150
  Isaac H. 55
  James 129
  James B. 156, 169, 186
  Jas. B. 165
  J. B. 148
  Johanna 223
  John 225
  Joseph 88
  Joseph S. 234
  Lucy 152
  Mandane 86
  Martha C. 207
  Mary 157
  Melberry 44
  Melcenia E. 143
  Perthana W. 1
  Reddick 44
  Rhoford 9
  Rutherford 38, 55
  William C. 132
  W. R. 211
Rutledge, Alexander 17, 67,
    73, 188
  Daniel L. 111
  Elijah 30 (See RUTTLEDGE)
  John 118
  John R. 182
  Mary 179
  Nancy 45 (See RUTCHLEDGE),
    71
  Richard 173
Rutter, Samuel 90
Ruttledge, Elijah 30

Ryan, Elmyra 194
  Martha Jane 228
  Mary Ann 185
  Sarah A. C. 167
Rye, Elizabeth 137
  E. W. 179
  Mary Jane 220
  Rebecca 45
Rynols, Betsey 18 (Reynolds?)
S_(?)_awce, Charity J. 181
S_(?)_rls, Payton 236
Sadler, Anderson 208
  Francis 208
  John N. 159
  Martha 212, 223
  Mary 217
  Sanford 207
  Sarah 150
  William 29
Saller, Peterson 177
Sally, Edwin C. 200
Sampson, James 101
Sandeford, Williford 177
Sanders, Alexander 183
  Asa H. 187
  Cullen 119, 132, 161
  Edna B. 108
  Eleanor 135
  Eleanor D. (Mrs.) 181
  Elizabeth 51, 117
  George 117
  George W. 200
  Isaac 13, 215
  James 135, 192
  Jarrott 231
  John 94, 111
  John H. 194
  John W. 111
  Julius 23
  Leah 218
  Levi L. 186
  Mary 132
  Nathaniel 60
  Polly 81
  Rebeccah 86
  Rhoda 73
  Robert 64
  Sally 161
  Samuel 132, 151
  Sarah Ann 145
  Thomas G. 148
  Washington 81
  Wiley 189
  Zilpha 217
Sanderson, Elizabeth 55
  Jane 223, 227
  M. 223
  Munroe 227
  Wm. 99 (See STANDERSON)
Sandiford, Mary 31
Sands, Bird 159
  Elizabeth C. W. 185
  Fanny 59
  George 29
  James 81
  James E. 139, 228
  Margaret A. 194
  Nancy 10
  Sally 38
  William 153, 159, 163, 173
Sanford, Anna 188
Saterfield, Anny 68
  Pheby 33
  Reuben 137
  William 49
Satterfield, Elizabeth 199
  E. W. 183
  J. 182

289

290

Shelton (cont.)
James 228 (See SKELTON)
James Monroe 227 (See SKEL-
    TON)
Jane 167
Mary Ann 132
R. P. 93
Susan 232
Thomas 167
Shepard, Lucinda 181
William 186
Shephard, Nancy 211
Shepheard, William 81 (?) (See
    SHEHEARD)
Shepherd, J. 202
John 60
Jno. 60, 88
Lititia 162
Martha 63
Mary Ann 129
Sarah H. 117
Thomas 173
Sheppard, Cary Ann 82
Elizabeth 19
James M. 207
Lewis 20
Louisa 123
Robert 60
Sherman, William 198
Sheron, Aaron 13
Sherrell, Jane 194
John W. 225
Lewis W. 186
Martha J. 218
Nancy 103
Polly 11, 224
Samuel W. 146
Saraphonia E. 214
William T. 81
Sherrill, Alanson 87
Alfred 49
Andrew S. 140
Archibal 44
Archibald 9
E. 78, 140
Elizabeth 233
Ephraim 64
Hugh 101
Hulda W. 51
Huldy 12
Mary Ann 103
Nancy 55
Peggy 49
Polly G. 63
P. S. 221
Rebecca 50
Renanna 87
Sam'l 99 (Sma'l?)
Samuel 10
Samuel W. 44, 140, 146, 150
Sma'l 99 (?)
Tursey 74
Wm. A. 172
Sherring, Thomas 81
Sherron, Aaron 13 (See SHERON)
Wood H. 146, 166
Shingleton, Ann 179
Ship, Benton 88
Mekins 88
Shoecraft, Drew 76
Shoecroft, Martha Jane 196
Shoemaker, Martha Ann 188
Samuel 193
Susan 114
Sholes (?), Jonathan 201
Shore, Jonathan 70
Shores, Elizabeth 34
Jane 197
Jonathan 159, 166

Shores (cont.)
Jonathan, Jr. 192
Martha 196
Philip 34
Rachel 164
Richard 166, 171
William 159
William M. 173
Short, Theophilus W. 48
Thomas 81
Shorter, James 11, 153
John 153, 192
Kindness 11
Mary 128
Purlena 78
Shours, Sousan 7
Shreves, John 211
Shryer, M. W. 210
Shuder, James M. 228
Siddle, Nancy 2
Sidwell, Lucy Ann 143
Sillamon, Sarah 85
Silliman, Cyrus C. 146
Elizabeth 89
Nancy 127
Sillivan, Barnard 38
Charles 92
Sim (?), James G. 193
Simmons, A. 152
Alexander 103, 212
Elam 153
Elisha B. 216
Hardena F. 176
John A. 94
Joseph 109
Lovely 78
Lucy 221
Nancy 125
Willis A. 188
Simms, James G. 168
Simons, John A. 107
Simpkins, Harriet 79
Simpson, Anderson 118
Charles W. 209
Edmund 81
Elizabeth 181
George 111
Harriet 57
Jane 47
John 2, 64
John T. 173
Martha 57
Mary 122
Nathan 34
Polly 56, 65
Presley 50
Presly 57
Robert 96, 132
Sterling 153
Valentine 140
William 29
Sims, Aseneth 133
Caswell S. 79, 81
Charlotte 122
Dudley B. 112
Edmund 67
Edward 21, 88
Elisha 34, 80
Frederick O. 231
(?), Hicksey A. 183
Isbel 168
James G. 173
James L. 224
James T. 155
Jane 95
John 70, 134, 140, 191, 218
Leonard H. 29, 36, 40, 42
Levi H. 22

Sims (cont.)
Margaret 108
Martha 134
Mary 47, 111
Matthius 140
Nancy L. 145
Parthena 180
Patsey 64
Polly 79
Robert 39
Sarah 189
Sephronia M. 237
Susannah N. 156
T. J. 156
(?), William 221
William W. 64
Sinclair, Alexander 194
Eli (2) 118, 160
Elias 88
Eliza 197
Elizabeth 160
Jane 118
William N. 94
Singleton, Andrew J. 217
Ann 179 (See SHINGLETON)
Harriet 200
James 159
Sarah Jane 204
Sinners, Lucy 159
Sinsett, John 1
Skean, Elizabeth 155
Hope 187
Mathew 155
Skeen, Hannah 78
Matthew 182
Skelton, James 228
James Monroe 227
Slate, James (2) 30, 32, 34, 74
Slavett, John 172
Sloan, John L. 93, 159
Sluder, Chelly Ann T. 162
Small, (?) Amos 1
Amos 3
George 24
Smart, Catharine 201
Frances 157
James 170
John A. 162
Joseph 24
Lusinda 83
Malinda 155
Martha 108
Philip 9, 34
Prisley G. 132
Sarah 157
Stpehen 11 (Stephen?)
William D. 221
Smith, Abner 88
Absolom 24, 34
Achilles 67
Agey 17
Agnes 149
Alexander 107
Aley 134
Allen 23, 38, 39, 47, 49
Alvin 206
Armelia W. 173
Aseneth 82
Betsey 6
Byrd 17
Caleb H. 170, 218
Catsey 67
Champ 112, 153
Charles B. 9
Daniel 53, 94
David 17, 54
David B. 94, 145
David J. 176

291

Spillam (?), John E. 195
Spillars, J. C. 148
Spillens, J. C. 127
Spinks, Elia J. 90
  James 193
  John 193
  Martha M. 215
  Nancy S. 205
Spradley (Spraklin), Agnes 101
  Andrew B. 101
  Calvin J. 140
  James 101
  Manerva 153
  Tavner 7
  William M. 153
  Wm. M. 153
Spradlin, Elizabeth 21
  James 70
  Larkin 80
  Margaret 70
  Obadiah 206
  Thomas E. (2) 227
Spradling, Susanah 41
Spraklin, Agnes 101 (See
    SPRADLEY)
Spring, Aron 10
  Benjamin (2) 71, 81, 98,
    105
  Catarine 81
  Margaret 61
  Martha R. 98
  Nancy 99
  Polly 71
  Rachel 36
  Sally 47
  William 115
  Winney 36
Springs, Aaron 14
  Betsy 97
  David 50
  Dorcas 174
  Elizabeth 84
  John 46, 54
  Margaret 101
  Mary M. 126
  Samuel 166
  Sarah 132
Sprinks, Emily M. 168
Spurlock, Byrd 94
  Francis 107
  John 76 (See SCURLOCK)
  Sarah 169 (See SURLOCK)
Stacey, John 122
Stacy, John 122
  Joseph 1, 17, 47, 50
  Nancy 1
  William 11
Stafford, William 38
Stambridge, Nancy 160
Stamps, A. 215
Standeford, Tabitha 5
Standerson, Wm. 99
Standford, Ruth 11
Standley, Anney 80
  Benjamin 64, 193
  David (2) 104
  Thomas 118
  Wm. 106
Standly, John 70
Stanfield, Robt. 119
Stanford, John 29
  William J. 191
Stanley, Benjamin 36, 55
  David 55
  James 166
  Lydia 65
  Mary Ann 180
  Moses 146
  Sarah 120

Stanley (cont.)
  Susannah 36
  Thomas 50
Stanly, Isaac 235
  Rebecca 37
Stanton, Elizabeth 238
Stapleton, Elizabeth 33
Starks, Peggy 207
Starnes, John 35
Starns, Moses 34
Starratt, Moses G. 174
Starrell, Lucinda 132
Steed, C. A. 216
  Emily H. 181
  James L. 198
  Martin 232
Steel, Geo. W. 21 (See STELL)
  Henry 215
  Sally (Stell?) 21
Steele, Alexander 3
  Caroline 129, 211
  Elenor G. 133
  Elizabeth 50
  George 50
  James 3, 13
  John W. 155
  Margaret 136
  Margarette 61
  Sally C. 232
  William 17, 32
  Wm. 50, 57, 84
Stell, George W. 23 (Still?)
  Sally 21 (See also STEEL)
Stembridge, Henry R. 94
Stephens, Eleanor 155
  James 64, 118
  Jeremiah 21
  Littleberry 53
  Penny 103
  Sanders 94
  Thomas E. 218
Stephenson, Benjamin 76
  Isaac 70
  John 50
  Sally 19
Sterritt, Moses 11 (Starratt?)
Stevens, Henry B. 235
  James 55
  James A. 205
  Jeremiah 21
  L. B. 164
  Littleberry 55, 56
Stevenson, Benjamin F. 38
  B. F. 70
  Clairnda R. 171 (?)
  Frances E. 223
  Manerva 191
Steward, Arretter 178
Stewart, Abner 5
  Alexander 35, 190
  Alijah 101
  Ann H. 127
  Barna 82 (?)
  Charles 125
  Charles P. 204
  Cyrus 70
  Ebenezer 153
  Eliza S. 119
  Elizabeth 127
  E. R. 134, 154
  Frances 214
  Gilley 64, 94
  Green 153
  Henry 115
  Herman 202
  Ira E. 118
  Isaac 205
  James 17, 19, 38, 132, 140,

Stewart (cont.)
  James (cont.) 183
  John (2) 140
  John A. 181
  John G. 146
  Joseph 35, 111, 112
  Joseph G. 188
  Lucy 104
  Matthew 208
  Nancy 115, 202
  Peggy 17
  Sally P. 135
  Sarah Ann 188
  Sarah H. 214
  Selina 132
  Tilley 7
  William 112
Stiblefield, Mahala 71
Stiles, Enoch 44
Still, Fanny 2
  George 12
  George W. 24 (See also
    STEEL, STELL)
Stites, Levy 60
Stobey, William 76
Stockard, John 3
Stockton, David 180
Stokes, Elizabeth 39
  Jordan 186
  Mary 235
Stone, Benjamin H. 125
  Charles 218
  Charlotte 219
  Coleman 44
  Elizabeth 152
  Fanny 105
  Fany 214
  James 52
  John W. N. 206
  Martha 52, 158
  Martha M. 94
  Mary 110
  Micajah 140
  Newbern 159
  Newbern P. 140, 147, 160
  N. P. 165
  Rebecca 42
  Ruth Jane 213
  Saml. 91
  Samuel 104, 106, 107, 109,
    111, 116, 117
  Thomas 26
  Thomas C. 35
  Wineford 118
Stoneman, Collin C. 13
  John H. 64, 76
Stoude (Troude), Menthey 99
Stovall, Beludar 87
  Julia F. 198
Str (?) d, James R. 216
Strain, Thomas 235
Strange, Josiah 128
Stratton, Elvira W. 204
  Thomas J. 148, 160
  Thos. J. 152
Strawn, Joseph J. 166
Strong, Elijah 140
  Green 223
  James 89
  James A. 74, 86
  Joseph J. 169
Strothers, Richard 214
Stroud, Andrew 209
  Archibald H. 204
  Catharine K. 239
  Elizabeth 185, 222
  Isabella 154
  James R. 216 (?)

293

Stroud (cont.)
John M. 94, 159
Mary 144
Ransom 5, 125
Thomas B. 187
Welles S. 200
Stuart, Alexander 47, 52
Christina 82
Cyrus 82
James 8
Jensey 8
John 45
Joseph 24, 160
Lucy 62
Mily 52
Rebecca 80
Sally 28
Saml. 88
William 76, 94
Stubblefield, James 218
John 220
Mahala 71 (See STIBLEFIELD)
Malinda 220
Mary 219
Studer, James M. 118
Stull, Susan 108
Valentine 82
Stutlesworth, Elijah 29
Styles (?), William J. 219
Sublett, Isaiah P. 217
Mary E. 194
William A. 160 (See
SYBLETT)
W. S. 140
Suggs (?), F. M. 213
Noah A. 60
Solomon 50, 55, 66
Sterling B. 218
Sullars, Martha W. 112
Sullivan, Ahasahael 166
Amanda M. 186
Azur 146
Barnard 38 (See SILLIVAN)
Barnet J. 160
Benjamin 70
Charles 64, 92 (SILLIVAN?)
Dennis 228
Eclemuel 94, 105
Eli 164
Elizabeth 209
Elizabeth Ann 196
Elizabeth Frances 217
Ely 174
Ethel (?) 187
Ethelbert 179
Euben 38
Holland (2) 21, 29
J. 69
Jacob 35, 43, (2) 55, 63,
64, 65, 77
Jas. 71
Jesse 21, 50
John 82, 231
John W. 237
Lavina 96, 224
Lydia 48
Martha Jane 232
Mary 90
Mary E. 224
Nancy 29
Parker 125
Parthena A. 228, 229
Paul 49
Peter 24, 30, 55, 60
Polly 23, 70
Polly M. 96
Rebecca 18
Rhoda Ann 183

Sullivan (cont.)
Sarah Jane 239
Simeon 29
Simion 41
Susannah 41
Sylvanus 174
William W. 146
Sumerhill, E. B. 155
Sumers, Naomi 60
Summars, Eli J. 196
Henry C. 140
Penelope J. 146
Summerhil, James A. 191
Summerhill, E. B. 155 (See
SUMERHILL)
Edward 154
Emily E. 119
J. P. 150
Lucy Ann P. 201
Martha E. 186
Wm. 154
Summers, Bazil 35
Eli 151
Geo. 24
Green 110
Henry D. 132
Jane E. 162
John 88, 238
John J. 182
Mary 96
Matthew 223
Rebecca J. 207
Summons, H. H. 183
Surlock, Sarah 169
Sutherland, William 50
Suthern, Henry 82
Suttle, LeRoy B. 154
Sutton, Anna 199
Jenney 20
Jesse 130, 140
Lewis 24, 46
Lucinda 130
Nancy 158
Nicy 103
Rebecca 37
Rebeccah 33
Rowland 33
Toliver 44
Swain, Ann 80
Caleb M. 98
Caleb W. 118
James M. 100, 146
James S. 114
John 107, 118
Malvina Jane 171
Rebecca 205
William M. 70, 81, 178
William W. 195
Swainey (?), William 224
Swan, Elizabeth G. 102
Elizabeth P. 146
Fanny 104
Geo. L. 36
George 36
James 75, 118, 174
Job 54
John 76, 84, 102, 104
Mary 171
Phillip 132
Susannah 75
T. 98
William 134, 177
William M. 49
Wm. S. 87
Swaner, Martha 168
Swann, Franklin P. 202
Galley 11
George 41

Swann (cont.)
Isaac 221
James 125
Margaret 215
Martha 225
Patsy 176
Richardson 166
William 125
Sweat, Cynthia 47
Edward 44
Elizabeth 119
Joseph 29
Robert 44
Sarah 120
Uriah 55
William 99, 119
Sweatt, Edward 204
George 185
Jane Frances 198
Jemima 188
John 68 (Seatt?)
Julia Ann 221
Martha 154
Mary P. 205
Nancy 183
Robert (2) 154
Robert P. 194
Sally 100
Sarah 140, 220, 229
William 101
William B. 220
William C. 146
Sweney, Nanny 54
Swift, Clevers W. 118
Swindall, William 222
Swindell, Kiziah 199
Jane 202
Pledge 81
Swindle, Isiah 50, 55
Joel 7, 140
Joel H. 180
John 118
John H. 82
Joseph 112
Pledge 55
Rachel 42
Swiney, John J. 154
Maria 36
Swingle, Equilla 53
Pledge 55
Swingley, Catharine E. 187
Elizabeth 22
John 207
Jonas 55
Joseph 23, 24, 28, 35
Mary Ann 169
Swinney, Amerilla 113
John J. 150
Swinny, William 232
Syblett, William A. 160
Sypcert, Lawrence 61
Sypert, Allison 114, 115
Ann 5
B. B. 121
Elizabeth 169
Hardy 71
H. S. 144
Jane 148
Lawrence 17, (2) 47, 123
Mary 32
Mary Ann 118
Mary D. 134
Minerva 99
Robert 34 (See SCYPERT), 64
Robert B. 132
Roxalana 107
Sarah 83
Sarah Ann 191

Winston (cont.)
Isaac 20, 123
James W. 49 (See WISPIN)
John 68, 89 (See WRISTON), 138
John J. 133
Lucy 68
Mary 123
Sarah W. 31
William C. 133, 147
Wm. C. 169
Winter, Alexander W. 115
Andrew J. (Dr.) 180
Elmira Jane 146
Frederick 108
James 108
Martha R. 112
Robert 225
Sarah E. 183
Wilbon R. 87
Wilburn 95
Winters, Elisha 35
John 119
Lodusky 230
Malinda 132
Rhoda 58
William 220
Wiseman, John 46, 99, 141
John B. 167
Rebecca Frances 203
Wisenir, William 24
Wispin (Winston), James W. 49
Wit, Abner 154
Witherspoon, Elihu L. 174
Elin 113
James 50
Sarah 11
Wimphrey 75
Witt, Alderson 178
Wittey, Elizabeth M. 151
Witty, Ezekerl C. 35
William A. 229
Wlatton (Patton?), James 87
Wollard, Allgood 162
Thersey C. 218
Womach, John 50, 62
Womack, J. S. 121
Mary Ann 193
Richard 8, 17
Susanah 8
Wommack, Agnes Julia Ann 143
Elijah 34
Jaes S. 161 (James?)
James S. 167
Joel 219
Lucy 33 (See WORMACK)
Mary J. 205
Patience Ann 114
Patsey 44
Richard 161
Samuel 177
Thomas 194
Wood, Ann G. 215
Benton 60
David F. 141
Edmund 60
Eliza Jane 206
Flemmings P. 154
F. P. 82
Frances 49, 195
George J. 187
Harriet 167
John 65
John C. 113
Joseph N. 188
Josiah 104
Levi 21
Luke 101, 119

Wood (cont.)
Margaret 190
Martha 84
Martha R. 166
Mary 92, 101, 151, 199
Moses A. 167
Nancy C. 234
Patsey 22
Peter S. 71
Polly 42
Reuben M. 167
Susan 130
Susannah 93
William 71
William G. 39
William J. 231
Woodal, Martha 152
Woodall, Bailey L. 176
Woodcock, Abraham 51
Jesse 51
Martha 29
Wooddall, John 9
Woodliff, Whitehead 142
Woodram, Jacob 56
Woodruff, Charles E. 191
Woodrum, Benjamin F. 174
Elizabeth 110
Frances Ann 226
John B. 185
Margaret 91
Martha 144
Mary E. 195
Obadia 12
Tabitha Jane 170
William 102
Woodrun, Rebecca 40
Stephen M. 232
Woods, Ann 177
Benton 93
Elizabeth 137
Isham 45
James 45, 202
John 141
Margarett 172
Martha J. 202
Mary Frances 236
Mills 35
Thomas 126
William 17
Woodvill, Henry 65
Margaret 65
Woodward, Baker 71
Delilah 11
Elenor 29
Frances 12
George 71
Hezekiah 87
Nancy 18
Permala 20
Sally 10, 19
W. 18 (See WOOWARD), 23
William 17
Winney 15
Woodwine, Obediah 6
Woolard, A. 222
Alleggood 50
Alligood 37, 210
Alygood 77
Celia 53
Emily 233
George W. 126
Harriet (2) 229
John 45
Louisa 37
Mariah 105
Simeon 45, 53
Wooldrid, Nancy 121
Wooldridge, Nancy 21

Wooldridge (cont.)
Pheby 45 .
Wooldrige, Fanny 24
Woolen, Joshua 39, 231
Levin 178
Levina C. 223
Leviniah 126
Manerva Jane 213
Martha Elvira 214
Moses 126
Woollard, Allgood 155
Allison 119
Cynthia 131
Elizabeth 140
George 154
Losen B. 141
Margaret 89, 102
Nancy 159
Woollen, John L. 77
John S. 68
Leven 74
Levin 77
Moses 39, 131
Woolridge, Thomas 3
Wooten, Bentsey 17
Wooward, W. 18
Word, Chany 110
Edmund 82
Fanny 5
Frances Ann 211
Harriet 91
Harrison 116
Hose 89
Isham 102
James 98
James T. 223
Jas. C. 168
J. C. 161, 164
John 56, 65, 95
Katharine 115
Martha 138
Mary Ann 213
Nancy 67
Polly 18
Rebecca 4
Sally 16
Sarah 192
Sarah F. 223
Thomas C. 138
William 95, 201
Wormack, Lucy 33
Worsham, Catharine 148
William B. 198
Wortham, Duke 7
Harriet J. 230
Mahaly 41
Nancy 21
Polly 25
Sarah 31
William H. 89
Zachariah 70, 71
Wrather, Baker 26
Cal (?) M. 208
Wray, Allison 108
Anna 206
Elizabeth 133
Elzi 174
Emely 203
Jane 81
Joseph 45
Luke 15
Margaret 15
Margaret Ann 225
Mary 72, 145
Oliva 197
Susannah 224
William 89
Willie 51

302

Wray (cont.)
  Willis 34
Wright, Abejah 34
  Abraham 83, 108
  Anderson 89
  Ann 35, 69
  Beedy 72
  Benjamin 215
  Berry 137
  Catharine Francis 235
  Charles 95
  Charlotte E. 122
  E. All 210 (See ALL WRIGHT)
  Edy 15
  Eliza 237
  Elizabeth 94
  Ellis G. 101 (See RIGHT)
  E. S. 134
  Francis 186
  Henry 17
  Hezekiah 21, 126
  Hollis 95, 107, 122
  Isaac 35, 174
  James 60, 196
  James N. 102
  James P. 233
  Jane 191
  Jesse 45, 51
  John 44, 56, 205
  John R. 94, 102
  John W. 147
  Joseph 133
  Josiah 130
  Lemuel 77, 108, 193, 226
  Lewis 46, 56
  Little Berry 135
  Littleberry 65
  Louisa 206
  Lucy 62
  Marchis H. 177
  Margaret 155
  Mary 212
  Mary Elizabeth 226
  Mourning 88
  Nancy Ann 225
  Patsey 68
  R. D. 161
  Rebecca 28
  Redding 39, 45
  Robertson 24
  Sally 10, 52, 216
  Sam'l 24
  Samuel M. 167
  Sarah 178
  Sarah Jane 232
  Solomon 133
  Solomon D. 108
  Thomas 102, 107, 227
  Wesley B. 235
  William 119, 126, 229
  Zechariah L. 228
Wriston (Winston), John 89
Wroe, Hiram S. 174
  Hiram T. 167
  Hyram S. 95
  Martha S. 215
  Mary 163
Wrye, Henry 45
Wskew, Alfred 163 (?)
Wyeen, William A. 175
Wyley, Polly 229
Wynn, Ann Eliza 147
  Martha 153
  Rebecca 102
Wynne, A. 86
  Alanson G. 219
  Albert 57
  Albert H. 55
  A. W. 79

Wynne (cont.)
  Chistley 89
  Frances 28
  Francis 24
  Irin 97 (?)
  Isham 3
  James 94, 102
  John L. 41, 49, 77
  John M. 159
  John W. 119, 127, 156, 162, 220
  Jno. L. 37, 73
  Judith 105
  J. W. 157, 170
  Lucy 74
  Margaret 50
  Martha 184
  Martha A. 134
  Polley 9
  Polly 30
  Polly L. 24
  Ridley 30
  Sam'l L. 24
  Thomas K. 91, 142
  Thomas R. 147
  William 65
  William H. 183
Wynns, James 161
Yand (?), John 110
Yandal, John 77
Yandell, Mary A. 132
  Samuel 167
  Thomas R. 132
  William 134
Yandle, James H. 154
Yanette, Thomas K. 179
Yarnell, Casa 43, 49
Yearnel, Delila 18
Yergen, Sam 160
Yerger, Amenda 115
  Mary L. 235
  Michael 67
  Michell 42
  Sam'l 128
  Saml. 155
  Samuel 77
Yergin, James 155
Yogk (?), James 35
York, Delila 144
  Edmund 35, 77, 103
  James 35 (See YOGK), 61
  Jonathan 175
  Jonathan S. 179
  Lucy 120, 132
  Robards 180
Youbanks, Hardy 56
Young, Alex S. 130
  Alexander 231
  Alexander S. 155
  Amanda 219
  Archibald 30
  Benjamin 167
  Berry 147
  Beverly 12, 134
  Cynthia 206
  Dake 161
  David 108, 181, 225
  Doak, 95
  Eliza 200
  Eliza Ann 227
  Elizabeth 39, 47, 72, 94, 104
  Elsa Ann 116
  Elvy 33
  Fanny 182
  Frances 89, 181
  Francis Ann 186
  George D. 207
  Gilbert 97 (Yojng?), 108

Young (cont.)
  Harbird 46
  Harriet 104
  Harvey 16
  Henry 77
  James (2) 39, 189
  James H. 34, 45, 233
  James L. 201
  James S. 168
  James W. 51
  Jimey 61
  John 77, 142
  Joseph 9, 17, 102, 232
  Levina 49
  Louisiana 234
  Lucinda 213
  Lydia Ann 207
  Manerva 219
  Martha 215
  Martha Jane 216
  Mary 51, 169, 225
  Mary D. 168
  Myrandy 9
  Nancy 22, 59, 117
  Parallee Catharine 232
  Priscilla C. 113
  Robert 49, 115, 181
  Sally 18
  Samuel M. 178, 214
  Sarah 165
  Stacy 142
  Susan 204
  Thomas 155
  Thomas M. 160
  William 12, 19, 82, (3) 89, 96, 102, 116, 129
  Wm. 155
Youngblood, William 113
Youree, Francis A. 189
  Frances F. 110 (Yourie?)
  James R. 120
  Maria 80
  Patrick 3, 89, 119
  Rachel Caroline 81
Yourie, Frances F. 110 (See YOUREE)
Zachary, A. 95
  Allen 89, 102, 126 (See AZACHARY)
  Delila N. 160
  Hartwell 89
  Hartwill S. 167
  Malekyah 83
  Milijah 176
  Stokes 95
Zachery, Nancy 232
Zackery, Nancy L. 231
  Susan E.. 226